T0323415

From the "Democratic Deficit"
to a "Democratic Surplus"

From the "Democratic Deficit" to a "Democratic Surplus"

Constructing Administrative Democracy in Europe

ATHANASIOS PSYGKAS

OXFORD
UNIVERSITY PRESS

Oxford University Press is a department of the University of Oxford. It furthers
the University's objective of excellence in research, scholarship, and education
by publishing worldwide. Oxford is a registered trade mark of Oxford University
Press in the UK and certain other countries.

Published in the United States of America by Oxford University Press
198 Madison Avenue, New York, NY 10016, United States of America.

© Oxford University Press 2017

CIP data is on file at the Library of Congress
ISBN 978–0–19–063276–2

1 3 5 7 9 8 6 4 2

Printed by Sheridan Books, Inc., United States of America

CONTENTS

ACKNOWLEDGMENTS

The conclusion of a large project, such as a book, offers a fitting opportunity to reflect on the scholarly debt to individuals and institutions that have made this work possible. I owe the biggest share of this debt to Susan Rose-Ackerman. The idea for this book was born in Professor Rose-Ackerman's Administrative Law class. From a preliminary discussion of the idea at the Yale Law School faculty lounge all the way through the publishing process, Professor Rose-Ackerman's excellent supervision, wise advice, and patient guidance were invaluable. Her insights challenged the way I approached administrative law, inspired me to pursue this project, and provided a new lens through which to view law more broadly. I am also so grateful to Professor Rose-Ackerman for teaching by example as a scholar, a teacher, and a mentor.

I can still remember the excitement that comes from fascinating scholarship when, by happy accident, I first read Bruce Ackerman's *We the People* as a first-year law student in Greece. I decided then that I had to apply to Yale in the future. To have Professor Ackerman as a faculty reader critiquing my work a few years later was an extraordinary privilege. I could not have asked for a more insightful reader, a more dedicated teacher, or a more generous mentor. I was equally fortunate to have Nicholas Parrillo's brilliant support. Professor Parrillo always asked incisive questions and offered profound and constructive comments that enriched my work and prompted me to think more about administrative law on both sides of the Atlantic.

The broader Yale Law School community offered an endlessly stimulating and encouraging environment. I wish to acknowledge very helpful conversations with Professors Douglas Kysar, Daniel Markovits, and visiting Professors Miguel Maduro, Amalia Kessler, and Peter Lindseth. I would also like to express my gratitude to my teachers, Professors Christine Jolls, Jerry Mashaw, James Whitman, Reva Siegel, George Priest, and Roberta Romano, and to Deans Robert Post and Harold Koh. I am especially grateful to the brilliant reference librarians and all the wonderful staff of the Lillian Goldman Law Library. A special note of recognition should go to the YLS Graduate Programs Office. Deans Toni Davis and Gordon Silverstein offered invaluable guidance. Director Maria Dino was incredibly supportive and encouraging and, together with Stephanie D'Ambrose and Caroline Curtis, she created "a home away from home."

This project required extensive fieldwork in several European countries. I completed most of this work (interviews, archival research) as a Fox International Fellow at the *Institut d'Etudes Politiques* (*Sciences Po*) in Paris. I am especially grateful to Professor Jean-Bernard Auby for welcoming me to the *Chaire Mutations de l'Action Publique et du Droit Public* and its many interesting activities and for his extremely kind support throughout my stay. Professor Renaud Dehousse, the Director of the *Centre d'études européennes*, provided another very helpful community of scholars to work with. Olivier Schrameck, then President of the *section du rapport et des études* of the French Council of State and currently President of the *Conseil supérieur de l'audiovisuel*, and Professor Yves Surel generously provided comments on my work at two conferences in Paris. My research needs also brought me to Brussels, London, and Athens. I wish to gratefully acknowledge support from the Onassis Foundation, the Propondis Foundation, and the Greek State Scholarship Foundation. Moreover, my gratitude extends to the many professionals (regulatory agency officials, industry and consumer group representatives) who took the time out of their busy schedules to grant me interviews. These individuals, most of whom are listed in the Appendix though others wished to remain anonymous, offered great insights into how regulation and accountability processes operate in practice and are viewed by stakeholders. I would like to add a special mention to the assistance of Vicki Nash, Julia Fraser, and Rachel Reeve at Ofcom in the United Kingdom, Stéphane Hoynck at ARCEP in France, and Vassilis Kondylis and Nikos Kitonakis at EETT in Greece.

I presented different parts of this book at workshops and conferences around the world and benefited from conversations with many individuals. I am afraid I would still miss a few names even if I attempted to list them all here. However, I wish to acknowledge the excellent insights on my work that I received from Professors Kim Lane Scheppele, Kalypso Nicolaïdis, Lorne Sossin, Mark Massoud, Hans-Martien ten Napel, Jacqueline Ross, Maximo Langer, Christoph Möllers, and Daniel Halberstam.

Furthermore, I would like to thank mentors, colleagues, and friends from around the globe who supported, inspired, and challenged me, and made this project better and the writing process more productive and enjoyable: my Greek professors and mentors, Despina Klavanidou and Eugenia Prevedourou, Diane Desierto, Florian Grisel, James Fowkes, Benjamin Berger, Conor Hanly, Marcelo Rangel Lennertz, Michaela Hailbronner, Jennifer Bond, Guillaume du Puy-Montbrun, Thomas Perroud, Diego Werneck Arguelhes, Scott Stephenson, Or Bassok, Alex Metz, Terra Gearhart-Serna, Stratos Pahis, Maya Munivrana, Nancy Yfanti, Jaclyn Neo, Johannes Reich, and Konstantinos Stylianou. I was fortunate to be a part of the Max Weber Programme at the European University Institute and owe particular gratitude to the wonderful "Weber crew," Phillip Ayoub, Ludivine Broch, Franziska Exeler, Valerie McGuire, and, of course, Eirini Karamouzi, for the travels, inspiring conversations, and support. I completed the book at the University of Bristol, where my generous colleagues have provided a supportive and stimulating research environment. I am especially grateful to Patrick Capps, Rachel Murray, Tonia Novitz, Julian Rivers, Albert Sanchez Graells, Phil Syrpis, and my mentor, Tony Prosser.

I am very grateful for the encouraging support of Scott Parris, my first editor at Oxford University Press (OUP), who guided this project from the very first stages through the review process, with the assistance of Cathryn Vaulman. The four anonymous reviewers for the press offered incisive and helpful comments, which benefited the final manuscript greatly. After Scott's retirement, I had the pleasure of working with other members of the OUP editorial team, David McBride, Anne Dellinger, Kathleen Weaver, and Emily MacKenzie. Finally, special thanks go to David Pervin, senior editor at OUP, who saw the book through to production and publication.

Last but certainly not least, I wish to thank my family. My grandparents, who were lovingly concerned about my having to be thousands of miles away, always offered their unconditional support and affection. I wish I could share the published book with them. Over the course of this work, two adorable members were added to the family: my niece and nephew, Kleio and Vassilis. Their presence has brought joy and endless fun (and some distractions . . .), especially when the writing process and data crunching seemed more challenging. My sister, Evi, has been there from the beginning. Finally, my parents, Stella and Vassilis, have always supported my steps, literal and academic. As my work has taken me around the world, their love has nurtured and encouraged me. This book is for you.

INTRODUCTION

When academics, policymakers, media commentators, and citizens talk about a European Union "democratic deficit," they often miss part of the story. This conventional narrative paints a picture of an opaque center that assumes more and more executive powers while remaining distant from the European citizens. This book argues instead that member-state regulatory processes that operate under EU mandates or influence may actually have become more democratically accountable, not less. EU law creates entry points for stakeholder participation in the operation of national regulatory agencies (NRAs); these avenues for public participation were formerly either not open or not institutionalized to this degree. In these cases, we see not a democratic deficit but a democratic surplus generated by EU law in the member states. Moreover, the decentralized EU regulatory structure may promote experimentation, innovation, and policy exchange between the member states.

This book discusses a series of case studies demonstrating how EU law and policy influenced telecommunications regulation in France, Greece, and the United Kingdom. It assesses how accountability processes operated on the ground by drawing on a compilation of more than 1,000 public consultations that telecommunications regulatory agencies carried out since the beginning of their operation, as well as some 8,000 consultation responses over a five-year period. The analysis is supplemented by interviews with agency officials as well as industry and consumer group representatives in Paris, Athens, Brussels, and London. The study finds increased participation by actors other than the traditional powerful firms as well as significant transparency gains compared to the previous regime. Nonetheless, the three countries did not respond to EU pressures in an identical fashion. The book compares how the same EU mandates were translated into divergent institutional practices as a result of the different administrative traditions, bureaucratic culture, and public law history of these countries. It also documents roadblocks and difficulties along the way. In some

cases, adjustment to the new accountability paradigm was particularly challenging. In other cases, administrative agencies moved beyond what I call the "EU
floor" (namely, the baseline participatory requirements imposed by the EU) to
experiment with other accountability tools. These good governance rules and
practices may, in turn, ultimately be generalized across the national administration as well as be diffused across borders in the EU.

More specifically, Chapter 1 constructs a model against which we can evaluate the accountability gains that EU law mandates may have produced at the
member-state level. My democracy-enhancement argument is based on a new
model of accountability, one that does not rest on the classic representative variant or the bureaucratic expertise model, the inefficiencies of which are pointed
out in this chapter. I call this proposed accountability model "deliberative-
participatory": it finds its normative underpinnings in Habermas's theory of
deliberative democracy, which I adapt and bring into the administrative sphere.
Chapter 1 contrasts this system with other models: the republican one; Dahl's
pluralistic account; the "directly-deliberative polyarchy" model proposed by
Cohen and Sabel, and Gerstenberg and Sabel; Robert Cover's work on "nomos
and narrative"; and, finally, the theory of "autopoiesis." In translating the theory into operational reality, I suggest four building blocks of the deliberative-
participatory model: open access, transparency, reason giving, and judicial review.

Chapter 2 elaborates on the institutional and procedural EU mandates that
I argue have enhanced the democratic accountability of regulatory agency operations in the member states. Although it might at first sound counterintuitive,
I submit that increased procedural accountability was not the primary intended
effect of EU law. Rather, the EU formally adopted these procedural mandates
to advance the substantive goal of creating an internal market in electronic
communications. Even so, I hypothesize that these EU requirements may have
significant implications for the nature of administrative governance in the
member states. Chapter 2 further assesses this impact against the backdrop of
the decentralized EU regime. It considers traditional theoretical arguments in
favor of decentralization and examines their applicability in the context of my
inquiry, which focuses on regulatory processes rather than substantive policymaking. I conclude that it is theoretically tenable to argue that the decentralized
EU structure may transform NRAs into individual loci of experimentation that
might, in turn, develop innovative results. The extent to which this has been
empirically true is a question for the case studies to address.

Chapter 3 presents the first country case. The French example is illuminating
because the EU procedural mandates were transposed into a policymaking environment rooted in the "republican" perception of the state, and traditionally
described as "statist" and suspicious of interest groups. The chapter examines
how the EU push for new mechanisms of public accountability has translated

into institutional practice in the area of electronic communications. It situates these developments in the historical context of the evolution of the French administrative model and state-society relations. It also discusses whether these new processes may gradually give rise to a different perception of the administrative state, one that will be more open to participatory influences in all sectors of administrative policymaking.

The fundamental tenets of the Greek case in Chapter 4 may seem similar to aspects of the French example. The chapter traces Greece's focus on conventional notions of administrative accountability through legislative delegation and the involvement of the Council of State as a consultative and judicial body. The pattern of state-society relations in the country has also been described as statist. Nevertheless, the Greek case is distinctive. I assess the transformative impact of EU law against the specific background of the Greek example and the historical, institutional, and cultural particularities of the country. Greece was facing the twin challenge of weak administrative capacity and an underdeveloped civil society. This was reflected in difficulties in transposing the EU requirements and a stark imbalance between industry and civil society involvement in regulatory decision making. Therefore, Chapter 4 illustrates that the introduction of participatory processes is a necessary but not always a sufficient condition for the new accountability paradigm to take strong roots. Institutional reform efforts, potentially including affirmative state intervention to build stronger civil society capacity, may also be required.

By contrast, at first sight the United Kingdom might appear to be a more challenging case for my argument regarding the accountability-enhancing effect of EU law: the British regulators had engaged in public consultations before the advent of the EU participatory mandates. However, the narrative in Chapter 5 spanning the last two centuries demonstrates that EU law did indeed lead to consequential changes in institutional structures and practices in the United Kingdom. These changes may not amount to a paradigm shift. Nevertheless, EU law did push significantly in the direction of formalized and institutionalized open public participation, adding impetus to and consolidating the domestic regulatory reforms that had been set in motion over the previous decades.

Chapter 6 concludes by exploring how the findings in the previous chapters can inform future developments in the EU regulatory system and further enhance democratic accountability at both the national and the supranational levels. The chapter first tells a story of convergence: in all three country cases, EU mandates transformed aspects of the preexisting administrative governance, and brought about accountability gains on all prongs of my deliberative-participatory model. However, cross-national variations still exist. This invites one to consider proposals for further EU-driven convergence through the creation, for instance, of a European telecommunications regulatory agency. The chapter suggests that at this stage this idea would result in losses in democratic account-ability and would therefore be unwise. Instead, I put forth a proposal that har-nesses the accountability benefits of the EU regulatory architecture by tapping into the institutional creativity of the member states and incrementally incor-porating further EU-level requirements through a system of feedback loops.

Questioning the European Union's "Democratic Deficit"

I. The different versions of the European Union's "democratic deficit"

The democratic legitimacy of the European Union has been subject to public debate and scrutiny since its inception.[1] The famous phrase "democratic deficit" was coined by David Marquand[2] in 1979 to describe a simple idea: given the range and depth of the EU's regulatory powers, the EU regulatory structure is insufficiently accountable from a democratic point of view.[3] The EU institutions themselves have raised such issues. The "classic" legitimating model is constructed around the paradigm of national parliamentary systems: the adoption and implementation of EU policies should be legitimized through the democratically elected European Parliament. Therefore, the "democratic deficit" depends on the role that the European Parliament plays in policymaking.[4] The European Commission has also acknowledged the public perception of the Union as "remote and at the same time too intrusive."[5] It is telling that, even as it recommended wide consultation with civil society organizations, the Commission was quick to make clear that "it goes without saying that, first and foremost, the decision-making process in the EU is legitimised by the elected representatives of the European peoples."[6] The European Council has also referred to the "democratic challenge facing Europe."[7]

Similar formulations have made recurring appearances in the literature on the EU's democratic deficit. For instance, it has been noted that "EC policymaking processes are largely dominated by bureaucracies and governments that provide little scope for parliamentary institutions (whether national parliaments or the EP) to intervene."[8] According to a more recent and provocative account, the specter of "bureaucratic despotism" haunts Europe: "Behind the fig-leaf provided by the rhetoric of economic and political integration is to be found a major development, the rapid accumulation of power in Brussels," in the process of which "democratic controls have suffered."[9] If we carry through this argument, legislative acts that are increasingly produced at the EU level and affect the member-state legal orders are "tainted" with a lack of democratic legitimacy. However, this description overly relies on a model of legitimacy that is "uploaded" from national parliamentary systems onto the EU level. Hence, it ignores or underestimates other effects that EU law has on the national legal orders that might undercut the notion of the EU "democratic deficit." Before proceeding to the bulk of this analysis, we need to briefly address two other versions of the EU democratic deficit.

According to the first version, the legitimacy of European integration is indirect: it proceeds from the democratic legitimacy of the member states.[10] The veto power of each member state in the Council was, in Joseph Weiler's words, a key element for the legitimacy of Community decisions. Consequently, the shift from unanimity to majority voting in an increasing number of policy areas since the Single European Act and continuing in subsequent Treaty revisions—including the Lisbon Treaty—exacerbates the democratic deficit problem by weakening national parliamentary control of the Council.[11]

Three brief responses could be made to this argument. First, this account seems to ignore a fundamental reality of the institutional architecture of the European Union which includes both an "intergovernmental component, where international features dominate" (e.g., in the European Council, and the Council of Ministers), and a "supranational component" where supranational features are most salient (e.g., in the European Parliament, the Courts, and the Commission). The perception of the member states as the most important—albeit indirect—source of legitimacy is not sufficient to provide an "adequate normative foundation for its supranational component,"[12] which as we saw becomes increasingly salient as integration proceeds. Relatedly, it does not square with the foundational jurisprudence of the European Court of Justice on the autonomy of the Community legal order and cannot accommodate the function of EU law as creator and protector of rights of the citizens of the EU, even against the member states.[13] Second, the flipside of this argument would be that the veto power itself might contribute, as Weiler acknowledges, to the democratic deficit since it allows only a few European citizens through their Minister in the Council to thwart the collective decisions of the rest of the Union.[14] Third, as will become apparent in subsequent chapters, the scheme in this book accommodates concerns about the role of member states in legitimizing the European project of regulatory integration by showcasing the importance of national regulatory authorities ("NRAs"). The literature has often neglected these national actors because of its narrower focus on more "traditional" bodies, such as national Ministers or Parliaments.

Another version of the democratic deficit emphasizes concerns about the "future of the national welfare state in an increasingly integrated European market." The fear is that while the policymaking capacity of member states is being weakened, the EU itself lags behind member states in social protection.[15] In essence, these arguments do not pertain to the democratic deficit as such. They do not point to a lack of democratic *processes*, but rather to a lack of *substantive* policy outcomes linked to a specific agenda. Our concern is more about the former than it is about the latter. The idea of a democratic deficit in the EU denotes a failure of the institutional infrastructure to provide a framework of democratic contestation that would lead to the adoption of one or another substantive policy agenda. To argue otherwise seems to put the cart before the horse. Hence, what captures the core of this democratic deficit critique is the "classic" version of this claim: that is to say, EU policies are adopted and implemented without going through a legitimating process abiding by standards derived from analogous national institutions or, more abstractly, from the majoritarian, "Westminster" model of democracy.

II. Diverse notions of legitimacy

One response to this broadly-held "classic" view of the democratic deficit was that what is perceived as a "lack of democratic structures and processes within the EU, in contrast to those that prominently exist at the national level,"[16] is, in fact, the flawed outcome of analyzing the EU against a democratic ideal that no modern government can meet.[17] As Andrew Moravcsik puts it, "the European 'democratic deficit' is a myth. Such criticisms rest on a vague understanding of what the 'democratic deficit' is, ignore concrete empirical data about whether one exists, and hold the EU to the impossible standard of an idealized conception of Westminsterian or ancient-style democracy."[18] Moravcsik's general "liberal intergovernmentalist" account of the EU reduces the latter to not much more than a traditional organization of sovereign states.[19] Thus, it downplays the supranational features of the EU, and is therefore subject to the same criticism discussed in Part I. However, if detached from his general theory about European integration, his specific assertion that the existence of a democratic deficit in the EU is overstated holds ground.

Indeed, the problem that accounts of the EU "democratic deficit" identify as distinctly "European" is not really so. Rather, it reflects a broader pattern of what could be called a "legislative democratic deficit" inherent in modern democratic systems, whereby easy associations between legislative performance and democratic preferences are viewed with skepticism.[20] The political science literature explains that the idea of "mandate representation"—according to which elections serve to identify a winning policy platform and select the politicians to be charged with implementing it fully—is at best fragile.[21] Moreover, incumbents make a series of decisions that cannot be placed on a single axis, are diverse, multi-layered and perhaps at times even internally inconsistent. In a purely majoritarian system, "citizens have only one instrument to control policy, their vote." However, a vote in a general election is clearly insufficient to have an impact on the content of thousands of decisions that affect citizen interests.[22] Against this backdrop, we can better appreciate the remark that classic democratic deficit theory "generally overestimates the importance of legislatures in national systems [and] is inspired by a somewhat reductive view of democracy, which is implicitly equated with the mere voting of laws by parliamentary assemblies."[23]

In assessing these accounts of a democratic deficit, in addition to the "decline of legislatures" thesis,[24] a version of which was analyzed above, we have to consider a parallel, and equally if not more important, related development: the rise of the administrative state.[25] These two developments are connected. As Wheare noted as early as 1968, "with a few important and striking exceptions, legislatures have declined in certain important respects and particularly in powers in relation to the executive government."[26] Therefore, there is an even stronger case today that in the modern regulatory state the quality of the democratic process should factor in the administrative rulemaking process since administrative rules are increasingly important, in terms of both their volume and their scope.[27]

The traditional model of administrative law, premised upon an idealized perception of representative democracy, would conceive of the administrative agency as a mere "transmission belt" for implementing specific legislative directions in particular cases.[28] The "transmission belt" theory fails both empirically and normatively. Empirically, because the application of broad legislative directives frequently requires agencies "to reweigh and reconcile the often nebulous or conflicting policies behind the directives in the context of a particular factual situation with a particular constellation of affected interests."[29] Normatively, because, beyond guiding principles, the complexity of modern problems requires policymakers to sift the changing scientific data in search of responsible regulatory solutions, for which parliaments have neither the time nor the expertise.[30] Therefore, we would want (and need) supplementary administrative policymaking. Furthermore, if the transmission belt theory were true, what would also be "transmitted" into administrative action would be the legitimacy inefficiencies of parliamentary institutions identified above. Last, even if the legislature exercises certain forms of oversight by means of parliamentary control (for example, hearings, commissions of inquiry) and its budgetary powers, this is far from ensuring the "transmission belt" ideal.[31]

A similar criticism would apply to a closely related construction which remains influential in European parliamentary systems. This is the "chain of legitimacy" idea. According to this view, administrative action is legitimate not only when (or because) it enacts specific legislative mandates, but because administrative institutions themselves draw their legitimacy from the public through this chain reaching down to the people. The picture is this: people elect their parliamentarians, who elect the Prime Minister, who selects her cabinet, which in turn appoints agency officials. This description should suffice to suggest its deficiencies. This chain of legitimacy seems to be too long, thus increasing the risk of an individual link breaking loose—in addition to the legitimacy lacunae associated with each individual stage. The picture becomes even more complicated if we take into account that many of these agencies are designed as independent authorities, thus challenging the very formal existence of this "chain of legitimacy" in the first place.[32]

The foregoing analysis confirms that "exclusive reliance on the parliamentary democracy tradition" in the EU context is misplaced:[33] it is misplaced both in overstating the role of parliamentary institutions and in underestimating the normative requirements for legitimate administrative action in modern democracies. But where does this leave us? The claim that the regulatory legitimacy problem exists at both the national and the European levels is valid,[34] yet it is still inadequate to fully address the democratic deficit question. Rejecting its uniqueness at the EU level offers a negative position, not a positive one. Hence, this book seeks to take the debate one step further and argue that the structure of the EU regulatory state may actually enhance certain aspects of the democratic accountability of national regulatory agencies at the member-state level through the creation of participatory channels for European stakeholders. Chapter 2 will elaborate on how EU mandates may have had this effect; Chapters 3, 4, and 5 will then test the claim in three case studies. The focus of this chapter, however, is on a preliminary, and foundational, conceptual issue. That is, the democratic accountability-enhancing view of EU law presupposes a different model of accountability: one that does not rest upon the classic representative variant, the inefficiencies of which have already been pointed out. I shall call this the "deliberative-participatory model."

Before analyzing the "deliberative-participatory" theory, we need to examine another model with increased appeal in the European context: the bureaucratic expertise model. According to this system, the regulatory state is legitimized because decisions are taken by an insulated body of independent experts. This "technical expertise" justification had found early support in the United States since the New Deal era.[35] The argument goes that, in today's pluralistic world, mediating between competing groups of actors demands neutrality, and is facilitated by the technical language of regulation.[36] This is probably the most salient normative justification for delegation to agencies. Delegation can reduce decision-making costs by helping overcome information asymmetries especially in complex technical areas of regulation. Legislators need expert information, but face both an increasing number of issues requiring their attention and limited resources. Agencies are therefore expected to develop and employ this expertise and thereby improve the quality of regulation thanks to their relative institutional competence.[37]

One of the most prominent supporters of the bureaucratic expertise model in Europe has been Giandomenico Majone who identifies two basic "logics" of delegation.[38] The first views delegation as a mechanism to reduce decision-making costs as described above. The second rationale is that delegation either to the regulatory branch in the domestic context or to supranational bodies, such as the Commission or the European Central Bank in the EU context, serves to enhance the credibility of policy commitments.[39] More specifically, the requirement of elections at regular intervals discourages the adoption of policies the positive effects of which for the electorate will come after the next elections. Furthermore, a current majority cannot bind future majorities to long-term policies and, in fact, new governments emerging from elections can renege on policies that the previously elected officials had deemed optimal. The proposal is then to delegate these decisions to outside expert bodies that can choose and implement the optimal policies credibly and over time.[40]

However, even if we assume that these bureaucratic bodies act in a disinterested manner,[41] this should not suffice as a legitimating mechanism given that most purportedly "expert" decisions are in essence politically charged. It is indeed difficult to disentangle cleanly the technical from the political aspects of a regulatory question since many perplexing distributional questions are usually implicated in seemingly technical issues.[42] Furthermore, accounts favoring a purely technocratic model seem to assume that citizen preferences are either irrelevant or predetermined and exogenous to the political process. This view, however, seems to ignore the question that initiated this inquiry, namely the question of *democratic* legitimacy, thus failing to provide a satisfactory answer.

III. A deliberative-participatory model of legitimacy

A. Habermas's theory of deliberative democracy

What is therefore required is an institutional design that acknowledges the reality of extensive administrative policymaking but self-consciously addresses the accountability challenges of the regulatory enterprise, and tries to bring citizens back into the policymaking process.[43] The model that arises as the most suitable alternative to evaluate the European regulatory integration is, I argue, a "deliberative-participatory democracy" model, a form of which was originally advocated by Jürgen Habermas. Under this model, the emphasis is shifted to political participation in deliberative processes:

> civil society, which provides the social underpinning of autonomous
> publics, is as distinct from the economic system as it is from the

public administration . . . [T]he integrative force of solidarity . . . should develop through widely expanded autonomous public spheres as well as through legally institutionalized procedures of democratic deliberation and decision making . . . The public opinion which is worked up via democratic procedures into communicative power cannot itself "rule" but can only channel the use of administrative power in specific directions.[44]

This theory of democracy ascribes a distinctive role to civil society, which is empowered to voice its opinions vis-à-vis the government. As Habermas puts it, "just those norms are valid to which all possibly affected persons could agree as participants in rational discourses." The public use of communicative freedom and the discursively produced and intersubjectively shared beliefs have a motivating force that appears as a generator of power potentials. This influence generated by the communication circulating in the public sphere, however, "can be converted into political power only if it passes through the sluices of democratic procedure and penetrates the constitutionally organized political system in general."[45] Habermas constructs a model of the circulation of power: "on the input side, influence generated in the public sphere is transformed through democratic procedures . . . into communicative power, which in turn is transformed through the legal programs and policies of parliamentary bodies into administrative power; at the output end, administrative programs create the necessary conditions for the existence of civil society, and hence of a vibrant political public sphere."[46]

The most important feature of the model, in this context, is that public opinion is transformed into communicative power through a *process* that provides channels for political participation. Later chapters will argue that it is precisely these channels of public participation that EU law creates for national actors, thus providing them with access which enables them to influence regulatory decision making at the member-state level. According to the Habermasian conception of democracy, the legitimating force of the democratic procedure can be found in the access to processes of such quality that facilitate publicly acceptable decisions.[47] His proceduralist paradigm of law, unlike the liberal and social-welfare models, does not favor a particular ideal of society or a particular political program.[48] Law's addressees are also its authors, in the sense that they accept legislative outcomes even if they cannot endorse them substantively, because they consent to the lawmaking procedures.[49]

A caveat needs to be made at this point. There are two ways in which we could talk about a legitimating effect through civil society participation in the EU. The first one pertains to participatory processes *at the EU level*.[50] The second one refers to such processes established under EU mandates or influence *at the member-state level*. As already stated, my emphasis is on the second category, namely, on the processes legitimizing agency operations in the member states. Habermas himself does not claim that his theory depicts a current trend in the evolution of EU "central" governance toward this deliberative ideal.[51] And this would be a tenuous assertion given the current state of affairs. The claim here is much more moderate: my argument is that the Habermasian account could provide the basis for a new accountability model that I call deliberative-participatory. This model could accommodate and shed light on the accountability-enhancing effects of EU law with respect to specific agency operations at the member-state level.

B. The relationship of Habermas's theory to other normative models of democracy

It is useful to situate Habermas's discourse theory of law and democracy in the broader context of other normative models of democracy. A first distinction would be between the republican and the deliberative model. Habermas describes the former as the system in which deliberation can rely "on a culturally established background consensus of the citizens, which is rejuvenated through the ritualistic reenactment of a republican founding act."[52] Habermas accepts the basic premise of this model, that is, the idea of citizen communication and participation in politics, but emphasizes that his theory "does not make the success of deliberative politics depend on a collectively acting citizenry but on the institutionalization of corresponding procedures."[53] In Habermas's deliberative model there is no unified deliberating subject, concentrated in a single entity of the united citizens or their assembled representatives. Instead, popular sovereignty takes effect in the circulation of "reasonably structured deliberations" and decisions in the context of a "decentered society."[54]

This perception of the citizenry not as an undifferentiated mass but as a network of voluntary associations participating in commonly accepted democratic processes brings us to a second necessary distinction between the deliberative and the pluralistic model. The pluralistic model, the leading exponent of which is Robert Dahl, recognizes that civil society is composed of a multiplicity of organizations with sets of preferences.[55] It is these organizations, and not the electorate in general, that exert pressure on the government. The political system is reasonably open to these multiple interests if they feel strongly enough about a cause to mobilize and campaign.[56] Therefore, the responsiveness of the political branches to these mobilized interests will depend on the political, and electoral, power of the interest groups.[57] Dahl presented the advantages of this model in a way that reflects the Madisonian ideal: competing interests are represented in the multitude of interest groups that can balance each other out so that not one of them can dominate the political system.[58] The pluralistic model could be an even better justification of the bureaucratic state: agencies, which have fewer members than legislatures and regulate a narrower set of issues, may be the locus on which interest groups could focus more effectively in the course of promoting their policy preferences.[59]

Nevertheless, there are both empirical and normative objections to the pluralistic model. With respect to the former, an aspect of the pluralistic model is that interest groups can influence political decisions because of their ability to deliver votes. However, agency members are not directly elected, so the influence of organized interests would have to pass through the elected branches, which would in turn monitor and control the agencies. Yet, these oversight mechanisms do not always perform "the job pluralistic theory requires of them."[60] Besides, this would assume that the behavior of legislators in the first place is dictated exclusively by their willingness to serve special interests, whereas public interest, constituent interest, and ideology also motivate legislative conduct.[61] Public choice scholars would then point to another way of powerful interest groups exerting direct influence on agency officials: even if the regulated entities cannot deliver votes to agency officials, they can still offer financial benefits and the prospects of lucrative positions in the private sector after the officials' term in the agency is over.[62] However, this can be prevented through the adoption of conflict of interest rules and "revolving door" restrictions.[63] Furthermore, it has been argued that it is unlikely that regulators would make decisions hoping to improve their future employment: any secret deal between the regulator and the industry would not be enforceable, and the idea that an interest group would hire a formerly favorable administrator "as a signaling device to present administrators who may be looking for a job later seems far-fetched."[64]

The pluralistic model of democracy could also arouse skepticism from a normative point of view. As Dahl observed, specific policies are instances of "minorities rule."[65] The question poses itself: Which minorities rule? In other words, the pluralistic theory does not ensure in and of itself that all interests will be recognized. Some individuals may not find their interests represented by any politically active organization, or the organization that represents them might be systematically excluded from the governmental process.[66] If we subscribe to the theory that the groups that care the most and organize most intensively to change the status quo have the most influence on policymaking, then this is hardly reconcilable with the assumption or the hope that different groups will balance each other out. Instead, powerful industry groups enjoying the most resources will predominantly steer policymaking at the expense of other less organized and less "traditional" associations. This problem is likely to be exacerbated in countries with limited civil society capacity and in which new groups have not yet developed sufficiently to constitute an effective counterweight to the established interest groups. Assuming this "influence asymmetry" to be empirically true, the skepticism against the pluralistic theory further lies in that, as structured, this model seems to provide space for the normative accommodation of these asymmetries.[67]

Even if this discussion were to take on a different meaning, namely that these "minorities" are not privileged elite groups but less powerful sections of the society, the question of determining these groups would persist. One place to look at would be the famous footnote four of the *Carolene Products* case professing concern for the status of "discrete and insular minorities."[68] However, as has been rightly noted, "discreteness and insularity" may be a source of bargaining advantage. Therefore, the concern should rather be protecting groups that possess the opposite characteristics, that is, groups that are "anonymous and diffuse" rather than "discrete and insular."[69]

These "anonymous circuits of communication" are precisely within the framework of Habermas's discourse theory. Democratic will formation is "anchored in the informal streams of communication emerging from public spheres that are open to all political parties, associations, and citizens,"[70] including "anonymous and diffuse" groups. In this context, we should distinguish the pluralistic theory as a normative model for democracy from social pluralism (or, better, plurality) as a sociological fact denoting a diversity of autonomous social organizations. The former, as noted previously, suggests that a preexisting distribution of power among competing, more or less organized interest groups is, and perhaps even should be, mirrored at the policymaking level. The latter, instead, may be a precondition for a robust and diverse deliberating public sphere[71] in which, however, not just organized interests but also diffuse and anonymous groups and individual citizens can participate.

In addition to illuminating Habermas's theory by contrast, the discussion about the pluralistic model serves another important function: it points to a challenge commonly facing both the pluralistic and the deliberative-participatory models. The deliberative-participatory account constructs an ideal picture of a rational discursive process in which the best argument wins. This alone does not suffice to ensure that this process is open and accessible to all groups and citizens—powerful and weak alike. However, the normative underpinnings of the deliberative-participatory model advocated in this chapter, contrary to the strand of the pluralistic model critiqued above, invite such broad participation. Whether this is the operational reality on the ground is a distinct issue that also pertains to questions of institutional design.[72] These questions underlie both the following section sketching the fundamental operative criteria of the deliberative-participatory model and the approach to the case studies in subsequent chapters.

Prior to the description of these operative criteria, a third distinction between Habermas's theory and other related theories of democratic legitimacy through deliberation proposed in the EU context is in order. One of the most interesting theories is the "directly-deliberative polyarchy" model proposed by Cohen and Sabel, and Gerstenberg and Sabel:[73]

> In a deliberative polyarchy local-, or, more exactly, lower-level actors (nation states or national peak organizations of various kinds within the EU; regions, provinces or sub-national associations within these, and so on down to the level of whatever kind of neighbourhood the problem in question makes relevant) are granted autonomy to experiment with solutions of their own devising within broadly defined areas of public policy. In return they furnish central or higher-level units with rich information regarding their goals as well as the progress they are making towards achieving them, and agree to respect in their actions framework rights of democratic procedure and substance as these are elaborated in the course of experimentation itself.[74]

This is an interesting model, certain aspects of which could map well onto the decentralized EU regulatory scheme described in chapter 2. For the purposes of the analysis here, however, the following clarification is important. Gerstenberg and Sabel seem to prefer to situate deliberation outside the existing state apparatus to actors that are granted autonomy. Likewise, in a 1997 article co-authored by Cohen and Sabel, the role of administrative agencies is essentially reduced to providing the "infrastructure for information exchange" between units to facilitate benchmarking and continuous improvement.[75] It is no surprise then that they criticize Habermas's claim that "communicative power cannot supply a substitute for the systematic inner logic of public bureaucracies. Rather, it achieves an impact on this logic 'in a siege-like manner'":[76] their argument is that in Habermas's account "even the most radical extension of the public sphere would be of limited consequence precisely because the technical demands, to which administration, parliament, and party must in turn respond, set limits—but which ones?—to the direction that might issue from a more encompassing, unrestricted discussion among citizens."[77]

Their "radical" response might look like an appealing normative account to some but it is of questionable feasibility. It certainly does not reflect the scope of the impact EU law has on NRA operations. What EU law does—as subsequent chapters will clarify—is employ state structures, in this context national administrative agencies, and mandate specific participatory processes with the aim of channeling public input and transforming popular participation into specific state-sanctioned policy outcomes. I will also argue that this may have long-term, even transformative, implications for the nature of administrative governance in the member states. This is not a small feat in itself: Habermas recognized that law—in this context we could say regulatory policy—can function as a "popularly inaccessible administrative code." However, when "law is formulated within a civil society of free associations, through deliberating political bodies . . . it is the best way of translating popular will into public policy."[78] But to claim that this would create and multiply autonomous decision-making units outside the established public policymaking mechanisms is to claim too much.

This is the basic distinguishing criterion between the deliberative-participatory model endorsed here and the two last theories to be examined: Robert Cover's work on "nomos and narrative" and the theory of "autopoiesis." As the previous analysis suggested, Habermas claims that the communicative power of citizens influences the production of legitimate law; it is therefore "jurisgenerative."[79] This formulation may, for some readers, invoke a connection with Robert Cover's famous 1983 article on "jurisgenesis": Cover argued that "the creation of legal meaning—'jurisgenesis'—always takes place through an essentially cultural medium. Although the state is not necessarily the creator of legal meaning, the creative process is collective or social."[80] He was interested first in the jurisgenera-tive processes of insular communities in their struggle to define and maintain the independence and authority of their "nomos," their normative universe; he also described how in the workings of groups dedicated to radical transformations of constitutional meaning as it affects the application of state power, the law grew through common symbols and discourse, through shared narratives and inter-pretations.[81] Habermas was similarly interested in the role of voluntary associa-tions and a robust public sphere outside of formal state institutions. However, a fundamental difference from Cover's theory is already apparent in the language Habermas uses to describe this jurisgenerative power: "a jurisgenerative com-municative power *must underlie the administrative power of the government*."[82] The distinction is in the same vein as the one we drew from Gerstenberg and Sabel's work. Habermas focuses on the interface between the public sphere and state power and examines how associations can influence the production of *state* law. In Cover's scheme, on the contrary, state institutions, and precisely courts, are characteristically "jurispathic": they usually destroy legal meaning.[83] Briefly put, "Habermas's idea of jurisgenesis is thus decidedly more 'statist' than Cover's."[84]

Last, Habermas's account should be distinguished from the "autopoiesis" the-ory, which is located in a broader social-theoretical framework, that of "systems theory." The "autopoiesis" strand found a prominent exponent in Niklas Luhmann, who described modern societies as systems of communication that have become differentiated into various functional subsystems through a process of social evo-lution.[85] Systems are "autopoietic" in the sense that "the states of the system are exclusively determined by its own operations. The environment can eventually destroy the system, but it contributes neither operations nor structures."[86] In another essay, Luhmann explained that "everything that is used as a unit by the system is produced as a unit by the system itself . . . . Autopoietic systems, then, are sovereign with respect to the constitution of identities and differences."[87]

This system/environment relation and the division of politics and law into different, recursively closed systems is the focus of Habermas's criticism against the autopoietic theory. Normatively, Habermas rejects Luhmann's account on the grounds that law "drop[s] any further-reaching claim to legitimation. There is no output the legal system could deliver in the form of regulations: interventions in the environment are denied it. Nor is there any input the legal system could receive in the form of legitimation: even the political process, the public sphere, and political culture present environments whose language the legal system cannot understand." This "autism" especially affects the political system. Furthermore, Habermas stresses that this assumed mutual indifference between law and other social subsystems does not correspond with empirically observed interdependencies.[88]

This account of autopoietic theory in *Between Facts and Norms* has been described as a caricature that exaggerates the distance between Habermas's and Luhmann's views in that it neglects another aspect of Luhmann's theory: the idea of "cognitive openness" and "structural coupling."[89] As Luhmann explains, systems are operatively closed but cognitively open, in the sense that communications within one system may, and ordinarily do, refer to events in the system's environment. Moreover, the idea of "structural coupling" is that one system presupposes specific states or changes in another system and relies on them.[90] However, even this qualification of a strong version of self-referential autopoietic systems does not alter the fact that each system develops its own codes which do not admit of mutual translation.[91] A form of communication proper to one system is just "noise" to another system. The system "has to contend with perturbations, irritations, surprises, and disappointments channeled by its structural couplings."[92] But this is precisely the point of differentiation. In a deliberative-participatory model the "voice" of societal actors should not be perceived as "noise" or "irritation," but as an essential precondition for the development of legitimate law. In turn, the law opens up institutional opportunities and encourages voluntary associations to supply this influence.[93] This interface is at the core of accountable policymaking.

IV. From theory to practice: Bringing the "deliberative-participatory democracy" theory into the administrative sphere

A. A question of scope: Is Habermas's theory applicable to the administrative state?

Having presented the deliberative model of democracy in Habermas's work and situated it in the landscape of normative models of democracy, we need to resolve what might seem a problem with the application of this model to the administrative state. The skeptic would say that it is a fundamental problem because it is one of scope of application. More specifically, one line of criticism of Habermas's theory has pointed to its "very traditional emphasis on legislation."[94] It is true that Habermas's main concern in *Between Facts and Norms* is parliamentary lawmaking.[95] However, skeptics would mainly point to Habermas's earlier two-volume work, *The Theory of Communicative Action*.[96] In that work, bureaucratic spheres are presented as "systems" the internal operations of which "are steered by 'media' that circumvent the process of reaching understanding through communicative action."[97] In Habermas's words, state and media-steered subsystems are "consolidated and objectified into norm-free structures . . . . [I]n modern societies, economic and bureaucratic spheres emerge in which social relations are regulated only via money and power. Norm-conformative attitudes and identity-forming social memberships are neither necessary nor possible in these spheres; they are made peripheral instead."[98] However, if administrative operations are irreducible to mechanisms of communicative interaction and citizens cannot "meddle" with the "steering media" of administrative systems, if the public sphere is reduced in essence to contributing only "taxes" and "mass loyalty" to the administrative system in exchange for "organizational performances" and "binding decisions,"[99] then at first sight Habermas's own language seems to defeat the project of applying his theory to the modern administrative state.

Nevertheless, this would be a hasty conclusion. *Between Facts and Norms* no longer views the administrative system in terms of "power as command." Rather, in multiple places it highlights that communicative power is translated into administrative power through the medium of law.[100] To be more specific, using Bernard Peters's model, Habermas depicts the circulation of power as a system of concentric rings.[101] At the "core" or the "center" of the system is represented each of the three branches of government: the parliamentary bodies, the judicial system *and* the "familiar institutional complexes of administration." Beyond the center, an "inner periphery" develops out of various institutions equipped with rights of self-governance or with other kinds of oversight and lawmaking functions delegated by the state (e.g., universities, public insurance systems, professional associations, foundations, etc.). Last, the "outer periphery" encompasses the civil society.[102] Therefore, when communicative power reaches the core of the political system, it influences the administration as well. As Habermas puts it, "binding decisions, to be legitimate, must be steered by communication flows that start at the periphery and pass through the sluices of democratic and constitutional procedures situated at the entrance to the parliamentary complex or the courts (and, if necessary, at the exit of the implementing administration as well)."[103] Contrary to what critics suggest on this count,[104] this evolution from *The Theory of Communicative Action* to *Between Facts and Norms* should be welcomed. It should also be expected: as scholars pointing out these "inconsistencies" note, *Between Facts and Norms* is a very different project investigating the explicitly normative principles of the constitutional state.[105]

Nonetheless, the skeptic would probably still remain unsatisfied. She would point to the very formulation of the last passage quoted in the previous paragraph to highlight the asymmetry between the "parliamentary bodies" and the "implementing administration." She would also quote in support the following: "the implementing administration [should be precluded from employing] the sorts of reasons that support legislative and judicial decision making. These normative reasons belong to a universe in which legislature and judiciary share the work of justifying and applying norms. An administration limited to pragmatic discourses must not change anything *in this* universe by its contributions; at the same time, it draws therefrom the normative premises that have to underlie its own empirically informed, purposive-rational decision making."[106] Limiting the executive branch to pragmatic discourses and to "employing administrative power according to the law,"[107] the critic would continue, dries out the role of the citizens' communicative power in the administrative sphere and puts us back to the starting position of the "transmission belt" theory, which both this chapter's earlier analysis and Habermas himself[108] reject.

However, these objections do not preclude the application of Habermas's deliberative model to the administrative state. What Habermas tries to do is offer a discourse-theoretical understanding of the separation of powers, which is in essence a functional account of the separation of powers. In this sense— namely, seen from a level of abstraction and "independently of any historical legal order and of any concrete form of institutionalization"[109]—the function of "administration" or, to make the distinction clearer, "implementation" does not coincide with the concrete form of the executive branch or the administrative apparatus. It would be fair to question the definitional clarity of terms such as "implementation"; however, Habermas makes clear that if the implementation of programmatic goals entails a further development of law, traditional legitimating structures would not suffice. Instead, "the logic of the separation of powers must then be realized in new structures, say, by setting up the corresponding forms of participation and communication or by introducing quasi-judicial and parliamentary procedures, procedures for compromise formation, and so on."[110] Habermas is well aware that modern administrations take on tasks that entail much more than the technical implementation of a statute. He therefore advocates shifting the functional separation of powers into the administrative system itself and introducing new elements of participation and control. He also argues that standards of effectiveness should not substitute for standards for the legitimacy of administrative action.[111] Instead, the administration needs to address the normative questions before it in a rational way. In Habermas's words,

> [this] cannot be contained within the professional confines of a normatively neutral task fulfillment. Consequently, procedural law must be enlisted to build a legitimation filter into the decisional processes of an

administration still oriented as much as ever toward efficiency. To this extent, my image of the democratically "besieged" fortress of the state apparatus was misleading. Insofar as the administration cannot refrain from appealing to normative reasons when it implements open legal programs, it should be able to carry out these steps of administrative lawmaking in forms of communication and according to procedures that satisfy the conditions of constitutional legitimacy.[112]

This passage should settle the issue of scope. The deliberative-participatory model can find its normative underpinnings in Habermas's theory. However, it still needs an account of its fundamental operative elements in practice. Habermas's response to this question is not conclusive. He supports a "democratization of the administration" but concludes that the specific form of innovations would result from the "interplay of institutional imagination and cautious experimentation."[113] The following section will provide a first sketch of the building blocks of the "deliberative-participatory" model. The case studies in subsequent chapters will also revolve around these features.

B. The fundamental operative elements of the "deliberative-participatory democracy" model in the context of the administrative state

When it comes to lawmaking processes in the context of legislative bodies, Habermas notes that they must be "regulated in the light of the discourse principle in such a way that the necessary communicative presuppositions of pragmatic, ethical, and moral discourses, on the one hand, and the conditions for fair bargaining, on the other, can be sufficiently fulfilled."[114] As observed in the literature, in using the word "sufficiently," Habermas acknowledges that the idealized version of rational discourse will not be fully realized within legislatures owing to constraints such as the majority rule and the pressure for timely action.[115] Besides, establishing representative bodies for deliberation and policymaking is, according to Habermas, the natural outgrowth of the inability of all citizens to join in the shared exercise of such powers.[116] Indeed, with some notable exceptions,[117] citizens cannot ordinarily be directly involved in the lawmaking process.

This means, in turn, that administrative agencies might provide an effective alternative locus for more direct forms of citizen participation in policymaking. As Jerry Mashaw has noted, "[a]dministrators at least operate within a set of legal rules (administrative law) that keep them within their jurisdiction, require them to operate with a modicum of explanation and participation of the affected interests, police them for consistency, and protect them from the importuning of congressmen and others who would like to carry logrolling into the administrative process."[118] Similarly, Mark Seidenfeld has remarked that the agencies' place in government, their structure, and their policymaking procedures suggest that the administrative state holds "the best promise for achieving the civic republican ideal of inclusive and deliberative lawmaking."[119]

The question then arises of what kind of administrative law we need to enact and support this deliberative-participatory ideal. I identify four basic building blocks: open access, transparency, reason giving, and judicial review.

1. Open Access

The deliberative-participatory model would require as a minimum that when an agency decides to adopt a policy, it give all interested parties a reasonable and equal opportunity to submit their comments on that policy before it is enacted. This language raises a number of issues.

First, the notion of "interested parties" does not suggest that individual citizens or citizen groups need to prove that they are directly or potentially affected by the agency policy to be granted access and send in their comments. Their interest is assumed in that they took the time to share their opinions with the agency.

Second, a "reasonable" opportunity entails that citizens are given a reasonable time frame within which they can participate in the rulemaking process. For instance, a two-week window for comments on a multi-page draft rule in a complex technical regulatory domain would fail the test of reasonableness.

Third, the idea of "equal" opportunity for participation is more challenging to define. It implies that one group should not be granted more privileged access to policymaking processes over another. Nevertheless, equal opportunity for participation does not mean equal influence on the actual final policy outcome. The latter will depend on a number of factors, including the policy issue at stake, for instance, the type of represented interests and their proximity to the regulated area, or the quality of the comments submitted. These factors already suggest that industry groups, which generally possess more resources and organized regulatory departments, are in a better position to provide more and more sophisticated comments, and might thus have a greater impact on the content of the final rule. This is not by definition incompatible with the foundational premises of the deliberative-participatory model, whereby the "best argument should win" in an open and transparent discursive process.[120] However, it does raise concerns and suggests that, as a matter of institutional design, it would be desirable under the deliberative-participatory model that agencies actively reach out and elicit the opinion of less salient, yet potentially affected, groups. Similarly, the deliberative-participatory model would accommodate, and even invite, reforms aiming at addressing gaps in the level of sophistication of comments submitted by individual members of the public.[121] Last, as a matter of research design, the deliberative-participatory model also requires that we keep track of the extent of the influence coming from different groups in the case studies.

The "equal access" prong could also serve as the criterion against which to evaluate rulemaking procedures, such as "negotiated rulemaking" (also known as "regulatory negotiation"). In the United States, this process found its first extensive justification in an article by Philip Harter and was endorsed by Congress.[122] Agencies use this procedure to bring interested parties into the rule-drafting process at an early stage, prior to beginning a rulemaking proceeding under the Administrative Procedure Act (APA). In negotiated rulemaking, the agency, with the assistance of one or more neutral advisers known as "convenors," assembles a committee of representatives of all affected interests to negotiate a proposed rule. The goal of the process is to reach consensus on a text that all parties can accept.[123] An extended discussion of the merits and disadvantages of this process is beyond the scope of this section.[124] However, it is useful to focus on one account describing negotiated rulemaking as negotiated compromise and arguing that it "fundamentally alters the dynamics of traditional administrative rulemaking from a search for the public interest, however imperfect that search may be, to a search for a consensus among private parties representing particular interests."[125]

This process of compromise does not automatically fail the deliberative-participatory standard. Habermas himself suggested as much: in complex societies there are cases, he noted, when the proposed regulations touch on diverse interests without any generalizable interest or clear priority of one value being able to vindicate itself. In such cases, he observed, "there remains the alternative of bargaining, that is, negotiation between success-oriented parties who are willing to cooperate." Nonetheless, he was quick to stress that the discourse principle should be brought to bear indirectly, namely, through procedures that regulate bargaining from the standpoint of fairness.[126] In this context, the "equal access" prong puts the emphasis on ensuring that the negotiating group represents all affected interests. But this is precisely where the challenge lies. For example, consumer federations purport to represent the interests of the consumer, but consumers are not a homogenous entity.[127] Similarly, it has been noted that even in the case of labor-management issues in the unionized sector, where the problem of representativeness does not appear to be of central importance, the ability of managers to represent shareholders may be questioned, only a small percentage of the workforce is unionized, and union leaders are not always good spokesmen for the rank and file. The problem is exacerbated in the case of negotiations about environmental pollution, in which "the diverse, geographically scattered individuals who breathe the air and drink the water cannot always be represented effectively by standard environmental groups."[128]

To sum up, the "equal access" requirement mandates caution regarding the compliance of regulatory negotiation as a rulemaking technique with the deliberative-participatory model. In the US context, this caution is arguably unwarranted because the agency will ordinarily publish the draft rule coming out of the committee in a notice of proposed rulemaking, and at that point anyone can participate by submitting comments. However, in practice it will be difficult at that stage to amend significantly a draft rule based on the consensus achieved by the committee. At any rate, a negotiated rulemaking scheme in a different context not including a public consultation component would entail a clear risk of introducing through the back door elements of corporatism that run explicitly counter to the deliberative-participatory model.

Fourth, the access granted to citizens under the deliberative-participatory model aims at ensuring public input on a *policy* to be adopted. That is to say, the public is brought into this discourse as a group of *citizens*; the agency does not simply conduct a consumer satisfaction survey. This distinction is important especially in the public utilities sector during the last three decades. The "New Public Management" theory that originated in the United Kingdom but spread to other European countries (often, chapter 2 will suggest, via EU law) led to the liberalization of markets, opening them up to private actors, and to the privatization of previously state-run services: this shifted the emphasis from "citizens" to "customers" of public services.[129] However, this customer model has its limitations and underplays the democratic character of agency action.[130] This transformation of "citizens" into "customers" should not relax the interface between the administration and the citizens in the production of policy. Public surveys constitute useful tools for agencies to sense public sentiment but, as even their proponents acknowledge, they cannot replace public participation in rulemaking.[131] Chapter 5 returns to these questions in more detail.

The fifth and last question to be considered in this subsection is: how much access is too much access? This question has also been posed in the terms of a tension between participation and deliberation,[132] a tension which, one could contend, might be obscured by my use of the term "deliberative-participatory" model. Participation is a precondition for deliberation: as the number of participants increases—and this might be the outcome of the agency reaching out to various groups itself—so does the possibility that more information and suggestions coming from more diverse sources will become available to the agency, thus potentially improving the quality of regulation.[133] However, it is argued in the literature that at some point increased participation stops being complementary and becomes detrimental to deliberation: a vast influx of comments may lead to information overload, encouraging poor analysis and superficial examination of alternatives.[134]

Although the numbers from our case studies do not suggest such a problem,[135] a general response is in order. We should distinguish between instances of mass participation in which the quality of the majority of comments is relatively poor and others in which the quality of the majority of comments is high. The latter, optimistic, case manifests the peak of the deliberative-participatory model: stakeholders are mobilized and contribute comments in high numbers and quality. This should not be a problem: if an agency is overwhelmed with input of high quality, this would suggest that the policy at stake has important implications and should be considered in depth before a final decision is made. However, the skeptics about the possibility of increased participation and deliberation being combined are concerned about the first scenario. A policy of differentiated treatment of comments may offer a solution in this case: a mass electronic postcard campaign should not be accorded the same weight as detailed comments that address the questions at hand in a sophisticated way and recommend solutions. This is by no means to say that mass comments should be disregarded.[136] However, a differentiated treatment is permissible since, as will be noted below, the deliberative-participatory model does not oblige the agency to respond to every individual comment but only the most important ones. This type of treatment is also confirmed empirically.[137]

2. *Transparency*

If open access lies at the core of the deliberative-participatory model, transparency is its necessary precondition. This is why in the context of the European Union the right to transparency has been described as a second-generation participation right laying the ground for the emergence of the third-generation right of civil society participation in administrative policymaking.[138] Transparency should be required at every stage of the policymaking process. The notice of the agency's intention to adopt a new policy and the draft rule itself must be publicized as widely as possible so that all potentially interested parties can take notice and participate in the process. At the end of the process, the agency must publish all the comments it has received (subject to restrictions for the protection of business secrets, restrictions that should nonetheless be narrowly construed) together with its justification for the final content of the rule pursuant to the third requirement analyzed right below. Publicizing the comments received allows interested parties and other actors, e.g., the media, to assess the influence that specific comments have had on the final rule. Moreover, this publicly available file can form the record on which citizens may base their application for judicial review of the published rule. Ideally, the administrative authority would publish the comments as soon as it receives them so that other parties can respond to them as well as to the original call from the agency, thus enhancing the deliberative nature of the enterprise.

3. *Reason giving*

For the administrative policymaking process to be truly deliberative, the interaction between the agency and the citizens must be a two-way street.

Administrators and citizens must be part of a give-and-take process in which citizens submit comments and administrators provide feedback to participants.[139] To ensure the latter, the deliberative-participatory model must introduce a reason-giving requirement so that agencies justify the reasons for their specific policy decisions.[140] The "deliberative" explanation could be added to other rationales proffered in the literature for the reason-giving obligation.[141]

The question that naturally arises is: what kind of reasons should the agency provide to comply with this requirement? In the US context, as Jerry Mashaw observes, a focus on an agency's reasons for a regulation has become the hallmark of judicial review under the APA.[142] For instance, in one case the Supreme Court rejected the rescission of a rule because of the agency's failure to consider amending its rule rather than rescinding it.[143] In another case a court of appeals struck down a regulation because the agency did not disclose the scientific data upon which it relied and did not find the facts on which it based its choice among the evidence in the record.[144] But does the agency have to respond to each individual comment it receives? The answer is no and is derived from balancing the deliberative and participatory aspects of the normative model that this chapter defends. An obligation to address every single comment submitted would place an unbearable logistical burden on the agency and would vindicate those maintaining that deliberation and participation are irreconcilable goals. The ideal of participation would suggest that it is not realistic to expect widespread participation and a detailed agency response to all the comments submitted. On the other side, however, the ideal of deliberation would require that the agency address the fundamental issues raised by a high number of comments or by fewer comments of higher quality.[145]

4. *Judicial Review*

The role of courts in securing the deliberative-participatory promise has already emerged at previous points and is supported by scholars advocating a deliberative model of democracy. Habermas indicates that "the communicative and participatory rights that are constitutive for democratic opinion- and will-formation acquire a privileged position [in judicial review]."[146] Mark Seidenfeld's civic republican model explicitly provides that the reviewing court's proper function is to ensure that the agency has interpreted the statute in a deliberative manner: this means that the court must make sure that the agency permitted open discourse, responded to all significant comments, and explained adequately how its decision furthers the public interest.[147]

Judicial review of agency action along these lines might therefore facilitate the proper operation of the deliberative-participatory model. However, for purposes of analytic clarity we need to draw a distinction here. Judicial review could serve an instrumental purpose in supporting the operative elements identified above: open access, transparency, reason giving. Strictly speaking, it does not constitute in itself an independent conceptual building block of the normative model advocated in this chapter. Viewing judicial review as a *sine qua non* of the deliberative-participatory model would be unnecessarily (and perhaps even falsely from a theoretical standpoint) tied to the US experience of courts expanding their reach under the "arbitrary and capricious" standard.[148] In fact, even in the US literature there have been prominent voices challenging the tendency to view the value of notice-and-comment processes through the lens of their judicial vindication.[149]

Therefore, participation and judicial review should be unbundled in such a way as to accept that it is tenable that an administrative system complies with the deliberative-participatory ideal even when the three prongs of the model (open access, transparency, reason giving) are not judicially enforceable. This thesis acquires increased significance in the European context in which, as both the following section and subsequent chapters will point out, judicial review of administrative policymaking processes is, for the most part, not equally developed. An empirical question concerns the extent to which these systems meet the deliberative-participatory ideal notwithstanding the lack of stringent judicial review in the US fashion. The answer to this question will determine whether judicial review is operationally, albeit not definitionally, a requisite part of the deliberative-participatory model.[150]

V. European administrative law under siege. Is the United States a model?[151]

Administrative law in Europe is changing.[152] Subsequent chapters will argue that EU law is a major driving force for this transformation: more specifically, in the example of electronic communications, EU law is moving the domestic administrative systems in a direction closer to the deliberative-participatory model. If we look closer at the operative elements of this model identified earlier (open access, transparency, reason giving, judicial review), we will notice a striking similarity with the informal rulemaking process as organized by the US APA. Section 553 of the APA stipulates that, when making rules or regulations having binding effect on private parties, the agency must provide notice of its proposal, an opportunity for affected parties to comment, and "a concise general statement" of the basis and purpose of the rules. Furthermore, the APA empowers a reviewing court to hold unlawful and set aside agency action, findings, and conclusions found to be "arbitrary, capricious, an abuse of discretion, or otherwise not in accordance with law."[153] Does this suggest that the US APA model should be the operational model for the transformation of administrative law in European countries?

This question invokes the discussion about the US "adversarial legalism" model potentially spreading to Europe.[154] The theory of "adversarial legalism" describes American methods of policy implementation and dispute resolution as more adversarial and legalistic compared with the systems of other economically advanced countries. According to the same account, Americans more often rely on legal threats and lawsuits and US laws are generally more complicated and prescriptive, adjudication more costly, and penalties more severe. As to governance, compared with European democracies, regulatory policymaking in the United States entails "more legal formalities, more interest group participation, and more aggressive judicial review."[155] Comparative law scholars have asked whether this "adversarial legalism" is spreading across Europe. The argument is that increases in economic liberalization and political fragmentation have undermined traditional, opaque, informal approaches to regulation and have generated functional pressures and political incentives to shift toward a more formal, transparent, adversarial legal style, similar to that found in the United States.[156]

My preliminary response would be that EU law, by moving the regulatory system closer to the deliberative-participatory model described in this chapter, seems to accept the basic premises of the "adversarial legalism" picture in terms of adopting formal, open, transparent and participatory regulatory processes. However, there is one fundamental part of the "adversarial legalism" description that does not capture fully the current state of affairs in all European countries; this is the lack of extensive litigation of the sort we witness in the United States. As I have already noted and will have the opportunity to explore further in the case studies, with the exception of some cases in the United Kingdom, European courts do not enforce routinely these participatory requirements to strike down measures on the basis, for example, of lack of *effective* consultation.[157] This does not *ipso facto* preclude the application of the deliberative-participatory model. Nor does it suggest that a more robust judicial review in this direction is unlikely to develop in Europe in the future. After all, the US APA introducing rulemaking procedures was passed in 1946, and it was not until a few decades later that US courts beefed up those provisions and imposed increasingly more obligations on US agencies with respect to participatory processes. However, what it does suggest is that a US "adversarial legalism"-style regulatory system is currently not in (full) operation in Europe.

To sum up, in the search for a model of democratic accountability, the account proposed in this chapter moves beyond the paradigms of the French republican tradition, or a utopian Westminster type of representative democracy, or a German hierarchical bureaucratic model of legitimacy through expertise in favor of an operational deliberative-participatory model that provides avenues for stakeholder input in administrative proceedings. From this perspective, we end up not just questioning the existence of the so-called EU democratic deficit in the specific context of regulatory policy, but actually arguing for a potential "democratic surplus" through the initiation, encouragement or formalization of public consultation procedures at the member-state level. Therefore, the emphasis of the following chapters is on this access to processes created under EU mandates or influence that may promote the deliberative-participatory ideal. The book elaborates on this idea by using the electronic communications sector as a case study in the example of France, Greece, and the United Kingdom. Chapter 2 outlines the EU initiatives in the area of electronic communications with an emphasis on institutional and procedural mandates, and explains how these mandates may have an accountability-enhancing effect at the member-state level. The "democratic surplus" thesis is then examined in the context of three country cases: France (chapter 3), Greece (chapter 4), and the United Kingdom (chapter 5). Chapter 6 concludes by exploring what the country cases can teach us in terms of the direction that the decentralized EU regime should take in future reforms.

Notes

1. Stephen Sieberson, *The Proposed European Union Constitution—Will It Eliminate the EU's Democratic Deficit?*, 10 COLUM. J. EUR. L. 173, 174 (2004).
2. DAVID MARQUAND, PARLIAMENT FOR EUROPE 64–66 (1979).
3. DAMIAN CHALMERS & ADAM TOMKINS, EUROPEAN UNION PUBLIC LAW: TEXT AND MATERIALS 65–66 (2007).
4. *See, e.g.*, the European Parliament Resolution on the democratic deficit, (1988) OJ C 187/229 of 18.7.1988.
5. *See* Commission of the European Communities, European Governance: A White Paper, COM (2001) 428 final, Brussels, 25.7.2001, p. 3.
6. Commission of the European Communities, Communication from the Commission: Towards a reinforced culture of consultation and dialogue—General principles and minimum standards for consultation of interested parties by the Commission, COM (2002) 704 final Brussels, 11.12.2002, p. 4.
7. Presidency Conclusions, European Council Meeting in Laeken, 14 and 15 December 2001, SN 300/1/01 REV 1.
8. Juliet Lodge, *EC Policymaking: Institutional Considerations*, *in* THE EUROPEAN COMMUNITY AND THE CHALLENGE OF THE FUTURE 26, 30 (Juliet Lodge ed., 1989).
9. LARRY SIEDENTOP, DEMOCRACY IN EUROPE 104, 119 (2001).
10. *See* Giandomenico Majone, *Europe's 'Democratic Deficit': The Question of Standards*, 4 EUROPEAN LAW JOURNAL 5, 6 (1998) (describing these "traditional arguments"). This account reflects the position of the German Constitutional Court, which, ruling on the constitutionality of the ratification of the Lisbon Treaty, wrote: "The empowerment to exercise supranational competences comes, however, from the Member States of such an institution. They therefore permanently remain the masters of the Treaties. In a functional sense, the source of Community authority, and of the European constitution that constitutes it, are the peoples of Europe with their democratic constitutions in their states." (BVerfG, 2 BvE 2/08 Judgment of June 30, 2009, para. 231). Similar language had been used in the *Brunner* case, in which the German Constitutional Court ruled on the Maastricht Treaty (BVerfGE 89, 155, Judgment of October 12, 1993).
11. J. H. H. Weiler, *The Transformation of Europe*, 100 YALE L.J. 2403, 2473 (1991).

12. Majone, *supra* note 10, at 12.

13. *See* ECJ Case 26/62, *Van Gend en Loos*, Judgment of February 5, 1963; ECJ Case 6/64, *Costa v. Enel*, Judgment of July 15, 1964; Majone, *supra* note 10, at 12–13.

14. Weiler, *supra* note 11, at 2467.

15. For a presentation of these arguments, *see* Majone, *supra* note 10, at 6–7, Oliver Gerstenberg, *Law's Polyarchy: A Comment on Cohen and Sabel*, 3 EUROPEAN LAW JOURNAL 343, 347–48 (1997), Oliver Gerstenberg & Charles F. Sabel, *Directly-Deliberative Polyarchy: An Institutional Ideal for Europe?*, *in* GOOD GOVERNANCE IN EUROPE'S INTEGRATED MARKET 289, 300 (Christian Joerges & Renaud Dehousse eds., 2002), Fritz W Scharpf, *Democratic Policy in Europe*, 2 EUROPEAN LAW JOURNAL 136 (1996).

16. Stephen Sieberson, *The Treaty of Lisbon and its Impact on the European Union's Democratic Deficit*, 14 COLUM. J. EUR. L. 445, 446 (2008).

17. Andrew Moravcsik, *In Defence of the "Democratic Deficit": Reassessing Legitimacy in the European Union*, 40 JOURNAL OF COMMON MARKET STUDIES 603, 605 (2002); *see also* Andrew Moravcsik, *Despotism In Brussels? Misreading the European Union*, 80 (3) FOREIGN AFFAIRS May/June 2001 (vehemently critiquing Siedentop's take on the question of democratic deficit).

18. Andrew Moravcsik, *The Myth of Europe's "Democratic Deficit"*, INTERECONOMICS: JOURNAL OF EUROPEAN ECONOMIC POLICY 331, 332 (November-December 2008).

19. *See* ANDREW MORAVCSIK, THE CHOICE FOR EUROPE: SOCIAL PURPOSE AND STATE POWER FROM MESSINA TO MAASTRICHT (1998), describing European integration as "a series of rational adaptations by national leaders to constraints and opportunities stemming from the evolution of an interdependent world economy, the relative power of states in the international system, and the potential for international institutions to bolster the credibility of interstate commitments" (*id.* at 472) and concluding that the EC has been, for the most part, the deliberate creation of statesmen and citizens seeking to realize economic interests through traditional diplomatic means (*id.* at 501).

20. *See* SUSAN ROSE-ACKERMAN, RETHINKING THE PROGRESSIVE AGENDA. THE REFORM OF THE AMERICAN REGULATORY STATE 34–38 (1992). *See also* Yves Mény & Yves Surel, *The Constitutive Ambiguity of Populism*, *in* Democracies and the Populist Challenge 1, 7–11 (Yves Mény & Yves Surel eds., 2002).

21. Bernard Manin, Adam Przeworski & Susan Stokes, *Elections and Representation*, *in* DEMOCRACY, ACCOUNTABILITY, AND REPRESENTATION 29, 33 (Adam Przeworski, Susan C. Stokes, Bernard Manin eds. 1999) (noting that "mandate representation occurs when what politicians and voters want coincides or when politicians care only about winning elections, and to win they must promise and implement policies that are best for the public. But short of this happy coincidence, politicians may have incentives to . . . deviate from the mandate." The authors explain that this might also be attributed to incumbents gratifying special interests that helped them get elected by financially supporting their campaigns). *See also* Susan C. Stokes, *What Do Policy Switches Tell Us about Democracy?*, *in* DEMOCRACY, ACCOUNTABILITY, AND REPRESENTATION 98 (Adam Przeworski, Susan C. Stokes, Bernard Manin eds. 1999) (studying presidential elections in Latin America between 1982 and 1995, observing that politicians regularly deviated from their mandates, and noting that although violations of mandate are not inconsistent with representation narrowly construed, they should still raise alarms about the quality of democracies in which they are endemic).

22. *See* Manin, Przeworski & Stokes, *supra* note 21, at 50. *See also* John Dunn, *Situating Democratic Political Accountability*, *in* DEMOCRACY, ACCOUNTABILITY, AND REPRESENTATION 329, 336 (Adam Przeworski, Susan C. Stokes, Bernard Manin eds. 1999) (noting that "[a]t the very least, an analysis of how accountability can reasonably be hoped to work must take in a sophisticated division of political labor . . . and a far wider range of transactions than giving or witholding one's vote, and winning or losing elective office.").

23. *See* Renaud Dehousse, *Constitutional Reform in the European Community: Are there Alternatives to the Majoritarian Avenue?*, 18 WEST EUROPEAN POLITICS 118, 122 (1998).

24. *See* Valentine Herman & Juliet Lodge, *The European Parliament and the "Decline of Legislatures" Thesis*, 13 JOURNAL OF THE AUSTRALASIAN POLITICAL STUDIES ASSOCIATION 10, 10–12

(1978) (noting a decline in Parliaments' performance of their legislative, financial/budgetary, control and representative functions); JEAN BLONDEL, COMPARATIVE LEGISLATURES 5–7 (1973). This term was used by Lord Bryce (JAMES BRYCE, MODERN DEMOCRACIES 335 (vol. II, 1921)) to describe a disappointment with legislatures that had already appeared in the 19th century works of A. LAWRENCE LOWELL, GOVERNMENTS AND PARTIES IN CONTINENTAL EUROPE (vols. I, II, 1896) and JAMES BRYCE, THE AMERICAN COMMONWEALTH (vol. I, 1888).

25. Over sixty years ago, Justice Jackson characterized the rise of the administrative state as "probably the most significant legal trend of the last century" (*Federal Trade Comm'n v. Ruberoid Co.*, 343 U.S. 470, 487 (1952) (Jackson, J., dissenting)). The phrase "rise of the administrative state" can be found over 500 times in the literature (Jonathan R. Siegel, *Law and Longitude*, 84 TUL. L. REV. 1, 57 n.285 (2009)). For the rise of the administrative state in Europe, *see* Giandomenico Majone, *The Rise of Statutory Regulation in Europe, in* REGULATING EUROPE 47 (Giandomenico Majone ed., 1996). Notably, the administrative state has been accorded constitutional status in the U.S. constitutional theory; *see* Bruce A. Ackerman, *The Storrs Lectures: Discovering the Constitution*, 93 YALE L. J. 1013, 1051–57 (1984) and BRUCE ACKERMAN, WE THE PEOPLE: TRANSFORMATIONS 255ff. (1998). *See also* Cass R. Sunstein, *Constitutionalism After the New Deal*, 101 HARV. L. REV. 421, 447–48 (1987) (agreeing that the New Deal "altered the constitutional system in ways so fundamental as to suggest that something akin to a constitutional amendment had taken place"). *Contra* Gary Lawson, *The Rise and Rise of the Administrative State*, 107 HARV. L. REV. 1231, 1231–32 (1994) (declaring the post-New Deal administrative state unconstitutional, but acknowledging nonetheless that the essential features of the modern administrative state have been taken as "unchallengeable postulates by virtually all players in the legal and political worlds").

26. KENNETH C. WHEARE, LEGISLATURES 148 (2nd ed. 1968).

27. *See* Susan Rose-Ackerman, *American Administrative Law Under Siege: Is Germany a Model?*, 107 HARV. L. REV. 1279, 1295–96 (1994). *See also* CORNELIUS M. KERWIN, RULEMAKING. HOW GOVERNMENT AGENCIES WRITE LAW AND MAKE POLICY 13–20 (3d ed. 2003) (compiling data to document the "formidable volume" of rules). There are similar trends in other countries; see, e.g., the observation of a parliamentary committee in the UK that "[s]econdary legislation makes up the majority of the law of this country. When implemented it affects every sphere of activity" (House of Lords Merits of Statutory Instruments Committee, *What happened next? A study of Post-Implementation Reviews of secondary legislation* (HL 180 2008-09), [1]).

28. *See* A. A. Berle Jr., *The Expansion of American Administrative Law*, 30 HARV. L. REV. 430, 431 (1917) (noting that "administrative law is the law applicable to the transmission of the will of the state, from its source to the point of its application").

29. Richard B. Stewart, *The Reformation of American Administrative Law*, 88 HARV. L. REV. 1669, 1684 (1975). *See also* JERRY L. MASHAW, DUE PROCESS IN THE ADMINISTRATIVE STATE 22 (1985) (noting that congressional statutes themselves require administrative agencies to make trade-offs between, for example, the need for public health or safety and the need for employment, product diversity, and a vibrant economy).

30. Bruce Ackerman, *The New Separation of Powers*, 113 HARV. L. REV. 633, 694 (2000).

31. *See* Susan Rose-Ackerman, *Regulation and Public Law in Comparative Perspective*, 60 U. TORONTO L.J. 519, 526 ("just as the legislature does not have the time, expertise, or foresight to write detailed statutes *ex ante*, so, too, it lacks the ability to provide comprehensive oversight *ex post*").

32. The various puzzles posed by independent agencies and their position in the constitutional edifice have been addressed in the literature on both sides of the Atlantic. *See, e.g.*, in Europe, Mark Thatcher, *Independent Regulatory Agencies and Elected Politicians in Europe, in* REGULATION THROUGH AGENCIES IN THE EU: A NEW PARADIGM OF EUROPEAN GOVERNANCE 47 (Damien Geradin & Rodolphe Munoz & Nicolas Petit eds., 2005), Conseil d'État, *Les autorités administratives indépendantes* (Rapport Public 2001—Jurisprudence et avis de 2000), Etudes & Documents No 52, at 251–462 (2001). In the US literature, *see Symposium: The Independence of Independent Agencies*, 1988 DUKE L.J. 215–99 (1988), Marshall J. Breger & Gary J. Edles, *Established by Practice: The Theory and Operation of Independent Federal*

Agencies, 52 ADMIN. L. REV. 1111 (2000), Martin Shapiro, *The problems of independent agencies in the United States and the European Union*, 4 JOURNAL OF EUROPEAN PUBLIC POLICY 276 (1997).

33. *See* Francesca Bignami, *The Democratic Deficit in European Community Rulemaking: A Call for Notice and Comment in Comitology*, 40 HARV. INT'L L.J. 451, 452 (1999). *See also* Peter Lindseth, *Democratic Legitimacy and the Administrative Character of Supranationalism: The Example of the European Community*, 99 COLUM. L. REV. 628, 684 (1999) (arguing that "parliamentary democratization largely misses the point, because the democratic deficit is really an accountability deficit at the subordinate technocratic level due to the lack of transparency and legally-enforceable participation rights in the regulatory process").

34. *See* Giandomenico Majone, *Regulatory Legitimacy, in* REGULATING EUROPE 294, 294–95 (Giandomenico Majone ed., 1996). *See also* Yves Mény, *De la démocratie en Europe: Old Concepts and New Challenges*, 41 JOURNAL OF COMMON MARKET STUDIES 1, 9 (2002) ("there is certainly a case for emphasizing the weakness of popular input in European institutions, but the same kind of critique should also be addressed to national systems").

35. *See* JAMES M. LANDIS, THE ADMINISTRATIVE PROCESS 23–24 (1938) (noting that "[w]ith the rise of regulation, the need for expertness became dominant; for the art of regulating an industry requires knowledge of the details of its operation . . . . Efficiency in the processes of governmental regulation is best served by the creation of more rather than less agencies. And it is efficiency that is the desperate need").

36. Bronwen Morgan, *Technocratic v. Convivial Accountability, in* PUBLIC ACCOUNTABILITY. DESIGNS, DILEMMAS AND EXPERIENCES 243, 246–48 (Michael W. Dowdle ed., 2006) (presenting this technocratic account, and later rejecting it as inadequate).

37. *See, e.g.*, Mark A. Pollack, *Learning from the Americanists (Again): Theory and Method in the Study of Delegation, in* THE POLITICS OF DELEGATION 200, 207–08 (Mark Thatcher & Alec Stone Sweet eds., 2003).

38. Giandomenico Majone, *Two Logics of Delegation: Agency and Fiduciary Relations in EU Governance*, 2 EUROPEAN UNION POLITICS 103 (2001).

39. This is one of the different political reasons for delegation suggested in the literature in addition to the functional/prudential arguments. For instance, it has also been argued that delegation serves legislators' self-interest in reelection because they can supply facilitation services to constituents in approaching the bureaucracy. (Morris P. Fiorina & Roger G. Noll, *Voters, Legislators and Bureaucracy: Institutional Design in the Public Sector*, 68 (2) AMERICAN ECONOMIC REVIEW, PAPERS AND PROCEEDINGS 256 (1978)). Another reason for delegation—summarized as the blame-avoidance thesis—is the possibility of passing on hard choices for unpopular policies to agencies (Susan Rose-Ackerman, *Introduction, in* ECONOMICS OF ADMINISTRATIVE LAW xiii, xv (Susan Rose-Ackerman ed., 2007)). Of course, the different rationales for delegation may overlap (Mark Thatcher & Alec Stone Sweet, *Theory and Practice of Delegation to Non-Majoritarian Institutions, in* THE POLITICS OF DELEGATION 1, 4 (Mark Thatcher & Alec Stone Sweet eds., 2003).

40. *See* Giandomenico Majone, *Two Logics of Delegation: Agency and Fiduciary Relations in EU Governance*, 2 EUROPEAN UNION POLITICS 103, 105ff. (2001), Giandomenico Majone, *Theories of Regulation, in* REGULATING EUROPE 28, 40–44 (Giandomenico Majone ed., 1996), Majone, *supra* note 10, at 16ff.

41. Which should not be taken for granted, *see* Renaud Dehousse, *The legitimacy of European Governance: The need for a process-based approach*, 1 CAHIERS EUROPÉENS DE SCIENCES PO 1, 13–14 (2001).

42. *See* Stewart, *supra* note 29, at 1684. *See also* Cass R. Sunstein, *Factions, Self-Interest, and the APA: Four Lessons since 1946*, 72 VA. L. REV. 271, 281 (1986) (noting that technical information will rarely be conclusive and its usefulness will often depend upon value judgments); Morgan, *supra* note 36, at 257 (noting "a certain disingenuousness about the evasion of the value-laden issues [through the use of expert language and the technical rationalization of the reasons for a decision]"). A similar response to Majone's rather optimistic picture was that while regulatory policies are purely Pareto efficient, the current reality is rather different, for many such policies have identifiable winners and losers; *see* Andreas Follesdal &

Simon Hix, *Why There is a Democratic Deficit in the EU: A Response to Majone and Moravcsik*, 44 JOURNAL OF COMMON MARKET STUDIES 533, 543 (2006).

43. *See* Ackerman, *supra* note 30, at 694 (further suggesting that "[m]odern constitutions must take constructive steps to lay bare the crucial dimensions of normative bureaucratic judgment and to discipline its exercise by a host of techniques ranging from public participation to judicial oversight"). As subsequent chapters will show, our scheme is along these lines not just as a normative question of proper institutional design, but also as a descriptive account of the way in which the decentralized regulatory system works in the EU.

44. Jürgen Habermas, *Three Normative Models of Democracy*, in JÜRGEN HABERMAS, THE INCLUSION OF THE OTHER. STUDIES IN POLITICAL THEORY 239, 249–50 (Ciaran Cronin & Pablo De Greiff eds., 1998).

45. JÜRGEN HABERMAS, BETWEEN FACTS AND NORMS. CONTRIBUTIONS TO A DISCOURSE THEORY OF LAW AND DEMOCRACY 107, 147, 327 (William Rehg trans., MIT Press, 1996).

46. Ciaran Cronin & Pablo De Greiff, *Editors' Introduction*, in JÜRGEN HABERMAS, THE INCLUSION OF THE OTHER. STUDIES IN POLITICAL THEORY vii, xvii (Ciaran Cronin & Pablo De Greiff eds., 1998).

47. *See* Erik Eriksen, *A Comment on Schmalz-Bruns*, in DEBATING THE DEMOCRATIC LEGITIMACY OF THE EUROPEAN UNION 304, 306 (Beate Kohler-Koch & Berthold Rittberger eds., 2007).

48. HABERMAS, *supra* note 45, at 445.

49. Hugh Baxter, *Habermas's Discourse Theory of Law and Democracy*, 50 BUFF. L. REV. 205, 288 (2002); *see also* HABERMAS, *supra* note 45, at 285 ("a consistent proceduralist understanding of the constitution relies on the intrinsically rational character of a democratic process that grounds the presumption of rational outcomes").

50. Recent trends at the EU administration level indicate that the EU, in particular, the European Commission, might be moving toward recognizing a right of civil society participation in European governance—Francesca Bignami calls this the third generation of participation rights before the Commission (Francesca Bignami, *Three generations of participation rights before the European Commission*, 68 LAW AND CONTEMP. PROBS. 61, 72 (2004)). This was quite clearly indicated in the 2001 White Paper on Governance (*supra* note 5), in which participation figures prominently as one of the principles underpinning good governance in the Union. The Commission stresses that "the quality, relevance and effectiveness of EU policies depend on ensuring wide participation throughout the policy chain—from conception to implementation" (*id.*, at 10). In 2002, the Commission issued the "Communication on Consultation," which reiterates its commitment to encouraging "more involvement of interested parties through a more transparent consultation process" and provides general principles and standards for consultation that help the Commission to rationalize its consultation procedures (*supra* note 6, at 19–22). This emphasis on stakeholder participation is a recurring theme in Commission policy documents (see, e.g., the European Commission's Third strategic review of Better Regulation in the European Union, Brussels, 28.1.2009, COM(2009) 15 final, p. 7). Related provisions were included in the rejected Constitutional Treaty (Article I-47 of the Constitutional Treaty on the "principle of participatory" democracy) and currently in the Treaty of Lisbon (Article 11 TEU). For an interesting account arguing that the scope of participation rights in EU administrative law is too narrow and should be extended to new situations and new types of procedures, in particular those that generally fall within the category of rulemaking, *see* JOANA MENDES, PARTICIPATION IN EU RULE-MAKING: A RIGHTS-BASED APPROACH (2011).

51. Habermas acknowledges the discussion about the "oft-bemoaned democratic deficit." What he puts forth is, in essence, a normative account: he asserts that what is needed to promote a "European democracy" is the development of a European-networked civil society, a European-wide integrated public sphere in the ambit of a common political culture (Jürgen Habermas, *Does Europe Need a Constitution? Response to Dieter Grimm*, in JÜRGEN HABERMAS, THE INCLUSION OF THE OTHER. STUDIES IN POLITICAL THEORY 155, 159–61 (Ciaran Cronin & Pablo De Greiff eds., 1998)). In a more recent (and, one could say, more pragmatic) account, Habermas advocates a policy of graduated integration which would bind only member states in which citizens had voted in favor of a politically constituted Union (JÜRGEN HABERMAS, EUROPE: THE FALTERING PROJECT 78 (Ciaran Cronin trans.,

Polity, 2009). Chapter 6 revisits the question of civil society organization and participation at the EU level.

52. Habermas, *supra* note 44, at 246.

53. *Id.* at 248.

54. HABERMAS, *supra* note 45, at 136. This could respond to Rubin's criticism of deliberative democracy that "the image of civil society as a whole deliberating about some issue is an unproductive metaphor driven by the premodern image of democracy" (Edward L. Rubin, *Getting Past Democracy*, 149 U. PA. L. REV. 711, 749 (2001).

55. *See* Nicholas R. Miller, *Pluralism and Social Choice, in* THE DEMOCRACY SOURCEBOOK 133, 133 (Robert A. Dahl, Ian Shapiro & José Antonio Cheibub eds., 2003) ("The fundamental postulates . . . are that (1) all societies are divided along one or more lines of fundamental conflict or cleavage that partition its members into different sets, and (2) the preferences of members of society, with respect to alternative public policies, are largely determined by the set to which those members belong").

56. John F. Manley, *Neo-pluralism: A Class Analysis of Pluralism I and Pluralism II, in* THE DEMOCRACY SOURCEBOOK 381, 382 (Robert A. Dahl, Ian Shapiro & José Antonio Cheibub eds., 2003).

57. *See* ROBERT A. DAHL, PLURALIST DEMOCRACY IN THE UNITED STATES: CONFLICT AND CONSENT 130–31 (1967).

58. *Id.* at 24.

59. For the pluralistic justification of the administrative state, *see* Mark Seidenfeld, *A Civic Republican Justification for the Bureaucratic State*, 105 HARV. L. REV. 1511, 1521–23 (1992) (who argues, nonetheless, that the pluralistic democracy theory fails to fully justify the broad grants of policy-setting authority characterizing the present administrative state).

60. *Id.* at 1524, 1523–26 (elaborating on the argument made in the text).

61. *See* Rubin, *supra* note 54, at 745; Daniel A. Farber & Philip P. Frickey, *The Jurisprudence of Public Choice*, 65 TEX. L. REV. 873, 894–901 (1987); RICHARD A. POSNER, THE FEDERAL COURTS: CRISIS AND REFORM 265–67 (1985).

62. *See* George J. Stigler, *The Theory of Economic Regulation*, 2 BELL J.ECON. & MANAGEMENT SCI. 3, 11–12 (1971).

63. *See* SUSAN ROSE-ACKERMAN, CORRUPTION AND GOVERNMENT. CAUSES, CONSEQUENCES, AND REFORM 75–77 (1999).

64. Steven P. Croley, *Public Interested Regulation*, 28 FLA. ST. U. L. REV. 7, 30 (2000) (noting additionally that "[i]t seems more likely that the future employment prospects of administrative regulators depend entirely on the regulators' experiences with regulatory issues, not on particular decisions that were friendly to an interest group or groups. If so, regulated interests might well seek to hire those administrators who were most aggressive against them . . . . To that extent, future employment opportunities would make administrators less friendly towards groups who might hire them later—exactly the opposite of what the wisdom informed by "revolving door" imagines").

65. ROBERT A. DAHL, A PREFACE TO DEMOCRATIC THEORY 128 (1956).

66. Rubin, *supra* note 54, at 742–43.

67. *Cf.* John F. Manley, *Neo-pluralism: A Class Analysis of Pluralism I and Pluralism II, in* THE DEMOCRACY SOURCEBOOK 381, 391 (Robert A. Dahl, Ian Shapiro & José Antonio Cheibub eds., 2003) (noting that even updated accounts of pluralism—"Pluralism II"- are incompatible with substantive equality).

68. *United States v. Carolene Prods. Co.*, 304 U.S. 144, 152 n.4 (1938) ("whether prejudice against discrete and insular minorities may be a special condition, which tends seriously to curtail the operation of those political processes ordinarily to be relied upon to protect minorities, and which may call for a correspondingly more searching judicial inquiry").

69. Bruce A. Ackerman, *Beyond Carolene Products*, 98 HARV. L. REV. 713, 723–24 (1985).

70. HABERMAS, *supra* note 45, at 171 and 136 (referring to the "anonymous form" of popular sovereignty).

71. *Cf.* Jürgen Habermas, *On the Internal Relation between the Rule of Law and Democracy, in* THE INCLUSION OF THE OTHER. STUDIES IN POLITICAL THEORY 253, 259 (Ciaran Cronin & Pablo

De Greiff eds., 1998) (referring to democratic procedure which provides legitimating force to the lawmaking process "in the context of social and ideological pluralism").

72. *See, e.g.*, William E. Forbath, *Habermas's Constitution: A History, Guide, and Critique*, 23 LAW & SOC. INQUIRY 969, 1000–1001 (1998) (noting that forging and sustaining an institutional role for such associations in the deliberation and bargaining that attend policymaking frequently requires affirmative state intervention and support. In fact, "the broader, more diffuse, or more subjugated the potential 'publics,' the more pressing the need for state support," *id.* at 1001).

73. *See* Joshua Cohen & Charles Sabel, *Directly-Deliberative Polyarchy*, 3 EUROPEAN LAW JOURNAL 313 (1997) [hereinafter Cohen & Sabel, *Directly-Deliberative*]; Joshua Cohen & Charles F. Sabel, *Global Democracy?*, 37 NYU JOURNAL OF INTERNATIONAL LAW AND POLITICS 763 (2005); Oliver Gerstenberg & Charles F. Sabel, *Directly-Deliberative Polyarchy: An Institutional Ideal for Europe?*, *in* GOOD GOVERNANCE IN EUROPE'S INTEGRATED MARKET 289 (Christian Joerges & Renaud Dehousse eds., 2002).

74. Cohen & Sabel, *Directly-Deliberative, supra* note 73, at 291–92.

75. Cohen & Sabel, *Directly-Deliberative, supra* note 73, at 335 (further noting that "[i]nstead of seeking to solve problems, the agencies see their task as reducing the costs of information faced by different problem-solvers: helping them to determine which deliberative bodies are similarly situated, what projects those bodies are pursuing, and what modifications of those projects might be needed under local conditions").

76. Jürgen Habermas, *Further Reflections on the Public Sphere*, *in* HABERMAS AND THE PUBLIC SPHERE 421, 452 (Craig Calhoun ed., 1992).

77. Cohen & Sabel, *Directly-Deliberative, supra* note 73, at 339.

78. JOHN P. MCCORMICK, WEBER, HABERMAS, AND TRANSFORMATIONS OF THE EUROPEAN STATE: CONSTITUTIONAL, SOCIAL, AND SUPRANATIONAL DEMOCRACY 216 (2007).

79. HABERMAS, *supra* note 45, at 147 (employing the concept introduced dogmatically by Hannah Arendt).

80. Robert M. Cover, *Nomos and Narrative*, 97 HARV. L. REV. 4, 11 (1983).

81. *Id.* at 25, 39–40.

82. HABERMAS, *supra* note 45, at 147 (emphasis added).

83. Cover, *supra* note 80, at 40.

84. Baxter, *supra* note 49, at 266 n.276.

85. Hugh Baxter, *Autopoiesis and the "Relative Autonomy" of Law*, 19 CARDOZO L. REV. 1987, 1993 (1988).

86. Niklas Luhmann, *Operational Closure and Structural Coupling: The Differentiation of the Legal System*, 13 CARDOZO L. REV. 1419, 1424 (1992).

87. NIKLAS LUHMANN, ESSAYS ON SELF-REFERENCE 3 (1990).

88. HABERMAS, *supra* note 45, at 51 and 335.

89. Hugh Baxter, *System and Lifeworld in Habermas's Theory of Law*, 23 CARDOZO L. REV. 473, 607–09 (2002).

90. Luhmann, *supra* note 86, at 1432 (further explaining that "[w]alking presupposes the gravitational forces of the earth within very narrow limits, but gravitation does not contribute any steps to the movement of bodies. Communication presupposes awareness states of conscious systems, but conscious states cannot become social and do not enter the sequence of communicative operations as a part of them").

91. *See* HABERMAS, *supra* note 45, at 335. *Cf.* Marleen Brans & Stefan Rossbach, *The Autopoiesis of Administrative Systems: Niklas Luhmann on Public Administration and Public Policy*, 75 PUBLIC ADMINISTRATION 417, 428–29 (1997) (noting that in Luhmann's view, "politics and "government" are functionally and analytically differentiated, and that the relationship between the two is not easily translatable into a particular institutional boundary).

92. Luhmann, *supra* note 86, at 1432.

93. Other theorists have tried to modify the autopoietic theory to account for intersystemic effects by introducing, for example, the idea of "interference" between law and society (GUNTHER TEUBNER, LAW AS AN AUTOPOIETIC SYSTEM 64–99 (Zenon Bankowski ed., Anne Bankowska & Ruth Adler trans., Blackwell 1993). Habermas refutes this attempt as inconsistent with the

theoretical architecture Teubner desires on the grounds that it tacitly presupposes the kind of communication that systems theory must exclude (HABERMAS, *supra* note 45, at 52–56; *see also* William Rehg, *Introduction, in* HABERMAS, *supra* note 45, at xxiii).

94. Niklas Luhmann, *Quod Omnes Tangit. Remarks on Jürgen Habermas's Legal Theory, in* HABERMAS ON LAW AND DEMOCRACY. CRITICAL EXCHANGES 157, 166 (Michel Rosenfeld & Andrew Arato eds., 1998).

95. That is, how public influence is transformed into communicative power and "enters through parliamentary debates into legitimate lawmaking" (HABERMAS, *supra* note 45, at 371).

96. 1 JÜRGEN HABERMAS, THE THEORY OF COMMUNICATIVE ACTION. REASON AND THE RATIONALIZATION OF SOCIETY (Thomas McCarthy trans., Beacon Press, 1984), 2 JÜRGEN HABERMAS, THE THEORY OF COMMUNICATIVE ACTION. LIFEWORLD AND SYSTEM: A CRITIQUE OF FUNCTIONALIST REASON (Thomas McCarthy trans., Beacon Press, 1987).

97. Baxter, *supra* note 89, at 572.

98. 2 HABERMAS, *supra* note 96, at 154.

99. Baxter, *supra* note 89, at 588.

100. HABERMAS, *supra* note 45, at 150 (further noting that "[a]dministrative power should not reproduce itself on its own terms but should only be permitted to regenerate from the conversion of communicative power").

101. For the analysis that follows in the text, *see* HABERMAS, *supra* note 45, at 354–56.

102. Habermas explains that the "outer periphery" branches into "customers" and "suppliers." "Customers" are groups that attempt to influence the political process more from the standpoint of particular interests; on the contrary, "suppliers" give voice to social problems, make broad demands, and articulate public interests or needs. Naturally, as Habermas acknowledges, the distinction is not a sharp one.

103. HABERMAS, *supra* note 45, at 356.

104. *See* Forbath, *supra* note 72, at 998 (noting that "Habermas violates his own injunctions. He sternly excludes the unruly norms and practices of democracy from the economic and administrative realms; then, at critical points, he smuggles them back in. The result is a deeply ambiguous and ambivalent account of the relationship between democratic principles, practices, and public spheres on the one hand, and the realms of the economy and public administration on the other").

105. *See* Baxter, *supra* note 89, at 570–71, 589–90.

106. HABERMAS, *supra* note 45, at 192 (emphasis in the original).

107. *Id.* at 188.

108. *Id.* at 191.

109. *Id.*

110. *Id.* at 193; *see also id.* at 438 (noting that "[w]e can no longer focus on the abstract, general statute as though it were the sole support for the institutional separation of the legislative, adjudicative, and executive branches of government. Even during the so-called liberal period, the institutional separation of powers by no means fully coincided with the functional separation. To be sure, the differences emerged more clearly as the welfare state developed. In speaking of "legislature," "judiciary," and "administration" in overly concrete terms, one disguises the logic of a functional separation of powers").

111. *Id.* at 391, 429 (also noting that legitimation problems cannot be reduced to the inefficiency of administrative steering).

112. *Id.* at 440.

113. *Id.* at 440. Forbath (*supra* note 72, at 998) has criticized Habermas for the "deep ambivalence" that runs through his works and "impedes it from helping to answer some of the very questions Habermas hopes to illuminate," including the forms of public administration we need today.

114. HABERMAS, *supra* note 45, at 171.

115. Baxter, *supra* note 49, at 284.

116. HABERMAS, *supra* note 45, at 170.

117. *See, e.g., Doctors for Life Int'l v. Speaker of the National Assembly*, 2006 (12) BCLR 1399 (CC) (South Africa), in which the South African Court proffered an expansive reading of

participation rights within the context of legislative lawmaking. The Court's opinion also drew from international treaties and from the public law of other jurisdictions to argue for an enforceable right to public participation in lawmaking under the South African Constitution. *See also*, on this case, Athanasios Efstratios Psygkas, *Revitalizing the "Liberty of the Ancients" Through Citizen Participation in the Legislative Process. Thoughts on* Doctors for Life International v the Speaker of the National Assembly & Others, 5 ANNUAIRE INTERNATIONAL DES DROITS DE L'HOMME/INTERNATIONAL YEARBOOK ON HUMAN RIGHTS 719 (2010); Karen Syma Czapanskiy & Rashida Manjoo, *The Right of Public Participation in the Law-making Process and the Role of Legislature in the Promotion of this Right*, 19 DUKE J. COMP. & INT'L L. 1 (2008).

118. Jerry L. Mashaw, *Prodelegation: Why Administrators Should Make Political Decisions*, 1 J.L. ECON. & ORG. 81, 99 (1985).

119. Seidenfeld, *supra* note 59, at 1576. *See also* Robert B. Reich, *Public Administration and Public Deliberation: An Interpretive Essay*, 94 YALE L.J. 1617, 1631–40 (1985) (noting the potential of public administrators to foster public deliberation).

120. Of course, the story would be different were these groups to use their resources in order to exert illegitimate influence on agency officials through under-the-table transactions.

121. *See, e.g.*, Mariano-Florentino Cuéllar, *Rethinking Regulatory Democracy*, 57 ADMIN. L. REV. 411, 491–95 (2005).

122. Philip Harter, *Negotiating Regulations: A Cure for Malaise*, 71 GEO. L.J. 1 (1982); Negotiated Rulemaking Act of 1990, 5 U.S.C. §§ 561–70.

123. *See* JEFFREY S. LUBBERS, A GUIDE TO FEDERAL AGENCY RULEMAKING 212–17 (4th ed. 2006).

124. *See, e.g.*, Laura I. Langbein & Cornelius M. Kerwin, *Regulatory Negotiation: Claims, Counter Claims and Empirical Evidence*, 10 JOURNAL OF PUBLIC ADMINISTRATION RESEARCH AND THEORY 599 (2000) (studying the quality of the experience of the participants in both regulatory negotiations and conventional rulemaking and finding that on a wide range of criteria negotiated rulemaking received higher ratings than did conventional processes). *But see* Cary Coglianese, *Assessing Consensus: The Promise and Performance of Negotiated Rulemaking*, 46 DUKE L.J. 1255 (1997) (arguing that, with respect to both saving time and eliminating litigation, negotiated rulemaking so far has not proven itself superior to informal rulemaking).

125. William Funk, *When Smoke Gets in Your Eyes: Regulatory Negotiation and the Public Interest-EPA's Woodstove Standards*, 18 ENVTL. L. 55, 97 (1987) (referring to the case study of the EPA's proposed rule to establish emission limitations for residential woodstoves under the Clean Air Act).

126. HABERMAS, *supra* note 45, at 165–67 (adding that these procedures should "provide all the interested parties with an equal opportunity for pressure").

127. William Funk makes this point with respect to the role of the Consumer Federation of America (CFA) in the woodstove negotiation cited previously (*supra* note 125, at 95, noting that, the CFA "may have represented the interests associated with the mentality of a Consumers Reports reader, but it did not appear to lobby on behalf of poor, rural folk for whom the rule will provide little benefit and perhaps significant burden").

128. For both examples, *see* Susan Rose-Ackerman, *Consensus Versus Incentives: A Skeptical Look at Regulatory Negotiation*, 43 DUKE L.J. 1206, 1210 (1994).

129. A characteristic example is the "Citizens' Charter" in the United Kingdom (The Citizen's Charter: Raising the Standard, Cm 1599 (1991)), which uses the term "citizens" in its title but the core of its content pertains to consumer rights with respect to public services. The term "Citizens' Charter" was for this reason described as a misnomer and the term "public customer's charter" was suggested as more "fitting" (Robin Hambleton & Paul Hoggett, *Rethinking Consumerism in Public Service*, 3 CONSUMER POLICY REVIEW 103, 111 (1993)).

130. *Cf.* Morgan, *supra* note 36, at 258 (referring to the literature "excoriating the replacement of the citizen by the consumer as the prototypical 'figure' of political discourse" and noting that "[m]uch of this criticism has a neo-republican inflection, assuming that technocratic modes of accountability have the effect of marginalizing the active creation of community. Active political citizens are, it is feared, replaced by apolitical, passive consumers").

131. *See* Carol Harlow, *Public Service, Market Ideology, and Citizenship, in* PUBLIC SERVICES AND CITIZENSHIP IN EUROPEAN LAW. PUBLIC AND LABOUR LAW PERSPECTIVES 49, 54–56 (Mark Freedland & Silvana Sciarra eds., 1998) (noting that New Public Management techniques are not necessarily undemocratic because they are derived from the market, but acknowledging that policymaking involves choices which New Public Management sees as appropriate for management and inappropriate for citizen input); *see also* Lester W. Milbrath, *Citizen Surveys as Citizen Participation Mechanisms*, 17 JOURNAL OF APPLIED BEHAVIORAL SCIENCE 478, 489 (1981) (supporting the use of citizen surveys, but noting that they constitute a snapshot in time and are no substitute for the creative policymaking that can occur in good face-to-face discussion).

132. *See, e.g.*, DIANA C. MUTZ, HEARING THE OTHER SIDE. DELIBERATIVE VERSUS PARTICIPATORY DEMOCRACY 17 (2006) (asking whether "deliberation and participation can really be part and parcel of the same goal" and noting that "the prototypical deliberative encounter—a calm, rational exchange of views in near-monotone voices" might not convey the "passionate enthusiasm" potentially associated with political participation).

133. Heterogeneity can be conducive to higher-quality deliberation; *see, e.g.*, Cass R. Sunstein, *Deliberative Trouble? Why Groups Go to Extremes*, 110 YALE L.J. 71, 76 (2000).

134. *See* Jim Rossi, *Participation Run Amok: The Costs of Mass Participation for Deliberative Agency Decisionmaking*, 92 NW. U. L. REV. 173, 211–41 (1997).

135. *See infra*, chapters 3, 4, and 5. More specifically, the data from public consultations in the three country cases during the period studied (i.e., from the inception of each regulatory agency until 2010) show that the average number of responses submitted per public consultation was 13.2 in France, 8.2 in Greece, and 22.35 in the United Kingdom.

136. *See* Cuellar, *supra* note 121, at 485 (noting that a large number of such missives, notwithstanding their lack of sophistication, can signal to the agency's political leadership the political cost of proceeding with a certain kind of regulation). *See also* Nina A. Mendelson, *Rulemaking, Democracy, and Torrents of E-Mail*, 79 GEO. WASH. L. REV. 1343, 1380 (2011) ("We should strongly encourage agencies to engage comments on the value-laden questions more seriously, including the comments of lay persons submitted in large numbers"); Nina A. Mendelson, *Should Mass Comments Count?*, 2 MICH. J. ENVTL & ADMIN. L. 173, 183 (2012) (arguing that large volumes of comments should at least "trigger an agency to engage in further deliberation and investigation. They should also prompt a brief response in the rulemaking documents. At a minimum, if agencies decide that the public comment game—at least for comments filed in large volumes by ordinary citizens—is not worth the candle, complete candor with the public is essential"). *But see* Cynthia Farina et al., *Rulemaking vs. Democracy: Judging and Nudging Public Participation that Counts*, 2 MICH. J. ENVTL & ADMIN. L. 123, 130–45 (2012) (arguing, in particular, that the types of preferences expressed in mass comments "may be good enough for electoral democracy, but they are not good enough for rulemaking, even when rulemaking is heavily laden with value choices" (*id.* at 137), and further pointing to the unreliability of those comments as a gauge of citizen value preferences).

137. *See* Cuellar, *supra* note 121, at 484 ("Differences in sophistication . . . might . . . affect who has a realistic chance of being part of the process shaping how agency staff use their limited discretion. Being deprived of sophistication shuts someone out of that discussion").

138. *See* Francesca Bignami, *Three Generations of Participation Rights Before the European Commission*, 68 LAW & CONTEMP. PROBS. 61, 68–72 (2004).

139. *Cf. Home Box Office, Inc. v. F.C.C.*, 567 F.2d 9, 35–36 (D.C. Cir. 1977) ("a dialogue is a two-way street: the opportunity to comment is meaningless unless the agency responds to significant points raised by the public").

140. Martin Shapiro characterized the judicial demand for more complete and persuasive explanation of agency decisions as a conversion of administrative law from a pluralist to a deliberative basis (MARTIN SHAPIRO, WHO GUARDS THE GUARDIANS? JUDICIAL CONTROL OF ADMINISTRATION 168 (1988) ("[t]here is a swing of the pendulum from synoptic adjudication to prudential deliberation for the agencies, and the only way courts can check on this kind of agency discretion is by themselves engaging in prudential deliberation").

141. *See, e.g.*, Jerry L. Mashaw, *Reasoned Administration: The European Union, the United States, and the Project of Democratic Governance*, 76 GEO. WASH. L. REV. 99 (2007) (explaining that a right to reasons has an instrumental purpose facilitating hierarchical, legal, and political accountability, but also has a particular moral force in a democratic polity recognizing the individual as the basic unit of social value that should be given reasons to affirm law as serving recognizable collective purposes).

142. *Id.* at 110.

143. *Motor Vehicle Mfrs. Ass'n v. State Farm Mut. Auto. Ins. Co.*, 463 U.S. 29 (1983). According to the court, "[n]ot having discussed the possibility, the agency submitted no reasons at all" (*id.* at 50).

144. *United States v. Nova Scotia Food Prods. Corp.*, 568 F.2d 240, 252–53 (2d Cir. 1977).

145. *See* Cuellar, *supra* note 121, at 421 n.37 (suggesting in a similar vein that "the agency may not ignore qualitatively important dimensions of the problem raised in the course of the notice and comment process (i.e., by a cogently written comment, or by some substantial proportion of the reasonably intelligible comments in the aggregate.)").

146. HABERMAS, *supra* note 45, at 264.

147. Seidenfeld, *supra* note 59, at 1547–49.

148. *See* Patricia M. Wald, *Judicial Review in Midpassage: The Uneasy Partnership Between Courts and Agencies Plays On*, 32 TULSA L.J. 221, 233–34 (1996) ("'Arbitrary and capricious' has turned out to be the catch-all label for attacks on the agency's rationale, its completeness or logic, in cases where no misinterpretation of the statute, constitutional issues or lack of evidence in the record to support key findings is alleged. Frequently the arbitrary and capricious charge is grounded on the complaint that the agency has departed from its prior rationale in other cases without admitting it or explaining why. Sometimes the agency is rebuffed because it did not give adequate consideration to an alternative solution. But most often the court simply finds the agency's explanation for what it is doing 'inadequate.'" (internal citations omitted)).

149. *See* Richard J. Pierce Jr., *Seven Ways to Deossify Agency Rulemaking*, 47 ADMIN. L. REV. 59, 86 (1995) ("I see the primary benefits of the notice and comment procedure as independent of judicial review. Agencies are more likely to make wise and well-informed policy decisions if they solicit, receive, and consider data and views from all citizens who are likely to be affected by a policy decision . . . . Indeed, I see judicial review of the resulting policy decision through application of the malleable duty to engage in reasoned decisionmaking as the source of net social costs rather than net social benefits").

150. This seems to be the general position advocated by Hermann Pünder, *Democratic Legitimation of Delegated Legislation—A Comparative View on the American, British and German law*, 58 INTL. & COMP. L.Q. 353, 375 (2009) (arguing that judicial control is "necessary for the legitimising effect of public participation and to prevent 'agency capture' by strong interest groups").

151. I reverse here the title of the article by Rose-Ackerman, *supra* note 27.

152. *See* Matthias Ruffert, *The Transformation of Administrative Law as a Transnational Methodological Project, in* THE TRANSFORMATION OF ADMINISTRATIVE LAW IN EUROPE 3 (Matthias Ruffert ed., 2007).

153. 5 U.S.C. §§ 503 (b)-(c), 706(2)(A).

154. The term "adversarial legalism" appears in the works of Mirjan Damaska and Robert Kagan, *see* MIRJAN R. DAMAŠKA, THE FACES OF JUSTICE AND STATE AUTHORITY: A COMPARATIVE APPROACH TO THE LEGAL PROCESS (1986), ROBERT A. KAGAN, ADVERSARIAL LEGALISM. THE AMERICAN WAY OF LAW (2001).

155. Robert A. Kagan, *Should Europe Worry About Adversarial Legalism?*, 17 OXFORD JOURNAL OF LEGAL STUDIES 165, 167–68 (1997).

156. *See* R. Daniel Kelemen & Eric C. Sibbitt, *The Globalization of American Law*, 58 INTERNATIONAL ORGANIZATION 103 (2004), R. Daniel Kelemen, *Suing for Europe. Adversarial Legalism and European Governance*, 39 COMPARATIVE POLITICAL STUDIES 101 (2006), and more recently R. DANIEL KELEMEN, EUROLEGALISM: THE TRANSFORMATION OF LAW AND REGULATION IN THE EUROPEAN UNION 7*ff.* (2011) (arguing that European integration is encouraging the

spread of a European variant of adversarial legalism that is "more restrained and sedate" than the American version. Kelemen calls this hybrid "Eurolegalism").

157. *See, e.g.*, Rose-Ackerman, *supra* note 27, at 1294 ("[t]here is no judicial review of the adequacy of representation"); *id.* at 1300 ("[a]s a consequence of the anemic quality of judicial review, German executive-branch policymaking tends to lack formality and accountability. No judicially enforceable statute constrains administrative policymaking").

2

Legitimation through Decentralization in the European Union

Chapter 1 constructed a "deliberative-participatory model" of administrative accountability. It further suggested that EU law mandates may have moved domestic systems closer to this model in the example of the telecommunications sector. This chapter elaborates on these procedural and institutional EU mandates. It puts forth several hypotheses regarding the effects of these provisions at the member-state level, and considers them in the context of the decentralized EU regulatory regime.

Part I, in particular, offers some context by outlining the substantive EU regulatory initiatives in the area of electronic communications over the past three decades. Part II then focuses on the institutional and procedural EU mandates. The development and inclusion of these provisions in the EU regulatory framework was incremental and much slower. I submit, however, that these EU provisions have had the accountability-enhancing effect earlier described as the "democratic surplus." Interestingly, Part II suggests, this was not the primary intended effect of EU law. Rather, these procedural mandates were formally adopted to advance the substantive goal of creating an internal market in electronic communications within the EU. Nevertheless, I hypothesize that these mandates may have significant implications for the nature of administrative governance within the member states. As chapters 3, 4, and 5 will demonstrate, the nature of these implications hinges on the domestic public law traditions, administrative history and procedures that had been in place before the advent of EU law. Part III further assesses the impact of the procedural EU provisions against the backdrop of the decentralized EU regime. It considers traditional theoretical arguments in favor of decentralization and examines their applicability in the context of our inquiry, which focuses on regulatory processes rather than substantive policymaking. I claim that the decentralized EU regulatory structure may promote experimentation, innovation, and policy exchange between the member states. The extent to which innovation has occurred in the member states is an empirical question for the country cases to address. The way

in which best governance practice should be diffused within the EU is a norma-
tive/institutional design question for the concluding chapter.

I. Liberalization of telecommunications in Europe:
An EU-driven process

The European Commission has had a catalytic impact on the telecommunications
sector in Europe.[1] From the late 1960s onwards, technological and economic
developments as well as regulatory reforms in the United States began to undermine the ideas of "natural monopolies" and monopoly provision by state suppliers.[2] The liberalization of the telecommunications market was eventually viewed
as vital to the EU's global competitiveness and a precondition for Europe's transition to the information society.[3] At first, however, the Commission appeared
to be only a source of advice for member states, and one pressing for rather
limited change by means of non-binding calls for greater competition in customer premises equipment and advanced services.[4] In a similar vein, in 1984
the Council adopted non-legally binding Recommendations.[5] The Commission
took the first major step toward liberalization in 1987 with the publication of
the *Green Paper on the Development of the Common Market for Telecommunications
Services and Equipment* that called for an ambitious general reform of the regulatory framework.[6]

The publication of this Green Paper marked the start of the liberalization process in the telecommunications sector with the gradual introduction of a binding
legal framework.[7] The first "hard law" Community instrument was adopted in
1988 (the "Terminals Directive").[8] It mandated that member states withdraw
any special or exclusive rights over the supply of telecommunications terminal
equipment. This was followed by the 1990 "Services Directive"[9] that liberalized
the supply of telecommunications services—excluding, notably, voice telephony. The legal basis that the Commission used to issue both the Terminals and
the Services Directives was Article 90(3) of the Treaty establishing the European
Economic Community, currently Article 106 of the Treaty on the Functioning
of the European Union (TFEU). This meant that the Commission was able to
issue these directives unilaterally without requiring the formal approval of the
Council and the European Parliament, which would have been the case under
Article 100a of the Treaty dealing with harmonization measures for the functioning of the internal market. Both directives were challenged on these jurisdictional grounds before the European Court of Justice (ECJ); the Court, for the
most part, upheld the competence of the Commission under Article 90(3) in two
judgments on the Terminals Directive and the Services Directive.[10]

The jurisdictional character of this political tension has been described as
"typical of any attempt to shift the focus of regulation from the national to the

European perspective."[11] Indeed, conflicts between the Commission and certain national governments on questions of substantive regulatory policy and the direction of EC action toward liberalization were limited; instead, sharp disagreements occurred over broader constitutional questions about the allocation of powers between the Commission and the Council, as exemplified in the 1991 and 1992 ECJ cases.[12] This is not to say that all member states were fully on board with respect to substantive policy. In fact, certain countries (e.g., the United Kingdom and Germany) pressed for rapid EC deadlines for competition. By contrast, other member states—often led by France with its strong notions of service public (chapter 3)—pressed for longer transition periods, greater EC re-regulation and scope for member states to impose conditions on suppliers. The introduction of universal service requirements in the EU regulatory framework is a telling example of the compromises that settled these substantive conflicts.[13]

In spite of these substantive agreements, the liberalization of the telecommunications sector was primarily an EU-driven process. The Commission may have acted as "broker among member states"—facilitating agreement on EU legislation committing all member states to a similar pace of liberalization and aiding national governments in dealing with domestic resistance to reforms[14]—but it was the Commission that took the initiative and set the pace. Indeed, backed by the ECJ's 1991 and 1992 decisions, the Commission adopted a series of directives amending the 1990 Services Directive to encompass a broader range of telecommunications services: satellite communications, use of cable television networks, mobile and personal communications. In 1996, the Commission published the "Full Competition Directive," which obliged member states to withdraw all exclusive rights for the provision of telecommunications services. Notably, member states could maintain special and exclusive rights only until 1 January 1998 for voice telephony and for the establishment and provision of public telecommunications networks.[15]

Three years later the Commission issued the 1999 Communications Review, the objective of which was to review EU regulation in the telecommunications sector and propose the main elements of a new framework for communications infrastructure and associated services.[16] The Review noted that the convergence of the telecommunications, broadcasting, and IT sectors was reshaping the communications market and called for a coherent regulatory regime. The Commission's approach was that the primary responsibility for achieving the objectives of the sector-specific Community legislation should rest with the independent national regulators. The natural counterpart of this delegation would be greater coordination of member states' actions to avoid fragmentation of the internal market. This, in turn, would require closer Commission monitoring and quality assessment to ensure consistent and effective implementation of the Community legislation at the national level.[17] Parts II and III will return to these questions.

The Commission then announced that it would propose five directives, which would simplify and consolidate existing legislation. Recognizing that the policy issues at stake were vital for Europe, the Commission further sought the views of interested parties on its proposed policies over a three-month period. More than 200 responses were received from a wide range of interests, inside and outside the EU. In addition, more than 550 people attended a two-day public hearing held by the Commission in January 2000.[18] In 2002 the European Community adopted the new "telecommunications package" (second-generation directives) consisting of the "Framework Directive" (Directive 2002/21/EC)[19] and four specific directives covering authorizations, access and interconnection, universal service consumers' and users' rights and telecoms data protection.[20] The legal basis for the "telecommunications package" was Article 95 of the Treaty; this meant that the Council adopted the directives acting by a qualified majority, on the proposal of the Commission and after obtaining the opinion of the European Parliament, pursuant to the procedure detailed in Article 251 of the Treaty. Furthermore, the Commission adopted a directive on competition in the markets for electronic communications networks and services consolidating all the previous liberalization directives. [21]

From a substantive perspective, in response to the technological convergence highlighted in the 1999 Communications Review, the second-generation directives had a broader scope now covering "electronic communications" services and networks.[22] Content (e.g., broadcasting) fell outside the scope of the 2002 regulatory framework. With respect to individual directives, the objective of the Framework Directive was to establish a harmonized framework for the regulation of electronic communications networks and services. It contained horizontal provisions supporting the other measures: scope and general principles, basic definitions, general provisions on the national regulatory authorities (NRAs), the new concept of significant market power, and rules for granting certain essential resources such as radio frequencies, numbers or rights of way.[23]

The Authorization Directive's main innovation was the replacement of individual licenses by general authorizations, while a special scheme for attributing frequencies and numbers continued to exist.[24] According to the new regime, a telecommunications firm may be required to submit a notification, but it cannot be required to obtain an explicit decision or any other administrative act by the NRA before exercising the rights stemming from the authorization. The Access Directive established rights and obligations for operators and for undertakings seeking interconnection and/or access to their networks.[25] As noted previously, the liberalization of telecommunications was accompanied by measures to secure the delivery of universal service. Formal provisions regarding the EU's policy on universal service were initially included in a 1995 directive.[26] Subsequent directives addressed aspects of universal service and were ultimately incorporated and consolidated into the Universal Service Directive of 2002. The existence of a specific directive dedicated to universal service demonstrated the commitment of the EU to a minimum set of services (defined in Articles 4-7 and 9(2) of the directive) "of specified quality to which all end-users have access, at an affordable price in the light of specific national conditions, without distorting competition."

The 2002 regulatory package had a built-in mechanism for periodic reviews by the Commission with a view, in particular, to determining the need for modifications in the light of technological and market developments.[27] The Commission carried out the first such review in June 2006.[28] In November 2007, it published a new review of the regulatory framework together with a set of reform proposals.[29] These proposals were grouped under the three pillars of better regulation, completing the single market in electronic communications, and increasing the level of consumer protection. December 2009 marked the formal adoption of the latest amendments of the EU regulatory framework on electronic communications ("third-generation directives"): the "Better law-making" and the "Citizens' rights" Directives.[30] They were complemented by a Regulation establishing the Body of European Regulators for Electronic Communications (BEREC),[31] which Part III examines in more detail. The 2009 reforms gave room to the Commission to help ensure a higher level of consistency in the application of remedies by adopting opinions on draft measures proposed by national regulatory authorities. Even though these new directives did not alter significantly the scope of universal service, they provided that to prevent the degradation of service and the hindering or slowing down of traffic over networks, member states should ensure that NRAs are able to set minimum quality-of-service requirements. They also reinforced provisions for users with disabilities.

In September 2016, the Commission proposed a new European Electronic Communications Code.[32] The proposal consists of a horizontal recasting of the four existing Directives (Framework, Authorisation, Access, and Universal Service) to bring them all under a single directive. The proposed overhaul of the regulatory framework focuses on: (i) ubiquitous and high-quality connectivity, (ii) enhanced coordination of spectrum management, (iii) adaptation of the universal service EU obligation with the focus on voice and basic broadband affordability, (iv) a revised regulatory institutional framework with a minimum set of harmonized competences for NRAs and additional tasks given to BEREC. At the time of this writing, the Commission's proposal has entered the legislative process, which will likely result in various amendments before any formal legislation emerges in 2017–18.

II. From substantive regulation to institutional and procedural mandates in the EU regulatory framework

The successive waves of EU directives outlined in Part I are implemented at the domestic level by national regulatory authorities (NRAs). Historically, EU rules focused mostly on opening up the markets in the member states, homogenizing substantive law, and promoting the creation of an internal market in the telecommunications sector. The development and inclusion of procedural mandates in the EU regulatory framework was incremental and much slower, out of respect for the member states' "procedural" and "institutional autonomy."[33] Nevertheless, I argue that these perhaps less visible procedural provisions transformed domestic regulatory practices in the member states in crucial respects. The inquiry is organized around two headings: first, the organization and independence of national regulatory institutions—the "institutional provisions" (Section A); second, "procedural provisions" pertaining to the accountable exercise of regulatory powers by the national regulators (Section B). These mandates—especially those considered under Section B—are at the center of this book, because they have had the, perhaps counterintuitive, accountability-enhancing effect earlier described as the EU "democratic surplus."

A. Institutional requirements for national regulators—Independence

As late as 2002, the Commission noted that "[t]he way in which NRAs are organized and exercise their powers is *clearly* a matter for the national legal and administrative systems, *provided* the basic requirements of the EU framework are complied with."[34] Of course, this raises the question: what are the "basic requirements" of the EU framework and how "basic" are they? The first-generation liberalizing directives included few organizational provisions and essentially no provisions on issues such as the appointment process, and the terms and removal of national regulators.[35] Nonetheless, these requirements gradually increased.

The focus of this section is on the independence of the NRAs. But independent *from whom*? Here it is important to distinguish between market independence and political independence.[36] Market independence (or "independence from the industry") views NRAs as neutral and impartial arbiters of competition and sector-specific rules; it seeks to insulate them from the regulated interests and prevent "agency capture" by the market actors. Political independence views regulatory authorities as distinct public bodies insulated from the corrosive effect of politics and politicians. This strand seeks to keep the agencies at arm's length from their political principals, that is, the parliament and, perhaps more importantly, the central government.[37]

The first generation of EU directives in the telecommunications sector was preoccupied with the first of these two prongs, i.e., independence from the industry. For instance, the 1988 Terminals Directive mandated that several duties under the directive be "entrusted to a body independent of public or private undertakings offering goods and/or services in the telecommunications sector" (Article 6). In a similar vein, the 1990 Services Directive stipulated that member states should ensure that "the grant of operating licences, the control of type approval and mandatory specifications, the allocation of frequencies and surveillance of usage conditions are carried out by a body independent of the telecommunications organizations" (Article 7). This perception of independence from market actors was consistent with the case law of the Court of Justice as well.[38]

However, one of the market actors in the new liberalized environment—in fact, often the key market actor—from which the regulator should be independent under EU requirements, was the government itself. EU law mandated the gradual liberalization of the telecommunications sector but not the privatization of the state or state-owned incumbent operator. The Treaty did not speak to the ownership of the operators,[39] and the EU did not question the state ownership of the public telecommunications operators (PTOs). This meant that the pre-liberalization institutional regime was counter to the EU independence requirements: Prior to the opening up of markets, the institution responsible for regulating the sector, often a Ministry of Communications, was commonly also responsible for controlling the commercial activities of the incumbent operator.[40] This created an obvious conflict of interest.[41] Indeed, this problem was not limited to the immediate aftermath of the liberalization. Rather, it persisted even after the establishment of new markets had created competitive pressures on the incumbent public operator. Even if the latter was to be privatized, the divestiture of the government shareholding was phased, thus extending the dependency relationship over a long period of time.[42] A 1997 Directive clearly addressed this issue by including specific language on the separation of regulatory and commercial functions.[43]

In its 1999 Communications Review, the Commission reiterated the crucial role of NRAs to the operation of the regulatory framework, and expressed some concern about their independence. It, therefore, proposed a review of the existing legal provisions with a view to strengthening this independence.[44] The resulting 2002 telecommunications package consolidated preexisting provisions on NRA independence but did not alter or expand the scope of the notion of independence. More specifically, Recital 11 of the Framework Directive (Directive 2002/21/EC) stated:

> In accordance with the principle of the separation of regulatory and operational functions, Member States should guarantee the independence of the national regulatory authority or authorities with a view to ensuring the impartiality of their decisions. This requirement of independence is without prejudice to the institutional autonomy and constitutional obligations of the Member States or to the principle of neutrality with regard to the rules in Member States governing the

system of property ownership laid down in Article 295 of the Treaty. National regulatory authorities should be in possession of all the necessary resources, in terms of staffing, expertise, and financial means, for the performance of their tasks.

Article 3(2) of the same Directive specified that:

> Member States shall guarantee the independence of national regulatory authorities by ensuring that they are legally distinct from and functionally independent of all organisations providing electronic communications networks, equipment or services. Member States that retain ownership or control of undertakings providing electronic communications networks and/or services shall ensure effective structural separation of the regulatory function from activities associated with ownership or control.

The approach of the first and second-generation telecommunications directives to the concept of independence suggests that the primary motivation of EU law was insulating NRAs from industry influence, but not necessarily from political influence.[45] This continued to be a major concern of the European Commission.[46] An explanation for the emphasis on the "market independence" prong (in the form of impartiality and avoidance of conflict of interests) could be that the aim of those early directives was to gradually promote fair and undistorted competition in the sector, in other words, create a level playing field for all operators.[47] Consequently, at that stage, insulation from the government seemed to be a predominant concern only insofar as the state was itself involved in the industry as a stakeholder by retaining, for instance, ownership or control rights over the incumbent. Nevertheless, the separation of regulatory and operational functions did not signal a formal EU endorsement of the "political independence" strand. In the narrow case of government ownership or control of PTOs, the EU-mandated independence from the ministry was just a different facet of "market independence," that is, impartiality vis-à-vis the market actors because the government *was* a market actor.

This "thin" definition of independence was criticized in the literature, where it was pointed out that "the devil is often in the details and broad requirements of independence might not do much to ensure the absence of capture of regulatory agencies by commercial or political interests."[48] A thin definition was, however, understandable especially at the early stages of EU regulatory integration because it was closely linked to the idea of respect for the institutional autonomy of the member states; this autonomy can be curtailed only to the extent necessary to achieve effective and consistent implementation of EU law. Given the (political and occasionally constitutional) skepticism of certain member states vis-à-vis independent agencies in the first place, an EU Directive early in the liberalization process mandating *full* independence from the government could have been considered too far-reaching. In particular, the Commission may have believed that the goal of incrementally opening up the market could be achieved without imposing intrusive institutional mandates on member states. However, implementation varied, with member states establishing divergent domestic institutional arrangements. Furthermore, as the substantive regulatory goals of the EU became more ambitious—in particular, furthering regulatory integration and the internal market in electronic communications—the pressure for institutional coordination (and the curtailment of member-state institutional autonomy) increased. This resulted in more detailed independence requirements in the 2009 reforms of the EU regulatory framework for electronic communications, to which I shall return shortly.

Prior to 2009 the Commission did seek more independence for NRAs. For instance, in the 1999 Communications Review the Commission alluded to reforms aimed at strengthening political independence,[49] but, as we saw, this was not followed through in the 2002 regulatory framework. In a 2003 Communication, the Commission described as "noteworthy" that draft legislation under discussion in one member state required that a number of key decisions could not go forward without the consent of officials in the NRA appointed by the Ministry. Similarly, it pointed to draft legislation in some member states that would require the NRA's decisions to be reviewed by the ministry.[50] More interestingly, a subsequent Commission report noted, in the section on NRA independence, that "concerns [persisted] in Bulgaria and Luxembourg, and in particular in Poland in relation to the rules for the removal of the head of the NRA."[51] In Poland, Article 109 of the Telecommunications Act gave the President of the Council of Ministers full discretion to dismiss the President of the NRA at any time and without any justification. An amendment reintroduced a fixed five-year term of office for the head of the NRA together with a list of conditions for dismissal. This allowed the previous infringement proceeding regarding the independence of the NRA to be closed.[52]

Recognizing the risk to NRA independence posed by political interference, as manifested in certain member states (e.g., in the form of removals without cause), the Commission in its 2007 reform proposals pushed for the enhancement of the "political" strand of independence. Consequently, Directive 2009/140/EC included more detailed provisions to protect NRAs, as stated in Recital 13, "against external intervention or political pressure." Importantly, the 2009 Directive inserted a new paragraph 3a in Article 3 of the Framework Directive (Directive 2002/21/EC) that reads:

> [N]ational regulatory authorities . . . *shall act independently and shall not seek or take instructions from any other body in relation to the*

exercise of these tasks assigned to them under national law implementing Community law. This shall not prevent supervision in accordance with national constitutional law. Only appeal bodies set up in accordance with Article 4 shall have the power to suspend or overturn decisions by the national regulatory authorities. Member States shall ensure that the head of a national regulatory authority, or where applicable, members of the collegiate body fulfilling that function within a national regulatory authority . . . *may be dismissed only if they no longer fulfil the conditions required for the performance of their duties which are laid down in advance in national law*. The decision to dismiss the head of the national regulatory authority concerned, or where applicable members of the collegiate body fulfilling that function shall be made public at the time of dismissal. The dismissed head of the national regulatory authority, or where applicable, members of the collegiate body fulfilling that function shall receive a statement of reasons and shall have the right to request its publication, where this would not otherwise take place, in which case it shall be published. (emphasis added)

These amendments signal a shift from the "insulation from industry influence model," typical of the first two generations of directives, to an "insulation from industry influence *and* political pressures model." The independence from political influence strand is more relevant nowadays after the full privatization of PTOs. The completion of these privatization initiatives means that usually the state no longer has a financial stake in particular market actors, the former incumbents. Nonetheless, the government may still seek to interfere in the market for reasons of public policy (or electoral gain). This, in turn, has traditionally resulted in support for politically independent bureaucratic bodies so as to enhance the credibility of policy commitments, as discussed in chapter 1.[53]

Of course, enhancing both the market/conflict of interests and the political prongs of independence does not automatically guarantee the effectiveness of NRAs if they are, for instance, deprived of adequate resources to carry out their regulatory work. The European Commission has acknowledged this possibility.[54] Successive Directives had touched on the issue of agency resources in recitals.[55] Among them, the Framework Directive stated in Recital 11 that NRAs "should be in possession of all the necessary resources, in terms of staffing, expertise, and financial means, for the performance of their tasks." Directive 2009/140/EC introduced specific amendments stipulating that member states shall ensure that NRAs have adequate financial and human resources to carry out the task assigned to them. Moreover, member states shall ensure that NRAs have separate annual budgets, and the budgets shall be made public.

The development of the EU institutional mandates has not yet led to a strict legal mandate that sets either the precise legal form of NRA organization or the category of state authorities to which an NRA must belong.[56] Recital 11 of the Framework Directive, which has not been rescinded, states that the "requirement of independence is without prejudice to the institutional autonomy and constitutional obligations of the Member States or to the principle of neutrality with regard to the rules in Member States governing the system of property ownership laid down in Article 295 of the Treaty." As the analysis in this section demonstrates, however, the EU gradually curtailed the principle of member-state institutional autonomy.[57] The European Court of Justice succinctly described this important qualification to the principle in a 2008 case: "Although the Member States enjoy institutional autonomy as regards the organisation and the structuring of their regulatory authorities within the meaning of Article 2(g) of the Framework Directive, *that autonomy may be exercised only in accordance with the objectives and obligations laid down in that directive.*"[58]

This delicate balance between member-state institutional autonomy and EU institutional mandates is captured in a recent debate in the literature. One scholar has contended that national parliaments could be charged with performing some of the regulatory tasks that the EU regulatory framework specifically assigns to NRAs.[59] Professor Szydło's argument builds on an ECJ judgment holding that the EU regulatory framework "does not in principle preclude, by itself, the national legislature from acting as national regulatory authority within the meaning of the Framework Directive provided that, in the exercise of that function, it meets the requirements of competence, independence, impartiality and transparency laid down by those directives and that its decisions in the exercise of that function can be made the object of an effective appeal to a body independent of the parties involved."[60] The author then elaborates on why, with respect to certain regulatory functions, national parliaments could meet those EU requirements. Professor Weatherill was quick to offer a rebuttal. The main claim of his persuasive reply is that even assuming it is, in principle, possible that a national parliament could in conformity with EU law be designated as an NRA, this would not be desirable. His argument echoes the, by now familiar, distinction between "market independence" and "political independence," and highlights the importance of the latter: "Independence from market actors is vital—but so is independence from quotidian politics, inter alia because this is exactly where market actors are able to find channels through which to press their special concerns." Therefore, in Weatherill's view, designating a specialist agency as a NRA is preferable precisely because it achieves insulation from "raw politics." [61]

In the case of electronic communications, Recital 13 of Directive 2009/140/EC seems to settle the debate: "express provision should be made in national law to ensure that [a national regulatory authority] is protected against external intervention or political pressure liable to jeopardise its independent assessment of matters coming before it. *Such outside influence makes a national legislative body unsuited to act as a national regulatory authority under the regulatory framework"* (emphasis added). This is yet another example of the growing EU involvement in the institutional design of NRAs to ensure their independence and effective implementation of EU law. Nevertheless, adding further layers of regulatory independence by EU fiat brings to the fore a concern raised in Szydło's article. The author is highly critical of the European legislature and of the Court of Justice that he describes as mandating the "substitution of a parliament by the network-bound administrative expertocracy." According to the same account, this substitution "undermines the concept of the domain of the law very strongly, because it places in the foreground not the national parliament, but the administrative authorities that are authorized to take the most important political and regulatory decisions with regard to market players."[62] This is an important concern, and one which recalls the critique that independent regulatory agencies sit outside the "chain of legitimacy" described in chapter 1. The additional element here is that the independence requirements originate in the EU and restrict the institutional autonomy of member states. Hence, although Szydło's proposal is unworkable, his concern with democratic accountability needs to be addressed. One response would be to pair increased independence with a corresponding increase in regulatory accountability.[63] Section B will suggest that EU law heeded the call, but not necessarily with the conscious and clear aim of cabining the enhanced NRA independence; in so doing, however, EU mandates further curtailed the principle of member-state institutional autonomy.

The 2016 Commission proposal for a European Electronic Communications Code[64] is the most recent manifestation of the tendency to limit member-state institutional autonomy with the aim of regulatory consistency. The proposed EU amendments seek to strengthen the independence of national regulators by building on the 2009 reforms. Notably, the new independence requirements pertain to appointments as well (Article 7.1): the head of the NRA "shall be appointed for a term of office of at least four years from among persons of recognised standing and professional experience, on the basis of merit, skills, knowledge and experience and following an open selection procedure." The maximum tenure can be no more than two terms. Furthermore, if adopted, the new provision will stipulate that member states shall ensure continuity of decision making by providing for an "appropriate rotation scheme" for board members. The 2009 provisions on dismissals are repeated in the 2016 proposals with the additional stipulation that the decision to dismiss the head of the NRA is subject to review by a court, on points of fact and law (Article 7.3). Another proposed reform is that NRAs should have "autonomy in the implementation of the allocated budget." However, "financial autonomy shall not prevent supervision or control in accordance with national constitutional law" but any control on the budget of the NRAs "shall be exercised in a transparent manner and made public" (Article 9). It is not certain that these provisions will be included in the final EU legislation. Either way, however, they illustrate the ongoing pattern of enhancing political independence through EU law provisions—indeed at a level of detail covering institutional aspects such as staggered terms.

B. Procedural provisions for regulatory accountability—Stakeholder participation

The story of procedural EU mandates, as with the institutional ones, is again one of gradual development. The turning point was the second-generation regulatory package that included provisions on stakeholder participation. Before exploring these, however, this section first addresses two other accountability mechanisms: transparency and the right of appeal.

The first-generation directives imposed certain transparency requirements on NRAs.[65] For instance, Article 9(5) of the Interconnection Directive[66] mandated that NRA decisions on interconnection disputes be made public, and that the parties concerned be given a full statement of the reasons on which the regulatory decisions were based. Article 12(3) of the same Directive stipulated that NRAs shall ensure that the procedures for allocating numbers "are transparent, equitable and timely and the allocation is carried out in an objective, transparent and non-discriminatory manner." The 2002 Framework Directive enhanced and generalized these transparency obligations. More specifically, Article 3(3) of the Directive provided that member states shall ensure that NRAs exercise their powers "impartially and transparently." Pursuant to Article 5(4), "Member States shall ensure that, acting in accordance with national rules on public access to information and subject to Community and national rules on business confidentiality, national regulatory authorities publish such information as would contribute to an open and competitive market."

One of the ways in which the third-generation directives—in particular, Directive 2009/140/EC—enhanced the independence of NRAs was through a new paragraph 3a in Article 3 of the 2002 Framework Directive. Part of this new proviso stipulates that *only* appeal bodies set up in accordance with Article 4 (i.e., the provision on the "right of appeal") shall have the power to suspend or overturn the decisions of the NRAs. This express provision does indeed strengthen regulatory independence. The flipside, however, is that the EU reiterates its continued commitment to accountability through a mechanism of review of regulatory decisions. The right of appeal is not new, and certainly not a third-generation right. Article 1(6) of the Directive 97/51/EC provided that "Member States shall ensure that suitable mechanisms exist at national level under which a party affected by a decision of the national regulatory authority has a right of appeal to a body independent of the parties involved." Article 4 of the Framework Directive (2002/21/EC) clarified the scope and form of the right of appeal:

1. Member States shall ensure that effective mechanisms exist at national level under which any user or undertaking providing electronic communications networks and/or services who is affected by a decision of a national regulatory authority has the right of appeal against the decision to an appeal body that is independent of the parties involved. *This body, which may be a court, shall have the appropriate expertise available to it to enable it to carry out its functions.* Member States shall ensure that the *merits of the case are duly taken into account* and that there is an effective appeal mechanism. Pending the outcome of any such appeal, the decision of the national regulatory authority shall stand, unless the appeal body decides otherwise.

2. Where the appeal body referred to in paragraph 1 is not judicial in character, written reasons for its decision shall always be given. Furthermore, in such a case, its decision shall be subject to review by a court or tribunal within the meaning of Article 234 of the Treaty. (emphasis added)

Article 4 gives member states leeway on the institutional design of appellate bodies, which in most countries are courts, normally administrative tribunals.[67] It does, however, include an expertise requirement. Furthermore, it provides some direction as to the scope of review: the merits of the case are to be "duly taken into account." As the Commission explained in its Eighth Report, published a few months after the adoption of the 2002 regulatory package, "[t]he practice under the existing framework [i.e., prior to the second-generation directives] has in many cases been for the appeals bodies to examine process rather than substance. This situation must be remedied under the new regime, and is indeed changing: in France for example the Court of Appeal, assisted by an expert, can now examine the substance of an NRA decision in addition to its legality."[68] The interface between procedural and substantive review will appear again later in the country cases. Moreover, chapter 5 will detail how procedural and merits review are intertwined in the case of a UK specialist regulatory court, the Competition Appeal Tribunal, which decides Article 4 appeals.

A second point of particular concern to the European Commission, as evidenced by the numerous consecutive reports raising the issue, was the length of the procedures for appeals against NRA decisions. The Commission also pointed out that the problem was aggravated by the systematic suspension of NRA decisions pending appeal.[69] The 2009 reforms sought to address the problem. Nevertheless, whereas the recitals were more detailed (Directive 2009/140/EC, Recitals 14-15), concerns about interference in national judicial procedures[70] meant that the final provision simply states that, pending the outcome of the appeal, the NRA decision shall stand "unless interim measures are granted in accordance with national law" (Article 1(4) of Directive 2009/140/EC). Furthermore, under the same Article, member states are required to "collect information on the general subject matter of appeals, the number of requests for appeal, the duration of the appeal proceedings and the number of decisions to grant interim measures. Member States shall provide such information to the Commission and BEREC after a reasoned request from either." In its 15th Report, published after the adoption of the 2009 reforms but before their transposition into the national systems, the Commission described "access to an effective judicial review of NRA decisions" as a "fundamental right of all affected parties." At the same time, the Commission recognized that the "time and resources consumed by appeal proceedings remain a serious challenge for effective regulation and legal certainty" and referred to the concerns of some regulators that "the number of appeals and disputes is affecting their work plan."[71] The new obligation of member states to collect information on appeals may help to quantify this "problem," as well as allow comparisons and exchange of good practices to strike a balance between adequate access to review on appeal and timely agency action.

The watershed moment in terms of democratic accountability came in 2002 with the introduction of the second-generation regulatory package. Article 6 of the Framework Directive stated that

> Except in cases falling within Articles 7(6), 20 or 21 Member States shall ensure that where national regulatory authorities intend to take measures in accordance with this Directive or the Specific Directives which have a significant impact on the relevant market, *they give interested parties the opportunity to comment on the draft measure within a reasonable period.* National regulatory authorities shall publish their national consultation procedures. Member States shall ensure the establishment of a single information point through which all current consultations can be accessed. *The results of the consultation procedure shall be made publicly available* by the national regulatory authority, except in the case of confidential information in accordance with Community and national law on business confidentiality. (emphasis added)

Similar provisions were included in other directives of the "regulatory package."[72] The 2009 Reforms did not amend this public consultation mandate.[73] I argue that this novel provision and its implementation by the member states initiated a new period for regulatory processes at the national level with long-term implications for the nature of governance. As a matter of positive law, binding EU legislation for the first time mandated a "notice and comment"-like procedure. The fact that the pertinent provision was included in directives, which means that member states could choose the legal means through which these directives would be incorporated into their respective national legal orders, did not alter the central fact: member states had to enact public consultation procedures in addition to complying with further requirements, such as establishing a single information point through which all current consultations can be accessed, and publicizing the results of the consultation procedure. The 2016 Commission proposal for a European Electronic Communications Code[74] reiterates the public consultation mandate adding that the reasonable period for comments on draft measures should be set "having regard to the complexity of the matter" and not be shorter than 30 days "except in exceptional circumstances" (Article 23).

Part III will assess the significance of the Article 6 participatory mandate in the context of the EU's decentralized regulatory system—a system that may promote experimentation, policy exchange and learning between the member states. The case studies in chapters 3, 4, and 5 will explore the accountability-enhancing effect of the EU procedural mandates. The remainder of this Part, however, addresses a different puzzle: Why did EU directives include participatory procedural requirements in the first place? R. Daniel Kelemen offers a helpful starting point:

> [W]ith the single market project, the EU took on an ambitious program of reregulation at the EU level. It did so in a political context characterized by fragmentation between major political institutions and growing public distrust of distant Eurocrats. This bred demands for transparency and public participation that then manifested themselves in developments in EU administrative law. EU lawmakers and the ECJ developed an administrative law suited to the new regulatory environment, and in the process they created ample new bases for administrative law litigation and control of the national bureaucracies through adversarial legalism.[75]

However, this explains the incorporation of accountability mechanisms *at the EU level*,[76] but not by necessary implication of mandates for participatory processes *at the member-state level*. Surely, the Euroskeptics would acknowledge that NRAs are bureaucratic institutions but they are not the "distant EU bureaucrats"—they are "*our* bureaucrats." The accountability of the national bureaucracy, according to the same account, may pose democratic challenges but these constitute a fundamentally domestic issue. EU involvement on this question would further curtail the institutional autonomy of the member states, which was already restricted by the independence requirements of the EU framework. An external observer would then see no problem with EU accountability mandates provided that they simply reflected and responded to demands already voiced at the domestic level, i.e., national demands to enhance the accountability of domestic regulators by means of stakeholder participation in the form of notice-and-comment binding rules. However, there did not seem to be demands for accountability mechanisms of this sort in the member states. Traditionally, the emphasis had been instead on conventional modes of accountability that would strengthen the "chain of legitimacy" described in chapter 1. Even recent literature, discussed at the end of the previous section, lamented the "substitution" of *national parliaments* "by the network-bound administrative expertocracy" and thus called for the empowerment of the legislature.[77] Furthermore, even in the United Kingdom, as chapter 5 will demonstrate, the 2002 EU regulatory framework brought about significant changes; this suggests that the UK practice of consultation prior to 2002 was not simply uploaded and incorporated in the EU regulatory package.

Therefore, a different motivating force must have been behind the adoption of the EU public consultation provisions, one that the legislative history of the Framework Directive might help to unveil. Article 6 in the Commission's original legislative proposal included provisions on both domestic public consultations and consultations with the Commission and other NRAs—the latter constitute a mechanism of vertical and horizontal coordination and were ultimately addressed separately in Article 7 of the Framework Directive. The pertinent part of the proposal on national consultations read:

> Member States shall ensure that where national regulatory authorities intend to take measures in accordance with this Directive or the Specific Measures, they give interested parties the chance to comment within a reasonable period. National regulatory authorities shall publish their national consultation procedures.[78]

The opinion of the Economic and Social Committee on the Commission's proposal did not engage with the question of national consultation. The European Parliament, however, in its first reading proposed some amendments to the Commission's proposal. The new language of the relevant provision, according to the Parliament's proposal, is italicized:

> *Except as provided for in paragraph 5*, Member States shall ensure that where national regulatory authorities intend to take measures in accordance with this Directive or the Specific *Directives*, they give *all* interested parties the chance to comment within a reasonable period, *proportionate to the extent of the measures envisaged. To this end, the Commission shall establish a harmonised procedure to enable national regulatory authorities to establish standard consultation criteria.* National regulatory authorities shall publish their national consultation procedures. *The results of the consultation shall be made publicly available by the national regulatory authorities, without prejudice to any confidential information.*[79]

Interestingly, the Parliament's amendments put forth higher transparency requirements and a stronger harmonization role for the Commission in the

establishment of consultation criteria. Nevertheless, neither the legislative resolution of the European Parliament nor the report of the pertinent parliamentary committee[80] provided any justification or insights as to these amendments
or the national consultation process more broadly. As a result of the first reading, the Commission published an amended legislative proposal that incorporated some of the language on transparency (the italicized text indicates the
changes made to the original proposal of the Commission):

> *Except where provided for in paragraph 5,* Member States shall ensure
> that where national regulatory authorities intend to take measures in
> accordance with this Directive or the Specific Measures, they give *all*
> interested parties the chance to comment within a reasonable period.
> National regulatory authorities shall publish their national consulta-
> tion procedures. *The results of the consultation procedure shall be made
> publicly available by the national regulatory authority, except in the case of
> confidential information in accordance with Community and national law
> on business confidentiality. Member States shall establish a single informa-
> tion point where all current consultations are listed.*[81]

In contrast, the Council's common position on national consultations was closer
to the Commission's original proposal, namely, it was not particularly concerned
with the publication of the results of the consultation procedures.[82] During
the second reading, the European Parliament's resolution on the Council common position[83] reinserted the obligation of member states to establish a single information point through which all current consultations can be accessed,
and to publicize the results of the consultation procedure (except in the case of
confidentiality). At the end of the process, the Commission accepted all of the
Parliament's amendments in full,[84] and Article 6 of Directive 2002/21/EC was
formally adopted in the version that was cited earlier. Thus, we are left without much enlightenment. The back-and-forth between the EU institutions did
not pertain significantly to the national consultation processes (whereas there
were disagreements over the process of coordination between NRAs and the
Commission), and consequently we cannot deduce much from this material
about the underlying logic of these procedural mandates.

So back to the original puzzle: why these procedural mandates? Professor
Kelemen's interesting analysis quoted earlier connected the rise of EU bureaucratic power with the emergence of demands for accountability. In a similar
fashion, the end of Section A alluded to an expectation that increased independence should call for a corresponding increase in regulatory accountability
to maintain public legitimacy. However, in fact, the relationship between independence and accountability, or between institutional and procedural mandates
respectively, was not one of cause and effect. Instead, another common feature

of the two notions may help to account for the incorporation of procedural mandates in the EU regime: both types of mandates have a similar effect—namely,
the curtailment of the institutional and procedural autonomy of the member
states. Nonetheless, procedural mandates were not, as a matter of fact, formally
adopted to counterbalance the institutional ones. Rather, the common impact
of both types of mandates on the institutional autonomy of the member states
points to the common roots of their adoption—that is to say, the promotion of
the substantive goal of creating an internal market in electronic communications within the EU. Recital 15 of the Framework Directive states that

> [i]t is important that national regulatory authorities consult all inter-
> ested parties on proposed decisions and take account of their com-
> ments before adopting a final decision. In order to ensure that decisions
> at national level do not have an adverse effect on the single market
> or other Treaty objectives, national regulatory authorities should also
> notify certain draft decisions to the Commission and other national
> regulatory authorities to give them the opportunity to comment.

The placement of the rationale for domestic public consultations together with
that for consultation with the Commission and other NRAs (even though the
two are now addressed in two separate provisions, Articles 6 and 7, and not in
one as was the case in the Commission's original legislative proposal) does not
appear to be accidental. In fact, both types of consultation have similar goals,
that is, the coordination between national systems and the proper functioning of the internal market. This link is further corroborated by an addition to
Recital 15 that had not been a part of the original proposal of the European
Commission: "It is appropriate for national regulatory authorities to consult
interested parties on all draft measures *which have an effect on trade between
Member States*" (emphasis added). The domestic accountability requirements,
like the ones on intra-EU coordination, add another monitoring mechanism to
ensure the effective and consistent implementation of substantive EU law. In
other words, the EU not only *empowers* new domestic actors by creating markets
in which they can now participate but also *enlists* them in policing and monitoring the new EU regulatory framework by making their voices heard in a public consultation process that is transparent and open to all. Professor Kelemen
helpfully highlights an important aspect of this story, which is worth quoting in
some length:

> The economic liberalization unleashed by the Single Market initiative
> introduced new actors, many of them foreign, into previously sheltered
> domestic markets. For these new market players, opaque systems of
> national regulation that relied on insider corporatist networks did not

ensure a regulatory level playing-field. The opacity of these systems often functioned as a kind of 'non-tariff barrier' to trade, and the very attributes of these systems that many observers had lauded – such as their flexibility and informality – created opportunities for bias in favor of national incumbents and other forms of protectionism.[85]

Kelemen's account is consistent with both this book's argument about the crucial connection between procedural mandates and the substantive goal of market integration as well as with the practice of national public consultations. As to the latter point, in particular, the case studies in later chapters indicate that foreign (not even necessarily EU) actors do indeed participate in important domestic consultations, and NRAs, especially the French and Greek regulators, occasionally publish English translations of their consultation drafts as well. We can also hear echoes of the Commission's objective of empowering economic actors in its 1999 Communications Review, which emphasized "the need for transparency and impartiality in the conduct of public authorities . . . so that the fundamental economic and civil rights of citizens, economic operators and investors are protected."[86]

Even though the connection between procedural mandates and market integration may suggest that economic actors (foreign or domestic, and especially the non-incumbents) were the target addressees and beneficiaries of these novel procedural provisions, public consultations are open to all interested parties and nothing precludes the participation of individual European citizens, nongovernmental organizations (NGOs), other public authorities, etc. The extent to which these actors availed themselves of these participatory processes is an empirical question that the case studies will take up. My point here is that the enhancement of the democratic accountability of NRA operations was a side effect of efforts to ensure the proper functioning of the new electronic communications markets. Differently put, the accountability requirements of EU law did intend to promote the interests of Europeans; only they did so primarily as procedural tools that aimed to secure the correct implementation of EU law pertaining to the functioning of competitive markets. It is telling in this regard that, although Article 8 of the Framework Directive lists the promotion of the interests of the *citizens* of the European Union among the NRAs' objectives, the content of the provision stresses the maximization of *consumer* welfare, not the democratic empowerment of *citizens*.

The fact that the promotion of an internal market in electronic communications was the primary goal of the institutional and procedural EU mandates in no way detracts from the accountability-enhancing effect of these provisions. As Part III will explain and the country cases will demonstrate, in the context of the decentralized EU system, these participatory mandates have had significant implications for the nature of administrative governance in the member states.

These implications are especially worth exploring if one accepts this section's claim that they may not have been the primary intended consequences of the EU's activities in the electronic communications sector.

III. The accountability-enhancing effect of the EU regulatory regime

If the EU accountability mandates have an accountability-enhancing effect, the decentralized EU regulatory structure multiplies this effect by twenty-eight times. In other words, I aim to show that the EU procedural requirements *in conjunction with* the EU's decentralized structure have enhanced democratic accountability across all member states.

A. Legitimation through decentralization

Network industries provide a typical example of the mode of EU administration. Substantive regulatory frameworks (mandating, as we saw, the liberalization of the sectors but also re-regulating the new markets) were put in place at the EU level. When it came to the implementation of these regulatory frameworks, however, the EU did not possess the institutional or financial resources to fully administer them itself. More specifically, it did not and does not possess the power of direct taxation that would support a large central bureaucracy.[87] Therefore, it has to rely on member states to carry out the centrally enacted basic regulatory scheme; differently put, it has to transfer power back to the periphery. This creates a decentralized regulatory regime.[88]

This basic picture, however, does not create a clear-cut compartmentalization of labor or a limited interface between the center and the periphery. Indeed, the classic distinction between direct or indirect administration has become less and less relevant.[89] Rather, the current paradigm of administrative integration is one of "mixed or composite proceedings," in which both the EU and national authorities participate.[90] This model has also been described as "managed decentralization."[91] NRAs are empowered as full-fledged enforcers, but the Commission retains overall responsibility and exercises supervision.[92] This general regulatory structure maps well onto our case study of the electronic communications sector. As described earlier, the 2002 "regulatory package" strengthened the regulatory position of NRAs: they have powers pertaining to, among other things, the definition and analysis of the market, regulation of operators with significant market power, mobile termination prices, codes of conduct for operators, calculating and financing of the net cost of universal services. The recognition of the key role of NRAs in the EU regulatory regime together with the enhancement of their institutional position and their independence raised the stakes of coordination among them (horizontal coordination) and with the Commission (vertical coordination). As the committee of the European Parliament reviewing the Commission's proposal for the new 2002 regulatory framework described this,

> "*Custodes quis custodiet?*", becomes here "Who will regulate the regulators - and how?" In this new approach, the role of the "framework Directive" becomes essential to set the "meta-rules" that will ensure consistency in the Community and avoid the two pitfalls of an overly general approach that forgets the peculiarities of national or even local markets and of divergent behaviour by the national authorities, be they governments or NRAs . . . . [T]he question of how to retain this delicate balance between independence and consistency remains acute.[93]

The 2009 reforms of the EU regulatory framework strengthened the mechanisms of coordination. Among the most important responsibilities of NRAs are the definition and analysis of markets and the designation of operators that have "significant market power" (Articles 14–16 of the Framework Directive). EU law subjects these powers to several harmonization procedures at multiple stages. A detailed analysis of these is beyond the scope of the inquiry here.[94] The notification regime of Articles 7, 7a, and 7b of the Framework Directive (as amended in 2009) should suffice as an illustration of the system of networks set up to ensure vertical and horizontal coordination. Pursuant to article 7(3), when a NRA intends to take measures regarding market definition or the designation of an operator as having significant market power, it must notify the draft measure to the Commission, BEREC, and the national regulatory authorities in other member states. These institutions may then submit comments on the draft measures, of which the NRA concerned "shall take the utmost account" [Article 7(7)]. Furthermore, under Article 7(4), the Commission may delay the adoption of the draft measure for two months. More importantly, the Commission may also veto the draft measure [Article 7(6)]. The notification procedure for the adoption of remedies by the NRAs (i.e., the imposition of obligations on operators) under Article 7a is similar. The two differences from the Article 7 process is that the Commission can delay the adoption of the NRA decision for three months [Article 7a(1)] and, crucially, that it may not veto the draft measure [Article 7a(7)]. The 2016 Commission proposal for a European Electronic Communications Code[95] puts forward an amendment of Article 7a to introduce a "double-lock" system. If adopted, this would mean that in cases in which the Body of European Regulators for Electronic Communications (BEREC) shares the Commission's serious doubts about a notified draft remedy, the Commission may require the NRA to amend or withdraw the measure and, if necessary, to re-notify it (Article 33.5c of the proposal).

Horizontal cooperation also occurs through networks of regulators created to encourage cooperation between the NRAs in the telecommunications sector. In 1997 regulators from different member states initiated the Independent Regulators Group (IRG) to consult on liberalization experiences and best practices. The IRG is an informal group of independent European telecommunications regulators with a current total of 37 members, which include the regulatory authorities of all the EU member states.[96] In 2002, the Commission issued a Decision that established a more formal version, the European Regulators Group (ERG). The aim of the Group was to "advise and assist the Commission in consolidating the internal market for electronic communications networks and services" as well as to "provide an interface between national regulatory authorities and the Commission" (Article 3).[97] As part of the 2009 reforms of the EU "electronic communications package," the Body of European Regulators for Electronic Communications (BEREC)[98] replaced the ERG. BEREC is composed of the heads of all the NRAs. Among its most important duties is its role to develop and disseminate among NRAs regulatory best practice; provide assistance to NRAs on regulatory issues; deliver opinions on the draft decisions, recommendations and guidelines of the Commission; issue reports and provide advice and opinions to the European Parliament and the Council on any matter within its competence.[99] Furthermore, under Article 3(3b) and (3c) of the Framework Directive (introduced by Directive 2009/140/EC), member states are required to "ensure that the goals of BEREC of promoting greater regulatory coordination and coherence are actively supported" by NRAs, as well as that NRAs "take utmost account of opinions and common positions adopted by BEREC when adopting their own decisions for their national markets."

These forms of horizontal and vertical coordination focus on the promotion of the internal market and the consistent implementation of *substantive* regulation. They are, however, silent, and thus looser with respect to participatory regulatory *processes*. This does not mean that networks such as BEREC could not serve as fora for the diffusion of best accountability practices; in fact, chapter 6 will argue that this may be an important, and potentially underappreciated, role these networks can play. The point here is rather to highlight the flexibility that member states still enjoy will respect to the implementation of the procedural EU mandates, which notably are included in directives. Indeed, a special feature of the EU regime is that it sets a minimum for consultation proceedings—let's call this the "EU floor." Member states are then free to expand the scope of consultation procedures and/or implement alternatives, which might increase participation and transparency, as long as they do not fall below this floor. This, in turn, means that NRAs might develop into "breeding grounds" and "learning sites" for state-of-the-art participatory practices that further public input.[100] Given that member states are obliged to set up participatory mechanisms, yet without a detailed set of specifications on how to do this, they find themselves in a situation that could be conducive to experimentation and innovation. A related point is that although we are discussing a specific (albeit very important) domain of regulation, the EU mandate for consultation and its implementation at the member-state level may also create conditions that would ultimately lead to the expansion of this new accountability paradigm to other administrative areas in the member states. As national regulators become familiar with these new accountability tools and a culture of public consultation takes roots, my hypothesis (to be tested in the case studies in the following three chapters) is that one can expect these regulatory processes to be generalized across the spectrum of national administration.

The importance of innovation and experimentation becomes more salient in a decentralized system than in a unitary one. I have already argued and the country cases will show that the procedural EU mandates established avenues for public participation that had not previously been as open or formalized in most member states. I now consider the impact of decentralization in enhancing accountability. Briefly put, the structure of the EU regulatory system serves as a multiplier of public influence, for it increases the number of entry points initially created in each member state. To appreciate this point, it is useful to consider traditional arguments put forth in favor of decentralized regimes and examine their validity in the context of our inquiry.[101] We should keep in mind that these arguments originally pertained to the decentralization of substantive policymaking. By contrast, this book's focus is on the effects of decentralization with respect to regulatory *processes*. This fundamental distinction has implications for the applicability of these arguments outside their original context.

1. *The interstate competition and promotion of choice argument.* According to this argument, devolution induces competition between the states for residents, capital, and economic activity. Charles Tiebout developed the original concept in 1956, suggesting that a decentralized system with horizontally arrayed jurisdictions competing to attract residents on the basis of differing tax and benefit structures produces efficient outcomes.[102] This analysis originally applied to "public goods" provided by public authorities. However, regulatory competition theorists adopted an expanded concept of "public goods" that also included regulation.[103] Therefore, the argument is that state governments are "suppliers of legal rules" and engage in competition to attract citizens and firms in their jurisdiction. Under the optimistic scenario, this competition ends up being a "race to the top" that leads to high-quality regulatory standards.[104]

The question is whether this account could be further expanded to include not only substantive regulation but also regulatory processes in the context of the decentralized EU regulatory structure: let's call this the hypothesis of "regulatory processes competition." This would be a theoretically tenuous and empirically uncertain, if not implausible, claim. One challenge for the "regulatory competition" theory proper is that the choice it professes to offer comes with costs; notably, the cost of relocation from one state to another that is particularly acute for individuals who moreover, like firms, make this choice based on a set of criteria lumped together.[105] This challenge is exacerbated when applied to the theory of "regulatory processes competition." The choice of jurisdiction turns on many factors indeed, and it is not realistic to expect that democratic accountability processes top that list. In the electronic communications sector, the industry probably cares more about substantive regulatory outcomes than regulatory processes. To be sure, regulatory certainty is important to operators and investors (especially the non-domestic ones), and transparent and participatory regulatory processes contribute to the stability and openness of the regulatory environment. Nevertheless, assuming that baseline requirements are in place—and the EU law mandates address this—it is unlikely that firms will move to a different member state on the single basis of more innovative participatory processes in that second country.

A possible reaction to this claim could be that regulatory outcomes may well depend on innovative accountability processes because agencies rely on outside parties throughout the policymaking process,[106] and innovative processes that invite and facilitate stakeholder involvement will lead to better policymaking. Nonetheless, this argument would have to prove a very difficult counterfactual, namely, that the improved regulatory outcomes can be attributed to those innovative processes that go beyond the common EU baseline requirements. On top of that, the different outcomes produced by these novel regulatory processes must outweigh the costs of relocation to have an impact on attracting residents or economic activity. Briefly put, the regulatory competition theory is not transferable to my project. There is, however, another type of competition—"reputational competition"—that might be at play.

2. *Pluralism, experimentation and innovation.* The argument is that having more diverse governmental entities enables innovation and lowers the costs of trying new policies, since there are more individual loci of experimentation that might develop innovative results as opposed to a uniform, centrally and a priori mandated standard.[107] According to Justice Brandeis's famous expression, states can serve as "democratic laboratories."[108] At first sight, there is no reason why this experimentation idea would be limited only to substantive regulation and not extend to regulatory processes as well. As already explained, EU law contemplates a minimum of accountability mechanisms operating at the member-state level. This means that the member states are empowered (or even invited) to enact additional measures that would allow for more open and more participatory procedures above the "EU floor." From this perspective, apart from simply multiplying entry points as suggested earlier, the European decentralized regulatory system might enlist twenty-eight agencies in experimenting with

consultation procedures. Ideally, the argument would hold, this diversity will result in the emergence of innovative governance models in certain member states that would then spread to the rest of the EU members. However, as has been correctly noted, there can be no presumption that just because national authorities have similar tasks, somehow there will be spreading of best regulatory practices[109] (and, we should add, processes). This is a case that stresses the importance of horizontal networks, such as BEREC and the Independent Regulators Group discussed above. These networks constitute fora in which NRA officials could exchange their views about modes of governance and learn from each other. The extent to which innovation did occur in the member states is an empirical question for the country cases to address. The way in which best governance practice may or should be diffused through these regulatory networks is a normative/institutional design question for the concluding chapter.

This, however, is a good place to consider the original hypothesis from a theoretical perspective: Should we expect the EU "federal" regulatory structure to promote procedural innovation? Professor Rose-Ackerman challenged the general claim that federalism promotes innovation as early as 1980 by putting forth a model predicting that "[i]f state and local governments are supposed to be 'laboratories,' then . . . few useful experiments will be carried out in them."[110] A discussion of the various arguments raised in response to the model in the economics and political science literature is beyond the scope of this inquiry. A recent account helpfully assessed three decades of several such responses and concluded that Rose-Ackerman's main claim that states will not innovate at the socially optimal level still stands.[111] It is, however, useful to consider the critique of the "experimentation and innovation thesis" in the specific context of our case that presents two important particularities. Firstly, the potential "innovators" in our case are not elected politicians but NRAs, that is, expert bureaucrats. Secondly, the experimentation in our story is with regulatory processes not substantive policies.

Rose-Ackerman's account suggests that secure politicians are likely to behave as if they were "risk averse" even if their underlying preferences are risk neutral. In fact, if it were possible, they would like to avoid risk taking altogether. Low-risk projects may provide little electoral benefits in case of success (on which secure incumbents do not rely for reelection) but reduce the possibility of failure and consequent penalization. An insecure politician may have a greater incentive to carry out risky projects but may be unable to find projects that are both risky and promise quick results (i.e., results before the next election).[112] In a decentralized system, the overall incentive to take risks and innovate is further reduced because governments that would have sponsored some risky projects, if they believed they were isolated from outside influences, may now wait for other jurisdictions' results and free ride on successful innovative efforts.[113] The possibility of free-riding, however, does not necessarily destroy the incentive to innovate first.[114] As Galle and Leahy indicate, if there are substantial first-mover advantages, and these advantages outweigh any accompanying costs, then "the excess represents value that cannot be obtained merely by free-riding."[115]

Let us now focus on our specific case, namely, procedural experimentation and innovation driven by NRAs. A fundamental assumption of the model discussed previously is missing here. That is to say, contrary to elected officials, NRA officials are not motivated by electoral gains precisely because they do not need reelection to keep their job; they often, in fact, enjoy fixed non-renewable terms. It has been noted in the literature that bureaucrats may still be sensitive to a reluctance by elected officials to undertake risky policy because the latter may still be able to leverage their capacity to expand or constrict an agency's budget or policy authority.[116] Nonetheless, this would seem to be less of an issue in our case study as the institutional EU requirements discussed in Part II.A., especially after the 2009 reforms, have bolstered NRA insulation from political interference.[117] Even so, however, the fact that NRAs may be less risk-averse than politicians does not necessarily imply that national regulators will be innovators—especially when free-riding is a possibility.

I would suggest that a further dynamic may be at play here, one that can promote experimentation and innovation at the member-state level and has been described in the literature as "policy evangelism": officials may experiment with novel policies because they are motivated by a desire to see those policies spread, "whether out of love for humanity, ideology, social status, or simple hubris."[118] The same account indicates that this claim might be persuasive for the safest incumbents as well as for bureaucrats who do not face the constraints of reelection, and may thus be more sensitive to personal motives. The point, more specifically, is that "bureaucrats may derive increased social status among their peers from achieving expertise in new policy areas—they are invited to appear on panels at industry conferences, and to opine in trade journals and technical assistance training calls."[119] This introduces the element of "reputational competition"; the idea is that NRAs may have incentives to come up with novel accountability mechanisms because of the reputational benefits they may derive therefrom. These benefits may be realized at the domestic level, but more importantly at the EU level and in the context of regulatory networks such as BEREC and the IRG.[120]

Regardless of the motives of national regulators, innovation with respect to accountability tools would also be more likely because novel regulatory processes would be only a part of a bundle of regulatory output. Galle and Leahy plausibly assert that "low innovation costs, high costs of exit, and the ability to hedge risk" should contribute to innovation. As further support, they cite studies showing that large states are the primary sources of innovation; they explain that states with ample resources are better able to absorb the cost of experimentation in one or two budget areas, can more easily diversify against the risk of failure, and therefore face a lower risk that residents will leave due to any single policy decision.[121] This description is particularly applicable to accountability experiments: the risk associated with these is hedged because they are only a piece of the regulatory activity of NRAs that includes a host of substantive regulatory measures. Briefly put, if a democratic experiment fails, it is unlikely that firms will move. As I argued earlier when examining the hypothesis of "regulatory processes competition," member states cannot expect to attract firms and residents on the basis of accountability innovation alone. Conversely, and importantly for the analysis here, member states will not lead them to exit on this basis either. In other words, experimentation with respect to regulatory processes meets the criteria of lower innovation costs, high costs of exit, and the ability to hedge risk; at the same time, NRAs may still reap reputational benefits as innovators in that regard. Even so, however, the literature has suggested that bureaucrats in various jurisdictions may be less likely than elected officials to have differing views about the "best" innovation options, thus their race to the top may end up being a "race to the same summit."[122] I would argue that a "race to the same summit" is not necessarily a bad outcome in this context. In fact, as chapter 6 will suggest, agreement on new regulatory processes after a period of experimentation may be the optimal way of building up institutional and procedural mandates in future reforms of the EU regulatory regime. All in all, the argument in favor of decentralization on the basis of experimentation and innovation should not be dismissed—at least, not easily, not at a theoretical level, and not so early.

3. *Facilitating democratic participation, and especially the engagement of local civil society organizations.* The idea here is that moving the exercise of political power closer to those affected by that power may well increase the likelihood of political involvement and awareness.[123] In the EU case, this would mean that national civil society groups can participate more easily in consultation procedures that NRAs organize. However, the literature has put in doubt this posited advantage of devolution: in the case of environmental group participation in decision making in the United States, Daniel Esty has argued that "[a]t the centralized level, environmental groups find it easier to reach critical mass and thereby to compete on more equal footing with industrial interests."[124] A response to this idea was that

> the logic of collective action might suggest the opposite. The cost of organizing on a larger scale magnifies the free-rider problems faced by environmental groups. Moreover, because environmental concerns vary throughout the country, there will be a loss in the homogeneity of the environmental interests when they are aggregated at the federal level, thereby further complicating the organizational problems.[125]

These organizational problems are exacerbated in the EU context. A European civil society is far from being formed; historical, cultural, geographic or even language barriers might hinder the effective organization of pan-European public interest groups. For this reason, at this stage, the third argument in favor of devolution would seem to support the current decentralized settlement in the European Union. Chapter 6 will take up this question again in light of the experience from the country cases. As a preview, this is not necessarily to say that national public interest groups are currently in a position, in terms of resources, to exert significant influence on NRAs.[126] The case studies in the next three chapters, which have compiled data on stakeholder participation and included interviews with these actors (consumer groups, in particular), discuss this question in further detail. At this point, however, it is fair to expect that national stakeholders are better situated to provide input domestically.[127] At any rate, the increased functions that the new regulatory scheme provides them at the member-state level may offer opportunities for their further development.

B. The case studies

So far I have presented the main claim that procedural EU mandates have had an accountability-enhancing effect at the member-state level, an effect that can be better appreciated if considered in the context of the decentralized EU regulatory structure. This "democratic surplus" argument is premised on the deliberative-participatory model constructed in chapter 1. The following chapters will test this claim in three case studies: France, Greece, and the United Kingdom. The focus will be on the NRAs in these member states, namely, the Autorité de Régulation des Communications Électroniques et des Postes (ARCEP) in France, the Hellenic Telecommunications and Post Commission (EETT) in Greece, and the Office of Communications (Ofcom) in the United Kingdom.

There are two main questions regarding case selection. Why telecommunications and why these countries? Besides its obvious importance to our everyday lives and its economic significance, this particular sector was selected because, as Part I outlined, the telecommunications industry was the first one to which the European Commission turned its attention. It, therefore, set the tone for similar initiatives in other sectors.[128] Electronic communications is also the first sector in which the EU involvement included advanced institutional and procedural provisions,[129] that is, the type of mandates that this book argues generate the "democratic surplus." Furthermore, as we saw, there have been subsequent generations of directives pertaining to this industry, rendering it the most illustrative case regarding the evolution of EU law in this area as well as its function as a model for other sectors. Chapter 6 will return to this point. The scope of the case studies covers "electronic communications" as broadly defined in the 2002 EU regulatory framework. Following the EU directives, it excludes content (most notably, broadcasting) even though the UK regulator is responsible for the TV and radio sectors as well. The case studies also exclude posts, which fall under a different EU regime, even though in all three country cases, the NRAs have also taken on the regulation of this sector.

As to the country cases, France, Greece, and the United Kingdom were selected for their different constitutional structures, diverse administrative traditions, often divergent perceptions of the regulatory state but also for the different models of representative politics, and especially of state-society relations, they portray. My expectation is that these differences translated into variations in the extent and forms of impact that institutional and procedural EU mandates had on national administrative governance. Previous literature has suggested that, because of dissimilar institutional frameworks and organizational arrangements, countries may respond differently and follow distinctive "adjustment paths" even if faced by similar external pressures for change.[130] Chapters 3, 4, and 5 trace these adjustment paths in response to the EU pressures for institutional and procedural change. Thus, they bring to the fore the conditions of implementation of EU law through networks of regulators within the politically, historically, and culturally diverse member states. The cases examine institutional structures, legal mandates and formal policymaking processes but also informal practices and the operation of regulatory processes on the ground beyond the "law on the books."

This type of research necessitated the collection, through both online sources and archival research, and compilation of data on public consultations over the NRAs' life span; this included more than 1,000 public consultations, and some 8,000 consultation responses over a five-year period. I supplemented the research design with semi-structured interviews with agency officials, industry and civil society representatives (that is, actors from all sides of the table) in Paris, Brussels, Athens, and London. More specifically, I contacted—first by email, followed up, in case of no response, by an email reminder, and then by telephone—market actors and NGOs that were participating in consultation exercises both frequently (normally, large telecommunications firms) and sporadically. I also contacted the "consultation champions" and legal advisers of the regulatory agencies in the three countries. Snowball sampling then identified further participants within the regulators. My interviews ranged between 45 minutes and 1.5 hours and investigated several questions falling under the central research problem I was analyzing. They covered, for example, the impact of EU law on domestic regulatory practices and the opportunities and challenges facing national stakeholders in their efforts to provide input on administrative policymaking.

In other words, exploring the effect of EU law on member-state regulatory governance is a complex problem, the full appreciation of which warrants an expansive toolkit. Therefore, the book opts for a multidisciplinary approach that draws on democratic theory, aggregate quantitative analysis of consultation practice, in-depth qualitative case studies, and comparative law.[131] Using this approach, the following chapters examine the varying degrees of change that EU mandates brought about in the three jurisdictions depending on the public law traditions, administrative history and procedures that had been in place before the advent of EU law. In this respect, this is also an interesting experiment from the perspective of comparative institutional analysis: we have common accountability mandates adopted at the center but their implementation in the periphery will hinge on national variations. My second, and perhaps more challenging, hypothesis is the, by now familiar, "democratic surplus" hypothesis. It begins by noting a general pattern described in earlier literature; namely, that national procedures had been similar in that generally the administration had enjoyed "considerable discretion" and not been required legally to interact openly with members of the public during the regulatory process.[132] Against this backdrop, the remainder of the book will shed light on ways in which EU mandates initiated, encouraged or formalized accountability mechanisms—most importantly, participatory procedures. In doing so, EU law enhanced aspects of the democratic accountability of regulatory agency operations in the member states and brought them closer to the deliberative-participatory model advocated in chapter 1.

Notes

1. Gerhard Fuchs, *Policy-making in a system of multi-level governance—the Commission of the European Community and the restructuring of the telecommunications sector*, 1 JOURNAL OF EUROPEAN PUBLIC POLICY 177, 179 (1994); *see also* Mark Thatcher, *The Commission and national governments as partners: EC regulatory expansion in telecommunications 1979–2000*, 8 JOURNAL OF EUROPEAN PUBLIC POLICY 558, 560–61 (2001) ("the sector provides an example of maximalist Commission and EC action")
2. *See* Thatcher, *supra* note 1, at 561–62.
3. Opinion of the Economic and Social Committee on the "Proposal for a Directive of the European Parliament and of the Council on a common regulatory framework for electronic communications networks and services" (2001/C 123/13).
4. MARK THATCHER, THE POLITICS OF TELECOMMUNICATIONS: NATIONAL INSTITUTIONS, CONVERGENCE, AND CHANGE IN BRITAIN AND FRANCE 80 (1999).
5. Council Recommendation (84/549/EEC) of 12 November 1984 concerning the implementation of harmonization in the field of telecommunications, OJ L 298/49, 16 November 1984; Council Recommendation (84/550/EEC) of 12 November 1984 concerning the first phase of opening up access to public telecommunications contracts, OJ L 298/51, 16 November 1984.
6. Commission, Green Paper on the Development of the Common Market for Telecommunications Services and Equipment. COM (87) 290 final, 30 June 1987; Susanne K. Schmidt, *Commission Activism: Subsuming Telecommunications and Electricity under European Competition Law*, 5 JOURNAL OF EUROPEAN PUBLIC POLICY 169, 173 (1998).
7. A broad overview of the general EU legal framework in the telecommunications sector is available at http://europa.eu/legislation_summaries/information_society/legislative_framework/index_en.htm
8. Commission Directive 88/301/EEC of 16 May 1988 on competition in the markets in telecommunications terminal equipment OJ L 131/73, 27 May 1988.

9. Commission Directive 90/388/EEC of 28 June 1990 on competition in the markets for telecommunications services, OJ L 192/10, 24 July 1990.

10. European Court of Justice, Judgment of the Court of 19 March 1991 in *Case C-202/88: French Republic v Commission of the European Communities—Competition in the markets in telecommunications terminal equipment*, [1991] ECR I-01223 (in this case France was supported by Italy, Belgium, Germany and Greece); European Court of Justice, Judgment of the Court of 17 November 1992 in Joined *Cases C-271, C-281/90 and C-289/90: Kingdom of Spain, Kingdom of Belgium and Italian Republic v Commission of the European Communities—Competition in the markets for telecommunications services*, [1992] ECR I-05833.

11. Antonio F. Bavasso, *Electronic Communications: A New Paradigm for European Regulation*, 41 COMMON MKT. L. REV. 87, 89 (2004).

12. Thatcher, *supra* note 1, at 558–60 (further noting that formal and informal institutional controls made the Commission very sensitive to the preferences of national governments. These controls operated through four processes: the participation of national governments at all stages of decision making; incrementalism; compromises and linkages; national discretion in implementation). *See also* Schmidt, *supra* note 6, at 176 ("The Commission has, however, enjoyed exceptionally favourable circumstances for its actions . . . Because of the significant interests in liberalization, the Commission received strong support from private actors who issued complaints or lobbied governments for acceptance. Nor were the governments bypassed. Rather, the analysis shows considerable support from national governments, despite the fact that their constitutional interests were violated"); Fuchs, *supra* note 1, at 184 (noting that the challenges before the ECJ were "not on substance, given the existence of a consensus on liberalization, but on form").

13. *See* Thatcher, *supra* note 1, at 570, 572 (noting that "EC rules to protect universal service were an important counterbalance to liberalization, especially for France and other member states worried that competition would lead to fierce price wars and the abandonment of unprofitable services or areas").

14. *Id.* at 573–74.

15. Commission Directive 96/19/EC of 13 March 1996 amending Directive 90/388/EEC with regard to the implementation of full competition in telecommunications markets, OJ L 74/13, 22 March 1996. *See also* Ian Walden, *European Union Communications Law, in* TELECOMMUNICATIONS LAW AND REGULATION 143, 163 (Ian Walden ed., 2012).

16. Communication from the Commission to the Council, the European Parliament, the Economic and Social Committee and the Committee of the Regions of 10 November 1999. Towards a new framework for Electronic Communications infrastructure and associated services—The 1999 Communications Review, COM(1999) 539 final, 10 November 1999. A brief overview is available at http://europa.eu/legislation_summaries/internal_market/single_market_services/l24216_en.htm.

17. 1999 Communications Review, *supra* note 16, at 1–2, 15.

18. A list of respondents and summaries of the comments submitted in response to the policy proposals set out in the 1999 Communications Review are available in the Communication from the Commission, The results of the public consultation on the 1999 Communications Review and Orientations for the new Regulatory Framework, COM(2000) 239 final, 26 April 2000.

19. Directive 2002/21/EC of the European Parliament and of the Council of 7 March 2002 on a common regulatory framework for electronic communications networks and services (**Framework Directive**), OJ L 108/33, 24 April 2002.

20. Directive 2002/20/EC of the European Parliament and of the Council of 7 March 2002 on the authorisation of electronic communications networks and services (**Authorisation Directive**), OJ L 108/21, 24 April 2002; Directive 2002/19/EC of the European Parliament and of the Council of 7 March 2002 on access to, and interconnection of, electronic communications networks and associated facilities (**Access Directive**), OJ L 108/7, 24 April 2002; Directive 2002/22/EC of the European Parliament and of the Council of 7 March 2002 on universal service and users' rights relating to electronic communications networks and services (**Universal Service Directive**), OJ L 108/51, 24 April 2002; Directive 2002/58/

EC of the European Parliament and of the Council of 12 July 2002 concerning the processing of personal data and the protection of privacy in the electronic communications sector
(**Directive on privacy and electronic communications**), OJ L 201/37, 31 July 2002.

21. Commission Directive 2002/77/EC of 16 September 2002 on competition in the markets
for electronic communications networks and services, OJ L 249/21, 17 September 2002.
The legal basis for this directive was Article 86(3) (ex Article 90(3)) of the Treaty.

22. Article 2(c) of the Framework directive defined the term "electronic communications service" as "a service normally provided for remuneration which consists wholly or mainly in
the conveyance of signals on electronic communications networks, including telecommunications services and transmission services in networks used for broadcasting, but exclude
services providing, or exercising editorial control over, content transmitted using electronic
communications networks and services; it does not include information society services,
as defined in Article 1 of Directive 98/34/EC, which do not consist wholly or mainly in the
conveyance of signals on electronic communications networks."

23. A brief overview of the Framework Directive is available at http://europa.eu/legislation_
summaries/information_society/legislative_framework/l24216a_en.htm#amendingact.

24. A brief overview of the Authorisation Directive is available at http://europa.eu/legislation_
summaries/information_society/legislative_framework/l24164_en.htm.

25. A brief overview of the Access Directive, from which the summary in the text is drawn,
is available at http://europa.eu/legislation_summaries/information_society/legislative_
framework/l24108i_en.htm.

26. Directive 95/62/EC of the European Parliament and of the Council of 13 December 1995
on the application of open network provision (ONP) to voice telephony, OJ L 321/6, 30
December 1995; Walden, *supra* note 15, at 180.

27. *See, e.g.*, Article 25 of the Framework Directive ("Review procedures"): "The Commission shall
periodically review the functioning of this Directive and report to the European Parliament
and to the Council, on the first occasion not later than three years after [July 2003]."

28. Communication from the Commission to the European Parliament, the Council, the
European Economic and Social Committee and the Committee of the Regions on the
Review of the EU Regulatory Framework for electronic communications networks and serv-
ices, COM(2006) 334 final, 29 June 2006.

29. Communication from the Commission to the European Parliament, the Council, the
European Economic and Social Committee and the Committee of the Regions—Report on
the outcome of the Review of the EU regulatory framework for electronic communications
networks and services in accordance with Directive 2002/21/EC and Summary of the 2007
Reform Proposals, COM(2007) 696 final, 13 November 2007.

30. Directive 2009/140/EC of the European Parliament and of the Council of 25 November
2009 amending Directives 2002/21/EC on a common regulatory framework for electronic
communications networks and services, 2002/19/EC on access to, and interconnection
of, electronic communications networks and associated facilities, and 2002/20/EC on
the authorisation of electronic communications networks and services, OJ L 337/37, 18
November 2009; Directive 2009/136/EC of the European Parliament and of the Council of
25 November 2009 amending Directive 2002/22/EC on universal service and users' rights
relating to electronic communications networks and services, Directive 2002/58/EC concerning the processing of personal data and the protection of privacy in the electronic communications sector and Regulation (EC) No 2006/2004 on cooperation between national
authorities responsible for the enforcement of consumer protection laws, OJ L 337/11, 18
November 2009.

31. Regulation (EC) No 1211/2009 of the European Parliament and of the Council of
25 November 2009 establishing the Body of European Regulators for Electronic
Communications (BEREC) and the Office, OJ L 337/1, 18 December 2009.

32. Proposal for a Directive of the European Parliament and of the Council establishing the
European Electronic Communications Code (Recast), Brussels, 14.09.16, COM(2016) 590.

33. For the distinction between institutional autonomy (*autonomie institutionelle*) and procedural autonomy (*autonomie procédurale*), *see* EUGENIE PRÉVÉDOUROU, L'ÉVOLUTION DE

L'AUTONOMIE PROCÉDURALE DES ÉTATS MEMBRES DE L'UNION EUROPÉENNE 87 *ff.* (1999). For an overview of the role of "procedural autonomy," *see* Adelina Adinolfi, *The "Procedural Autonomy" of Member States and the Constraints Stemming from the ECJ's Case Law: Is Judicial Activism Still Necessary?*, *in* THE EUROPEAN COURT OF JUSTICE AND THE AUTONOMY OF THE MEMBER STATES 281 (Hans-W. Micklitz & Bruno De Witte eds., 2012).

34. Eighth Report from the Commission on the Implementation of the Telecommunications Regulatory Package: European telecoms regulation and markets 2002, COM(2002) 695 final, 3 December 2002, at 18 (emphasis added).

35. *See also* Thatcher, *supra* note 1, at 566 ("The NRAs had much discretion since EC legislation was broad and relied on their action, but laid down few stipulations on their organizational position and procedures").

36. *See also* James Fesler's definition of independence as "independence from control by the governor, legislature, or other political or administrative agency [and] independence of control by organized special interests" (JAMES W. FESLER, THE INDEPENDENCE OF STATE REGULATORY AGENCIES 13 (Public Administration Service No. 85, 1942)).

37. On the correspondence between regulation and economic interests, and the political process by which regulation is achieved, both of which elements could be viewed as underpinning the two strands of independence considered in the text, see the classic George J. Stigler, *The Theory of Economic Regulation*, 2 BELL J.ECON. & MANAGEMENT SCI. 3 (1971).

38. See ECJ (Fifth Chamber) Judgment of 13 December 1991 in Case C-18/88: Régie des télégraphes et des téléphones v GB-Inno-BM SA, [1991] ECR I-5941, at para 28: "Articles 3(f), 90 and 86 of the EEC Treaty preclude a Member State from granting to the undertaking which operates the public telecommunications network the power to lay down standards for telephone equipment and to check that economic operators meet those standards when it is itself competing with those operators on the market for that equipment."

39. See Article 295 EC Treaty (ex 222 EEC Treaty, and currently 345 TFEU): "This Treaty shall in no way prejudice the rules in Member States governing the system of property ownership."

40. Walden, *supra* note 15, at 171.

41. *See* Damien Geradin & Nicolas Petit, *The Development of Agencies at EU and National Levels: Conceptual Analysis and Proposals for Reform*, 01/04 JEAN MONNET WORKING PAPER 1, 9 (2004).

42. On the privatization of PTOs, *see* Thatcher, *supra* note 1, at 571–72. On the phased divestiture, *see* Walden, *supra* note 15, at 173.

43. Directive 97/51/EC of the European Parliament and of the Council of 6 October 1997 amending Council Directives 90/387/EEC and 92/44/EEC for the purpose of adaptation to a competitive environment in telecommunications, OJ L 295/23, 29 October 1997, Article 1(6) (inserting Art 5a into Directive 90/387/EEC).

44. *Supra* note 16, at 58–59.

45. *See* Geradin & Petit, *supra* note 41, at 25 ("liberalization directives tend to be more severe when it comes to protect regulator (*sic*) from undue influence from industry than to protect regulators from political interferences"); Phedon Nicolaïdes, *Regulation of Liberalised Markets: A New Role for the State? (or How to Induce Competition Among Regulators)*, *in* REGULATION THROUGH AGENCIES IN THE EU. A NEW PARADIGM OF EUROPEAN GOVERNANCE 23, 33 (Damien Geradin, Rodolphe Muñoz & Nicolas Petit eds., 2005) ("[t]he independence required by the Directive is different than the independence defined in the regulatory literature. The Directive in essence seeks to prevent conflicts of interest. The functional independence defined in the literature means protection from political interference").

46. *See* Communication from the Commission to the Council, the European Parliament, the European Economic and Social Committee and the Committee of the Regions, European Electronic Communications Regulation and Markets 2003—Report on the Implementation of the EU Electronic Communications Regulatory Package, COM(2003) 715 final, 19 November 2003, at 24 ("In certain Member States there is no explicit transposition of the requirements of the Framework Directive as to the NRAs' independence from operators or their impartiality").

47. This reading is also consistent with the case law of the ECJ. For instance, in the course of examining the legality of Article 6 of Directive 88/301, the Court explained that "a system of undistorted competition, as laid down in the Treaty, can be guaranteed only if equality of opportunity is secured as between the various economic operators. To entrust an undertaking which markets terminal equipment with the task of drawing up the specifications for such equipment, monitoring their application and granting type-approval in respect thereof is tantamount to conferring upon it the power to determine at will which terminal equipment may be connected to the public network, and thereby placing that undertaking at an obvious advantage over its competitors" (Judgment of the Court of 19 March 1991 in Case C-202/88: French Republic v Commission of the European Communities.— Competition in the markets in telecommunications terminals equipment [1991] ECR I-01223, at para. 51).

48. Geradin & Petit, *supra* note 41, at 25.

49. *Supra* note 16, at 58: "The Commission . . . will strengthen existing legal provisions to ensure that the independent national regulator can undertake its role of supervision of the market free from political interference, without prejudice to the government's responsibility for national policy."

50. Communication, *supra* note 46, at 25.

51. Communication from the Commission to the European Parliament, the Council, the European Economic and Social Committee and the Committee of the Regions, Progress Report on the Single European Electronic Communications Market 2007 (13th Report), COM(2008) 153, 19 March 2009, at 10.

52. *See* Communication from the Commission to the European Parliament, the Council, the European Economic and Social Committee and the Committee of the Regions, Progress Report on the Single European Electronic Communications Market 2009 (15th Report), COM(2010)253 final/3, 25 August 2010, at 310.

53. *See also* Geradin & Petit, *supra* note 41, at 25, who, writing before 2009, lamented the focus of liberalization directives on protecting the regulators from undue influence from the industry rather than from political interference, adding that this was "regrettable as one of the main historic reasons for creating regulatory agencies was to remove politically-sensitive issues from the hands of the government."

54. 13th Report, *supra* note 51, at 10: "the Commission is examining continuing concerns as to resource constraints in Bulgaria, Greece, Luxembourg, Poland and Slovakia. The NRAs in the small Member States in particular can find it difficult to muster the expertise and resources needed to conduct market reviews and monitor implementation of remedies in increasingly complex markets."

55. See Directive 95/62/EC, Recital 10: "whereas [NRAs] should have the necessary means to carry out these tasks fully"; Directive 97/51/EC, Recital 9: "whereas the national regulatory authorities should be in possession of all the resources necessary, in terms of staffing, expertise, and financial means, for the performance of their function."

56. *See* Marek Szydło, *National Parliaments as Regulators of Network Industries: In Search of the Dividing Line Between Regulatory Powers of National Parliaments and National Regulatory Authorities*, 10 INT'L J. CONST. L. 1134, 1140–41 (2012).

57. This development seems to reflect a broader trend. *See* Ján Klucka, *The General Trends of EU Administrative Law*, 41 INT'L LAW. 1047, 1051 (2007) ("Apart from the Community institutions, the national administrations are also bound by procedural requirements when they implement Community law (indirect implementation). Those common procedural principles counterbalance the procedural autonomy principle, which has led to diversity among the national administrative proceedings. One can observe that, due to this development, the national administration autonomy in the implementation of EC legislation has been progressively reduced and framed by Community principles").

58. ECJ (Second Chamber), Judgment of 6 March 2008 in Case C-82/07, *Comisión del Mercado de las Telecomunicaciones v. Administración del Estado*, [2008] ECR I-01265, at para. 24 (emphasis added).

59. Szydło, *supra* note 56.

60. ECJ (Fourth Chamber), Judgment of 6 October 2010 in Case C-389/08, *Base NV and others v. Ministerraad*, [2010] ECR I-09073, at para 30.
61. Stephen Weatherill, *National Parliaments as Regulators of Network Industries: A Reply to Marek Szydło*, 10 INT'L J. CONST. L. 1167, 1167–68 (2012).
62. Szydło, *supra* note 56, at 1164.
63. *See also* Geradin & Petit, *supra* note 41, at 25 (noting that "the fact that NRAs need to be independent should not be an excuse to exempt them from any form of control. A balance must be struck between independence and accountability").
64. *Supra* note 32.
65. *See* Geradin & Petit, *supra* note 41, at 28–29.
66. Directive 97/33/EC of the European Parliament and of the Council of 30 June 1997 on interconnection in Telecommunications with regard to ensuring universal service and interoperability through application of the principles of Open Network Provision (ONP), OJ L 199/32, 26 July 1997.
67. *See* Commission Eighth Report, *supra* note 34, at 19.
68. *Id.*
69. *See* Communication from the Commission to the European Parliament, the Council, the Economic and Social Committee and the Committee of the Regions—Fifth report on the implementation of the telecommunications regulatory package, COM(1999) 537 final, at 11 ("In some Member States the procedures for appealing against decisions by the regulator may create lengthy delays (Denmark, Greece, Austria), or have suspensory effect (Ireland)"); Communication from the Commission to the Council, the European Parliament, the European Economic and Social Committee and the Committee of the Regions, European Electronic Communications Regulation and Markets 2004, COM(2004) 759 final, at 11; Communication from the Commission to the Council, the European Parliament, the European Economic and Social Committee and the Committee of the Regions, European electronic communications regulation and markets 2005 (11th Report), COM(2006) 68 final, at 11 ("The Commission is considering . . . the length of time taken for appeals to be settled and the fact that in a number of Member States the NRA's decision is often suspended automatically in accordance with national practice. Following Commission infringement action, automatic suspension is being abolished in Poland"); Communication from the Commission to the European Parliament, the Council, the European Economic and Social Committee and the Committee of the Regions, European electronic communications regulation and markets 2006 (12th Report), COM(2007) 155 final, at 15 ("the length of the appeal process is an issue in a number of Member States, for example Italy and Portugal, where proceedings can last from four to six years, and Greece, where the highest administrative court has not yet issued decisions despite the fact that some cases have been pending since 2001"); Communication from the Commission to the European Parliament, the Council, the European Economic and Social Committee and the Committee of the Regions, Progress Report on the single European electronic communications market 2008 (14th Report), COM(2009) 140 final, at 13 ("Systematic appeals and lengthy procedures continue to undermine legal certainty and effective implementation of the framework in a number of Member States (e.g., Belgium, Hungary, Portugal, Romania and Sweden). In contrast, efforts to address these issues have been made in Greece and Poland").
70. Walden, *supra* note 15, at 176.
71. Communication from the Commission to the European Parliament, the Council, the European Economic and Social Committee and the Committee of the Regions, Progress Report on the single European electronic communications market 2009 (15th Report), COM(2010) 253 final/3, at 6.
72. *See, e.g.*, article 33(1) of the "Universal Service Directive."
73. Recital 17 of Directive 2009/140/EC only added that the national consultation provided for under Article 6 of the Framework Directive should be conducted prior to the Community consultation provided for under Articles 7 and 7a of that Directive (a process that will be outlined in Part III in the discussion of horizontal and vertical coordination), to allow the views of interested parties to be reflected in the Community consultation. This would also

avoid the need for a second Community consultation in the event of changes to a planned measure as a result of the national consultation.

74. *Supra* note 32.

75. R. Daniel Kelemen, *Adversarial Legalism and Administrative Law in the European Union*, *in* COMPARATIVE ADMINISTRATIVE LAW 606, 614–15 (Susan Rose-Ackerman & Peter Lindseth eds., 2010).

76. As Kelemen further observes (*id.*, at 610), "mounting criticism of the EU's supposed 'democratic deficit' and public distrust of distant, 'faceless' Eurocrats has further encouraged the spread of adversarial legalism—particularly in the sphere of administrative law. Critics of the democratic deficit have called for increasing transparency and public participation in the EU's regulatory processes. *Opaque regulatory processes that were long tolerated at the national level are deemed unacceptable at the EU level*, where voters demand greater transparency. EU policymakers have responded to these demands by putting in place more transparent administrative procedures, more formal procedures for public participation and stronger 'access to justice' provisions" (internal citations omitted and emphasis added).

77. Szydło, *supra* note 56, at 1164.

78. Proposal for a Directive of the European Parliament and of the Council on a common regulatory framework for electronic communications networks and services, COM(2000) 393 final, OJ C 365 E/198, 19 December 2000, at 204.

79. European Parliament legislative resolution on the proposal for a directive of the European Parliament and of the Council on a common regulatory framework for electronic communications networks and services, OJ C 277/100 (Amendment 33).

80. Committee on Industry, External Trade, Research and Energy, Report on a proposal for a directive of the European Parliament and of the Council on a common regulatory framework for electronic communications networks and services, Final A5-0053/2001.

81. Amended proposal for a Directive of the European Parliament and of the Council on a common regulatory framework for electronic communications networks and services, OJ C 270 E/199, 25 September 2001, at 214.

82. Common Position (EC) No 38/2001 adopted by the Council on 17 September 2001, OJ C 337/34, 30 November 2001.

83. European Parliament legislative resolution on the Council common position for adopting a European Parliament and Council directive on a common regulatory framework for electronic communications networks and services, OJ C 177 E/142, 25 July 2002.

84. COM(2002) 78 final.

85. Kelemen, *supra* note 75, at 608. *See also* R. DANIEL KELEMEN, EUROLEGALISM: THE TRANSFORMATION OF LAW AND REGULATION IN THE EUROPEAN UNION (2011) (elaborating on the argument that the increased volume and diversity of players in the liberalized single market and the concomitant demands for a level playing field pressure EU policymakers to rely on a more formal, transparent approach to regulation backed by vigorous enforcement, often by private parties. For instance, Kelemen argues that decentralization of regulatory authority in the field of competition policy allows the EU to co-opt and harness national competition authorities, national courts and regulated firms as the agents of EU law, *id.* at 146).

86. *Supra* note 16, at 15.

87. According to an interesting depiction of this, "[w]ho implements most EU regulations? Not the Brussels bureaucracy. For the EU's employees, which number less than 30,000—of which 4-5,000 are real decision-makers—constitute a workforce no larger than that of a medium-sized European city. They number about one-fortieth of the civilian federal workforce in the US, a country noted for the small size of federal civilian employment." (Andrew Moravcsik, *The EU ain't broke*, PROSPECT 38, 40 (March 2003)).

88. As Renaud Dehousse puts it, "European technocratic structures have a clear multilevel character, given their role as a connecting device between the EU and national administrations" (Renaud Dehousse, *Misfits: EU Law and the Transformation of European Governance*, 2/02 JEAN MONNET WORKING PAPER 1, 5 (2002)). Interestingly, in one case in which the Community had first decided to keep enforcement centralized as well, it subsequently

shifted to the decentralization model: to be more specific, in competition law, the original enforcement system had been fairly centralized with the Commission retaining the relevant powers and the national competition authorities (NCAs) not being empowered to apply the pertinent provisions (Articles 81 and 82 of the EC Treaty). Nonetheless, Council Regulation (EC) 1/2003 [OJ L 1/1] marked a shift back to the norm, i.e., a decentralized enforcement system, and entrusted NCAs as well with enforcing EU competition law.

89. *See* Herwig C. H. Hofmann, *Mapping the European Administrative Space*, 31 WEST EUROPEAN POLITICS 662, 667 (2008).

90. *See* Sabino Cassese, *European Administrative Proceedings*, 68 LAW & CONTEMP. PROBS. 21, 24 (2004) (further noting that "[b]ecause the Community opted from the start for implementation by 'indirect rule,' these composite proceedings now make up the bulk of European administrative proceedings"). *See also* Giacinto della Cananea, *The European Union's Mixed Administrative Proceedings*, 68 LAW & CONTEMP. PROBS. 197, 198 (2004) ("Another trend in the administration of EU policies is that when making decisions . . . both national authorities and either the Commission or EU agencies take part in multiphase processes. These sequences of activities may be characterized more precisely as mixed administrative proceedings"); Klucka, *supra* note 57, at 1049–50 ("According to the traditional model of administrative action, the Community administration is essentially a steering body that leaves the execution of European laws in the hands of national administrations . . . . Today, one can observe a major shift from this model since many decisions are now made through mixed administrative proceedings"); Johannes Saurer, *Supranational Governance and Networked Accountability Structures: Member State Oversight of EU Agencies, in* COMPARATIVE ADMINISTRATIVE LAW 618, 618–19 (Susan Rose-Ackerman & Peter Lindseth eds., 2010) (noting "[t]he transformation of European administration from the paradigm of indirect administration to the governance of administrative networks").

91. Geradin & Petit, *supra* note 41, at 16.

92. *See* PAUL CRAIG, EU ADMINISTRATIVE LAW 50–51 (2006).

93. Committee on Industry, External Trade, Research and Energy, Report on a proposal for a directive of the European Parliament and of the Council on a common regulatory framework for electronic communications networks and services, Final A5-0053/2001, at 59.

94. See the concise presentation in Walden, *supra* note 15, at 168–70.

95. *Supra* note 32.

96. Further information is available on the IRG website at www.irg.eu.

97. Commission Decision 2002/627/EC of 29 July 2002 establishing the European Regulators Group for Electronic Communications Networks and Services, OJ L 200/38, 30 July 2002.

98. Regulation (EC) No 1211/2009 of the European Parliament and of the Council of 25 November 2009 establishing the Body of European Regulators for Electronic Communications (BEREC) and the Office, OJ L 337/1, 18 December 2009.

99. More information on BEREC is available on its website (http://berec.europa.eu). Regulation (EC) No 1211/2009 includes further provisions on other issues, such as the composition, decision-making processes and budget of this body.

100. This phrase has been used to describe the function that European Agencies might develop (Deirdre Curtin, *Delegation to EU Non-Majoritarian Agencies and Emerging Practices of Public Accountability, in* REGULATION THROUGH AGENCIES IN THE EU. A NEW PARADIGM OF EUROPEAN GOVERNANCE 88, 113 (Damien Geradin & Rodolphe Muñoz & Nicolas Petit eds., 2005)). However, this characterization could also apply in the context of NRAs, as will be examined later in the text.

101. My definition of a "decentralized regime" is purposely broad. The defining characteristic is the division or sharing of power between multiple levels. This covers, for instance, federal systems, devolution arrangements and, importantly for our purposes, the "managed decentralization" model of EU administration. On the well-established nature of these arguments, *see* Heather K. Gerken, *Foreword: Federalism All the Way Down*, 124 HARV. L. REV. 4, 6 (2010) ("we are intimately familiar with [federalism's] benefits: federalism promotes choice, competition, participation, experimentation, and the diffusion of power. The [U.S. Supreme] Court reels these arguments off as easily as do scholars"). See also the cautionary note of

Barry Friedman, *Valuing Federalism*, 82 MINN. L. REV. 317, 317–18 (1997) ("Constitutional decisions of the nation's highest court contain paeans to the federal system. And academic literature richly extols the oft-expressed reasons underlying the American invention of divided government. Much of this is just talk, however, evidencing little real effort to understand the tangible benefits of a federal system") (internal citations omitted).

102. Charles Tiebout, *A Pure Theory of Local Expenditures*, 64 J. POL. ECON. 416 (1956); Daniel C. Esty & Damien Geradin, *Introduction*, *in* REGULATORY COMPETITION AND ECONOMIC INTEGRATION: COMPARATIVE PERSPECTIVES xix, xxiii (Daniel Esty & Damien Geradin eds., 2001).

103. *See* Damien Geradin & Joseph A. McCahery, *Regulatory Co-opetition: Transcending the Regulatory Competition Debate*, *in* THE POLITICS OF REGULATION: INSTITUTIONS AND REGULATORY REFORMS FOR THE AGE OF GOVERNANCE 90, 94–95 (Jacint Jordana & David Levi-Faur eds., 2004).

104. *See* Wallace E. Oates & Robert M. Schwab, *Economic Competition Among Jurisdictions: Efficiency Enhancing or Distortion Inducing?*, 35 J. PUB. ECON. 333 (1988) (concluding that in their basic model interjurisdictional competition is efficiency-enhancing, but also discussing three distinct sources of potential distortion). There is, however, the pessimistic story of a race to the bottom. *See, e.g.*, in the area of environmental regulation, Richard B. Stewart, *Pyramids of Sacrifice? Problems of Federalism in Mandating State Implementation of National Environmental Policy*, 86 YALE L.J. 1196 (1977). *But see* the reply of Richard L. Revesz, *Rehabilitating Interstate Competition: Rethinking the "Race-to-the-Bottom" Rationale for Federal Environmental Regulation*, 67 N.Y.U. L. REV. 1210 (1992). For more applications of the regulatory competition theory in the US, EU and global context, *see* REGULATORY COMPETITION AND ECONOMIC INTEGRATION: COMPARATIVE PERSPECTIVES xix, xxiii (Daniel Esty & Damien Geradin eds., 2001).

105. *See* Susan Rose-Ackerman, *Risk Taking and Reelection: Does Federalism Promote Innovation?*, 9 J. LEGAL STUD. 593, 608 (1980) ("First, moving is costly . . . . Second, people cannot diversify. They must choose a single state in which to reside. Third, in choosing a place to live, a person is not simply making a choice about the jurisdiction's innovation strategy. Current public service levels, commuting time, and environmental conditions are all linked together. Since in realistic situations this lumpiness will reduce the number of choices available, a voter may seek to change policy within his current jurisdiction instead of moving").

106. *See* Brian Galle & Mark Seidenfeld, *Administrative Law's Federalism: Preemption, Delegation, and Agencies at the Edge of Federal Power*, 57 DUKE L.J. 1933, 1956–57 (2008). *See also* David P. Dolowitz & David Marsh, *Learning from Abroad: The Role of Policy Transfer in Contemporary Policy-Making*, 13 GOVERNANCE 5, 10 (2000).

107. Nestor Davidson, *Cooperative Localism: Federal-Local Collaboration in an era of State Sovereignty*, 93 VA. L. REV. 959, 1007 (2007).

108. *See New State Ice Co. v. Liebmann*, 285 U.S. 262, 311 (1932) (Brandeis, J., dissenting) ("It is one of the happy incidents of the federal system that a single courageous State may, if its citizens so choose, serve as a laboratory; and try novel social and economic experiments without risk to the rest of the country").

109. *See* Phedon Nicolaïdes, *Regulation of Liberalised Markets: A New Role for the State? (or How to Induce Competition Among Regulators)*, *in* REGULATION THROUGH AGENCIES IN THE EU. A NEW PARADIGM OF EUROPEAN GOVERNANCE 23, 36 (Damien Geradin & Rodolphe Munoz & Nicolas Petit eds., 2005).

110. Rose-Ackerman, *supra* note 105, at 594.

111. *See* Brian Galle & Joseph Leahy, *Laboratories of Democracy? Policy Innovation in Decentralized Governments*, 58 EMORY L.J. 1333, 1397 (2009).

112. Rose-Ackerman, *supra* note 105, at 596-06.

113. *Id.*, at 610–11 (further explaining that "[w]hile states, like firms, can sometimes protect their innovations through the patent laws, the outcome of a risky project is often an organizational or methodological change that cannot be patented. With low cost diffusion and no higher level subsidies, few differential benefits exist and not many risks are likely to be taken").

114. Ian Ayres, *Supply-Side Inefficiencies in Corporate Charter Competition: Lessons from Patents, Yachting and Bluebooks*, 43 U. KAN. L. REV. 541, 548 (1995).

115. Galle & Leahy, *supra* note 111, at 1361.

116. *Id.*, at 1374–75.

117. Even the skeptics of the "experimentation and innovation thesis" acknowledge that "the bureaucratic innovation theory is a more compelling one than the politician account" (*id.*, at 1387).

118. *Id.*, at 1386. According to a similar account that recognizes several reasons underlying the motivation to innovate, "[t]he possibility of free riding may be reduced to the extent that policy makers value the possibility that their innovation will spread beyond their jurisdiction. If one assumes that rather than being egoists, policy makers are promoters of policies and their spread, then the rate of innovation in the networked scenario will be greater than the rate of innovation in the island scenario. That is, those who seek to maximize their impact on the world rather than their jurisdiction will have greater opportunities to affect a networked world. Alternatively, it is conceivable that emulation by other states will increase the prestige of the leaders of the state that originated the innovation, creating an incentive to innovate even if most of the benefits of the innovation go to others" (David Lazer, *Regulatory Capitalism as a Networked Order: The International System as an Informational Network*, 598 ANNALS AM. ACAD. POL. & SOC. SCI. 52, 61 (2005)).

119. Galle & Leahy, *supra* note 111, at 1386.

120. *See* Dorit Rubinstein Reiss, *Administrative Agencies as Creators of Administrative Law Norms: Evidence from the UK, France and Sweden*, in COMPARATIVE ADMINISTRATIVE LAW 373, 384 (Susan Rose-Ackerman & Peter Lindseth eds., 2010) (noting that there is informal reputational competition between national regulators concerning how well they regulate and that this peer pressure seems to extend to transparency and consultation norms as well).

121. Galle & Leahy, *supra* note 111, at 1367.

122. *Id.*, at 1388–89 (clarifying, with further citations, that "bureaucrats tend to share more information with one another, rely on similar sources of authority, and take a less ideological attitude toward policymaking").

123. DAVID SHAPIRO, FEDERALISM: A DIALOGUE 91–92, 139 (1995).

124. Daniel Esty, *Revitalizing Environmental Federalism*, 95 MICH. L. REV. 570, 650 n. 302 (1996) (adding that "[t]he difficulty of mobilizing the public in many separate jurisdictions is well-established," id., at 650–51).

125. Richard Revesz, *Federalism and Regulation: Some Generalizations*, in REGULATORY COMPETITION AND ECONOMIC INTEGRATION: COMPARATIVE PERSPECTIVES 3, 9–10 (Daniel Esty & Damien Geradin eds., 2001).

126. *See, e.g.*, SUSAN ROSE-ACKERMAN, CONTROLLING ENVIRONMENTAL POLICY. THE LIMITS OF PUBLIC LAW IN GERMANY AND THE UNITED STATES 11 (1995) (noting that "Germany has many private groups, but few have the technical capacity to mount a challenge to the conventional policy-making and standard-setting processes. Most are poorly staffed and funded. No organizations resemble the Environmental Defense Fund and the National Resources Defense Council in their ability to invest millions of dollars per year intervening in administrative processes and bringing lawsuits").

127. *Cf.*, in the different context of courts and not agencies, Francesca Bignami, *The Democratic Deficit in European Community Rulemaking: A Call for Notice and Comment in Comitology*, 40 HARV. INT'L L.J. 451, 511 (1999) (noting "the current imbalance in Community interest representation" and that under her proposal "[n]ational courts would serve as point of access to the judicial review component of rulemaking and therefore interest groups would not need to be well-organized in Brussels with the resources to employ expensive Brussels lawyers").

128. *See* DORIT RUBINSTEIN REISS, REGULATORY ACCOUNTABILITY: TELECOMMUNICATIONS AND ELECTRICITY AGENCIES IN THE UK, FRANCE AND SWEDEN 38 (2007) (Doctoral dissertation, UC Berkeley, on file with author) (noting that "when other sectors were liberalized, many ideas were borrowed from the telecommunications sector").

129. *See* Geradin & Petit, *supra* note 41, at 29–30 (discussing several network industries and noting that "[n]one of the first-generation directives contained provisions designed to ensure the participation of stakeholders in regulatory processes. *Except in the case of the new telecommunications regulatory package*, second-generation liberalizing directives do not deal with this issue either" (emphasis added)).
130. THATCHER, *supra* note 4, at 16, 18 (with further citations).
131. *See also* KELEMEN, *supra* note 81, at 17 (noting, in the context of his study, that "while indicative of broad trends, aggregate data cannot definitively establish a causal link between European integration and shifts in regulatory style . . . . To explore and understand the causal pathways linking European integration and adversarial legalism, we must turn to detailed case studies of particular policy areas.") Like Kelemen, I share the methodological maxim that "[t]he prudent social scientist, like the wise investor, must rely on diversification to magnify the strengths, and to offset the weaknesses, of any single instrument" (ROBERT D. PUTNAM, MAKING DEMOCRACY WORK: CIVIC TRADITIONS IN MODERN ITALY 12 (1993)).
132. Francesca Bignami, *Creating European Rights: National Values and Supranational Interests*, 11 COLUM. J. EUR. L. 241, 316 (2005).

3

France

France is an illuminating case. It was a late liberalizer, only opening fully its telecommunications market to competition in 1998. What renders the French case more interesting is that these participatory processes occur in a policymaking environment traditionally described as "statist"[1] and suspicious toward interest groups. This pattern has its origins in the French Revolution and the "republican" perception of the state, "in which elected governments are mandated to carry out the will of the people directly," without the mediation of organized interests that contradict the "political culture of generality."[2] This chapter examines how the EU procedural mandates have translated into institutional practice in the area of electronic communications in France. It situates these developments in the historical context of the evolution of the French administrative model and state-society relations. It also discusses whether these new processes might gradually give rise to a different perception of the administrative state that will appear to be more open to participatory influences through all sectors of administrative policymaking.

I. The French republican tradition and its reflection in public law

It is a commonplace to highlight Jean-Jacques Rousseau's influence on the French Revolution. One of the excerpts that succinctly showcases certain key features of the early French republican tradition comes from the Fourth Book of *The Social Contract*: "when the State close to ruin subsists only in an illusory and vain form, when the social bond is broken in all hearts, when the basest interest brazenly assumes the sacred name of public good; then the general will grows mute, everyone, prompted by secret motives, no more states opinions as a Citizen than if the State had never existed, and iniquitous decrees with no other goal than particular interest are falsely passed under the name of Laws."[3]

We can trace three building blocks of the French republic at the moment of its foundation: the idea of the indivisible "national sovereignty," the "general interest" as the aim of all state action, and the celebration of the supremacy of the law (*la loi*), or more fittingly the supremacy of the statute. This description, with certain variations, maps well onto the three principal dimensions of the founding moment of the Revolution constituting what Pierre Rosanvallon has termed the "political culture of generality": as social form (the celebration of the "grand national whole"), as political quality (the faith in the virtues of immediacy), as mode of regulation (the cult of law).[4] A common thread running through these features of the early French republican tradition is that they are hardly compatible with the picture drawn in chapter 1: that of an administrative state open to direct influence from individuals and groups in a deliberative-participatory system.

A. The general will emanating from an indivisible national sovereignty...

The revolutionaries aspired to unity by assembling all parties into a single body politic that would be the source of all sovereignty.[5] The Commune of Paris issued a manifesto symbolizing this attachment to the *grand tout*: "We only have one desire: to lose ourselves in the great whole."[6] Abbé Sieyès, a key figure of that period, the "constitution maker" and an original political thinker,[7] reiterated the same idea: "France is a unique whole composed of integral parts" and "subject in all its parts to a common legislature and administration." At a different point of that speech he stresses: "There isn't but one Order in a State, or rather there are no longer Orders as long as representation is common and equal."[8] These ideas of an indivisible Nation that expresses the general will above and beyond every individual will and from which stems all sovereignty were reflected in a fundamental text of that period. Article III of the Declaration of the Rights of Man and of the Citizen of 26 August 1789 enunciated: "The principle of all sovereignty resides essentially in the nation. No body, no individual may exercise any authority which does not proceed directly from the nation."

In view of the spirit of those times and the emphasis on the notion of the sovereign will of an indivisible nation, it should come as little surprise that a corporatist spirit of separate orders or *corps* challenging the unity of the general will did not fit into this vision. Sieyès clearly expressed this perception in another passage: "Everyone today feels the need to establish social unity upon the destruction of orders and of all the big corporations."[9] Since the Nation was affirmed as a totality that could not be reduced to any of its constitutive elements, the various mediating social structures were considered suspect of contradicting the access to generality and potentially corrupting the general will.[10] This hostility toward corporate bodies was quickly incorporated into binding official texts. On 2 March 1791, a decree (*décret d'Allarde*) abolished guilds (*corporations*). A couple of months later, the law *Le Chapelier* of June 14, 1791, reinforced and expanded this prohibition. This piece of legislation reaffirmed the abolition of any kind of citizens' guild in the same trade or of the same profession as one of the fundamental bases of the French Constitution (art. 1). Article 3 stipulated that "all administrative or municipal bodies are forbidden to receive any address or petition in the name of an occupation or profession, or to make any response thereto." Furthermore, in 1810, Article 291 of the Criminal Code instituted the offense of the unauthorized association composed of more than twenty people. Part II of this chapter will describe that these strict restrictions were gradually relaxed and eventually abolished.

The ghost of *Le Chapelier* might seem long gone in a country of more than 1.1 million active associations, 12 million volunteers and 1.9 million employees in this sector with a cumulated budget exceeding 59 billion Euros, and a public that predominantly (87%) looks favorably on associations.[11] However, it is telling that two French lobbyists in separate interviews drew a distinction between the French and the US culture vis-à-vis interest groups by mentioning the same example: "while in 1791 the Americans were adopting the First Amendment, in France the Assembly was passing the law *Le Chapelier*."[12]

B. ... taking the form of statute and resulting in the "cult of law" ...

The procedural embodiment of this indivisible national sovereignty is the statute produced in the representative legislative body. Article 6 of the Declaration of the Rights of Man and of the Citizen reflected this idea: "Law is the expression of the general will." Furthermore, eight out of the seventeen articles of the Declaration refer to the functions of the law demonstrating its centrality in the early French republic.[13] The preeminence of the representative body was not in itself a Rousseauian idea: in the *Social Contract* it is the body of the citizens that directly exercises legislative power by itself. However, the French revolutionaries, in a pragmatic fashion, chose to combine the general will with the parliamentary will (of a unicameral body) and identify their representative institutions with Rousseau's definition of the law as the product of the general will.[14] In Sieyès' words, the "representatives are the sole depositories of the general will."[15] To the democratic perception of the statute as emanating from the general will was added the liberal perception of the law as a guarantee against arbitrary rule and a safeguard for liberty owing to the impersonal and general character of the norm.[16]

This legicentric tradition (*légicentrisme*) was translated into the jurisprudence of the Conseil d'État under the Third Republic (1870–1940). The constitutional texts of 1885 followed the current of ideas just described (and also reflected in the Declaration of 1789) regarding the predominance of the law.[17] It was precisely this superiority of the law that the Conseil d'État reaffirmed in establishing the theory of the statute-screen (*théorie de la loi écran*): In examining the legality of an administrative act taken in conformity with a statute that petitioner claims to be unconstitutional, the court may not strike down the administrative act. This would imply a power to review the constitutionality of the statute, and—as the court stated—"in the current state of French public law this course of action may not be discussed." In other words, the statute, the embodiment of parliamentary sovereignty, creates a screen between the administrative act and the Constitution but also between the judge and the Constitution.[18] The connection between the *théorie de la loi écran* and the sovereignty of the statute was expressed in clear terms in the conclusions of the *Commissaire du gouvernement*, Roger Latournerie, who even invoked Rousseau.[19] This jurisprudence of the Conseil d'État was subsequently affirmed on several occasions under the Fourth and the Fifth Republic.[20]

C. … and aiming at the general interest.

If the general will was the source of public power and the statute its procedural expression of choice, the general interest was the "teleology of the public action," encompassing both the legislature and the executive.[21] Rousseau had defined the content of the law in the same way: "When I say that the object of the laws is always general, I mean that the law considers the subjects in a body and their actions in the abstract, never any man as an individual or a particular action."[22] Sieyès reiterated the central importance of the general interest: "Public salvation requires that the common interest of the society be maintained pure and unadulterated."[23]

The French republican tradition subscribes to a voluntaristic approach to the "general interest": The *intérêt général* is transcendent—it surpasses private interests, and is not simply the sum of particular interests as the utilitarian approach would suggest.[24] This republican vision of the public interest constitutes "the heart of the French republican model,"[25] and the highest courts of the land likewise acknowledged the role of the legislator in determining the general interest.[26]

D. Administration bound: The distrust vis-à-vis a strong executive power

The recognition of parliamentary sovereignty as the genuine expression of the general will aspiring to the common interest went hand in hand with the distrust of the executive branch. The sovereignty of the law signified not only a government of law but also the legislator's ambition to assume all political functions, including those of the executive and judiciary.[27] In revolutionary France that strong suspicion toward executive power resulted in the latter being understood solely as a delegated power. The revolutionaries would not cease to stress that the ministers were simply serving the legislative power.[28] According to Sieyès, the executive power and whatever belonged to it only existed after the Law had been completely formed.[29]

This perception was inserted in the Constitution of 1791, the first French written Constitution.[30] Article 2 of the second section of Chapter IV of Title III read: "The administrators do not have any representative character. They are agents temporarily elected by the people to exercise, under the surveillance and the authority of the king, the administrative functions." This text is interesting in that it illustrates the fundamental distinction between the sovereign representative body and the civil service and casts it in principal-agent terms to use the familiar 20th century terminology. Furthermore, it reflects another telling terminological issue. When describing the executive, the term "power" is dropped in this passage in favor of "functions." Other articles of that Constitution refer to the "executive power," but, as Rosanvallon suggests, the tendency at that time was to avoid the use of the term "power" to qualify the executive. The "execution" was reduced to the narrowest and most mechanic meaning that this expression could have to ensure that it could in no way challenge the predominance of the law as the expression of the generality.[31] The dominant understanding of the era was that the law representing the general will defined from its sacrosanct position the general interest, in the name of which the administration merely applied this will. This picture recalls the "transmission belt" idea of chapter 1 depicting the administration as the machinery mechanically applying legislative directions.

In the early 20th century the perception of the administration changed. Léon Duguit, dean of the law school at the University of Bordeaux, introduced a particularly influential theory of the state (with a lasting impact on French public law until today) linking the administration to the realization of the general interest through the model of the *"service public."* In Duguit's approach, the public power may not be legitimized by its origin but only by the services it renders to the public in conformity with the law.[32] The emphasis is on the general interest of the collectivity and not on the public power (*puissance publique*) as his intellectual rival, Maurice Hauriou, argued.[33] Duguit's account shifted the emphasis from the commanding power to the public tasks of the administration, to its mission serving the *intérêt général*.[34] Thus, in order to establish the legitimacy of administrative power, the "school of public service" substitutes the notion of the general interest for that of executing the general will.[35]

This connection between the *intérêt général* and the administration assumed a noticeable place in the jurisprudence of the *Conseil d'Etat* as well. In 1901 the highest administrative court stated: "the administration cannot take a decision except for reasons of general interest."[36] The replacement of the element of public power by the element of the aim of public activity led to the emergence of a new cause of action to invalidate administrative acts in cases of distortion of this aim: the abuse of power (*détournement de pouvoir*).[37] Beginning in the late 19th century and through the 20th century, administrative acts were invalidated on the grounds that they did not serve the aim of the law or the general interest, thus constituting an abuse of power. The connection between the mission of the administration, the general interest and *détournement de pouvoir* continued under the Fifth Republic.[38] In this context, the emphasis on the general interest as the aim of administrative policymaking resulted in severe skepticism vis-à-vis the effort of groups and individual citizens to influence administrative action. This "administrative lobbying" would seek to steer administrative action in the direction of "particular interests," which is what the tool of *détournement de pouvoir* purported to cover.[39]

Therefore, the perception of the administration in both variants that this section presented would be hostile to the idea of direct citizen involvement in administrative policymaking. The original perception focusing on the administration as a subject mechanically executing the general will enshrined in the statutes that the representatives of the Nation had voted left no room for any public participation outside the selection of those representatives. Likewise, the later account by its emphasis on the notion of the general interest as the sole purpose of all administrative action was hardly more hospitable to the direct expression of group or individual interests.

In conclusion, in view of the four features described in this Part, the early French "republican model" could not accommodate any individual or group interests that would seek access to the policymaking process. Indeed, it squarely opposes the deliberative-participatory model of chapter 1: the latter challenges the idea of an indivisible nation expressing a unified general will; it views with skepticism the perception that there is a single general interest that the representative body or the administration can easily detect on their own and then singlehandedly serve; that the statute can cover all types of economic and social regulation and clearly delineate a restricted role for the executive power in applying these rules. Had the early republican model remained fixed in time, the deliberative-participatory model and the EU mandates described in chapter 2 would have brought about cataclysmic changes. My claim is not that we are witnessing such cataclysmic changes given precisely that the early republican model has indeed evolved. However, aspects of the founding moment of the French republic were embedded in the culture of the French administration and public law and determined the extent to which those early traditions evolved, and consequently the degree of change effectuated by EU mandates. The following pages assess these developments.

II. The descriptive inadequacies and the evolution of the "early republican model"

Part I was painting the early French republican tradition with a broad brush. Qualifications to the "jacobinist model" in terms of the recognition of "*corps intermédiaires*" and their role in the late 19th century and especially the 20th century are necessary (A). In a related vein, the Fifth Republic marks a considerable break from the preexisting institutional relationship between the legislative and the executive power as well as the preeminence of the statute in the French constitutional system (B).

A. The descriptive inadequacies of the pure "jacobinist model"

The "jacobinist model" was massively criticized even though it was at the same time generally described as dominant. Furthermore, it did not remain frozen in its original form and was largely amended to give space first to labor unions in 1884 and subsequently to associations in 1901.[40]

As Rosanvallon details, the legal recognition of syndicates came as a result of the realization on the part of elected officials that unions could function as a "source of order and social regulation" and would "moderate the workers' movement," especially at the height of the strike movement. Moreover, the emergence of the discipline of sociology in the 1870s contributed the intellectual challenge to the dominant jacobinist understanding thus rendering it more vulnerable.[41] The official recognition of labor unions by means of the 1884 law came with restrictions of its own: It permitted the creation of professional syndicates while all other associations were still prohibited under the criminal code; it specified that the *exclusive* objective of professional syndicates was the study and defense of economic, industrial, commercial and agricultural interests (Art. 3) therefore originally purporting to exclude any thoughts of "political" aims;[42] it provided that labor unions could be financed by member dues, but could not acquire any property other than what was necessary for their meetings, libraries and professional instruction. On the other hand, they could set up special funds for mutual aid and pensions (Art. 6).

In the coming years labor unions saw their role continuously expand. After World War I, the law of March 25, 1919, set up the first institutional framework for collective bargaining agreements. What is important for our purposes is that syndicates were gradually recognized as interlocutors of the public authorities and the more representative of them were brought into the elaboration of the economic policy of the country.[43] 1946 marks the constitutional recognition of labor unions. Paragraph 6 of the Preamble of the Constitution of 1946—a preamble that is incorporated in the Constitution of 1958 currently in effect—provides that "everyone may defend their rights and interests through union action and may belong to the union of their choice." Paragraph 8 further stipulates that "all workers shall, through the intermediary of their representatives, participate in the collective determination of their conditions of work and in the management of the work place." This right takes practical form in Article L101-1 of the Labor Code (*Code du travail*), pursuant to which the government should organize a prior concertation with the representative employees' and employ-ers' unions when it intends to adopt a project for reform having an impact on individual or collective labor relations, employment or professional training and which might be the topic of a national negotiation.

The official recognition of other, i.e., generic, associations would only come seventeen years later, in 1901; the development of their role in and vis-à-vis the French state did not follow a similar path. In fact, Rosanvallon described the dis-crepancy between the regimes of 1884 and 1901 as a "scandalous gap." Article 6 of the 1901 law imposed strict constraints on the finances and property of associations: they could only rely, without prior authorization, on member dues and possess only an office for the governing board and meetings of its members and other property "strictly necessary" to the accomplishment of their goals, a condition that was narrowly construed. In Rosanvallon's terms, "the right of association was conceived far more narrowly, in such a way as to structure the freedom of association without actually acknowledging the social function of the resulting institution." In contrast, labor unions were gradually recognized as "quasi-public" organizations.[44]

This gap between labor unions and other associations in terms of their rec-ognition in the context of public policymaking was bridged under the Fifth Republic and especially during the last quarter of the 20th century.[45] In 1971, the Conseil Constitutionnel solemnly declared that the freedom of association was among the fundamental principles of the Republic thus elevating it to the status of a constitutional value.[46] More importantly for the purposes of this chapter's inquiry, intermediary bodies were enlisted as "functional auxiliaries of the state,"[47] notably through their participation in consultative committees. The increasing recourse to such committees, with estimates of their number reaching up to 5,000, led to the emergence of what is termed a "consulting administration" (*administration consultative*).[48] Concerns were voiced against a potentially exces-sive use of these consultative bodies saturating the institutional landscape.[49] In 2006, two decrees sought to remedy the problem by introducing the rule that the committees created prior to the publication of these decrees would be abolished after three years except in cases where their "indispensable character" would have been established. Furthermore, the duration of new committees would be five years. A study establishing their necessity would precede their creation, and at the end of the five years, the need for renewal would have to be re-evaluated.[50] Newer reports reiterated the issue of heavy use of consultative committees.[51]

In the literature on state-society relations in France, these developments were often perceived in opposing terms. For instance, Frank Wilson recognized the numerical prevalence of statutory institutions purporting to accommodate direct contacts between government officials and representatives of authorized interest groups. However, the vast majority of his interviews with interest group leaders showed a pessimistic outlook on the importance and effectiveness of these processes.[52] Therefore, Wilson's conclusion was rather that the predominant pattern in France is pluralist. "The most frequent activities, and the ones regarded as most effective in shaping policies, were formal and informal contacts between separate interest groups and political or administrative officials. Other basically pluralist practices, especially legislative lobbying and public relations campaigns, are important forms of group action."[53]

Other students of the French interest group structure did not share Wilson's pluralist account. For instance, John Keeler noted that "[d]espite the fact that the French system remains less fully corporatized than those of many other polities, the French case has featured a neocorporatist trend, . . . [but] it is important to acknowledge that interest group dynamics in France have been unevenly corporatized."[54] One of his arguments buttressing the claim that the French system seems to conform much better to the norms of the corporatist model than to those of the pluralist model pertained to the politics of group recognition. He described the benefits accompanying interest groups' participation in consultative committees viewing them as an explanatory factor for why the privileged groups value their exclusive status and the excluded groups almost always seek recognition.[55] According to a third account, France represents a "statist pattern [of policymaking, whereby] government decision-makers and decision-making organizations take a leadership role in policymaking and have primary control over structuring the 'state-society relationship.'"[56]

We do not have to resolve definitively the question of the state-society configuration in France to suggest that the gradual recognition of the increasing role of labor unions and other associations remained far from the deliberative-participatory ideal that emphasizes open access for all interested parties. If we begin with Schmitter's definition of corporatism "as a system of interest representation in which the constituent units are organized into a limited number of singular, compulsory, noncompetitive, hierarchically ordered and functionally differentiated categories, recognized or licensed (if not created) by the state and granted a deliberate representational monopoly within their respective categories in exchange for observing certain controls on their selection of leaders and articulation of demands and supports,"[57] we can observe that certain elements of this definition, primarily those related to the state recognizing and licensing interest groups, are met in the French case. Nevertheless, the fragmented structure of French interest groups[58] sharply contradicts the idea of the monopoly of representational activity. The key feature in the French model of interest representation is not only that the state selects its privileged interlocutors in the context of consultative bodies but also that it retains the upper hand both in the process of the official recognition of civil society groups and, more importantly, in restricting the power of these bodies.[59]

The Economic, Social and Environmental Council is another manifestation of this idea.[60] Its membership—in terms of the organizations selected to be represented—is determined by decrees although the selection of the specific representatives is an internal matter of these groups. In fact, it was described as another instance "participating in the absorption of the economic sphere by the political sphere, characteristic of the Gaullian era."[61] The mission of the Council is to "advise the government and the parliament and participate in the elaboration of the economic, social and environmental policy." However, as industry actors stressed repeatedly, this consultative institution, despite its constitutional recognition, is not of the highest visibility or influence.[62]

Therefore, we could say that during the 20th century we witness a move from the "corporatism of the universal" (*corporatisme de l'universel*)[63], associated with the revolutionary tradition viewing society as a grand national whole, to a "state corporatism" (*corporatisme étatique*)[64] in which the state largely determines both the interests it will officially admit into public policymaking and the terms of their, often limited, involvement. This system presents certain drawbacks. One of them has to do with the difficulty of selecting the interlocutors of the state. The impulse (or an imperative of accountable government) would be to ensure that, in making those choices, the state not arbitrarily "award a privilege." The criterion of "representativeness" would *prima facie* appear to serve the need for objectivity when accompanied by specific metrics.[65] Nevertheless, the fact remains that the state will always draw the line, and thresholds set unilaterally entail some degree of arbitrariness.

There is a second, and potentially more pernicious, drawback of the decision to exclude intermediate associations from effectively participating in postwar economic policymaking, due to a distrust that, as Part I suggested, goes back to the early republican tradition: coupled with institutional choices that deprived consultative bodies of any influential say (when the state did decide to consult with interest groups), these exclusionary practices resulted in what has been described eloquently as "Tocqueville's revenge." That is to say, the state *invited* societal actors to intervene, but it did not *empower* them to intervene,[66] reducing the influence of those privileged actors to a largely inconsequential participation in a host of consultative bodies. Therefore, this anti-Tocquevillian strategy did not break the circle of a historically weak and underdeveloped civil society. As Jack Hayward noted succinctly in 1976, French interest groups are "pressured rather than pressure groups."[67] This, in turn, deprived French authorities of valuable resources and the positive contributions of associations and individuals, thus undermining the effectiveness and the legitimacy of statist policymaking.[68]

This presentation reflects the inherent tensions in the French model trying to reconcile the role of interest groups with the "culture of generality" that was especially dominant in the early republican tradition. Just as the Fourth and Fifth Republics try to incorporate the voice of interest groups into the policy-making process, article 27 of the Constitution of 1958 clearly states that no member of parliament shall be elected with a binding mandate:[69] this provision illustrates that the value of the "general interest," which the legislature shall redeem insulated from any pressure from specific groups representing "partial interests," persists.

Just as the government, especially after 1975, would demonstrate a new attitude toward the potential public role of associations,[70] other accounts would talk about the "flourishing of associations, leagues, syndicates and organizations of all sorts that atrophy the representative function of the assemblies capturing wills that up until then had only the function to express themselves."[71]

Just as non-governmental organizations (NGOs) try to increase their access to policymaking, the journal of perhaps the most influential consumer group, *UFC-Que Choisir*, would draw a distinction, often difficult to sustain, between the "activity of associations serving the general interest and the lobbying of big groups more concerned with promoting corporate interests";[72] lobbyists would tell me that there is a persistent suspicion toward interest groups and a perception that "lobbying entails bringing briefcases full of cash to policymakers." I, too, would occasionally notice somewhat skeptical looks when in casual conversations I would initially present this project to French lawyers, including both senior and younger ones, as a "study of citizen and interest group participation in administrative rulemaking," and more often when I later described it—more provocatively to gauge reactions but less accurately—as a study of "lobbying in administrative policymaking."

Just as the Institut d'Études Politiques de Paris (Sciences Po), which traditionally produces the political and economic elite of France, was offering eight courses on lobbying when I was visiting during the academic year 2010–2011 (namely, many more than the sections of other "traditional courses") others described how French students, from an early age in school and even more so if they pass from *Sciences Po* and the National School of Administration (ENA) are "educated to sincerely adhere to the founding myth according to which the State is at the same time the incarnation, the depository of the general interest and its sole guarantor."[73]

These tensions underscore that despite the considerable evolution of the jacobinist tradition, public involvement in policymaking in the context of an open participatory system is not a given. The following section examines another major change to the early republican model regarding the relations between parliament and the executive or between the statute and administrative policymaking.

B. Changes to the legislature-executive balance and the centrality of the statute under the Fifth Republic

Parliament would maintain its preeminent role vis-à-vis the executive until the end of the Fourth Republic. This is not to say that the executive remained circumscribed in the narrowly defined limits envisaged by the revolutionaries.[74] As the history of the relations between the legislature and the executive shows, there were institutional arrangements to accommodate the regulatory authority of the executive power.[75] The scope of regulatory power developed continuously; in particular, since the end of the 19th century this rulemaking power could be exercised not only to execute the laws but also even in the absence of preexisting legal provisions, what would be called an "autonomous" rulemaking authority. Since the Third Republic, the rulemaking power increased considerably by means of enabling statutes (*lois d'habilitation*), then at the end of the Fourth Republic by the practice of framework laws (*lois-cadres*). However, notwithstanding these developments, until 1958 the default rule was that there were no limits on the domains in which a statute could be adopted. By contrast, administrative regulations were subordinate in nature, only completing and never contradicting a statute; they had a limited scope and especially the autonomous rulemaking power could only be exercised in specific domains that had been customarily delineated.

The Constitution of 1958, and specifically Articles 34 and 37, reversed the balance between the legislature and the executive, this time in favor of the latter.[76] Article 34 introduces a list of specific domains in which the statute may intervene. Article 37 stipulates that matters falling outside the scope of statutes shall be matters for regulation. In other words, Article 37 places residual policymaking authority with the executive. This in principle rulemaking power is further enhanced by an increasing recourse on the part of the government to Article 38. This provides that "the Government may ask Parliament for authorization, for a limited period, to take measures by ordinances (*ordonnances*) that fall normally within the domain of statutes. These ordinances shall be issued by the cabinet, after consultation with the Conseil d'État. They shall come into force upon publication, but shall lapse in the event of failure to table the bill of ratification before Parliament by the date set by the enabling Act (*loi d'habilitation*)." Over the past few years the executive has been resorting increasingly to the use of *ordonnances* to make rules to such an extent that the Conseil d'État in its 2006 report noted that this practice has become the "principal mode of legislation."[77]

Under the Fifth Republic, the omnipotence of the statute was similarly challenged: In a famous 1985 case, the Conseil Constitutionnel declared that the statute "does not express the general will except to the extent to which it respects the Constitution."[78] However, the most important changes came about with the constitutional revision of July 23, 2008, introducing the "priority preliminary ruling on the issue of constitutionality" or *question prioritaire de constitutionnalité*. According to the new Article 61-1 of the Constitution, "if, during proceedings in progress before a court of law, it is claimed that a legislative provision infringes on the rights and freedoms guaranteed by the Constitution, the matter may be referred by the Conseil d'État or by the Cour de Cassation to the Conseil Constitutionnel which shall rule within a determined period." A provision declared unconstitutional "shall be repealed as of the publication of said decision of the Conseil Constitutionnel or as of a subsequent date determined by said decision" (Art. 62). This constitutional amendment introduced a posteriori constitutional review of statutes by the Conseil Constitutionnel. In turn, this suggests that the *théorie de la loi écran*, which Part I described as the outgrowth of the "cult of the statute," is significantly modified if not altogether abolished. The statute no longer forms a screen between the (administrative) judge and the Constitution, since the Conseil d'État may refer the law at stake to the Conseil Constitutionnel for constitutional review, which might lead to its invalidation.

These developments in the French constitutional structure under the Fifth Republic indicate a fundamental shakeup in the balance between the legislature and the executive as well as the centrality of the statute: Parliament is no longer considered the incontestable locus of sovereignty and the product of its will, the statute, is no longer the fundamental instrument of policymaking. The implication of this, as chapter 1 also explained, is that elections may no longer be considered as the exclusive (not even the most crucial) tool of legitimacy. Instead, these developments bring to the fore the increased importance of accountability mechanisms that link administrative policymaking directly with the citizens, what was called briefly "administrative democracy."

In conclusion, both strands of the development of the early republican tradition (under Sections A and B above) lead to the same conclusion: the call for the emergence of "administrative democracy." The rise of the executive highlights the increased need for accountability mechanisms outside the classic representative model but also in lieu of the system of *corporatisme étatique* that favored specific groups selected by the state which would in any event keep a firm grip on policy formation. The following Part examines whether participatory processes developed in the late 20th century have met these needs.

III. Forms of "administrative democracy" in the late 20th century but without a paradigm shift

In 1983 Frank Wilson noted: "the remote and sometimes authoritarian power of the executive in the Fifth Republic places important limits on interest group influence. The executive exercises controls over most of the avenues of access for interest groups. It closes off some of these points of access to certain groups deemed too hostile, too demagogic, not representative, or not 'serious' enough."[79] This Part examines whether subsequent developments in the area of "administrative democracy" might refute this claim. During the last two decades of the 20th century France has had its share of experimentation with mechanisms to solicit citizen input on state projects: *enquêtes publiques, concertation, débat public*, participation in local government.

Public hearings/inquiries (*enquêtes publiques*) were introduced in 1983 and covered projects of urban planning or other works that were susceptible, due to their nature or the character of the zones concerned, to affect the environment.[80] A special commissioner, called *commissaire enquêteur*, is responsible for carrying out the *enquête* by notifying the public about the project and then receiving their comments, suggestions and counter-proposals for a period that may not be less than one month. At the end of the process, the *commissaire enquêteur* prepares a report (*bilan*) and submits to the prefect a favorable or unfavorable opinion on the project. A common criticism against the *enquêtes publiques* is that they come too late in the process and the comments are usually complaints that do not further public debate.[81]

The procedure of concertation (*concertation*) is enshrined in Article L300-2 of the code of urbanism and is mandatory before the elaboration or the revision of local urban plans or other significant projects of urban planning. The municipal council runs this process which resembles more a dialogue and comes early in the process, namely before the elaboration of the project. However, the modalities of the *concertation* are not stipulated in the code of urbanism but are determined by the municipal council itself, which could lead to a less structured process. Furthermore, according to article L. 121-16 of the environmental code (in its formulation until 1 January 2017), the person responsible for a project with an impact on the environment *could* proceed to a *concertation* before launching the *enquête publique*. As is clear from the language of this provision, this decision was purely discretionary.

The procedure of public debate (*débat public*) was first introduced in French law in 1995 as an optional process throughout the elaboration of a project of urban development.[82] This law also created the National Commission on Public Debate (Commission nationale du débat public—CNDP) to guarantee the organization and the quality of this process. Following the adoption of the Aarhus Convention (UNECE Convention on Access to Information, Public Participation in Decision-making and Access to Justice in Environmental Matters) on June 25, 1998, a 2002 law[83] inserted a new chapter into the environmental code entitled "participation of the public in the elaboration of big projects." The CNDP was transformed into an independent administrative authority. The detailed description of these processes, which vary depending on the nature and the cost of the project, is beyond the scope of this section.[84] The important element is that the *débat public* pertains again to important projects of urban development and transformation. Furthermore, the selection of the members of the CNDP is largely controlled by government ministers or other official bodies.[85]

We could add to these participatory processes another mechanism of public involvement, that is, citizen panels (*conférences de citoyens*).[86] The goal of these panels is to allow a dialogue between citizens and representatives of the political, economic life as well as experts on unresolved and controversial questions. After some preparatory training over a couple of weekends organized by scientists, a public debate takes place for about four days. At the end of this process, the panel issues a report with opinions and recommendations that is published and submitted to political authorities. Three such *conférences de citoyens* have been organized in France: one in 1998 on GMOs, one in 2002 on climate change, and the last in 2003 on the fate of domestic wastewater sludge. However, these processes are highly discretionary as there is no legal provision mandating that they be carried out for specific questions or in a specific way.

As to direct citizen involvement in local affairs, in 1992 a law provided for the *possibility* of local consultations on decisions falling under the competence of the community.[87] Local democracy was enhanced in 2002 with a law rendering mandatory the creation of neighborhood councils in communities exceeding 80,000 citizens, and providing for the same option for communities with a number of citizens between 20,000 and 80,000.[88]

A few observations on all the above participatory mechanisms are in order. First, these processes were limited in scope. They were (and are) often highly discretionary in nature, they applied mostly to the local level,[89] their enumeration was limited, and they pertained most characteristically to urban planning and environmental projects often of special concern to specific communities, which is not a distinctively French phenomenon.[90] Furthermore, they did not cover administrative rulemaking. The most important deficit is that these diverse provisions underscored the lack of a comprehensive and systematic reflection on the *procédure administrative non contentieuse*,[91] i.e., the procedure within the administration and not before the courts. This is why, in view of the nature of these processes and the lack of a holistic approach to citizen participation, we could not at that point talk about a paradigm shift and a transition to a new model of deliberative-participatory administration.

This brings us to a last point. As the title of this Part suggests, the analysis is limited to forms of "administrative democracy" in the late 20th century, thus leaving outside its scope three important developments of the 21st century. The first one is the case study of this book, that is to say, the consultation processes employed by the ARCEP, on which Part IV will elaborate. The second development pertains to the emergence of the so-called "environmental democracy." This principle was enshrined in Article 7 of the Charter for the Environment of 2004 (*Charte de l'Environnement*) to which the plenary of the Conseil d'État accorded constitutional value.[92] Article 7 of the Charter reads: "Every person has the right, in the conditions and to the extent provided for by law, to have access to any information pertaining to the environment in the possession of public bodies and to participate in the elaboration of public decisions likely to affect the environment." The general assembly of the Conseil d'État adopted a "broad and pragmatic interpretation" of the notion of "public decisions likely to affect the environment" covering regulatory acts (*actes de nature réglementaire*) including *ordonnances*.[93]

The so-called "law Grenelle II" of July 12, 2010,[94] affirmed this interpretation by introducing Article L120-1 in the environmental code which thenceforth stipulated: "Except for particular provisions related to public participation included in this code or other applicable legislation, the regulatory decisions (*décisions réglementaires*) of the State and public authorities are submitted to public participation when they have a direct and significant impact on the environment. They are subject either to a prior publication of a draft decision by electronic means under conditions allowing the public to submit comments pursuant to the modalities set out in paragraph II or to a publication of a draft decision before the issue is brought before a consultative body bringing together representatives of the categories of people concerned by the decision at stake pursuant to the modalities set out in paragraph III." In other words, the law *Grenelle II* introduced a consultation requirement that now covered regulatory acts as well.

The public consultation component of *Grenelle II* was strengthened by a new law that the Hollande administration passed in December 2012.[95] Under Article 2 of this new law, the draft rule must now be made available to the public along with a statement explaining its context and objectives. The public can then submit comments within a minimum of 21 days. After the close of the consultation period, the public authority must wait at least four days before issuing the final rule. At that point, it must also provide a statement of reasons and a synthesis of the comments received. These documents must remain available online for a minimum of three months. These developments in the environmental area are important, yet they still face important limitations. The time periods for public comment and for government review of these responses are short, and the government can decide how it wishes to summarize the comments.[96] The requirement that these documents be available online for a minimum of three months (meaning that they can then be removed) seems to curtail unnecessarily the transparency of the public consultation exercise. Moreover, the legislative initiatives in the environmental sector occurred subsequent to the adoption of a new consultation regime in the electronic communications sector. This in no way detracts from the importance of the latest environmental legislation, but highlights the pertinence of the case study in this book.

The third development is the enactment in October 2015, after two failed attempts in 1996 and 2004, of a French administrative procedure code entitled "the code on the relations between the public and the administration" (CRPA 2015).[97] The absence of an administrative procedure code in France had been an anomaly[98] and, as noted earlier in this section, attracted academic criticism. The code is intended to constitute a *lex generalis* of the relations of the public with the administration, codifying case law, statutory and regulatory provisions.[99] It consists of five main parts (entitled "exchanges with the administration," "unilateral acts," "access to administrative documents and re-use of public data," "resolution of disputes with the administration," "provisions applying overseas"). The CRPA 2015 introduces a third type of public inquiries in addition to those provided for in the environmental code and the code of expropriations.[100] Most notably, it codifies provisions on open public consultations; these provisions are assessed in Part V at the end of this chapter.

Parts I, II, and III of this chapter aimed at re-constructing the institutional setting in which the provisions for public consultation in the telecommunications sector are inscribed so as to better appreciate their innovative nature. Part IV will now present these processes, and examine their novelty as well as the degree of change that they have brought about.

IV. Toward an enhanced culture of consultation: The example of the ARCEP

A. The creation of an independent telecommunications regulator

The Autorité de Régulation des Télécommunications (ART) was created by a 1996 statute[101] to prepare the opening of the telecommunications sector to competition following the liberalization efforts of the European Commission detailed in chapter 2. This sector, except for mobile telephony, had previously been a legal monopoly with France Télécom being the historic operator and the Ministry of Posts and Telecommunications retaining many powers over the sector as well as *tutelle* (formal responsibility) for France Télécom.[102] The ART was entrusted with regulating competition ensuring that there would be no significant barriers to entering the market; however, it was also responsible for overseeing the market to guarantee the provision and financing of the "public service of telecommunications." The agency was renamed the Autorité de Régulation des Communications Electroniques et des Postes (ARCEP) in 2005 when it also took on the regulation of postal services.

The ART (since 2005 ARCEP) was created as and describes itself as an independent administrative authority (*autorité administrative indépendante*). Its Executive Board is composed of seven members (previously five for ART) who are appointed for staggered six-year terms "on the basis of their economic, legal and technical qualifications in the areas of electronic communications, post and regional economy." These members' terms are irrevocable and non-renewable. They are appointed by the President of the Republic (who appoints three members), the President of the Senate (who appoints two members) and the President of the National Assembly (who appoints two members).[103] This institutional arrangement reflects an "institutional balance" model, since different branches of government or legislative bodies appoint the Board. This, in turn, means that the structure of the French constitutional system may lead to different parties appointing board members because the legislative branch and the presidency of the republic may be controlled by different parties (in the case of *cohabitation*). Hence, this configuration might also follow the "party balance" model of appointments.[104]

The composition of the ARCEP represents a clear example of the "independence through expertise" idea, whereby independence is thought to be guaranteed by the agency members' professional trajectory and the fact that their reputation as established experts is at stake during their tenure at the agency. Furthermore, it illuminates the discussion of informal networks between politicians and members of independent regulatory authorities.[105] Chairmen of the ARCEP have been commonly graduates of the École Nationale d'Administration, members of the Conseil d'État, and have held positions in the various ministries. Other board members (former and current) include a Senior Member of the Court of Auditors and policy officer to the Prime Minister, a professor and technical advisor for higher learning and research at the Prime Minister's office, many Councilors of State, a councilor for justice at the Prime Minister's office, a professor and technical advisor for media, cinema, postal affairs and electronic communications regulation at the Prime Minister's office, and professors with experience in the industry.

The background of the aforementioned members suggests that the French appointment method following the "institutional balance" ideal is not in itself sufficient to guarantee political insulation. As is the case with a considerable percentage of the administrative elite, the vast majority of the board members of the ARCEP and other high ranked agency members, e.g., unit directors, have followed the traditional path leading to the upper echelons of the French administration: they received an elite education at one of the *grandes écoles*, e.g., the École Nationale d'Administration (National School of Administration), the École des Mines (School of Mines), the École des Ponts et Chaussées (School of Bridges and Roads), the Institut d'Études Politiques de Paris (Paris Institute of Political Studies). They then became members of one of the *grands corps de l'État*; more specifically, they joined either one of the *grands corps administratifs*—that is, the Conseil d'État, the Cour des comptes (Court of Auditors) or the Inspection générale des finances (General Inspection of Finances)—or one of the technical corps (*grands corps techniques*).[106] In other words, it would be a quite challenging task to separate the politicians from the top civil servants (the "*haute fonction publique*") due to their common training and early careers. This difficulty is accentuated by the permeability of the worlds of politics and the high civil service on account of an increasing mobility within the top public service and the ministries.

This picture is complemented by considering a pattern of "revolving doors" practices (or what the French call "pantouflage"), namely, the mobility between the public and the private sector, in this case telecommunications firms. Some noteworthy examples include a director of public affairs at Orange-France Télécom, who had previously served as the head of ARCEP's unit on mobile operators and worked in three ministerial cabinets. His counterpart at SFR had similarly had experience in the public sector, including having served as director at a Ministry. Furthermore, the senior Vice-President in charge of Public Affairs at Alcatel-Lucent had served at the ARCEP for six years. Last, a director of regulatory affairs and relations with local authorities in the Group Iliad had similarly worked at the ARCEP for six years, first as head of the interconnection unit, then as chief of the broadband section. To be sure, French law regulates aspects of this practice to prevent the risk of a severe "conflict of interests."[107]

The point of these remarks is not to challenge the independence of the ARCEP but to suggest that the mode of appointment neither results in the complete political insulation of the agency nor exhausts the guarantees for an impartial and neutral regulator. At the same time, however, appointments have rarely been motivated by or led to party politicization.[108] The criteria of appointment ultimately aim at a high level of expertise by incorporating into agency operations a prior knowledge of how the administration works in addition to technical competence.[109] These guarantees are coupled with and reinforced by additional mechanisms of oversight implicating other actors:

Political oversight: Every year the ARCEP submits a public report to the government and Parliament in which it outlines its annual activity and goals for the future. Furthermore, agency representatives participate in hearings by parliamentary permanent committees. Another way to bring the ARCEP in contact with elected officials is through the *Commission supérieure du service public des postes et des communications électroniques* (CSSPCE). This committee is composed of seventeen members: seven members from the National Assembly, seven members from the Senate and three "qualified personalities." It was created in 1990 when France Télécom was transformed from a service of the State (*service de l'État*) into a form of public corporation with operating and financial autonomy.[110] The aim was to assuage parliamentarians by establishing another mechanism of parliamentary oversight that would "guarantee the public service of telecommunications." This mechanism consists in the requirement or the possibility that the CSSPCE issue an opinion before the ARCEP adopts a policy. Over the years, the committee has kept its responsibilities and even seen its domain of intervention expand; however, its powers are not particularly expansive or influential. These tools of parliamentary oversight demonstrate that the ARCEP retains its independence vis-à-vis the legislature, but must commit to explaining its actions.

The trade-off between the independence of the regulator on the one hand and the need for some kind of political oversight and coordination with elected officials on the other was not just an issue of the 1990s at the moment of the creation of these independent agencies. In fact, this question came to the fore more recently in France (2010-2011) when the government attempted to assign a government commissioner (*commissaire du gouvernement*) inside the ARCEP on the occasion of a bill that would transpose certain provisions of the 2009 EU regulatory package.[111] During the first reading of this bill in the National Assembly (and somewhat late in the process), the government introduced an amendment, Article 13. This new article provided that a government commissioner nominated by the Minister and placed within the ARCEP would "communicate the analysis of the government," in particular with respect to policy in the domain of posts and electronic communications. The commissioner would retire during the deliberations of the agency. However, she could put on the agenda any question related to sectoral policy and "the examination of this question could not be refused." In the discussion in the National Assembly,[112] the Minister, Éric Besson, defended the amendment by highlighting that the government commissioner would have limited power and her presence would "reinforce the dialogue" between the agency and the government, which is indispensable given that their regulatory powers are intertwined. The amendment prompted strong reactions on the part of the ARCEP and members of the opposition that pointed out the risk of undermining the independence of the agency. Interestingly, the European Commission threatened that it would consider initiating the procedure of violation of the EU directives against France.[113] In February 2011, the Senate deleted the amendment, a position that was affirmed by the *commission mixte paritaire* (i.e., a committee bringing together seven deputies and seven senators with the aim of reconciling the two legislative bodies on the basis of a common text).

Judicial control: the decisions of the ARCEP are reviewable by courts, most notably by the Conseil d'État. Decisions concerning dispute settlements fall under the jurisdiction of the Cour d'Appel de Paris (Paris Court of Appeal) that has an economic regulation division specializing in regulation and competition disputes.[114] Subsequent sections will elaborate on judicial review of agency policymaking.

External control: As detailed in chapter 2, the ARCEP is bound by EU law, as are all NRAs, to submit its draft decisions concerning relevant market analyses for the electronic communications sector to the European Commission for its opinion as well as to its European counterparts.

Public control: Most interesting for present purposes is the oversight from actors affected by the actions of the ARCEP, i.e., the regulated industry, civil society groups (particularly, consumer groups), other public authorities, individuals. The adoption of participatory regulatory processes is therefore inscribed in this idea of public oversight to promote transparent and accountable policymaking on the part of the ARCEP. The following sections take up these questions.

B. A consultation practice on the rise

Since its inception, the ARCEP (then ART) emphasized the priority it assigned to taking action in concertation with the regulated entities. In the Annual Report of 1997, documenting the activities of the ART during the first eighteen months of its existence, Chairman Jean-Michel Hubert identified dialogue with all market actors as a method of attaining the aim of balanced, fair and sustainable competition consistent with the objectives of the *service public*. However, another excerpt from that Report highlights the initial approach to participatory processes:

> ART's first task is to gather feedback from participants to ensure that the decisions it takes are relevant to the market situation. To this end, it organizes regular consultation through the two consultative commissions placed under its authority by the Act. It can also gather information through the existing consultative committee on numbering as well as the interconnection committee established by the decree on interconnection. These consultative bodies consist of operators' representatives, users' representatives and other qualified persons. ART has also taken its own initiatives to facilitate regular contact with market players and key figures. This is done through public consultation exercises, special hearings before ART's executive board, informal meetings and a discussion group on the Internet.[115]

As Figure 3.1 will illustrate later, the prioritization in this passage of the methods for soliciting public input reflects both the actual legal regime of that era and the practice of the agency in the first stages of its operation. When the Report refers to consultation, it means, first and foremost, consultation within the two consultative commissions established by the law of 1996: the telecommunications networks and services consultative commission (Commission consultative des réseaux et services de télécommunications [CCRST]) and the radiocommunications consultative commission (Commission consultative des radiocommunications [CCR]). These commissions, which had formerly been under the authority of the direction générale des postes et télécommunications (DGPT) of the Ministry, were responsible for examining draft regulations on radiocommunications and on telecommunications networks and services. They could also be consulted on any issue falling within their field of competence. The impulse of the legislator to create these commissions is consistent with the pattern of *corporatisme étatique* described in Part II of this chapter: the (real or declared) wish of the state to bring the industry and civil society groups into the policy-making process translated into the creation of a body that was nonetheless not entrusted with significant powers. The interconnection committee that was also mentioned in the previous excerpt from the Report was established by a decision of the ART on 4 June 1997.[116] The consultative committee on numbering was set up in 1996 by the DGPT and constituted an informal discussion group consisting of representatives of all those market participants–operators, service providers, businesses, users—concerned by numbering.

The formal consultation with the CCRST and the CCR contrasts with the process of public consultations that the ART launched during that period. The latter only occurred on an ad hoc basis and were highly discretionary in nature. The Report alludes to a number of public consultations held over the past eighteen months; these, however, were not published on the agency's website and there is no (or very little) information about who responded to these consultations, and even less about the content of the replies. The informal, loosely structured, voluntary and rather non-transparent way in which those public consultations were carried out is attributable to the legal regime guiding the ART's activity. The telecommunications law of 1996 did not contain any provisions on public participation through open consultation processes. On the contrary, it envisaged stakeholder participation via the two corporatist bodies mentioned just above. It is thus understandable that whenever the ART conducted a public consultation, it proceeded in an unregulated environment that included no specific mandates with respect to the openness and transparency of this procedure, which was still commendable in itself.

These optional informal consultation processes are even more commendable if we consider the situation of the telecommunications sector a few decades before that point. The following example is illustrating: When the French Association of Telecommunications Users (Association Française des Utilisateurs de Télécommunications) was created in 1969 to promote the cause of the expansion of telephony in France, it found itself in the environment of a state administrative monopoly. In that environment, an association of consumers of a *service public* was viewed not simply as something unfamiliar or incomprehensible, but occasionally even as an "intruder representing particular interests" that were potentially opposed to the general interest; this was another manifestation of the foundational principles and perceptions described earlier in this chapter. The idea was instead that the syndicates representing the personnel of the administration that provided telephone services in the context of the public monopoly (briefly put, the labor unions of the civil service) represented the interests of consumers as well![117] The description of a status quo that was state-dominated, fixed and suspicious toward interest groups, as well as the established role and privileged position of recognized labor unions similarly reflect, in this specific case, the broader patterns that Parts I and II of this chapter identified. Therefore, they help us appreciate the changes that occurred gradually in the 1990s with new market actors rising and the ART trying to involve them in its activities, albeit in a limited, informal, discretionary, state-corporatist and not always particularly transparent way.

The analysis in the previous Parts and its easy application to this case study, i.e., the telecommunications sector in the first stages of its liberalization, help us appreciate even more the new phase that was opened in June 2004 with the transposition into French law of the 2002 EU "electronic communications package" described in chapter 2. The new statute specifically modified the 1996 law to include the exact wording of the Framework Directive regarding consultation procedures.[118] Article L 32-1 of the *Code des postes et des communications électroniques* (CPCE) reads as of 2004:

> Whenever, in the context of the provisions of this code, the minister in charge of electronic communications and the *Autorité de régulation des communications électroniques et des postes* intend to take measures which have a significant impact on the market, they shall publicize the intended measures within a reasonable period before their adoption and receive comments on them. The result of these consultations is made public except in the case of confidentiality protected by law. The authority puts in place a service allowing access to those consultations.

Other provisions oblige the agency to launch a public consultation on specific questions, such as the management and allocation of frequencies owing to their scarcity, or the imposition of obligations of interconnection.[119] The general provision of L.32-1 and the specific mandates just mentioned were immediately reflected in the practice of the ARCEP regarding public consultation. Figure 3.1 illustrates the number of consultations on electronic communications matters (thus excluding postal services that fall outside the scope of this study)[120] that the ARCEP launched since its creation in 1996.

Figure 3.1 shows a spike in 2004, namely, the year of the adoption of the new legislative regime, with the number of consultations per year remaining stable or increasing thereafter. This peak in 2004 can be explained by the new regulatory requirements that the new law transposing the EU "regulatory package" introduced. Instead of unilaterally imposing obligations or regulations, the new law mandated a series of periodic market analyses to determine the operators with significant market power in each respective market and subsequently adopt remedies. These procedures came with the obligation to

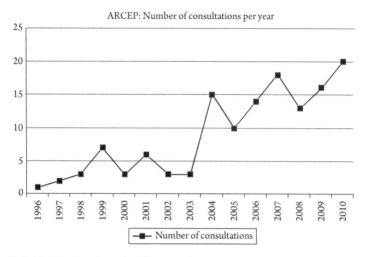

Figure 3.1 ARCEP: Number of public consultations per year

Source: Own elaboration with data from the website of the ARCEP

launch public consultations, a significant number of which were carried out that year. Subsequently, the familiarization of agency officials with these participatory processes and the development of a culture of consultation resulted in a more frequent organization of public consultations. These pertained to subjects that were not necessarily related with market analysis, and might not even lead to a binding measure and consequently a prior consultation was not required by law.

The consultation on "orientations" regarding net neutrality in the summer of 2010 is one such telling example. The final document issued by the ARCEP at the end of the consultation process only included "proposals and recommendations." The Authority underscored that its "overall approach is primarily one of prevention, as the threats to the internet's neutrality lie more in practices that could develop, rather than current malfunctions in the marketplace. The Authority's current line of action is therefore one of recommendation . . . . In future, this action could be completed by more prescriptive measures should they prove necessary."[121] In other words, the agency would consider intervening only if the market failed to follow those recommendations.[122] In a similar vein, despite the absence of a legal obligation to do so, the ARCEP launched another public consultation in May 2012 on a draft report it was preparing to present to Parliament and the government on the topic of net neutrality.[123] In another example, in April 2011 the ARCEP launched a public consultation on a project of recommendations concerning the modalities of access to optical fiber lines in "small houses" in very dense zones. On June 15, 2011, the Authority published its decision on market analysis but also the recommendation on which it had consulted.

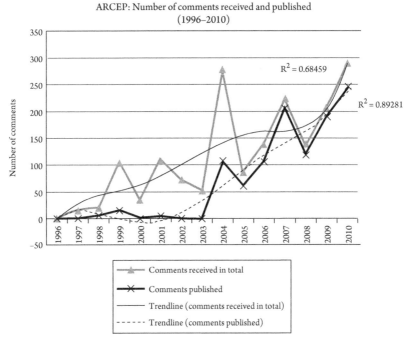

Figure 3.2 ARCEP: Number of comments received and published during public consultations in the telecommunications sector (1996–2010)

Source: Own elaboration with data from the website of the ARCEP

The trend reflecting the influence of EU mandates on the consultation practices of the ARCEP is more clearly demonstrated in other qualitative characteristics, such as the number of comments received during these consultations and, more importantly, the number of comments published (Figure 3.2). These features are probably more important for they reflect the dynamism of the market, the willingness of the actors to engage in the public consultation processes and the commitment of the ARCEP to transparency.

These trends suggest that the new regime that France adopted following EU mandates brought primarily significant transparency gains. This observation is also consistent with the perception of the agency itself, as indicated in an interview, that public consultation is an instrument of good governance that ensures the transparency of its operation.[124] Furthermore, these trends map well onto stakeholders' impressions regarding the rising importance of public consultations. In a couple of interviews, I asked experienced market actors to draw the data series line in an empty chart so as to illustrate their expectations of the evolution of the number of consultations as well as the number of comments received/published over the past 10 to 15 years. Figure 3.3 is indicative of the responses I received.[125]

Number of consultations per year

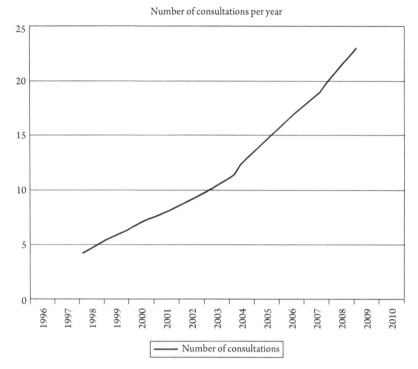

Figure 3.3 Stakeholders' perception of the development of public consultations in France from 1996 to 2010

C. Evaluating ARCEP's regulatory processes against the fundamental operative elements of the deliberative-participatory model

Chapter 1 identified four blocks constituting the deliberative-participatory model and contributing to accountable administrative policymaking. Applying these criteria to the consultation practices of the ARCEP, we could note the following.

1. *Open Access*

This criterion is met by the consultation practices of the ARCEP. All interested parties can submit their comments on the draft measures. In fact, on several occasions and at the request of stakeholders, the agency decided to extend the deadline for the submission of comments to ensure that interested parties had the opportunity to participate. A question that arises pertains to the alternative methods of soliciting public input that single out and involve only specific actors in specific committees, for instance in the context of the *commission consultative des communications électroniques.* The following section will address this question in more detail, but since the role and influence of this consultative body were rather limited until its abolition by Decree 2015-1566 on December 1, 2015, its existence did not seem to contradict the open access prong of the deliberative-participatory model.

2. Transparency

The launch of every public consultation is now sufficiently publicized. In particular, stakeholders that have signed up for email notifications are informed when a new consultation is about to begin. As to the publication of comments, even though there have been instances in which we had no available data whatsoever as to the comments received[126] (which is problematic in view of the specific statutory requirements described above), the data suggest that this criterion is, to a large extent and increasingly so, met. In fact, as the previous section (and especially Figure 3.2) demonstrated, transparency gains are probably the most important contribution of the EU regulatory regime of 2002.

3. Reason giving

In France, there is no general principle imposing a reason-giving obligation for regulatory acts unless there is a specific statutory requirement to this effect. The duty to provide reasons, which is imposed by a 1979 statute, applies to unfavorable individual decisions (*actes individuels défavorables*) and more specifically to eight types of them.[127] By contrast, with some exceptions,[128] it does not extend to general rules (*actes réglementaires*).

The CPCE introduces explicit reason-giving obligations in certain cases, e.g., in article L34-8 when the ARCEP determines the modalities of interconnection and access to the network. Other provisions mandate reason giving in cases of sanctions, thus following the general rule for unfavorable individual decisions. Interestingly, when there is no such textual obligation, the consultation process enhances the justification of administrative acts since the Authority will often publish a synthesis or overview (*synthèse*) of the comments received. This increases the transparency of the reasons that led to the adoption of the final text and constitutes another accountability gain stemming from these participatory processes. However, the CPCE imposes no specific obligation on the ARCEP to publish such syntheses nor does it specify any requirements as to the content of these documents. This has led to variations in terms of the number of consultations for which the ARCEP published syntheses and the mean number of pages of these syntheses (Table 3.1).

In view of this heterogeneity, the lack of any binding obligations to this effect, and the importance of the reason-giving requirement even in the form

Table 3.1 **ARCEP's syntheses following public consultations**[1]

Year	Percentage of cases in which a synthesis was published	Mean number of pages of the synthesis
2004	47%	31.3
2005	30%	14.3
2006	50%	13.4
2007	50%	26.7
2008	62%	24.4
2009	38%	27.3
2010	40%	12.1

[1]Own elaboration with data from the website of the ARCEP.

of a synthesis, this appears to be an area for reform of the CPCE in the direction of introducing an explicit requirement on the part of the ARCEP to publish such syntheses (Section E below).

4. *Judicial review*

The fourth operative element is a key feature because, as chapter 1 also suggested, it might constitute a significant distinguishing factor between the American and the European models of administrative democracy. Court cases involving public consultations in France could be placed on a spectrum, with judicial involvement becoming more controversial as we move along the spectrum.

The spectrum of judicial review: From a checklist obligation (participatory processes as a formalité substantielle) *to a potential "hard look approach"*[129] *à la française (by means of the introduction of the* théorie du bilan *in the electronic communications sector)?*

The types of judicial review on the one end of this spectrum include the relatively "easy" cases, in which consultation constitutes what I call a "checklist obligation." In other words, the court simply inquires whether the agency has fulfilled a statutory obligation to hold a consultation or not.[130] In this context, participatory processes constitute a substantial formality (*formalité substantielle*); this means that if the administrative authority does not give full effect to these processes, its decision will be annulled. For instance, in the *Association Le Réseau Sortir du Nucléaire* case, the petitioners asked for the annulment of the authorization to the Electricity of France (Electricité de France), the major electric utility company in France, to proceed to the definitive termination and complete dismantlement of a nuclear facility. The court held that the consultation with an observatory of dismantlement of old nuclear facilities, composed of elected officials, union representatives, associations and the state, and whose objective was to inform its members about the progress of the works, did not respond to the objectives of the directive. Among those objectives was the possibility offered to the concerned public to be informed and express its opinion prior to the award of the authorization. Therefore, the authorization in question was given following a procedure of informing the public that was incompatible with the objectives of that directive. As a result, the Conseil d'État invalidated the act.[131] Interestingly, in this case the consultation of a consultative body did not suffice. The public itself, i.e., all the interested parties, should have been informed and given the opportunity to express their opinion.[132] This is another instance showcasing the difference between consultation as traditionally perceived, that is to say, in the context of a formal consultative administrative body, and the new understanding of consultation as an open procedure in which everyone can participate.

There are also, however, less clear-cut versions of the checklist obligation. In *Association des Renseignements pour Tous*,[133] a second round of consultations was required prior to the modification of the obligations imposed on a player exerting significant influence on the market. The Conseil d'État held that the ARCEP may not release itself from the obligation to carry out a new market analysis and proceed to all corresponding consultations unless the analysis and the consultations that had preceded the original decision that it now sought to amend permitted the appreciation of the adequacy and the proportionality of the intended modification. In another interesting passage in this decision, the court noted that consultations constitute guaranties for the consumers as well as for the operators themselves.

Other cases showcase the role of consultation as part of the reason-giving process. In *Orange et SFR* the court noted that "during a series of consultations preceding the contested decision as well as in its justification, the ARCEP clarified the principles it employed to estimate the incremental long-term costs of an efficient operation and responded to the operators' criticism against its choices."[134] This remark by the Conseil d'État did not have any specific impact on the outcome of the case; in other words, the annulment of the act on the grounds of lack of sufficient reasons was not at stake in this case. Nevertheless, it does indicate that the court took notice of the process through which the agency had reached its decision. This, in turn, could suggest that in the future the adequacy of the process might, explicitly or not, advocate for or against the validity of an administrative action.

A very interesting aspect of the French case is a striking particularity it presents: Judicial review imposes an implicit obligation on market actors to avail themselves of the consultation process and be consistent. We can see this in a line of cases related to the allocation of a fourth license for 3G mobile phone services, which Free Mobile ended up receiving. In the first case, Bouygues, a French telecommunications company, attacked the obligation (imposed by the ARCEP) to return part of the frequencies it had been assigned. The Conseil d'État held that the decisions that the ARCEP had taken since 2000 and the consultations preceding them had alerted every operator so as to prepare to restitute, when and should the moment come, certain frequencies that had been assigned to them in the frequency band of 900 MHz. Besides, the court continued, the contested decision had been preceded by a profound concertation that the ARCEP had carried out in 2006 and 2007 with all the operators; during that process, it was notably possible for every one of them to evoke the specific problems that could stem from the intended schema of restitution that had been clearly presented to them. The Conseil d'État concluded that it appeared from oral argument and the record that during that concertation, Bouygues had not proposed an alternative schema or calendar that could resolve the risks that it only put forward in the context of its petition for judicial review.[135]

In the next case, Bouygues attacked the legality of the decision to assign a fourth license to Free Mobile on the grounds, among other things, of violation of the principle of transparency and legitimate expectations. In a similar vein, the Conseil d'État responded that, before the adoption of the contested decree, the determination of the amount of the license fee had been, on the one hand, the subject of a public consultation that the ARCEP carried out in the summer of 2008 at the behest of the government, and, on the other hand, the topic of opinions requested from the Commission des participations et des transferts, the ARCEP, and the Commission consultative des communications électroniques. All these procedural stages had taken place with the knowledge of the interested parties, notably the 3G operators already present on the market (Bouygues was included among them), who had had the opportunity to submit their comments to the government before the determination of the amount of the license fees by the decree.[136]

The most interesting feature of these decisions is that normally we would expect the consultation process to lead to the creation of a record ("*dossier*"); this would subsequently figure in judicial review assisting the judge in evaluating the legality of the official act in question. In the two cases outlined above, from a mechanism for reviewing agency action, consultation is transformed into a tool for assessing the conduct of private actors.

Let us now turn to what could be described as the "expected" function of consultation in judicial review and move toward the other end of the spectrum as described in the introduction of this section. First, the default rule is that these are cases of applications for judicial review in order to invalidate an administrative act on the grounds of excess of power (*recours pour excès de pouvoir*).[137] In cases of discretionary administrative power, the judge will apply a standard of limited judicial review (*contrôle restreint*), whereby she examines whether there has been a manifest error of appreciation (*erreur manifeste d'appreciation*) on the part of the agency.[138] I argue that the *dossier* produced during the public consultation phase would support the judge in this examination of the potential existence of such a manifest error, which is generally difficult to prove. More specifically, consultees might have pointed in their submissions to manifest major flaws in the merits of the challenged decision or in the decision-making process itself. Courts could then assess whether the agency neglected to address any of these major issues. In this sense, the consultation record would not expand the narrow contours of *contrôle restreint*, but rather orient it toward manifest errors emerging, for instance, from multiple consultation responses.

The second more controversial point concerns the introduction of the *théorie du bilan* (roughly translated as "balancing theory") in this sector: The *théorie du bilan* first appeared in the subject matter of expropriations in the jurisprudence of the Conseil d'État in 1971.[139] This theory was used to assess the legality of the *déclarations d'utilité publique*—that is to say, the decisions affirming that the expropriation of an asset is useful for a public purpose—and was described as "full proportionality review."[140] In other words, the *théorie du bilan* introduces in effect a more searching judicial review: The judge performs, in essence, a cost-benefit analysis of the measure balancing the restrictions on "private property, the financial cost and eventual disruption to the social order" that should not be "excessive in view of the interest it serves."

This is a theory in expansion.[141] I argue that we could see it expand into the telecommunications sector as well, even if it were not to be explicitly stated in those exact terms. The vehicle for that would be Article 32-1-II CPCE. This provision lists twelve goals that the Minister and the ARCEP should pursue when taking regulatory measures that must be, according to the language of the Code, "reasonable and proportionate in light of the aims pursued." These goals are often contradictory: *service public*, effective competition, encouragement of investment, interoperability, consumer protection, confidentiality of communications, public safety, etc. The enunciation of the principles that should guide administrative action in the telecommunications sector in addition to the textual reference that these administrative measures should be proportionate suggest that we could envisage the expansion of a version of the *théorie du bilan* in this area. In such a case, the usefulness of the record produced during public consultations would acquire increased importance in guiding the judicial enterprise: it would provide a valuable resource and a more stable reference for the judge to go more deeply into the substance of the agency decision and the consideration of alternative administrative measures, a move that the *théorie du bilan* may permit.[142] This would not necessarily result in the introduction of a "hard look" doctrine in the French case law. It might, however, invite courts to take consultation as a serious aid not only to assess the consistency of the conduct of market actors but also that of the agency by means of clear signposts.

Having considered the four criteria of the deliberative-participatory model, the following section addresses questions challenging the idea that public consultations do indeed matter.

D. Does consultation matter?

1. Who participates?

One of the most plausible first questions a reader might ask at this point is: who are empirically the market players that are involved in the public consultations that the ARCEP increasingly launches? Figure 3.4 provides an answer for the consultation practices of the French regulator over a recent five-year period.

If we also look at the break-down of stakeholder participation per year, we generally find no significant variations from year to year, with the exception of 2009 in which the percentage of the participation of local authorities was double the average over the five-year period. We could explain this by taking into account the topics of the public consultation that year: they included the development of the optical fiber and questions of ultra high-speed mobile coverage that have implications for regional development in which local authorities have an obvious interest.

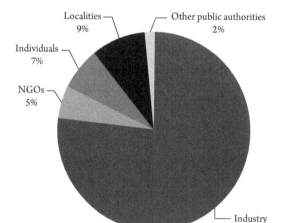

Figure 3.4 ARCEP: Type of actors responding to consultations (2006–2010)

Source: Own elaboration with data from the website of the ARCEP

In light of these data we could easily imagine a line of criticism that would describe these participatory processes as a charade: the industry dominates the process, therefore the same powerful industrial actors determine the content of regulation as was the case under the previous regime. There is a set of responses to this plausible critique: First, putting to one side the admittedly very high percentage of industry involvement, these processes facilitate the engagement of even a small number of actors that would otherwise be left outside the regulatory process, namely, individuals, smaller NGOs, and even certain local authorities that were traditionally not very powerful lobbyists. Second, as consumer groups themselves acknowledge, not all consultations are of interest to consumers since some of them have a very narrow technical scope that only concerns the industry.[143] Third, the category that we term as "industry" is broad as it encompasses both traditionally strong industries, such as the incumbent operator, but also smaller companies that are involved in the telecommunications business. It is also not uncommon that foreign companies participate in the public consultations that the ARCEP organizes.[144]

Moreover, depending on the type of consultation, these diverse firms may have divergent interests. For example, in the example of net neutrality, operators and content providers (both groups including smaller and bigger companies) would prefer the ARCEP to go in opposite directions. More specifically, the break-down of the stakeholders that participated in the public consultation on network neutrality (20 May–2 July 2010) does not deviate from the general pattern shown in Figure 3.4: industry participation amounted to 82% (indeed, this was somewhat higher than the average 77% in Figure 3.4); NGOs (consumer groups) accounted for 7% of the comments submitted to the Authority, individuals for 9%, while 2% came from public authorities. However, the alignment of interests on the topic of net neutrality cuts across different stakeholder groups and cannot be captured by the traditional industry-civil society divide.

In particular, content and application providers (e.g., Skype, Dailymotion, VON Europe), consumer groups (e.g., UFC-Que Choisir) and end users on the one hand generally supported a robust regime of network neutrality that minimizes the interference of network operators, prohibits blocking or hindering unfettered access to internet services, and allows for free exchange and flow of data. On the other hand, operators (e.g., AT&T, Cable & Wireless) expressed concerns about heavy restrictions on traffic management and service differentiation by ISPs and the significant costs and practical difficulties such restrictions would cause for operators. These actors pointed out that substantial new investment is needed to support the unprecedented growth of Internet traffic and the increasing demands of its changing traffic mix and to extend broadband networks. They underscored that, to fund these investments, network providers need to be able to price their services in manners that are attractive and affordable to customers.[145] In the context of this public consultation, operators found an ally in equipment manufacturers (i.e., manufacturers of the network infrastructure). Firms, such as Qualcomm and Tekelec, expressed skepticism toward strict regulation of traffic management, and support for the idea of different fee schedules for differentiated quality of service on the basis of consumer choice. Other stakeholders, namely, copyright collection societies, could not be clearly placed into one or the other camp of the debate and raised different concerns pertaining primarily to piracy. This discussion demonstrates that lumping together the 20% of comments coming from content providers, the 40% of comments coming from network operators, and the 9% of comments coming from equipment manufacturers all under the heading of "industry," while accurate and an indication that well-funded industry groups do participate in higher numbers, may not always reflect fully the nuances of interest alignment and representation in particular cases.

In any case, public consultation processes increase transparency. Therefore, even assuming that powerful pressure groups dominate the process, the procedural mandates described earlier make it easier for competitors, NGOs, and the public to trace the impact of specific points of view on the final policy outcome.

2. Alternatives to consultation in soliciting input from key stakeholders: Complementary or antagonistic processes?

The critic would then jump on this last point about transparency to point to additional methods through which stakeholders may influence agency policymaking circumventing the public consultation process.

> Private meetings with actors: Everyone acknowledges, the critic would say, that public consultations do not preclude the agency from having private informal meetings with key market actors. Briefly put—the critic would go on perhaps with an extra dose of cynicism—public consultations merely serve as a façade to give an air of legitimacy to a policymaking process that still occurs in obscure meetings behind closed doors in which old boy networks have the usual bearing.

I would respond that multilateral or bilateral meetings between agency officials and stakeholders might complement but do not severely undermine the public consultation process, and in no case bring us back to the old status quo of secrecy as that grim picture would suggest. Here is why: All the lobbyists that I interviewed suggested that participating in public consultations is a necessary prong of their strategy, as it helps to identify them as a reliable and expert market player and contributes to establishing a stronger presence in the sector. Many were quick to assert that while the involvement in public consultations might be a necessary step, it is usually not sufficient: "you need to try to schedule an appointment to ensure that you have an additional opportunity to get your message through." Given this multi-pronged strategy, another experienced lobbyist underscored the importance of consistency in the presentation of your message in various forums and before different officials in order to preserve your credibility as an interlocutor.[146] This, in turn, means that an actor presenting different arguments in private meetings and in public or omitting a crucial part of her argumentation in one of the two processes (presumably in the public consultation) would risk seeing her credibility undermined. As another industry representative explained, a response to a public consultation provides actors with the opportunity to address all points of interest, including second-order questions, while in informal meetings they have to focus on select first-order issues that are more crucial to them. They will then repeat these focal points in their official public response that might even at that point exert some influence on the agency, although he added that he found this would rarely be the case.[147]

Besides, an ARCEP official himself observed during an interview that when justifying the policy it adopted, the agency cannot rely on an informal private meeting when there is a public record of positions available by means of the public consultation. In fact, the agency expects market actors to publicly take a position at some point thus formalizing their participation in informal meetings. Furthermore, in a formal document ARCEP explains that "on the whole, all [its] areas of responsibility result in technical consultations with market stakeholders, on either a regular basis or as the need arises. These discussions are completed by more formal, systematic public consultations on the actions the Authority plans to take."[148]

The added value of formalization, and the increased transparency accompanying it, was similarly acknowledged by a consumer group representative who pointed out that it is beneficial to the organization to have an official record to publicly demonstrate that it defended a position and potentially moved the public authority in the direction of protecting consumer interests.[149]

Formal consultative bodies: Earlier sections explained that the ARCEP also relies on consultations with statutorily constituted bodies, such as the *commission consultative des communications électroniques*. A problem that could be identified with respect to these bodies is that they might reproduce the corporatist fallacies of the old administrative tradition. More specifically, their members are preselected and usually come from traditional experienced actors. Moreover, there are no public records of their meetings: the committee members do not usually agree on a final text that garners consensus and is published, minutes are generally not produced, and citizens in any event would not normally have access to them under the French Freedom of Information legislation because those documents would be of a preparatory nature and thus exempt from disclosure requirements.[150]

However, we should not view consultations with those consultative bodies as an antagonistic process undermining the public consultation process. According to an interview with a former member of the *commission consultative des communications électroniques*, these bodies saw their role gradually decrease concomitantly with the rise of public consultations. Furthermore, they come late in the decision-making process, namely, at the end of the public consultation process; hence, during these meetings actors repeat comments that they had previously had many occasions to express.[151] As other actors suggested, these committees might have some influence when participants raise questions for the future,[152] but again if the agency decides to take up these issues, it will still need to hold public consultations. Moreover, consultative bodies might have a pedagogic function informing actors of new developments and directions for the future and also offer a useful opportunity for different actors to meet and discuss, e.g., within the GRACO that brings together representatives from the ARCEP, local authorities and operators.[153] However, again, the functions just described by actors having had experience participating in these committees suggest that these consultative bodies do not compete considerably with the public consultation process in that they rarely have a concrete impact on specific policy outcomes.

E. Proposals for reform

As chapter 2 explained, EU mandates establish a minimum set of procedural requirements, what I called the "EU floor." Member states are free to move beyond that and promote accountability mechanisms better reflecting the deliberative-participatory ideal. This section offers certain proposals that France could consider in the direction of reform.

First, I suggested earlier that an initiative enhancing the accountability of regulatory agency operations would be the introduction in Article L32-1 of the CPCE of an obligation to publish a synthesis after every public consultation that the ARCEP concludes. Even when this would not result in the agency providing explicit reasons for the changes it made to the original draft linking them to specific comments, a summary and categorization of the contributions would help structure the debate. This, in turn, would facilitate the public's understanding of the stakes in the policy under consideration as well as the positions of the relevant actors. Furthermore, even the relatively simple task of organizing and providing an overview of the comments received would occasionally open a window to understanding the agency's hierarchization of the issues raised during the consultation. Besides, the formalization of the obligation to publish a synthesis would not impose a significant additional burden on the agency given that its staff already carries out this work to a certain extent while processing the responses; in practice, the difference would be that this work would now be mandatory, more structured, and public.

Second, in this mandatory overview the agency should also mention every bilateral or multilateral meeting held with market actors to discuss the policy under consideration. This obligation would not extend to the content of these meetings. However, it would mandate that the ARCEP publish the dates and names of the firms, non-governmental organizations (NGOs), public authorities, and individuals audited. Hence, it would offer a picture of the importance of each policy to specific actors as evidenced by their willingness to participate in informal meetings with agency officials outside the formal public consultation process. Consequently, it would also direct the attention of the public and their competitors to the positions that these market players took in the public consultation. This reform would not impose the burdensome requirement to publish the minutes of every single meeting,[154] a suggestion that met the skepticism of French actors from opposing sides of the table as to its practicability in the French context.[155] Rather, it would go in the direction of increased transparency without significantly disturbing the French traditions or abolishing bilateral meetings altogether, which may be unfeasible or even undesirable.[156] After all, the agency itself has decided on several occasions to refer in public reports to meetings with stakeholders without any legally binding obligation to do so.

Third, one of the concerns regarding the effectiveness of consultative bodies but also of the public consultation procedure itself is that they come too late in the process to have a substantial impact on the final policy. A way to remedy this potential problem would be to encourage the ARCEP to generalize a practice it already increasingly appears to adopt, that is, to launch public consultations earlier in the policymaking process. At the earlier stages, the outcome of the consultation will not be the promulgation of a final rule, but of "recommendations" or "orientations" as these are usually called. This would not be limited only to cases in which the agency does not have formal decision-making powers anyway; it would also prepare gradually and more smoothly the development of binding rules in the areas in which the ARCEP may adopt binding action. This reform proposal does not go so far as to suggest a hard-law mandate for this broader scope of consultations. In other words, I do not recommend a rewriting of Article L32-1 of the CPCE to prescribe a prior public consultation when the ARCEP intends to adopt policy recommendations as well—that is, in addition to "measures which have a significant impact on the market" as the wording currently is. Rather, a soft-law instrument, e.g., internal guidelines with permissive language that would not give rise to legitimate expectations formally, would be an effective way for the ARCEP to declare its commitment to a practice that is both beneficial and not unfamiliar to the agency, while maintaining the requisite flexibility.

Fourth, the previous section suggested that participation in the policymaking process by traditionally weaker actors (NGOs, individuals) may be higher than under the preexisting regime, which had not allowed for civil society input in an open process. Nonetheless, NGO and individual participation still lags considerably behind industry participation. The question then is: how can the Authority reach out to these stakeholders and facilitate their involvement in public consultations? One policy response would go beyond the remit of the ARCEP and address the more general issue of building civil society capacity on the ground, e.g., by increasing public funding for civil society groups. The following chapter will return to this broader set of points, as Greece seems to face starker challenges when it comes to a weak civil society. There are, however, measures that the ARCEP itself could adopt. For instance, a fundamental problem for groups that lack robust regulatory departments with the resources and expertise to decipher jargon (technical, legal, engineering, economics) is that the consultation document itself may be difficult to access, hence discouraging participation in the consultation exercise. The Authority should therefore include executive summaries in the consultation documents that present the issues in a clear and concise fashion. The draft under consultation should include, where applicable, a specific, clearly designated section on the impact of the proposed measures on traditionally underrepresented stakeholders. Furthermore, more elaborate companion "layman's documents" should be issued and publicized more broadly than usual when the agency is consulting on matters that affect a wide range of actors.

Relatedly, the ARCEP should continue the practice of online chat sessions that allow citizens to ask questions directly to agency staff members working on a matter that will be or is at that point under public consultation. For instance, in October 2010, the ARCEP organized an online chat that brought together a total of 487 people with a peak of 262 simultaneous connections. 102 questions were submitted in total (42 had been posed prior to and 60 during the chat session). Although this was an informative and commendable exercise, scheduling it before or, at least, during the public consultation on network neutrality in the summer of 2010 might have clarified issues earlier and thus facilitated increased participation in the consultation process itself.[157] Moreover, all questions submitted during the chat session should be acknowledged and answered, even briefly, after the end of the exercise if there is not sufficient time to address them during the session. Last, as was noted in Part IV.D.2., consultative bodies might play a similar pedagogic role in informing actors of new developments and directions for the future.

The fifth and final consideration concerns the appropriate degree of the Conseil d'État's involvement in the policymaking process. The French example supports the claim first raised in chapter 1 that judicial review is not a necessary definitional element of the deliberative-participatory model: the ARCEP developed a consistent practice of public consultation even in the absence of US-style judicial review. At the same time, however, this country case also buttresses the argument that a credible mechanism for judicial review of the adequacy of the agency's participatory processes and the ways in which these processes feed into the substantive administrative decisions may enhance the other prongs of the democratic accountability model proposed in chapter 1. Judicial monitoring of the agency's compliance with the "checklist obligation" described in Part IV.C.4.[158] cannot by itself meet fully the criterion of a "credible mechanism for judicial review." Taking into account the public consultation to assess the consistency of the stakeholders' positions (as in the *Bouygues* cases examined in Part IV.C.4.)[159] means that the consultation exercise figures in judicial reasoning in a more nuanced way than in the paradigm of "checklist obligation"; this potentially increases the salience and importance of the exercise. Nevertheless, it does so in way that, as we saw, effectively enhances the scrutiny of the conduct of the market actors but not necessarily that of the agency. Instead, the analysis in Part IV.C.4. suggested that more searching judicial scrutiny of administrative action would enhance other aspects of the deliberative-participatory model (namely, reason giving and transparency), as the existence of credible and substantial judicial review would feed back into the agency's decision-making process and especially its reasoning.[160] In this respect, my fifth reform proposal reinforces the first recommendation of this section: more robust judicial review may result in more consistent publication of syntheses and increased attention to their quality. Lastly and importantly, as Part IV.C.4. explained in more detail, my recommendation for enhanced judicial review could fit well into the French statutory and doctrinal framework.

V. Conclusion: Looking to the future—Generalizing public participation in administrative policymaking

Chapter 2 suggested that one of the consequences of the Europeanization of sector-specific regulatory processes at the member-state level might be that these processes could spill over into other regulatory domains and ultimately be generalized across the board. The question then is whether we have reached, under the influence of EU law, a "critical mass" of participatory processes in different sectors that would facilitate the generalization of such a right across the administration and in all forms of policymaking in France.

We could try to offer an answer by looking first at an initiative that was signed into law in 2011[161] after having passed, not easily, through both legislative bodies and the scrutiny of the Conseil Constitutionnel. The "Warsmann law" (from the name of the deputy, Jean-Luc Warsmann, who sponsored the bill) or, officially, the law for the "simplification and improvement of the quality of the law" included the following provision (Article 16):

> When an administrative authority is obliged to consult an organization prior to the promulgation of a regulatory act, it may decide to organize an open consultation allowing for the collection of comments from affected persons, on a website or by all other means.

> At the end of the consultation, it produces a synthesis of the comments received by the agency, eventually accompanied by complementary elements of information. This synthesis is made public.
>
> This open consultation substitutes for the mandatory consultations in application of a legislative or regulatory provision. The organizations whose opinion must be received in application of a legislative or regulatory provision may offer their comments in the context of the consultation provided for in this article.
>
> As an exception to the provisions of this Article, the following consultations remain mandatory: those concerning an independent administrative authority, those requiring the assent (*avis conforme*) [of the consultative body], those regarding the exercise of a public freedom and those pertaining to the social dialogue.
>
> A decree following consultation with the Conseil d'État shall determine the conditions of application of this article, notably the modalities of the organization of the consultation, the duration of which might not be less than fifteen days.

Therefore, this statute introduces a system of "open consultation" that may replace the formal, institutionalized process of agencies consulting consultative bodies. This "open consultation" comprises elements that sound familiar to those knowledgeable of the US notice-and-comment model.[162] More importantly, this process is not sector-specific. Could we then talk about an open consultation practice generalized across the wider spectrum of French administration similar to the American A.P.A.?

I will contend that the features of this new system provide a clear negative answer to this question, but it would be interesting to first point out the "adventures" this Article 16 (or 8, as was the number in the original bill) had to go through before its final adoption. The legislative history of the "Warsmann law" suggests that it was included in the final text with opposition. Article 8 was part of the legislative proposal as submitted by Jean-Luc Warsmann. The National Assembly accepted this Article in the first reading. However, the Senate deleted it in the first reading. Then the National Assembly reinserted it in the second reading. The Senate, again, deleted it in the second reading. Consequently, Article 8 was one of the questions that the *commission mixte paritaire* had to resolve. This committee ended up including Article 8, as adopted by the National Assembly, in the final text of the law–with the *rapporteur* for the Senate still appearing reluctant. In its decision, the Conseil Constitutionnel was not asked to and did not rule on the constitutionality of Article 16 (most complaints were of a procedural nature).[163] Therefore, this provision became positive law with no further complications.

Does this mean that we are witnessing the emergence of a notice-and-comment process *à la française*? Even if one overlooks the obvious reluctance of the legislature to adopt this Article, a fair characterization of the "Warsmann law" would be that it introduces a watered-down version of the US notice-and-comment process. First, even though the statement of reasons accompanying Warsmann's legislative proposal mentions the goal of associating the citizens with administrative decision-making, the purpose of the text is not so much to strengthen administrative democracy as to streamline administrative operations. The concern is that the latter are often delayed because in the traditional process the consultative commissions do not always meet promptly to issue their opinions; this process may now be replaced by "open consultations." Second, Article 16 is limited in scope: It provides for open electronic consultation *only* when the original statute stipulates that specific consultative bodies be consulted. It may only substitute for mandatory consultation (*consultation obligatoire*) and even though there might be many instances of such *consultations obligatoires*, the provision still falls short of general applicability. Third, and more importantly, this process is not mandatory. It permits but does not oblige the agency to opt for the open consultation. Thus, it keeps with the tradition of discretionary open consultations in other areas.

Article 16 of the "Warsmann law" was incorporated in the 2015 administrative procedure code (CRPA 2015) discussed earlier in this chapter. This type of open consultations which substitute for consultation of consultative committees (L132-1 to R132-7 CRPA 2015) is therefore subject to the same critical observations that applied to the "Warsmann law." The CRPA 2015 also covers a second type of consultations which have been termed "purely optional public consultations": these can occur both cumulatively with a traditional consultation but also when there is no obligation to consult a committee (L131-1).[164] This second type of discretionary consultations is subject to another set of general principles: the consultation procedure must be published; relevant information on the proposed project or act must be provided; a "reasonable" comment period must be ensured; the outcome or envisaged follow-on activities must be made public "in due course."

Article L.131-1 CRPA 2015, is commendable in its attempt to provide a uniform set of guiding principles for purely optional public consultations. Furthermore, its broad wording, which refers to "the conceptualization of a reform, the design of a project, or the making of an act" without any qualifier (e.g., "regulatory" act), could be interpreted as applying to both "legislative and non-legislative rules." If this broad interpretation is adopted, the French CRPA will stand out among general administrative procedure acts in covering soft law as well.[165] At the same time, the list of principles in Article L.131-1 is limited and far less ambitious than those included in the relevant 2011 report by the Conseil d'État; as such, the CRPA 2015 does not realize fully the authorization given to the government in the enabling statute to "reinforce citizen participation in rulemaking."[166] Furthermore, the abstract formulation of Article L.131-1 means that not only is the original decision to launch these public consultations completely discretionary (in the absence of another specific statutory mandate) but also that, once initiated, the details of the process are very much still set by the administrative authority itself.

Admittedly, the aforementioned initiatives should not necessarily be judged against the criterion of the older (one might say, traditional) US notice-and-comment model nor were they cast in such terms. The way in which the "Warsmann law" and now the CRPA 2015 processes are designed allows for trial and error, and is therefore a step forward toward the generalization of participatory administrative processes in France. I would risk the prediction that by the end of the next decade, with the increasing familiarization of public authorities with these regulatory processes adopted under EU mandates and influence over the past few years, a general binding provision for citizen participation in administrative policymaking will be enshrined more smoothly in the French legal system.[167]

Notes

1. *See, e.g.,* LARRY SIEDENTROP, DEMOCRACY IN EUROPE 23–24 (2001).
2. VIVIEN SCHMIDT, DEMOCRACY IN EUROPE. THE EU AND NATIONAL POLITIES 121 (2006); PIERRE ROSANVALLON, LE MODÈLE POLITIQUE FRANÇAIS: LA SOCIÉTÉ CIVILE CONTRE LE JACOBINISME DE 1789 À NOS JOURS 13 (2004) [hereinafter ROSANVALLON, LE MODÈLE POLITIQUE]. *See also* PIERRE ROSANVALLON, DEMOCRACY PAST AND FUTURE 98, 108 (Samuel Moyn ed., 2006) (underscoring the traditional perception that pluralism was divisive).
3. JEAN-JACQUES ROUSSEAU, THE SOCIAL CONTRACT AND OTHER LATER POLITICAL WRITINGS 122 (Victor Gourevitch ed. & trans., Cambridge University Press, 1997).
4. ROSANVALLON, LE MODÈLE POLITIQUE, *supra* note 2, at 13.
5. *See* RAYMOND CARRÉ DE MALBERG, LA LOI, EXPRESSION DE LA VOLONTÉ GÉNÉRALE 16–17 (Sirey, 1931, reed. Economica, 1984).
6. Cited in PIERRE ROSANVALLON, THE DEMANDS OF LIBERTY. CIVIL SOCIETY IN FRANCE SINCE THE REVOLUTION 13 (Arthur Goldhammer trans., 2007).
7. Bronislaw Baczko, *The Social Contract of the French: Sieyès and Rousseau,* 60 JOURNAL OF MODERN HISTORY S98, S100 (suppl. 1988).
8. *Dire de l'abbé Sieyès, Sur la question du veto royal* (Séance du 7 septembre 1789) (Paris: Gaudin), p. 10, 15, 5–6. A famous quote from Sieyès was: "In whatever manner a nation wills, it suffices that it does will" (EMMANUEL JOSEPH SIEYÈS, QU'EST-CE QUE LE TIERS-ÉTAT? 116 (3e éd. 1789)).
9. Abbé Sieyès, *Projet d'un décret provisoire sur le clergé* (12 février 1790) (Paris: Imprimerie Nationale), at 5.
10. Rosanvallon, Le modèle politique, *supra* note 2, at 13.
11. Luc Ferry & Conseil d'analyse de la société, La représentation du monde associatif dans le dialogue civil—Rapport au Premier Ministre 10, 12 (2010).
12. Interviews n. 75104 and 75107.
13. It has been pointed out in the literature that the role played by law in the Declaration was originally the product of a compromise between the radical and the moderate wings of the National Assembly. "The first wanted to guarantee the supremacy of the new legislative power; the second wanted to limit the 'anarchic' tendencies linked with the claims of rights" (Philippe Raynaud, *The "Rights of Man and Citizen" in the French Constitutional Tradition, in*

THE LEGACY OF THE FRENCH REVOLUTION 199, 207 (Ralph C. Hancock & L. Gary Lambert eds., 1996)).

14. *See* C. Bradley Thompson, *The American Founding and the French Revolution, in* THE LEGACY OF THE FRENCH REVOLUTION 109, 141 (Ralph C. Hancock & L. Gary Lambert eds., 1996) ("the Rousseauans faced a dilemma. How could they embody and institutionalize the General Will constitutionally? . . . It was in this context that Condorcet, Sieyès, and the other radicals were forced to go beyond Rousseau's admonitions outlined in *The Social Contract* against representative government. They had to accept representation as a necessary evil, unavoidable in a large nation . . . . Because party, factions, and interests are the antipodes of the General Will, the Rousseauans argued that any vestiges of the ancien régime must be eliminated, particularly the representation of the nobility in a bicameral legislature. Only in a unicameral legislature could popular sovereignty and the General Will be expressed in their true and unalloyed form"); MALBERG, *supra* note 5, at 157; Jeremy Rabkin, *Revolutionary Visions in Legal Imagery: Constitutional Contrasts between France and America, in* THE LEGACY OF THE FRENCH REVOLUTION 219, 231 (Ralph C. Hancock & L. Gary Lambert eds., 1996) ("the leading figures in the new National Assembly persuaded themselves that a representative assembly could somehow assume the role of Rousseau's citizen body and pronounce the general will").

15. SIEYÈS, *supra* note 8, at 154.

16. *See* ROSANVALLON, LE MODÈLE POLITIQUE, *supra* note 2, at 85–88. Carbonnier's description eloquently captures that spirit: "It is the *law*, the faceless order, aspiring to universality and eternity, similar and equivalent to divinity, the order projected into space and time, meeting an anonymous crowd and yet invisible generations" (Jean Carbonnier, *La passion des lois au siècle des Lumières, in* JEAN CARBONNIER, ESSAIS SUR LES LOIS 240 (2nd ed., 1995)).

17. MALBERG, *supra* note 5, at 27–28.

18. Conseil d'État [CE], Décision du 6 novembre 1936, *Arrighi* (Rec., p. 966); RENÉ CHAPUS, DROIT ADMINISTRATIF GÉNÉRAL (TOME 1) 33 (15th ed., 2001).

19. In his own words, "In our system the principle of separation of powers presents a very special character that the particular historic circumstances have imprinted onto it . . . . The conception is entirely dominated by the sovereignty of the law. We do not have to examine here in detail the role that the theory of that time, and notably the ideas of the Genevan philosopher, played on this point." *See also* ARNAUD HAQUET, LA LOI ET LE RÈGLEMENT 121 (2007) (noting that the *théorie de la loi écran* refers implicitly to the high quality of the legislator).

20. *See, e.g.*, CE, Décision du 10 juillet 1954, *Fédération des conseils de parents d'élèves des écoles publiques* (Rec., p. 449); CE, Décision du 15 octobre 1965, *Union fédérale des magistrats et Sieur Reliquet*; more recently, CE, 23 avril 1997, G.I.S.T.I. (N° 163043).

21. GRÉGORY HOUILLON, LE LOBBYING EN DROIT PUBLIC (VOL. I) 428 (2008) (doctoral dissertation, on file with author).

22. ROUSSEAU, *supra* note 3, at 67.

23. SIEYÈS, *supra* note 8, at 90.

24. CONSEIL D'ÉTAT, RAPPORT PUBLIC 1999—"RÉFLEXIONS SUR L'INTÉRÊT GENERAL" (1999).

25. ELISABETH ZOLLER, INTRODUCTION AU DROIT PUBLIC 11 (2006).

26. Conseil Constitutionnel [CC], Décision n. 83–162 DC du 20 juillet 1983, *Loi relative à la démocratisation du secteur public* ("the appraisal of the general interest lies with the legislator"); CC, Décision n° 87–232 DC du 07 janvier 1988, *Loi relative à la mutualisation de la Caisse nationale de crédit agricole* ("the legislator was able to take into account the general interest, which, according to its appraisal . . . "); CC, Décision n° 93–322 DC du 28 juillet 1993, *Loi relative aux établissements publics à caractère scientifique, culturel et professionnel* ("considering the objective of the general interest to which this seems to correspond"); *cf.* CE, 29 juin 1951, *Syndicat de la raffinerie de soufre française*, Rec. p.377; Rec. Dalloz, p. 661 (with a Note by Marcel Waline maintaining, however, that in this case the way in which the administration used an option to serve the general interest in executing the legislation constituted an abuse of power (*détournement de pouvoir*)).

27. ROSANVALLON, *supra* note 6, at 57.

28. PIERRE ROSANVALLON, LA LÉGITIMITÉ DÉMOCRATIQUE. IMPARTIALITÉ, RÉFLEXIVITÉ, PROX-
    IMITÉ 60–61 (2008).
29. *Dire de l'abbé Sieyès, supra* note 8, at 8.
30. The Constitution was drafted and adopted by the National Assembly and formally accepted
    by the king who signed it in the presence of the Assembly on September 14. On the drafting
    history and acceptance of the Constitution, *see* MICHAEL P. FITZSIMMONS, THE REMAKING
    OF FRANCE: THE NATIONAL ASSEMBLY AND THE CONSTITUTION OF 1791 129–39 (1994).
    The Constitution of 1791 retained the monarchy and declared both the legislative assem-
    bly and the king as representatives, but delegated the legislative power to one National
    Assembly. It would, however, be short-lived. Even though it was the product of elaborate
    work from 1789-1791, it only lasted less than a year. *See* FRANÇOIS FURET & RAN HALÉVI, LA
    MONARCHIE RÉPUBLICAINE: LA CONSTITUTION DE 1791 239ff. (1996) (exploring reasons for
    the Constitution's "failure").
31. ROSANVALLON, *supra* note 28, at 102. Carré de Malberg similarly connected the positive side
    of the statute as the expression of the general will with the negative side of excluding the
    executive from representing this will (MALBERG, *supra* note 5, at 47, 20).
32. LÉON DUGUIT, TRAITÉ DE DROIT CONSTITUTIONNEL, TOME I: LA RÈGLE DE DROIT—LE PROB-
    LÈME DE L'ETAT IX (3rd ed., 1927).
33. *See* Maurice Hauriou, *An Interpretation of the Principles of Public Law*, 31 HARV. L. REV. 813
    (1918).
34. This link is clear in his very definition of *service public*: "Every activity of general interest
    which is of such an importance to the entire collectivity that those in authority are under a
    duty to insure its accomplishment in an absolutely continuous manner, even by the use of
    force" (Léon Duguit, *The Concept of Public Service*, 32 YALE L.J. 425, 431 (1923)). The role of
    the government, in this view, is the development of social solidarity, notably by taking on
    the activities of general interest (JACQUES CHEVALLIER, SCIENCE ADMINISTRATIVE 167 (4th
    ed., 2007)).
35. LÉON DUGUIT, LES TRANSFORMATIONS DU DROIT PUBLIC XIX (1913) ("the will of the gover-
    nor has no force as such; it only has value and force to the extent it pursues the organiza-
    tion and functioning of a public service. Thus, the notion of public service replaces that of
    sovereignty").
36. CE, Décision du 22 mars 1901, *Sieur Pagès*, Rec. p. 315.
37. *See* DUGUIT, *supra* note 35, at 205–14.
38. RAYMOND ODENT, CONTENTIEUX ADMINISTRATIF (TOME 2) 581(1978, reed. Dalloz, 2007)
    ("the mission of the administration is . . . a mission of general interest . . . . Therefore, there
    is abuse of power (*détournement de pouvoir*) when an administrative authority, betraying the
    spirit of the mission entrusted to it, uses its prerogatives for aims that are not of the general
    interest, thus for illegitimate aims").
39. *See* HOUILLON, *supra* note 21, at 483–87.
40. ROSANVALLON, supra note 2, at 11, 18; Loi "Waldeck-Rousseau" du 21 mars 1884 relative à la
    création de syndicats professionnels; Loi du 1 juillet 1901 relative au contrat d'association.
41. *See* ROSANVALLON, *supra* note 6, at 153–57 and 161–67.
42. To the 21st-century reader this exclusion of political aims might seem not to follow from
    the definition of action of trade unions under Article 3 except under a very
    special view of "politics"—in fact, as is suggested later in the text, labor unions did start to
    play a role in policymaking and politics in the 20th century. However, this is indeed another
    indication of the narrow equation of politics with the general interest/will during that per-
    iod. This is confirmed by the legislative history of the 1884 statute: More specifically, the
    word "exclusively" was added later in the drafting process, thus conveying at least the inten-
    tion to limit union action strictly to the economic and social realm, namely, to representing
    the "particular interests" of specific groups (ROSANVALLON, *supra* note 6, at 171). Relatedly,
    a proposal to include a reference to the "general interests" of the occupational groups was
    rejected (*id.*, at 172).
43. HOUILLON, *supra* note 21, at 417.
44. ROSANVALLON, *supra* note 6, at 208, 8, 207.

45. *Id.*, at 261.
46. Décision n. 71–44 DC du 16 juillet 1971, Loi complétant les dispositions des articles 5 et 7 de la loi du 1er juillet 1901 relative au contrat d'association.
47. ROSANVALLON, *supra* note 6, at 231.
48. The term appeared in the literature in the 1960s (*see* YVES WEBER, L'ADMINISTRATION CONSULTATIVE (1968)) as this practice became more salient.
49. CHRISTOPHE GUETTIER, INSTITUTIONS ADMINISTRATIVES 456 (5th ed., 2010).
50. Décret n°2006-672 du 8 juin 2006 relatif à la création, à la composition et au fonctionnement de commissions administratives à caractère consultatif and Décret n°2006-665 du 7 juin 2006 relatif à la réduction du nombre et à la simplification de la composition de diverses commissions administratives. These provisions were incorporated in Article R. 133-2 of the 2015 "code on the relations between the public and the administration," which is discussed later in the text.
51. *See* CONSEIL D'ÉTAT, RAPPORT PUBLIC 2011—"CONSULTER AUTREMENT. PARTICIPER EFFECTIVEMENT" 35–37 (2011). Another senatorial report published in February 2007 focused only on consultative bodies placed at the level of the Prime Minister—their number was, again, non-negligible, forty-four. The report pointed, among other things, to the heterogeneity of these committees, their annual budgetary cost of 15 million Euros, the fact that they occupied 3,200 square meters of office space, and similarly called for their rationalization (Les commissions et instances consultatives ou délibératives placées directement auprès du Premier ministre: Une nécessaire rationalisation, Rapport d'information n° 244 (2006-2007) de MM. François Marc et Michel Moreigne, fait au nom de la commission des finances).
52. Frank L. Wilson, *French Interest Group Politics: Pluralist or Neocorporatist?*, 77 AMERICAN POLITICAL SCIENCE REVIEW 895, 900 (1983). According to certain telling quotes: "we are usually listened to but not heard" or "sometimes I feel that there are several ways to ignore the ideas of others: never consult them or consult them so often that they don't have time to really think out the problem."
53. *Id.*, at 907.
54. John T. S. Keeler, *Review: Situating France on the Pluralism-Corporatism Continuum: A Critique of and Alternative to the Wilson Perspective*, 17 COMPARATIVE POLITICS 229, 244–45 (1985).
55. *Id.*, at 232–33.
56. VIVIEN A. SCHMIDT, FROM STATE TO MARKET? THE TRANSFORMATION OF FRENCH BUSINESS AND GOVERNMENT 47 (1996).
57. Philippe C. Schmitter, *Still the Century of Corporatism?*, 36 REVIEW OF POLITICS (SPECIAL ISSUE: THE NEW CORPORATISM: SOCIAL AND POLITICAL STRUCTURES IN THE IBERIAN WORLD) 85, 93–94 (1974).
58. Into which one should factor additional considerations such as, for example, the very low unionization rate in France (7.7% in 2008), which was the second lowest in the OECD after Turkey (OECD.stat data on trade union density, available at http://stats.oecd.org/Index. aspx?DataSetCode=UN_DEN).
59. *See also* Wilson, *supra* note 52, at 909 ("In France the government clearly controls the use of corporatist forms. It has formed statutory bodies to promote 'concertation' among groups and government representatives, but it has refused to give these bodies decision-making or other powers").
60. Introduced in the Constitution of 1946, the *Conseil économique* was later renamed into *Conseil économique et social*, and is since 2008 called the *Conseil économique, social et environnemental*.
61. STÉPHANE DESSELAS, UN LOBBYING PROFESSIONNEL À VISAGE DÉCOUVERT. ENQUÊTE SUR L'INFLUENCE DES FRANÇAIS À BRUXELLES 178 (2007).
62. *See* Wilson, *supra* note 52, at 901 (noting that the interviews he carried out confirmed the reputation of the Economic and Social Council having at best a negligible effect on the policy process: 59% of the respondents "saw the ESC as having very little or no effect on policy. Even though they felt that the ESC advisory opinions were often of outstanding quality, most group spokesmen, including those who served personally on the Council, admitted

that neither the government nor the parliament paid much heed to its work"). A 2011 interview I had with an experienced lobbyist, who wished to remained anonymous because of their evaluation of the Economic, Social and Environmental Council as "an institution of little or no use," echoed the same sentiment.

63. To use the term that Rosanvallon borrows from Pierre Bourdieu and applies to a different setting (ROSANVALLON, *supra* note 28, at 67).

64. This term might have a negative connotation referring to fascist Italy. However, the meaning I ascribe to it is different and explained in the text. *See also* HOUILLON, *supra* note 21, at 425: "The state masters those interests. It can approve them, solicit them when it needs them, even arbitrate them without necessarily being bound . . . . This difference between lobbying and 'corporatisme étatique' shows to what extent lobbying is still, in the era of national sovereignty, irreconcilable with representation."

65. *See, e.g.*, the law n. 2008-789 of 20 August 2008 "on the renewal of social democracy and the reform of work time," inserting criteria of representativeness (e.g., in the professional branches one of the criteria is that the syndicate had 8% of the votes cast during the last internal election).

66. JONAH D. LEVY, TOCQUEVILLE'S REVENGE. STATE, SOCIETY, AND ECONOMY IN CONTEMPORARY FRANCE 12 (1999) (noting that "[t]he solution is not *less* state, but a *different* kind of state-an *empowering* state, a state that gives societal and local actors the financial, regulatory, and institutional means to assume their responsibilities").

67. Jack Hayward, *Institutional Inertia and Political Impetus in France and Britain*, 4 EUROPEAN JOURNAL OF POLITICAL RESEARCH 341 (1976).

68. LEVY, *supra* note 66, at 10–11.

69. In its literal translation, "Any binding mandate is null and void."

70. Also influenced by the new spirit growing out of the events of May 1968, *see* ROSANVALLON, *supra* note 6, at 257–63 (referring to reforms leading to an increased role for associations).

71. GEORGES BURDEAU, TRAITÉ DE SCIENCE POLITIQUE—TOME IX (LES FAÇADES INSTITUTION-NELLES DE LA DÉMOCRATIE GOUVERNANTE) 168 (2nd ed., 1976) (situating this remark within the broader discussion of the "general phenomenon" of the "decline of Parliaments" and adding that "the new circuits of representation do not limit themselves to competing with the parliamentary representation. Rising to de facto powers, they often purport to substitute it").

72. Interview with Patrick Beaudouin, QUE CHOISIR Argenet, N. 116 (October 2009), at 55. Interestingly, the interviewee, a parliamentarian sponsoring legislation to regulate lobbying in the National Assembly, replied that is not necessarily evident how to distinguish between these two types of lobbying as to their aims; hence, "it is not only more equitable but also more efficient to submit everyone to the same rules."

73. Preface of Benoît Le Bret *in* DESSELAS, *supra* note 61, at 17.

74. *See, e.g.*, Constitution of 1791, Chapter IV, Section I, Article 6: "The executive power can make no law, even provisional, but only proclamations in conformity with the laws to order their execution."

75. The outline of the development of those relations in the text is drawn from YVES GAUDEMET, TRAITÉ DE DROIT ADMINISTRATIF (TOME I) 548–51 (16th ed., 2001).

76. HENRI OBERDORFF, LES INSTITUTIONS ADMINISTRATIVES 17 (6th ed., 2010).

77. CONSEIL D'ÉTAT, RAPPORT PUBLIC 2006—"SÉCURITÉ JURIDIQUE ET COMPLEXITÉ DU DROIT" (2006), at 270. *See also* Pierre Delvolvé, *L'été des ordonnances*, 21 REVUE FRANÇAISE DE DROIT ADMINISTRATIF 909 (2005). Indeed, three times since 2000—in 2004, 2005 and 2009—the number of *ordonnances* was higher than the number of regular statutes (Secrétariat Général du Gouvernement, *Lois et règlements en vigueur. Approche statistique* (January 2011).

78. Décision n° 85–197 DC du 23 août 1985—Loi sur l'évolution de la Nouvelle-Calédonie.

79. Wilson, *supra* note 52, at 909.

80. Loi n°83–630 du 12 juillet 1983 relative à la démocratisation des enquêtes publiques et à la protection de l'environnement.

81. *See* Susan Rose-Ackerman & Thomas Perroud, *Policymaking and Public Law in France: Public Participation, Agency Independence, and Impact Assessment*, 19 COLUM. J. EUR. L. 225, 256

(2013) (noting that the process "is essentially a way for the national government to exert some control over spending priorities and economic development at the local and regional levels" and that it has been criticized as being "too closed, too ineffective, and for coming too late in the policymaking process").

82. Article 2 of the loi du 2 février 1995 relative à la protection de l'environnement, called "loi Barnier", and decree of application of 10 May 1996.

83. Loi n° 2002-276 du 27 février 2002 *relative à la démocratie de proximité*.

84. More information on these procedures is available at https://www.debatpublic.fr.

85. Rose-Ackerman & Perroud, *supra* note 81, at 259.

86. More information on this mechanism is available at http://www.debatpublic.fr/notions_generales/autres_experiences.html.

87. Loi n. 92–125 du 6 février 1992 relative à l'administration territoriale de la République.

88. Loi n. 2002-276 du 27 février 2002 relative à la démocratie de proximité.

89. *See* GUETTIER, *supra* note 49, at 560 (noting that the local initiatives aiming at improving the functioning of local democracy by means of public consultation processes or the involvement of citizens in the management of local affairs remain very limited).

90. For examples of participation in town planning in Germany and England, *see* Theodora Ziamou, *Public Participation in Administrative Rulemaking: The Legal Tradition and Perspective in the American and European (English, German, Greek) Legal Systems*, 60 ZEITSCHRIFT FÜR AUSLÄNDISCHES ÖFFENTLICHES RECHT UND VÖLKERRECHT 41, 83ff. (2000).

91. See the remarks of Jean-Bernard Auby, Remarques introductives au colloque "Vers une démocratie administrative? Des administrés aux citoyens" (Pôle Européen d'Administration Publique, Strasbourg, 19–20 Mars 2010).

92. CE, Ass., Décision du 3 octobre 2008, *Commune d'Annecy*.

93. See the speech of the Vice-President of the Conseil d'Etat, Jean-Marc Sauvé, *La démocratie environnementale aujourd'hui* (17 November 2010), at 3 (available at http://www.conseil-etat.fr/Actualites/Discours-Interventions/La-democratie-environnementale-aujourd-hui).

94. Loi n. 2010-788 du 12 juillet 2010 portant engagement national pour l'environnement.

95. Loi n. 2012-1460 du 27 décembre 2012 relative à la mise en œuvre du principe de participation du public défini à l'article 7 de la Charte de l'environnement. For a discussion of the Conseil Constitutionnel decisions that led to the adoption of this statute, *see* Rose-Ackerman & Perroud, *supra* note 81, at 268–72.

96. Rose-Ackerman & Perroud, *supra* note 81, at 272.

97. Code des relations entre le public et l'administration (Statutory provisions: Ordonnance n° 2015-1341 du 23 octobre 2015; Regulatory provisions: Décret n° 2015-1342 du 23 octobre 2015); Dominique Custos, *The 2015 French Code of Administrative Procedure: An Assessment*, *in* COMPARATIVE ADMINISTRATIVE LAW (Susan Rose-Ackerman, Peter Lindseth & Blake Emerson eds., 2d ed) (forthcoming 2017); Maud Vialettes & Cécile Barrois de Sarigny *Questions autour d'une codification*, 2015 ACTUALITÉ JURIDIQUE, DROIT ADMINISTRATIF 2421. For a collection of articles on the CRPA 2015, see the special *dossier* in 2016 REVUE FRANÇAISE DE DROIT ADMINISTRATIF 1–74.

98. Daniel Labetoulle, *Le code des relations entre le public et l'administration: Avant-propos*, 2016 REVUE FRANÇAISE DE DROIT ADMINISTRATIF 1, 1.

99. Vialettes & Barrois de Sarigny, *supra* note 97, at 2422.

100. Livre I: Titre III: Chapitre IV. For commentary, *see* Pierre Bon, *L'association du public aux décisions prises par l'administration*, 2016 REVUE FRANÇAISE DE DROIT ADMINISTRATIF 27, 28–29.

101. Loi de réglementation des télécommunications n° 96–659 du 26 juillet 1996.

102. MARK THATCHER, THE POLITICS OF TELECOMMUNICATIONS: NATIONAL INSTITUTIONS, CONVERGENCE, AND CHANGE IN BRITAIN AND FRANCE 157 (1999). Before France Télécom became autonomous in 1990, telecommunications services in France had been supplied by the Ministry of Posts, Telegraphs and Telecommunications (PTT). This government Ministry was divided into various general directorates (*directions générales*), including after 1946 the *Direction Générale des Télécommunications*, headed by a civil servant, the *Directeur général des telecommunications* (*id.*, at 102–104).

103. The chairman of the Authority is appointed by the President of the Republic on the proposal of the Prime Minister. Since the Act of 5 March 2007 on the future television, the appointment is preceded by consultation with the relevant parliamentary committees on electronic communications and the postal sector. Information on appointments is available on the website of the agency at http://www.arcep.fr/index.php?id=12&L=1.

104. For a discussion of different systems of appointing agency officials, *see* Susan Rose-Ackerman, *Regulation and Public Law in Comparative Perspective*, 60 U. TORONTO L.J. 519, 531–33 (2010).

105. *See* Mark Thatcher, *Independent Regulatory Agencies and Elected Politicians in Europe, in* REGULATION THROUGH AGENCIES IN THE EU. A NEW PARADIGM OF EUROPEAN GOVERNANCE 47, 59*ff.* (Damien Geradin & Rodolphe Munoz & Nicholas Petit eds. 2005).

106. *See also* Mark Thatcher, *Regulatory Agencies, the State and Markets: A Franco-British Comparison*, 14 JOURNAL OF EUROPEAN PUBLIC POLICY 1028, 1035 (2007) (reporting that, over the period 2002-2006, 50 per cent of the members of the French independent regulatory agencies came from the *grandes écoles* and 33 per cent from the *grands corps*, thus concluding that the creation of those agencies has reinforced the power of the existing administrative elites).

107. Article 432–13 of the penal code (*prise illégale d'intérêts*, literally: "illegal assumption of interests") provides for the offense of *pantouflage* ("*délit de pantouflage*") stipulating that a civil servant or public agent may not assume a position in a private firm that he or she was in charge of overseeing or concluding contracts with until after three years have elapsed from the date he or she left the public sector. In case of violation, the penalty may reach up to two years imprisonment and a fine of 30,000 euros. For more details on these provisions, and more broadly the "conflict of interests" regime in France, including an evaluation of its weaknesses and proposals for reform, see the report of the Commission de réflexion pour la prévention des conflits d'intérêts dans la vie publique, *Pour une nouvelle déontologie de la vie publique* (2011).

108. Thatcher, *supra* note 106, at 1034–35 (further reporting that only 5.3% of French market IRA members had stood for elected office in the 2002–06 period, as against 9% in the 1990–2001 period).

109. *Cf.* Martin Hirsch, *L'expertise scientifique indépendante dans un établissement public: l'exemple de l'Agence française de sécurité sanitaire des aliments, in* CONSEIL D'ÉTAT, RAPPORT PUBLIC 2001, "LES AUTORITÉS ADMINISTRATIVE INDÉPENDANTES" 428 (2001) (suggesting—in the context of another authority, the French Food Agency (Agence Française de Sécurité Sanitaire des Aliments)—that it is entrusted with developing independent expertise).

110. THATCHER, *supra* note 102, at 212.

111. Projet de loi portant diverses dispositions d'adaptation de la législation au droit de l'Union européenne en matière de santé, de travail et de communications électroniques, n° 2789, déposé le 15 septembre 2010.

112. Available at http://www.assemblee-nationale.fr/13/cri/2010-2011/20110097.asp.

113. *Arcep: UE menace la France de sanction* (LE FIGARO, 8 February 2011) (available at http://plus.lefigaro.fr/article/arcep-ue-menace-la-france-de-sanction-20110208-396423/commentaires), *Il n'y aura pas de commissaire du gouvernement à l'Arcep* (LE MONDE, 16 February 2011) (available at http://www.lemonde.fr/technologies/article/2011/02/16/il-n-y-aura-pas-de-commissaire-du-gouvernement-a-l-arcep_1481174_651865.html).

114. ARCEP, Annual Report 2011 (2012), at 44.

115. Autorité de régulation des télécommunications, Annual Report 1997—Unabridged Version (1998), at 5, 201.

116. Decision No. 97-155. The interconnection committee was established pursuant to Article D. 99-6 of the Code des postes et des télécommunications, stemming from Decree No. 97-188 of 3 March 1997 on interconnection.

117. On this example, *see* JACQUES POMONTI, L'AVENTURE DU TÉLÉPHONE: UNE EXCEPTION FRANÇAISE 53,73, 87, 75 (2008).

118. Article 3, Loi no 2004-669 du 9 juillet 2004 relative aux communications électroniques et aux services de communication audiovisuelle.

119. Arts. L.42-2, L.34-8 and D.99-11 CPCE.
120. An additional methodological clarification is in order: When the ARCEP lumped together an initial public consultation on a question (or a series of questions, as is most commonly the case) with the consultation on the final draft of the decision (*projet de décision*), which is often simultaneously notified to the European Commission or the Conseil de la Concurrence as well, I followed the methodology of the agency and treated them as a single public consultation for the purposes of Figure 3.1. In case any comments were received during the final round, those were added to the first for the purposes of Figure 3.2. Examples of this sort of lumping together include, for instance, the consultation on value-added services (*Consultation publique sur les services à valeur ajoutée*) [23 November 2006–5 January 2007] that was followed by a consultation on the text of the decision (*Consultation publique sur le projet de décision n° 2007-0213*) [8 March–10 April 2007]. Since I did not count public consultations on the same issue as distinct ones, but attached subsequent rounds to the original consultation, these follow-up consultations were counted in the year in which the first round of consultation began (e.g., in the example of value-added services, that was the year 2006).
121. ARCEP, Internet and network neutrality: Proposals and recommendations (September 2010), at 19.
122. In September 2012, the ARCEP reiterated this point in a report to the Parliament: "ARCEP has observed a decrease in the use of [traffic management] practices, in particular thanks to competition, and especially on mobile networks where they were the most frequent. Nevertheless, certain current practices are still contrary to the framework proposed in 2010. ARCEP is therefore calling for the steady elimination of service blocking (VoIP, P2P) on mobile networks. If the market fails to make sufficient progress on its own, the Law gives ARCEP the powers needed to enforce its recommendations" (ARCEP, Report to Parliament and the Government on Net Neutrality (September 2012), at 4).
123. This is not to say that public consultations preceded only non-binding actions, such as reports and recommendations, in this area. In December 2011, while the ARCEP was in the process of preparing the introduction of a quality of service (QoS) monitoring mechanism for fixed internet access, it held a public consultation on proposed "orientations." In June 2012, the agency submitted to public consultation a draft decision that set the QoS indicators for internet access, giving precise details on the measurement methods to be used for these new indicators. The final decision (no. 2013-0004) was issued in January 2013.
124. *See* interview n. 75301.
125. Interviews n. 75203 and 75105.
126. There were four such cases in 2006, four in 2007, two in 2008, one in 2009 and three in 2010.
127. Loi n°79-587 du 11 juillet 1979 relative à la motivation des actes administratifs et à l'amélioration des relations entre l'administration et le public.
128. For instance, one introduced by a 2002 law (Loi n°2002-276 du 27 février 2002 *relative à la démocratie de proximité*) regarding declarations of public utility (*déclarations d'utilité publique*) in the case of expropriations for a public purpose.
129. This is an approach associated with a searching judicial review even of the substantive content of agency action in the United States. Courts decided to review the policy considerations and technical evaluations of administrative agencies. However, since they lacked the institutional competence and technical resources to perform this intense scrutiny themselves, they imposed on the agencies the obligation to create a voluminous record during the elaboration of the rule.
130. On the other hand, administrative authorities have discretion to freely proceed to consultations or not when these consultative processes are not mandatory (CHAPUS, *supra* note 18, at 1073).
131. CE, N° 292386- Lecture du 6 juin 2007—*Association le Réseau Sortir du Nucléaire*.
132. A more recent decision of the Conseil Constitutionnel, *Association France Nature Environnement*, reviewed a different type of "checklist obligation," *see* Conseil Constitutionnel, Decision No. 2011-183/184QPC, 14 October 2011 (available in English

at http://www.conseil-constitutionnel.fr/conseil-constitutionnel/english/priority-preliminary-rulings-on-the-issue-of-constitutionality-qpc-/sample-of-decisions-qpc/2011/decision-no-2011-183-184-qpc-of-14-october-2011.103823.html). In this case, it was the legislature and not the administration that failed to meet a consultation obligation under Article 7 of the Charter for the Environment of 2004. As a reminder, this, now constitutional, mandate provides that "each person has the right, in the conditions and to the extent provided for by law, to have access to any information pertaining to the environment in the possession of public bodies and to participate in the elaboration of public decisions likely to affect the environment." More specifically, the case involved the list of facilities that are subject to various licensing criteria due to environmental hazards they might pose. The Environmental Code provided that the responsible minister may issue general requirements for these installations. Prior to that, she should obtain the opinion of the "Supreme Council of classified installations" and consult with the "concerned ministers." The Constitutional Council found, however, that neither the contested provisions nor any other legislative provision assured the implementation of the principle of public participation. This was in violation of Article 7 of the Charter for the Environment, and therefore the specific provisions of the Environmental Code were unconstitutional. In other words, the "checklist obligation" imposed by Article 7 of the Charter was that some form of public consultation be included in the statute. In this case, there was none: the only requirements were that the minister consult with an expert body, the "Supreme Council of classified installations," and within the government. The Constitutional Council reached similar conclusions in a series of other related environmental law cases in 2012, *see* Conseil Constitutionnel, Decision No. 2012-262QPC, 13 July 2012; Conseil Constitutionnel, Decision No. 2012-269QPC, 27 July 2012; Conseil Constitutionnel, Decision No. 2012-270QPC, 27 July 2012; Conseil Constitutionnel, Decision No. 2012-283QPC, 23 November 2012; Conseil Constitutionnel, Decision No. 2012-282QPC, 23 November 2012. For further discussion of this jurisprudence of the Conseil Constitutionnel, *see* Rose-Ackerman & Perroud, *supra* note 81, at 268–70.

133. CE, N° 310453 -Lecture du 19 juin 2009—*Association des Renseignements pour Tous.*
134. CE, N° 324642- Lecture du 24 juillet 2009—*Orange et SFR.*
135. CE, No 312741- Lecture du 27 avril 2009—*Bouygues.*
136. CE, N° 332393- Lecture du 12 octobre 2010—*Bouygues.*
137. For this cause of action, *see* RENÉ CHAPUS, DROIT DU CONTENTIEUX ADMINISTRATIF 208*ff.* (12th ed., 2006).
138. *See* CHAPUS, *supra* note 18, at 1061; GUY BRAIBANT & BERNARD STIRN, LE DROIT ADMINIS-TRATIF FRANÇAIS 286–87 (7th ed., 2005); GAUDEMET, *supra* note 75, at 501.
139. CE, 28 mai 1971—*Ministre de l'équipement et du logement c/ Fédération de défense des personnes concernées par le projet actuellement dénommé "Ville nouvelle Est"*—Rec. Lebon p. 409.
140. CHAPUS, *supra* note 18, at 1078.
141. *Id.*, at 1078–82 (outlining other areas in which courts applied this doctrine); GAUDEMET, *supra* note 75, at 503; BRAIBANT & STIRN, *supra* note 138, at 289.
142. The *théorie du bilan* could do this work more effectively if interpreted in a fashion that would give full effect to the doctrine, that is, if the judge could consider alternatives that would strike a better balance. *See* Bertrand Seiller, *Pour un contrôle de la légalité extrinsèque des déclarations d'utilité publique*, 2003 ACTUALITÉ JURIDIQUE, DROIT ADMINISTRATIF 1472 (elaborating the idea of "balancing the balances"- *bilan des bilans*).
143. Interview n. 75201.
144. *See* interviews n. 75202 and 75203.
145. See AT&T, Comments of AT&T Global Network Services France, SAS: ARCEP Consultation Paper on Internet and Electronic Communications Network Neutrality (July 13, 2010), at 3. On this question of funding network expansion, see also ARCEP, Report to Parliament and the Government on Net Neutrality (September 2012), at 29 ("This thriving ecosystem . . . raises the question of how to share the value and to pay for the infrastructures . . . . Content and application providers are generally satisfied with the current situation, but some of the operators would like the investment burden to be allocated differently. Some ISPs are thus working to develop new business models").

146. Interview n. 75106.
147. Interview n. 75105.
148. ARCEP, Annual Report 2011 (2012), at 54.
149. Interview n. 75202.
150. Article 2, Loi n. 78-753 du 17 juillet 1978 portant diverses mesures d'amélioration des relations entre l'administration et le public et diverses dispositions d'ordre administratif, social et fiscal.
151. Interview n. 75103.
152. Interview n. 75201.
153. *See* interview n. 75105; see also the minutes (*compte rendu*) of GRACO's meeting on 28 September 2010 (available at http://arcep.fr/uploads/tx_gspublication/cr-travaux-graco-sept-2010.pdf).
154. *Cf.* the express prohibition of ex parte communications in the context of formal rulemaking in the US, 5 U.S.C. §§ 556, 557(d). With respect to informal rulemaking, US courts have held that "ex parte contacts do not per se vitiate agency informal rulemaking action, but only do so if it appears from the administrative record under review that they may have materially influenced the action ultimately taken" (*Action for Children's Television v. F.C.C.*, 564 F.2d 458, 476 (D.C. Cir. 1977)). Courts were more concerned in cases involving "massive evidence that industry parties financially interested in the rulemaking secretly lobbied with" agency staff (*see, e.g., United Steelworkers of Am., AFL-CIO-CLC v. Marshall*, 647 F.2d 1189, 1215 (D.C. Cir. 1980), interpreting *Home Box Office, Inc. v. F.C.C.*, 567 F.2d 9 (D.C. Cir. 1977)). Moreover, the strict restrictions on ex parte contacts do not apply to intergovernmental communications. However, the D.C. Circuit recognized that "there may be instances where the docketing of conversations between the President or his staff and other Executive Branch officers or rulemakers may be necessary to ensure due process. This may be true, for example, where such conversations directly concern the outcome of adjudications or quasi-adjudicatory proceedings. . . Docketing may also be necessary in some circumstances where a statute [like the Clean Air Act in this case] specifically requires that essential 'information or data' upon which a rule is based be docketed" (*Sierra Club v. Costle*, 657 F.2d 298, 406–407 (D.C. Cir. 1981)).
155. Interview n. 75100 (industry), n. 75201 (consumer group).
156. Dorit Reiss explains, reporting on interviews with officials of the telecommunications and electricity regulators in the UK, France, and Sweden, that agencies see bilateral meetings as critical to their job in multiple ways (Dorit Rubinstein Reiss, *Participation in Governance from a Comparative Perspective: Citizen Involvement in Telecommunications and Electricity in the United Kingdom, France and Sweden*, 2009 J. DISP. RESOL. 381, 393–94 (2009)).
157. As a general matter, this would not, of course, preclude the possibility of a follow-up chat session after the end of the public consultation and while the agency is considering the adoption of the final measure if there is sufficient demand for that or the Authority thinks that there is a need for such an exercise.
158. As a reminder, this is the binary "has the ARCEP carried out a public consultation or not?"
159. *See* Cyril Roger-Lacan, *Remarques*, 2010/23 REVUE LAMY DE LA CONCURRENCE 162, 162 (2010) (mentioning that the court's consideration of the "game of economic actors" is an example of the particularity in the judicial review of ARCEP's decisions that distinguishes the latter from the more "classic" review on the grounds of excess of power (*excès de pouvoir*)).
160. *See id.*, at 165 (noting that it is very important that a regulator entrusted with extremely broad powers should know that its reasoning will be revisited if the operators challenge its decisions; and adding that the existence of a real and substantial review has a balancing role on the relations between the regulator and the regulated sector).
161. Loi n° 2011-525 du 17 mai 2011 de simplification et d'amélioration de la qualité du droit.
162. The US Administrative Procedure Act (A.P.A.), adopted in 1946, provided early on a model a direct public involvement in administrative policymaking, especially with respect to informal rulemaking. Section 553 of the A.P.A. stipulates that, when making rules or regulations having binding effect on private parties, the agency must provide notice of its proposal, an

opportunity for affected parties to comment, and "a concise general statement" of the basis and purpose of the rules.

163. Décision n° 2011-629 DC du 12 mai 2011.

164. Custos, *supra* note 97.

165. *Id.*

166. Bon, *supra* note 100, at 27–28. *See also* Custos, *supra* note 97 (noting that this provision "does not even explicitly require that a synthesis of comments be published, nor does it require reach-out efforts to all interested persons, let alone the giving of reasons").

167. Rose-Ackerman and Perroud (*supra* note 81, at 312) are more cautious on this point: "It remains to be seen whether the glimmers of change that we have isolated are passing fancies or a real reformulation of policymaking that takes account of modern political and technocratic realities."

4

Greece

The fundamental tenets of the Greek model may strike readers as akin to those in the French case study. Greece is a unitary state with a traditional focus on conventional notions of administrative accountability through legislative delegation and the involvement of the Council of State (Symvouleio tis Epikrateias) both prior to the promulgation of administrative rules and at the judicial review stage. In fact, since Greece is a parliamentary and not a semi-presidential system, the role of the executive branch looks, at least formally, more circumscribed with a much more limited place for autonomous rulemaking power (the picture, as this chapter will explain, is more nuanced than this). The pattern of state-society relations in the country has similarly been described as statist.[1] Furthermore, like France, Greece was a late liberalizer—indeed, the latest one, as full liberalization in telecommunications services was completed only in January 2001, namely, three years later than in France.[2] These basic commonalities anticipate the effect of the 2002 EU mandates on the Greek administrative law regime: the participatory provisions of the EU directives shook up traditional statist relations and introduced new accountability mechanisms. In this respect, the story told in this chapter will sound familiar to readers of chapter 3.

Nevertheless, the transformative impact of EU law must be assessed against the specific background of the Greek example and the historical, institutional, and cultural particularities of the country. The EU public consultation mandates were transposed into an institutional environment that, like France, was not particularly hospitable to the idea of open and direct public involvement in policymaking. Greece, however, was facing to a greater extent the additional challenge of weak administrative capacity marked by excessive formalism in conjunction with an underdeveloped civil society. The following pages will discuss these features and elaborate on how the EU participatory provisions were mapped onto the Greek administrative system and reflected these implementation challenges. The country case in this chapter may, therefore, serve as an illustrating example of the idea that the introduction of participatory processes is a necessary but not always sufficient condition for the new accountability paradigm to take strong roots. Institutional reform efforts, including policies aimed at building stronger civil society capacity on the ground, might also be required.

I. Traditional notions of administrative accountability in Greek public law

The Greek legal order pursues administrative accountability through two main mechanisms: parliamentary sovereignty (primarily expressed in this context as a textually strict doctrine on permissible delegations of legislative authority) and control by the Council of State. Both of these modes of accountability are enshrined in the current Constitution[3] but their historical pedigree goes farther back.

A. Parliamentary sovereignty and rules of delegation

The principle of popular sovereignty found its way into the third revolutionary Constitution that was adopted during the Greek War of Independence against the Ottoman Empire: the "Political Constitution of Greece," signed in 1827, declared that "sovereignty lies with the people; all powers derive from the people and exist for the people."[4] This formulation was kept intact in all Greek Constitutions following 1864.[5] As in France, the principle of popular sovereignty was translated institutionally into the principle of parliamentary sovereignty. The centrality of the statute—*légicentrisme*, to quote the French term from the previous chapter, or *nomarchy* (rule of the statute) to use a Greek term reflecting a similar idea—was a key characteristic of the first period of Greek constitutionalism.[6] This preeminence of the statute stemmed from the recognition of the legislative body's omnipotence, but in the 19th century its roots were mostly liberal: the statute was perceived as a guarantor of freedom and individual rights.[7]

The recognition of the sovereignty of the nation as expressed in Parliament by means of statutes was manifest in the case law through most of the 19th century as well. The underlying theory of the time was that courts would apply the law (statute), any law, provided that it formally existed.[8] In the words of the *Areios Pagos*, the Supreme Court in civil and criminal matters,

> the will of the legislator must guide judicial decisions, and this can only be deduced from the statutes and decisions stemming from the legislative power. The courts, however, have no jurisdiction to examine the content of the legislative decisions, for it cannot be assumed that the authority representing the sovereignty of the nation, acts unlawfully . . . . The judge must implement the statute and adjudicate on the basis of the law, but cannot criticize it or reverse it on the grounds that

the authority of the sovereign nation did not have the power to issue that law.[9]

Even after the formal judicial recognition in 1897 of the power of all courts to disapply statutory provisions that they deem unconstitutional, and for almost a century up until the salient rise of constitutional judicial review in the 1980s,[10] deference to the legislature and thus the judicially sanctioned preeminence of the statute remained the norm.[11] As one of the towering figures of Greek constitutional law in the 20th century, Aristovoulos Manesis, put it echoing the French political axiom, "within the framework of the Constitution, the sovereign people may will as they please provided that they will."[12]

For the purposes of our discussion, the most interesting aspect of the principle of parliamentary sovereignty and the "rule of the statute" is its implications for administrative action. In this context, parliamentary sovereignty undergirds the principle of legality: administrative agencies may only act *intra et secundum legem*, that is, based on a preexisting statute that delegates policymaking authority and delineates the limits of this secondary lawmaking power.[13] This prong of parliamentary sovereignty was highlighted early on in the constitutional law literature. It is, however, especially relevant under the Constitution currently in operation, in particular its provisions that regulate the process of legislative delegation in some detail.

The current Constitution of Greece was adopted in 1975 following the reinstatement of democracy in July 1974 after the overthrow of the seven-year-long military junta. Article 1 describes the form of government as a *parliamentary republic*. There was, however, a conscious effort to strengthen the role of the executive. This was perceived by the drafters of the Constitution to be "the central demand of the new era."[14] The executive was accordingly organized in a centralized way around two offices: the President of the Republic (head of state) and the Prime Minister (head of government). According to Article 82 of the Constitution, the Prime Minister (PM) shall direct the actions of the Government, which in turn is responsible to "define and direct the general policy of the country." The Constitution of 1975 had vested the President of the Republic with broad authority.[15] The President's powers were curtailed significantly during the first constitutional revision in 1986 which introduced a "clear parliamentary system of governance."[16]

Inscribed in the principle of parliamentary sovereignty, and specifically the principle of legality, are both a very limited recognition of autonomous rulemaking power to the executive and a strict delineation of statutory delegation in the Constitution of 1975.[17] As we consider the constitutional regulation of legislative delegation, we should keep in mind Article 35(1) of the Constitution, which stipulates that no act of the President "shall be valid nor be executed unless it has been countersigned by the competent Minister who, by his signature alone shall be rendered responsible." In other words, in the case of presidential decrees the power may nominally belong to the President but is essentially exercised by the cabinet or the individual ministers.[18] The Constitution allows the President to issue, upon the proposal of the cabinet, "acts of legislative content" only "under extraordinary circumstances of an urgent and unforeseeable need." These acts need then be submitted to Parliament for ratification within forty days or they "henceforth cease to be in force" (Article 44(1)). Furthermore, pursuant to Article 43(1), the President may issue "the decrees necessary for the execution of statutes" but may never suspend the application of laws nor exempt anyone from their execution. These decrees simply execute, that is, "concretize law" which, otherwise, could not be applied immediately; they do not create new rights or obligations.[19]

The highest proportion of executive decree power, however, is delegated by ordinary legislation.[20] There are three types of delegation: specific, specialized, and general. Under the so-called "specific statutory delegation" of Article 43(2), a statute allows for the issuance of regulatory decrees, on the proposal of the competent minister, "within the limits of the delegation." The authorizing statute defines the object and the general principles of the regulation.[21] Second, the exercise of delegated rulemaking authority can also take the form of acts issued by administrative organs other than the President. This type of "specialized delegation" under the second clause of Article 43(2) may concern only the "regulation of more specific matters or matters of local interest or of a technical and detailed nature." This is an important provision for the modern administrative state, as it constitutes the basis for rulemaking by independent administrative agencies.[22] The last type of delegation is the so-called general statutory authorization, which is included in "framework statutes." In contrast with "specific delegation," framework statutes specify only the broad framework of the matters to be regulated by decree.

The discussion of these provisions highlights the conscious choice of the Greek constitutional legislator to circumscribe strictly the rulemaking authority of the administration, thus defining it as a secondary power subject to the primacy of and limits set by the statute. The commitment to the institutionalization of executive rulemaking found clear judicial support in the 1990s when the Council of State ruled on the constitutionality of what had been until then a widely held executive practice. More specifically, it had been common for ministers to issue regulations without prior statutory delegation. These administrative acts would later be ratified retroactively by the Parliament (controlled by the same majority as the executive), thus acquiring the force of statute. This rubberstamping practice also meant that challenges against the original administrative acts which had been pending before administrative courts would no longer be reviewable post ratification. The Plenary of the Council of State held that this practice was unconstitutional because it violated the principles of separation of powers and legality of administrative action, as well as the express and exhaustive regulation of legislative delegation in the text of the Constitution.[23] This example brings to the fore the second key mechanism of administrative accountability, namely, the operation of the Council of State.

B. The role of the Council of State and judicial review

The Greek Council of State, in its present form, was established by the Constitution of 1911 and has been in continuous operation since 1929.[24] During the discussions in the Constitutional Assembly, the majority MPs had referred repeatedly to the French Conseil d'État as a source of inspiration and guarantor of the rule of law.[25] Importantly, the Council of State was entrusted with two sets of competences—consultative and judicial—that it has retained under the current Constitution of 1975.

The consultative function of the Council of State is described in Article 95(1)(d) of the Constitution as the "elaboration of all decrees of a general regulatory nature." This is an a priori review of legality. Once the minister has signed the draft decree, she sends it to the Council, which examines whether all mandatory decision-making procedures have been followed correctly, whether the decree falls within the limits of the statutory delegation and conforms to the Constitution and other laws. Furthermore, the Council reviews the quality of the drafting and may also offer advice on substantive issues and the "expediency" of the draft decree.[26] In practice, this advisory role of the Council is very important because the administration almost always follows the Council's recommendations.[27] In fact, it has been noted that because of its high technical standards the Council of State has won a reputation as a "tough guardian of legality;" consequently, some ministers have "opted to prepare a legislative amendment or ministerial decision" so as to avoid the rigorous a priori scrutiny under Article 95(1)(d) of the Constitution.[28]

The central function of the Council of State is that of Supreme Administrative Court. Pursuant to Article 95(1)(a) of the Constitution, the Council is in principle responsible for deciding on petitions for annulment of enforceable administrative acts (*aitisi akyroseos*)—these cases are called "annulment disputes" (*akyrotikes diafores*). Certain annulment disputes may be transferred to ordinary administrative courts depending on their nature or importance, under Article 95(3) of the Constitution. On the contrary, it is the ordinary administrative courts (administrative courts of first instance and administrative courts of appeal) that have the original competence to rule on the so-called "substantive disputes" (*diafores ousias*) by exercising full jurisdiction.[29] Examples of "substantive disputes" include notably taxation and social security cases. Last, the Council of State may also hear "substantive disputes" by virtue of either an express constitutional provision or a statute issued on constitutional authorization

[Article 95(1)(c)].[30] The distinction between annulment and substantive disputes has important implications for the scope of review and available remedies. Annulment disputes entail a narrower scope of review, limited, in principle, to the legality of the administrative act and not the factual circumstances of the case. The only available remedy is the annulment of the act (or omission) that is challenged before the court. By contrast, in substantive disputes the judge may go deeper in examining the existence of a right and establishing the prejudice or damage that the applicant has suffered as a result of administrative action. Moreover, judicial redress may take the form of both annulment but also amendment of the administrative act in question.

I will return to this distinction—particularly, the scope of review—in the next Part and in Part III.D.4. The broader point that this section seeks to underscore, however, is the presumption of reviewability under Article 95(1)(a) of the Constitution. In other words, the jurisdiction of the Council of State to review administrative acts in annulment proceedings is determined as the default rule at the highest level; exceptions are permitted only to the extent allowed by constitutional provisions. Therefore, a legislative provision that abrogates or restricts the jurisdiction of the Council of State is unconstitutional.[31] Together with the constitutional protection of the right of access to courts under Article 20(1) of the Constitution,[32] these provisions constitute the judicial reflection of the principles of administrative legality and the rule of law.

II. The inadequacy of the traditional forms of public accountability and the need for a new participatory model

A. The inefficiency of the conventional modes of accountability

Chapter 1 addressed the deficiencies of the conventional mode of democratic accountability more broadly. With respect to Greece in particular, developments over the past three decades further highlight the limitations of the traditional modes of accountability discussed in Part I.

First, the Third Hellenic Republic has seen a continuous strengthening of the executive since the Constitution of 1975. The internal structure of political parties marked by strong party discipline in conjunction with the so-called "reinforced PR" electoral system, which allocated supplementary seats only to the largest parties, led to strong parliamentary majorities and durable single-party cabinets.[33] The constitutional revision of 1986 removed powers from the President of the Republic, thus reinforcing the concentration of executive power in the cabinet, and especially the Prime Minister.[34] These developments challenge the supremacy of the statute and the position of Parliament as the uncontested site of democratic accountability: the PM-centered parliamentary system means that the government, relying on a strong, unified majority in Parliament, could easily translate its political choices into law.[35] The historical pattern of a single party controlling both Parliament and the executive was recently disrupted; political and party fragmentation and a strongly divided electorate did not produce a single-party majority in the elections of June 2012, January 2015, and September 2015. The fragmented Parliament, which no longer rubberstamped quickly and easily the government's choices, may account for a problematic practice: the last three coalition governments (similarly to the two previous administrations facing less sympathetic Parliaments) resorted increasingly to the exercise of autonomous rulemaking power under Article 44(1) of the Constitution discussed in Part I.A. It was not always clear that this practice met the high constitutional threshold of "extraordinary circumstances of an urgent and unforeseeable need," which points to an attempt to bypass detailed parliamentary scrutiny. This phenomenon further exemplifies my broader claim that the traditional methods of accountability cannot always confront adequately the legitimation challenges stemming from an expanding executive power.

Second and relatedly, statutory delegation is still prominent.[36] Despite the institutionalization of delegation rules in the Constitution, the application of these rules is not as narrow as a strict textual reading might suggest. According to the case law, the statutory authorization has to be concrete, in the sense of containing the general principles and directions that will govern the regulation of the relevant topics. The latter, however, do not have to be expressly cited in the authorizing statute; it suffices that they can be deduced from the whole of the statutory provisions or from the existing relevant legislation.[37] Indeed, as has been correctly observed, parliamentary majorities have repeatedly given governments "much discretion in using their decree power."[38] Similarly, the modern meaning of the principle of legality has expanded as most of the times the administration is accorded discretion and is bound only as to the fulfillment of a goal that is itself mentioned in the statute in broad terms.[39]

Third, judicial review, albeit important, must be viewed in its proper context. Annulment review before the Council of State remains the norm even though the number of substantive disputes, and the jurisdiction of ordinary courts, has increased significantly since 1975.[40] This default review in annulment, however, is more restricted compared to full jurisdiction review. More specifically, the Constitution and presidential decree 18/1989 set out the following express, narrow grounds for annulment:[41]

a. lack of power of the administrative authority that has issued the act under review;
b. infringement of procedural law ("procedural ultra vires");

c. infringement of substantive law: Importantly, the administrative agency's *evaluation* of facts is not subject to review except in the case of review of flagrant "abuse of discretion." This form of judicial scrutiny still only covers the margins, the "extreme limits" in the exercise of discretion.[42]

d. abuse of power: This is of very limited practical importance as the applicant is required to prove that the administrative authority intentionally pursued an aim different from that laid down in the empowering statute. Furthermore, the Council of State considers this heading to be non-applicable in the specific context of regulatory acts.[43]

The literature, however, has noted a recent move toward a "substantialization" of annulment review. This entails more flexibility and broader judicial scrutiny primarily on the grounds of review of the agency's reasoning. This development—together with the increase in the number of cases transferred to ordinary administrative courts as substantive, "full jurisdiction," disputes—casts doubt on the doctrinal soundness and practical significance of the distinction between annulment and substantive cases.[44] Nonetheless, judicial review of general rules (as opposed to individual administrative acts) remains strictly within the jurisdiction of the Council of State.[45] Furthermore, the scope of review in these annulment cases is very narrow, mainly out of respect for the principle of separation of powers and the idea that "the judge may not become the lawmaker." Review of the substantive legality of a regulatory act is essentially confined to an assessment of the compliance of the act with the conditions and limits set out in the empowering statute under which it has been issued. The Council abstains from reviewing whether the challenged rule is "advisable or effective."[46] Therefore, a proper understanding of the effectiveness of conventional accountability tools should not lose sight of the limitations of judicial review, particularly with respect to policymaking.

Fourth and particularly important for our case study, the conventional accountability model does not apply aptly to independent agencies. The 1990s saw the creation of many independent authorities in the areas of protection of rights, regulation of politically sensitive issues (e.g., recruitment to the civil service and broadcasting), and economic regulation.[47] Five of them—however, not the Hellenic Telecommunications and Post Commission—are now enshrined in the Constitution ("constitutionalized independent authorities").[48] This constitutionalization means that a statute may not disband these agencies, and results in further constitutional guarantees. More specifically, Article 101A of the Greek Constitution, as inserted during the 2001 constitutional revision, provides that

1. In cases where the establishment and functioning of an independent authority is provided by the Constitution, its members shall be appointed for a fixed tenure and shall enjoy personal and functional independence, as specified by law.

2. . . . The members of the independent authorities must possess the corresponding qualifications, as specified by law. Their selection is made by decision of the Conference of Parliamentary Chairmen seeking unanimity or in any case by the increased majority of four fifths of its members. Matters relating to the selection procedure are specified by the Standing Orders of Parliament.

Law 3051/2002, which was passed to implement this constitutional provision further specifies the guarantees of personal and functional independence of agency members. Article 2 provides that independent agencies are not subject to internal hierarchical review or supervision by any organs of the executive branch. This 2002 statute applies only to the "constitutionalized independent authorities." Nevertheless, the literature has correctly noted that subjecting independent agencies to hierarchical administrative review would undermine the effort to place them outside the central administration.[49] This lack of internal review led to a scholarly focus on the need for parliamentary scrutiny as an important compensating mechanism of public accountability.[50]

The constitutional legislator answered this call by providing for two means of parliamentary involvement in the operation of independent authorities: at the selection stage and subsequently through parliamentary control. As to the former, the selection of the agency boards is made, as noted above, by decision of the Conference of Parliamentary Chairmen seeking unanimity or in any case by the increased majority of four fifths of its members. The Conference of Parliamentary Chairmen is a multipartisan body composed of the President and Vice Presidents of the Parliament, former Presidents of the Parliament if they are still MPs, the Chairs of Standing Committees, the Chair of the Special Permanent Committee on Institutions and Transparency, the leaders of all parliamentary groups, and a representative of independent MPs (if they are more than five). The composition of this body and the requirement of unanimity or a four-fifths majority on appointments mean that board members are usually politically neutral or, often, that the choices reflect a party balance.

Parliamentary control, on the other hand, is significantly weaker. Parliamentary censure may not lead to the dismissal of an agency member, for they enjoy constitutionally guaranteed fixed terms.[51] Furthermore, since these independent authorities lie outside the administrative hierarchy and no principal-agent model is in operation, MPs may not exercise the traditional forms of scrutiny against ministers, the agencies' would-be political principals. Therefore, in practice and under the Standing Orders of Parliament, parliamentary control translates into the obligation of the independent authorities to present an Annual Report of their activities.[52] Furthermore, standing committees may invite agency members to a hearing. These committees may also submit reports of their findings on the agency's activities to the President of the Parliament. These reports are publicized and may also include dissents; this suggests that an agency may be publicly criticized, and this process could, in fact, be politicized.[53]

Nevertheless, prior practice suggests that these parliamentary committees have not demonstrated excessive zeal in holding such hearings and issuing reports. This is an additional indication that parliamentary control is weak;[54] its main aim is that agencies inform and communicate with the legislature rather than the latter scrutinizing the former. This "gap" in the conventional forms of accountability for independent authorities becomes particularly salient in the case of strong regulatory agencies. As will become apparent in Part III, EETT is one of these agencies. Indeed, the Greek telecoms regulator has been described as the strongest and most "productive" agency in terms of regulatory decision making.[55] Interestingly, EETT's legal adviser noted in a speech that EETT's extensive regulatory competencies differentiate it from other independent authorities and make it necessary that the agency respect the "criteria of good regulation."[56]

In conclusion, all the above developments underscore the expansion of the Greek administrative state—notably the rise of independent regulatory agencies. They also reveal the inadequacy of the traditional institutional and procedural set-up, and call for the emergence of a new model of administrative accountability.[57] Part III will argue that EU law introduced and institutionalized such new regulatory processes, which enhanced the democratic accountability of regulatory agency operations in the telecommunications sector. To assess the novelty of these participatory mandates, the challenges associated with their implementation domestically, and the extent of their transformative impact, we should first examine two other sets of issues: the structural deficiencies existing in the background of the Greek state (Section B) and the status of citizen participation in Greek administrative law prior to the advent of EU law (Section C).

B. The structural deficiencies of the Greek state

Long-term patterns in what I termed the "background conditions of the Greek state" have been described to include: "patronage in the recruitment to the civil service, centralizing tendencies in state organization, and the heavy presence of the state in the economy. These are indications of a historical trajectory of state-society relations."[58] This section explores these ideas around two axes: weak state (1) and weak civil society (2).

1. A weak state

The problem has been succinctly described as follows: The Greek public administration "has taken on the appearance of a *quasi*-Weberian bureaucracy."[59]

The historical development of the Greek state may account for the administration's structural deficiencies. After the end of World War II and the Greek
civil war (1946–1949), Greece underwent a period of significant growth. This
development, however, was linked with the emergence of a "ubiquitous, over-
interventionist, over-regulating, paternalistic and protectionist state."[60] George
Pagoulatos has described post-war Greece as a "developmental state," characterized by a "state-driven policy pattern" corresponding to a protected market.[61]
The strong interest of successive governments in undertaking a wide range of
economic activities—which included, importantly for present purposes, service provision—reinforced the state's centralizing tendencies and resulted in an
overgrown and sluggish public sector.[62]

Indeed, a gigantic state did not mean an administratively effective state. This
idea was captured in the picture of the Greek state as "a Colossus with feet of
clay." Dimitri Sotiropoulos has further explained that the historical development
of the state and civil society in Greece in conjunction with the polarizing electoral system favoring majoritarian party governments resulted in an "imbalance
of organizational strength" between the political parties and the state in favor of
the former. This, in turn, meant that the two major parties alternating in power
succeeded in "bending the state to their own needs."[63] Another scholar similarly
identified a trend towards "bureaucratic clientelism," a distinct form of clientelism consisting of systematic infiltration of the state machine by party devotees
and the allocation of favors through it.[64] A related facet of this overgrowth and
the concomitant window for corruption is the excessive legalism and formalism
characterizing the Greek system. In the Greek case, formalism did not necessarily mean standardization, formalization, predictability, and stability.[65] Quite
the contrary. The plethora of laws led to a "vast and inflexible legal framework,"
which provoked the "rise of informal arrangements and corrupt practices," thus
resulting in selective enforcement and circumvention of formal rules.[66]

The above structural challenges were exacerbated by an organizational feature
that further distinguishes Greece from France: Greece lacked a strong, well-trained
bureaucracy, an administrative elite.[67] As a consequence of clientelism at the top,
"waves of civil servants" were hired on non-meritocratic criteria. Furthermore,
they lacked strong historical traditions of their own and an *esprit de corps*.[68]
Different governments have made some efforts to remedy this problem. An independent authority, the Supreme Council for Civil Personnel Selection (ASEP), was
established in 1994 to monitor the neutrality, transparency, and meritocracy of
the process of civil service appointments.[69] Even though political support for this
institution has not always been universal and party officials, especially at the local
level, have often tried (and managed) to find loopholes and circumvent the formal
appointment procedures in the past, ASEP has seen its jurisdiction expand over
the past years and was incorporated into the Constitution in 2001.

Moreover, a 1983 statute created the National Center of Public Administration and entrusted it with two main missions: produce highly-skilled civil service officials though pre-entry training in the National School of Public Administration and Local Government (ESDDA); and provide in-service training for civil servants.[70] The rationale underlying the establishment of the National School of Public Administration was similar to that for the French ENA. Nonetheless, the actual importance of the ESDDA in Greece has been nowhere near close to the prominence that ENA and its graduates enjoy in France and their impact on that country's institutional life. In fact, as Spanou and Sotiropoulos explain, the effort to produce the top cadres of the civil service through the ESDDA has run against resistance from within the civil service. The National Center of Public Administration has been more successful in meeting its second objective of training output.[71] Nevertheless, improvements of this type do not suffice to address the deeper structural problems of the Greek state. These problems of state inefficiency are evident, for example, in Greece's poor record in the transposition of the EU's single market rules and the high rate of infringement proceedings brought against it.[72] As Part III will show, these implementation challenges were reflected in the telecommunications sector as well.

2. A weak civil society

The "hegemonic position of the Greek state left little room for the development of an articulate civil society."[73] The culture of "bureaucratic clientelism" meant that the governing party acted "as a collective patron to its active supporters who [became] the clients of the state bureaucracy" thus hindering the emergence of strong, independent civil society actors.[74] As this idea has been described more starkly, state-economy relations were marked by "an incestuous and sometimes corrupt relationship with respect to the allocation of favors and contracts."[75]

More specifically, post-dictatorship state-society relations in Greece, particularly in the 1980s, were described as befitting "some form of state corporatism" with the government manipulating or co-opting professional associations.[76] George Pagoulatos has contested the state corporatist argument noting that it "overstates the degree of state control over organized interests and the possibility of state-imposed concertation, and underestimates the fragmented and often rent-seeking character of interest mobilization." Instead, he describes these state-society relations as a "sui generis case of parentela pluralism," whereby certain (usually sub-sectoral) groups pursue access to state resources through their attachment to the politically dominant party.[77] A third account has termed the Greek patterns of interest intermediation and policymaking as a case of "'disjointed corporatism' whose fragmented functioning bears the marks of the asymmetric statist–corporatist past."[78]

Even in the absence of scholarly agreement on a specific label, state-society relations as depicted in all the above accounts demonstrate the point of a weak civil society. Parties "colonized" interest groups, especially labor unions[79] that were prone to extensive internal political factionalization; this was particularly strong within the trade union confederation (GSEE).[80] On the contrary, Greek business has been described to present "a striking organisational and strategic contrast to Greek labour: it retained much of its organisational autonomy from the state and developed considerable capabilities vis-à-vis political institutions."[81] Nevertheless, this is not to say that the industry, albeit less party-dominated, has been immune to the corrosive effect of financial ties with the Greek state.[82]

In light of the grim accounts of the role and independence of Greek civil society,[83] it is no surprise that interest groups have historically been considered to be particularistic and "largely disruptive factors."[84] However, the argument has been made that a more positive approach is slowly developing[85] as "a more mature Greek democracy has been gradually allowing market forces to play a greater role in the economy while favouring more open participation of civil society in the policymaking process."[86] Importantly for our purposes, the EU has been described as a strong force in support of Greek civil society: "the Europeanization process has encouraged in several ways (institutional, financial, etc.) the formation of an increasing number of social associations, especially non-governmental organizations (NGOs)."[87] This chapter's case study offers an opportunity to test this Europeanization claim. As Part III will show, EU mandates empowered new actors, yet the form and numbers of participation reflect embedded features of the weak Greek civil society.

C. The unmet need for an alternative participatory model of democratic accountability

These structural challenges in the background conditions of the administrative state underscore the difficulty of administrative reforms aiming at enhancing democratic accountability. At the same time, they bring to the fore the importance of precisely this type of reforms. Throughout the 20th century, however, this call had mostly gone unanswered.

Greek law provides for the participation of individuals in administrative decision-making only in the form of the right to a prior hearing before adverse administrative action is taken against a specific individual or firm. Indeed, the right of defense against individualized acts, originally developed in the jurisprudence of the Council of State as a general principle, is now enshrined in the Constitution and codified in the Administrative Procedure Code (APC) of 1999 (Law 2690/1999).[88] Nevertheless, the APC included no provisions on public participation in rulemaking. The courts refused to step in and fill the gap.[89]

This is not to say that the Third Republic did not provide for any forms of civil society involvement in policymaking. With respect to labor relations in particular, beginning in the 1980s, reforms have strengthened syndicate participation in national policymaking.[90] These institutional changes culminated in Law 1876/1990 on free collective bargaining that consolidated the roles of both the trade union (GSEE) and the industry (SEV) confederations.[91] This gave effect to Article 22(2) of the Constitution which stipulates that "general working conditions shall be determined by law, supplemented by collective labor agreements concluded through free negotiations and, in case of the failure of such, by rules determined by arbitration." Interestingly, Law 1876/1990 provided that these private agreements of these stakeholders could become generally binding, i.e., sources of law, if sanctioned by a ministerial decision. However, this form of public participation has been curtailed recently; it is also more in a corporatist vein, which, as chapter 1 discussed in more detail, does not meet the criteria of the deliberative-participatory model. Relatedly, an assessment of this type of stakeholder involvement should take into account the low unionization rates in Greece.[92]

Moreover, social dialogue occurs through a formal consultative mechanism, the Economic and Social Committee (ESC). The ESC was formed in 1994 (Law 2232/1994) to represent interest groups in Greece: employers and businessmen as one group; employees and civil servants as another; and citizens, local authorities, and independent professions as the third.[93] The 2001 constitutional revision offered formal recognition to this body in Article 82(3). The ESC issues opinions primarily on laws relating to "labor relations, social security, taxation measures, as well as socio-economic policy in general" on its own initiative or at the request of the competent minister.[94] Nevertheless, despite the argument that consulting the ESC on the most important bills should be a minimum requirement,[95] this body has no enforcement powers. As a result, ministers choose when they want to consult the ESC and if they wish to accept its opinion.[96] The head of a major consumer group with experience of participation in the ESC's work explained in an interview[97] certain reasons for ESC's limited role even though MPs acknowledge that the Committee's opinions are generally well substantiated. First, the ESC often does not deliver unanimous opinions; this lack of consensus reduces its influence. Second, its public visibility has increased only recently. Third, consumers, a group of particular interest for our case study, constitute only 1/60 of the interests represented. In any event, the membership of the ESC is predetermined and even though it does try to represent a broad array of actors (albeit in a rather disproportionate manner), it does not employ open participatory practices.

By contrast, specific statutes provided for limited forms of public participation that were generally open to the public. As early as 1923, a legislative text provided that a town plan should, before its approval, be exhibited in the town hall for 15 days and the public informed of this by general notice by the mayor. Interested parties could then submit written objections to the municipality, and these were forwarded to the authority in charge of issuing the town plan. This 1923 legislation has been described as pioneering since it established a form of public participation almost a century ago.[98] Law 947/1979 sought to remedy some of the deficiencies of the original process by means of requirements for further publicity and longer time periods for these participatory processes. Furthermore, Law 1337/1983 reflected a stronger effort to bolster citizen engagement by providing for additional participatory mechanisms, such as open meetings, as well as publicity through the press. Citizens were now empowered to submit not only "objections" (as had been the case under the 1923 regime) but also comments and opinions. Thus, they could contribute to the drafting of the general urban plan in a positive, substantive fashion. A similar public consultation requirement (without the use of the term itself) has been included in the environmental sector. Law 1650/1986 (as amended by Law 3010/2002) gives citizens the opportunity to submit comments on the environmental impact assessments accompanying projects that may affect the environment.

The above examples of direct public consultation are important but serve primarily as an exception that highlights the rule. These binding requirements for public participation were mostly limited to the local level (urban planning and environmental projects of particular concern to local communities) and did not cover policymaking at the national level. By contrast, mechanisms for nationwide consultation were left largely to the discretion of individual ministers or senior officials.[99] On several occasions, ad hoc or standing consultative committees[100] were established within ministries but these were not open to the public. More open forms of public participation were rare and highly discretionary. Consequently, at the turn of the 21st century, the Organisation for Economic Co-operation and Development (OECD) publicly highlighted the need for a notice-and-comment process.[101]

Part III demonstrates that Greece eventually introduced a formal notice-and-comment process. Nevertheless, it did so in a specific case, the electronic communications sector, and in response to EU pressures. The transformative effect of these EU mandates becomes more salient when considered against the historical and institutional backdrop that Parts I and II have set up. Furthermore, Part IV discusses whether the use of public consultation processes in the telecommunications area may have paved the way for the generalization of such accountability tools across the administration.

III. The emergence of participatory processes in telecommunications regulation: The Hellenic Telecommunications and Post Commission (EETT)

A. The rocky path to the liberalization of telecommunications in Greece

The road to the full liberalization of the electronic communications sector was not uncomplicated. Telecommunications was quickly described as a public service and organized as a unit directly connected with the ministry.[102] The Greek Telecommunications Organization (OTE) was then founded in 1949 as a "public enterprise" and given exclusive rights for the operation of telecommunication services. In other words, the strongly embedded notion of public service was originally equated with public monopoly and state ownership in public utilities. The jurisprudence of the Council of State subsequently transformed this understanding into a constitutional requirement for state supervision over the provision of these services.[103] This attachment to public service did not ultimately pose a constitutional obstacle to liberalization and privatization. Nonetheless, together with the weak administrative capacity of the Greek state described in Part II, it helps to explain Greece's slow and occasionally deficient adaptation to EU requirements.[104]

Indeed, as noted earlier, Greece was the last member state to liberalize its telecommunications market. Until 1992, all telecommunications services were supplied by OTE. In 1992 Greece began services in the cellular telephony market through licenses to two private operators, Panafon and Telestet. In December 1995, a third mobile license was awarded to OTE that was transferred to its subsidiary, Cosmote, in April 1997. Internet provision services, electronic data interchange services, and other value added networks had been liberalized since 1994, but restrictions of access to OTE leased lines for providing the liberalized services were only lifted in 1996 and the incumbent delayed access of other operators until 1998.[105] Complete liberalization of the market, and in particular termination of the OTE monopoly on voice telephony, only took effect on January 1, 2001.

More specifically, in June 1996, the Greek state (at that point the majority shareholder of OTE) and OTE itself applied for a five-year extension of the EU's January 1, 1998, deadline for full liberalization. The request was made on the grounds that OTE needed further time and revenues for the digitalization and modernization of its public network infrastructure. The European

Commission, in rejecting most of the arguments used by the government to justify a derogation, granted Greece an extension until December 31, 2000, to remove all restrictions on the provision of voice telephony and the underlying public network infrastructure. The Commission agreed to this derogation solely on the basis of one justification, that is, to allow OTE sufficient time to rebalance its tariffs.[106] The wisdom of this derogation was questioned.[107] However, it is an illustrating example of the challenges associated with an overgrown and interventionist, yet weak, state that Part II.B.1. identified: Greece was not fully prepared to accommodate swiftly structural market reforms that ran counter to the long-standing tradition of monopoly provision of telecommunications services.

This factor accounts not only for the pace of adjustment to EU requirements but also, relatedly, for deficiencies in this adjustment process. This was demonstrated, for example, in the infringement proceedings that the European Commission initiated in 1999 against Greece for failure to comply with Directive 96/2/EC on mobile and personal communications. In a 2001 judgment, the European Court of Justice (ECJ) found that Greece had indeed failed to fulfill its EU obligations fully.[108] Implementation challenges continued into the 21st century even after the full liberalization of the sector. In a series of cases, the ECJ found that Greece had infringed its EU obligations due to its failure to transpose the 2002 electronic communications regulatory package.[109] Greece ultimately met its commitments under the second-generation directives by means of Law 3431/2006. Finally, a more recent statute (Law 4070/2012) incorporated the third-generation directives into the Greek legal order.

Furthermore, EU law had an indirect yet consequential effect on privatization initiatives. As was noted in chapter 2, EU law mandated the gradual liberalization of the telecommunications sector but neither spoke to nor questioned the ownership of the public telecommunications operators. Instead, privatization emerged "as a logical corollary of competition-driven sectoral and structural liberalisation in the EU." As new firms entered the market, the incumbent felt the competitive pressure to adapt to private sector standards and raise capital to modernize its infrastructure.[110] The privatization efforts in the telecommunications sector were part of a broader momentum that had begun in the 1990s under indirect EU pressures. Since 1994, Greece had adopted a series of convergence programs to meet the criteria for admission to the European Monetary Union (EMU).[111] The privatization initiatives were inscribed in these programs to reduce the public deficit and debt, although OTE itself was one of the most successful public enterprises.[112] Therefore, those identifying themselves as pro-EU "modernizers" supported the privatization agenda in addition to the liberalization agenda directly mandated by the EU; in the relevant political discourse, "the two agendas became largely synonymous."[113] The first phase of OTE's privatization began in 1996 and continued over the next fifteen years.

B. The creation of an independent telecommunications regulator

The regulatory agency for the sector was originally set up by Law 2075/1992 under the name Hellenic Telecommunications Committee (EET) to supervise the transition to competition; it began its operation in the summer of 1995. After the enactment of Law 2668/1998 on the organization and operation of the postal services sector, EET was also entrusted with responsibility for this domain, and was renamed the Hellenic Telecommunications and Post Commission (EETT). Law 2867/2000 enhanced the EETT's supervisory, monitoring, and regulatory roles, as did Law 3431/2006[114] and Law 4070/2012, which is currently in effect.

Article 6 of Law 4070/2012 expressly states that EETT is the National Regulatory Authority on matters of network supply and electronic communications services, and that it is an independent administrative authority. We can assess the validity of this description around three axes: appointments of the agency's board members, the financial and administrative autonomy of the agency, and its relationship with the political branches. As to the first of these independence prongs, EETT is run by a board of nine members: the President, two Vice Presidents (in charge of electronic communications and postal services, respectively), and six other members. According to the governing statute, they are "persons of established prestige" with scientific expertise and "wide societal acceptance." Board members serve four-year staggered terms, and they can be reappointed only once.

The selection process has gone through a series of amendments over the past several years. Pursuant to Article 3(3) of Law 2867/2000, EETT's board members were designated by the Conference of Parliamentary Chairmen and formally appointed by the Minister of Transports and Communications. As noted in Part II.A., the Conference of Parliamentary Chairmen is the multipartisan body involved in the selection of members of the constitutionalized independent authorities with the aim of safeguarding the members' political neutrality. Nevertheless, Article 72(1) of Law 3371/2005 amended that provision and stipulated that the President and two Vice Presidents would be selected and appointed by the cabinet following a recommendation by the Minister of Infrastructure, Transports and Networks and consultation with the Parliamentary Committee on Institutions and Transparency. The remaining six members of the board would be appointed by the Minister. These changes were correctly criticized in the literature as compromising the institutional independence of the regulator.[115] Indeed, under the 2005 statute, the majority of the Board was directly selected by the Minister, which could leave room for political appointments. The special procedure for the appointment of President and Vice Presidents did add an element of transparency as the hearings before the Parliamentary Committee on Institutions and Transparency were public and gave MPs the opportunity to vet the candidates briefly. However, the fact that the minister was present in the hearings and proposing a candidate to a committee with a majority of MPs of her own party did not preclude the potential politicization of the process.

Even though these 2005 procedural changes did not lead to stark differences in the types of appointments made in practice, recent reforms reintroduced the previous model of appointments. Article 6(1) of Law 4070/2012 stipulates that all board members are selected by the Conference of Parliamentary Chairmen subsequent to a recommendation by the Parliamentary Committee on Institutions and Transparency. The involvement of both the Parliamentary Committee on Institutions and Transparency and the Conference of Parliamentary Chairmen seems more consistent with the spirit of the 2009 EU Directives, which strengthened, as chapter 2 described, the political independence of NRAs. Furthermore, this model of appointments mirrors Article 101A of the Greek Constitution on the appointment of members of the constitutionalized independent authorities. Considering that EETT enjoys wide powers and its decisions have important implications for the national economy and the citizens' everyday life, it is appropriate that the guarantees it enjoys in terms of appointments are akin to those for the agencies enshrined in the Constitution.

As to the second prong of independence identified above, Article 6(2) of Law 4070/2012 states that EETT enjoys full financial and administrative autonomy.[116] By contrast, under Law 2246/1994, the Minister of Finance and the Minister of Transports and Communications were given the authority to decide on the way EETT administered its financial resources.[117] Relatedly, before 2001, EETT had been severely understaffed. Almost all experienced staff had been seconded from OTE and eventually recalled to that company. Due to personnel shortages, external experts and advisors often assisted EETT in its duties. The fact that EETT was severely understaffed resulted in slow decision-making in certain areas, such as dispute resolutions and licensing. Importantly, the use of OTE personnel by EETT did not serve to enhance the reputation of the agency's independence among market participants.[118] These problems reflected the weak administrative capacity that permeated the whole administration as described in Part II.B.1. However, these deficiencies became particularly acute in this example because of the highly technical and complex decisions required for the regulation and monitoring of the new liberalized telecommunications environment. This problem has been remedied under the last two governing statutes.[119]

The last piece of agency independence pertains to EETT's relationship with the other branches of government. Article 6(2) of Law 4070/2012, like Laws 2867/2000 and 3431/2006 before it, states that EETT's members "enjoy full personal and operational independence in exercising their duties." Pursuant to the same provision, EETT is not subject to hierarchical control from the ministry or any other institution in the exercise of its duties. This stands in clear contrast with Law 2246/1994 which had given the Minister of Transport and

Communications the power to exercise "suppressive legality review"[120] thus restricting EETT's decisional independence. Moreover, under that same 1994 law, the Minister and EETT nominally shared regulatory tasks for the sector; however, in essence EETT had insufficient powers and was reduced to an advisory body.[121] In its December 1999 report on Greece's progress on the Implementation of the Telecommunications Regulatory Package, the European Commission had remarked that the boundaries between EETT's powers and those of the ministry had not always been clearly defined and called the ministry to address issues of division of power through a new framework law.[122] As was previously noted, Law 2867/2000 addressed these concerns and reinforced EETT's position by providing for the full personal and operational independence of its members. Law 4070/2012 currently in force moves further in this direction.

Furthermore, according to Article 6(2) of Law 4070/2012, EETT must submit an annual report of its activities to the Minister of Infrastructure, Transports and Networks as well as to the President of Parliament. Members of EETT are also invited to parliamentary hearings; this offers the agency an additional opportunity to inform Parliament about its activities. However, as Part II.A. explained in the case of independent administrative authorities more broadly, these forms of parliamentary supervision are loose, have primarily an informational goal, and cannot threaten the independence of the agency. Last, Article 78 of Law 4070/2012 provides for various forms of judicial review of EETT's decisions depending on the type of decision. Section D.4. will examine these questions in further detail.

The increased guarantees of independence came together with a gradual increase in the powers of the regulator. Under its current statute, EETT has 45 sets of competences, the broader array of powers in its history. These range from market analysis to the management of radiofrequencies, numbering, domain names, electronic signature, codes of practices, etc. Importantly, EETT may "issue regulatory or individual administrative acts to regulate any matter in relation to its powers" (Article 12(ma) of Law 4070/2012). This broad rulemaking power in conjunction with the wide range of specific competences enables the regulator to intervene in the sector with relative flexibility in terms of regulatory tools.[123] At the same time, these extensive powers highlight the importance of expertise and democratic accountability in the agency operations. As the following section demonstrates, the latter requirements only gained salience under the 2006 governing statute.

C. The timid rise of public consultation

The challenges facing the regulator in light of the longstanding tradition of state monopoly and the technical complexity of regulation in this sector were considerable. In the efforts to build up administrative capacity and create an expert

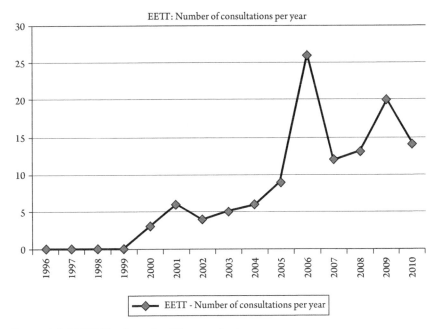

Figure 4.1 EETT: Number of public consultations per year

Source: Own elaboration with data from the website of the EETT and archival research

regulator that could monitor the liberalization initiatives effectively, democratic accountability was not at the top of the domestic regulatory agenda.[124]

Indeed, Laws 2246/1994 and 2867/2000 contained no general provisions on public consultation. More specifically, before 2006 the only provisions mandating public consultation covered two specific topics: the allocation of special licenses for frequencies and the regulation of roaming contracts between mobile operators. My research, however, has not shown any instances in which these particular provisions were applied. As Figure 4.1 shows, EETT had launched public consultations prior to the formal adoption of the 2002 regulatory package at the EU level. The peak, however, both in the number of public consultations and the comments submitted [Figure 4.2], came in 2006 with the formal, and delayed, transposition of the EU requirements by virtue of Law 3431/2006. Article 17 of Law 3431/2006 transposed the wording of Article 6 of the 2002 Framework Directive. More specifically, the text of the 2006 statute read:

1. Except in cases falling within Article 16(5) and Articles 18 and 19, EETT may proceed to consultation when it deems necessary, on the request of the Minister of Transports and Communications, and in any event before it takes measures that have a significant impact on the relevant market in

application of this law. It shall give interested parties the opportunity to submit comments on the draft measure within a reasonable period of time.

2. EETT carries out this public consultation following the process that it determines by a decision. EETT shall, for this purpose, issue within a month a Regulation that will determine all the details regarding public consultations, deadlines, forms of publication, the collection and analysis of responses, record keeping, and every other relevant detail.

3. EETT shall keep a single information point listing all consultations, their results and EETT's conclusions from the consultations except in the case of confidential information in accordance with Community and nationallaw.

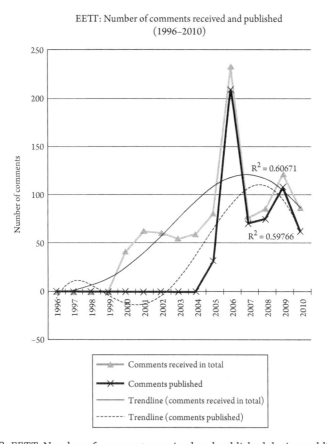

Figure 4.2 EETT: Number of comments received and published during public consultations in the telecommunications sector (1996–2010)

Source: Own elaboration with data from the website of the EETT and archival research

The only aspect that the domestic legislation added to the transposition of the EU mandate was the possibility of EETT to launch public consultations proprio motu or when so requested by the Minister, in other words, even in the absence of an EU obligation to do so. Article 17 of Law 4070/2012 did not amend the requirement for public consultations under the 2006 statute.

An interview with EETT's legal adviser indicated that, even before the formal adoption of the EU public consultation mandates in 2006, the agency had been aware of the Commission's proposals and the forthcoming introduction of the new participatory requirements.[125] Nevertheless, since EETT was not yet bound by EU law, the decision to resort to public consultations was highly discretionary and infrequent. In 2001, the Undersecretary of Transports and Communications issued a decision on public consultations.[126] This document reiterated that the Minister and EETT had the discretionary power to launch a public consultation. Moreover, the same ministerial decision stipulated that all stakeholder submissions would be strictly confidential. As Figure 4.2 demonstrates, EETT complied with this direction: the comments received during the public consultations launched prior to the 2006 statute were for the most part not published.

Another interesting, and original compared to the other two country cases, feature of EETT's consultation practices during those first years was that the Greek regulator outsourced the first four public consultations in 2000–2001 to teams from the National Technical University of Athens.[127] However, this should not come as a particular surprise, as it reflects again the broader pattern of weak administrative capacity described in Part II.B.1. Besides, as noted in Section B, due to personnel shortages, external experts often assisted EETT in other duties as well. The problem of understaffing was dealt with after 2001, and particularly under the 2006 and 2012 statutes. Consequently, EETT acquired the in-house capacity to carry out public consultations and assess their outcomes.

Indeed, in implementation of Article 17(2) of Law 3431/2006, EETT issued the Regulation of Public Consultations in 2006.[128] This Regulation sets the duration of the public consultation to 30 days in principle, with a possibility for the agency to opt for a shorter or longer time period. Several public consultations have lasted for two months. After the public consultation has begun, the authority may also organize an open meeting to present the subject of this exercise [Article 6(2)]. At the end of the process, EETT publishes on its website the comments submitted; within 60 days, the agency must also publish the "results" of the consultation and its own "conclusions" (Article 10). The extent to which EETT follows its own guidelines as well as the four prongs of the deliberative-participatory model is examined in the following section.

D. Evaluating EETT's regulatory processes against the fundamental operative elements of the deliberative-participatory model

1. Open Access

EETT's public consultations are expressly open to all "interested parties."[129] In this sense, the Greek regulator meets the requirement of open access under the deliberative-participatory model. As in the other case studies, however, the question is how this textual provision translated into practice. Figure 4.3 provides an answer regarding the type of actors that participated in public consultations over a recent five-year period.

The figures are striking and unlike those we see in the other country cases. Responses came overwhelmingly from the industry (91%). Participation on the part of NGOs and individuals amounted to a meager 3% and 2%, respectively. EETT seems to be aware of this discrepancy, and has taken measures that

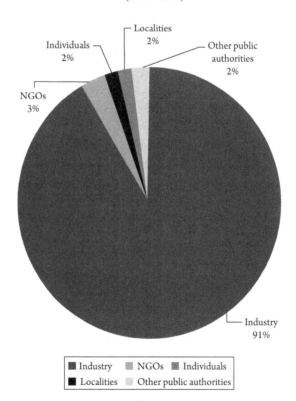

EETT: Type of actors responding to consultations
(2006–2010)

Figure 4.3 EETT: Type of actors responding to consultations (2006–2010)

Source: Own elaboration with data from the website of EETT

could be viewed as attempts to remedy this imbalance. For instance, the 2007, 2008, 2009, and 2010 Annual Reports included a specific chapter regarding consumers and how they benefited from EETT's activities during those years.[130] Moreover, in January 2009, EETT established the Consumer Service Sector for Telecommunication Services (CSSTS). The CSSTS is a special team for assessing the complaints filed by telecommunications consumers and detecting issues that demand the mobilization of its auditing mechanism. Nonetheless, this initiative was not concerned with public consultations per se even though it did try to engage consumers more.

Furthermore, in the framework of resolving requests and complaints by consumers, in 2008 EETT organized a series of meetings with consumer organizations as well as with public organizations such as the General Secretariat for the Consumer and the Consumer Ombudsman. The aim of these meetings was to inform these organizations of a series of issues, such as the way complaints were handled by EETT and the official procedure to follow when filing a complaint; the jurisdiction of EETT over consumer issues; the leaflets and the regulatory documents that EETT had issued (for example the "Guide for the Informed Consumer" and the "Code of Practice for Electronic Communications"); and the publication of comparative tables with the quality indicators of electronic communications services.[131] Useful as these informational meetings may have been, they did not amount to active participation in policymaking. Moreover, I did not find evidence of related follow-on activities. In fact, major consumer groups that had participated in EETT's public consultations in the past expressed dissatisfaction with the level of their current involvement in the agency's activities.[132]

This is not to say that consumer groups have never had an impact on policymaking outcomes. For example, after a public consultation on a "Code of Practice in the provision of electronic communications services" (April 23, 2008–May 30, 2008), EETT incorporated a few of the suggestions that the two major consumer groups had submitted. By contrast, a comment submitted by an individual citizen had no relation to the actual Code of Practice; instead, it pertained to that individual's dispute with a particular telecommunications provider and as such it did not contribute to the policymaking process.

OTE, the incumbent operator, provided an interesting response in an interview when I raised the question of imbalance in stakeholder engagement: "In principle, EETT's regulatory decisions aim at protecting consumers, especially if one takes into account the contrast with the previous monopoly regime. The agency receives complaints from individual consumers, is aware of their concerns and responds to these by proposing regulatory action. It is, therefore, natural that telecoms companies participate in public consultations to this extent because they react to decisions that predominantly affect them."[133] The claim of a pro-consumer orientation inherent in the regulation of the sector relies on an outdated, and thus flawed, benchmark—the pre-liberalization conditions. Furthermore, it is empirically uncertain in the absence of the counterfactual, namely, the effect that increased NGO participation would have on the formation of policies that the former incumbent has already described as pro-consumer. In fact, the complaints of the two major consumer groups noted earlier point to a further difficulty with OTE's position.

Instead, the problem of limited NGO and citizen involvement is more fundamental. It reflects the persistence of the historical features of a weak civil society discussed in Part II. It also offers a useful lesson: the supply of participatory processes does not necessarily guarantee that all stakeholders will avail themselves of these engagement opportunities. It may, however, helpfully turn the spotlight on structural deficiencies in crucial background conditions—in this case, on the lack of civil society capacity on the ground and the need to correct this. Part IV.A. will discuss such corrective interventions. My point here is that it is easier to make the case for such affirmative measures when it is apparent that although a participatory process is in place, its intended audience is not empowered to use it.

2. Transparency

The Council of State has declared the principle of transparent administrative action as an aspect of the rule of law.[134] This reflected earlier jurisprudence of the same court that had recognized a right of access to administrative documents.[135] Subsequently, this right was codified in Article 16 of Law 1599/1986, and currently in Article 5 of the Administrative Procedure Code. The provision currently in force provides for a broad right of access with a specific set of exceptions.[136] Furthermore, all administrative regulatory acts have to be published; otherwise they are considered non-existent.[137] By contrast, publication of individual administrative acts is only mandatory when an express legislative provision so stipulates.[138] EETT goes beyond these general publication requirements and publishes all its decisions—namely, individual acts as well—because they may have broader implications for the operation of the market.[139] The agendas of EETT board meetings are also posted on its website.

There is an RSS feed through which public consultations on proposed measures are publicized. However, the structure of the website is not always particularly helpful. The syntheses (or "results") of the public consultations are often not listed under a common thread together with the main consultation documents on the specific topic. Sometimes they are available on separate pages, which may hinder effective monitoring of particular consultations. Before 2006, syntheses would discuss the content of stakeholder responses, often in some detail, but would not disclose the names of the participants. This practice complied with the 2001 ministerial decision on public consultations discussed in Section C, but foreclosed full transparency.[140] Since 2005, the transparency of the process has increased as stakeholder submissions are generally published. However, this is still not always the case, which suggests that there is room for improvement on this prong. Nonetheless, even skeptical industry representatives who challenged the practical importance of public consultations overall (because they usually occur late in the policymaking process) recognized the transparency gains stemming from these participatory processes.[141]

3. Reason giving

Regulatory acts do not, as a rule, require reasoning unless a specific provision expressly mandates this.[142] Therefore, the publication of the agency's conclusions at the end of the public consultation process—as is required by EETT's Regulation of Public Consultations (2006)—enhances the justification of regulatory action. Nonetheless, my data suggest that this is not universal practice: syntheses were publicly available for 57% of all public consultations in the period between 2000 and 2010. This is unfortunate: both industry and NGO representatives[143] explicitly acknowledged in interviews the importance of the agency responding to, substantively[144] engaging with stakeholder submissions and publishing an overview at the conclusion of public consultations.

4. Judicial review

Interestingly, various actors from all sides of the table have endeavored to restrict the judicial enforceability of public consultation mandates. Examples from the industry include a consultation response by Wind Hellas which expressly stated that "the positions expressed herein do not legally bind Wind." In a similar vein, Telebox's submission in another consultation clarified that "these views are comments on the draft on which EETT is conducting a public consultation; under no circumstances do they limit our right to challenge the legality or constitutionality of the Code [i.e., the final measure] in the future."

EETT's own Regulation of Public Consultations (2006) stipulates in Article 3(7) that "the draft of the public consultation and the submissions of interested parties do not bind EETT as to the content of the final regulation it may adopt." This is probably a self-evident statement, but it is interesting that the agency chose to highlight this as a general principle. One reason may be that this language precludes the rise of legitimate expectations as to the final policy outcome. Moreover, the express limitation of the binding nature of the consultation steps may also be intended to cabin judicial involvement in what has transpired during the public consultation process. EETT's legal adviser further explained in an interview: "We have never used the parties' submissions against them. They bind neither the stakeholders nor the agency. This is, of course, not to say that they can provide false or inaccurate data (and this has not occurred in the past anyway). We want public consultations to be an important part of regulatory decision making and not an obstacle to stakeholder engagement."[145]

On the judicial side, a major Council of State decision in 2010 ultimately resulted in confining the scope of review.[146] Some brief context is necessary to appreciate this judgment better. Prior to Law 3431/2006, EETT's acts were generally challenged directly by petition for annulment before the Council of State following the default rule described in Part I.B. Article 67 of Law 3431/2006 amended this and provided that all agency decisions were to be contested by means of petition of full jurisdiction before the Administrative Court of Appeal of Athens. This meant that the merits of the case would be duly taken into account and there would be an effective appeal mechanism, in accordance with Article 4 of the 2002 Framework Directive.[147]

The question of the constitutionality of this transfer of all cases from the Council of State to the Administrative Court of Appeal ended up before the Plenary of the Council of State. The Council held that the transfer was unconstitutional as to review of general rules. In this category of cases, the Council explained, full jurisdiction would entail an impermissible interference of the judiciary in matters for which the executive is exclusively responsible: the amendment of a regulatory act (which is one of the remedies in full jurisdiction cases) would constitute in effect an issuance of a new rule. However, pursuant to Article 43 of the Constitution, only organs of the executive branch may issue rules.[148] Consequently, in the Council's opinion, transforming these annulment disputes into full jurisdiction ones may result in courts substituting their judgments for the rulemaking authority of the executive. Moreover, with respect to review of individual acts issued by EETT, the Council held that the permissibility of full jurisdiction review would be determined on a case-by-case basis. The criteria for this assessment include the object of these acts, the preconditions for their issuance, the nature of review required to ascertain these preconditions, and the consequences of their amendment. A sizeable dissent held that the provision at stake (Article 67 of Law 3431/2006) was unconstitutional in its entirety because it did not differentiate between types of acts on the basis of these criteria.

The impermissibility of full jurisdiction review of regulatory acts had been widely accepted in the literature.[149] A line of cases following the 3919/2010 judgment of the Council of State have similarly reiterated that regulatory acts must fall under the jurisdiction of the Council as annulment disputes.[150] By contrast, other cases involving individual acts have held that administrative sanctions are properly within the jurisdiction of the Administrative Court of Appeal as substantive disputes.[151] Furthermore, the Council of State has held that the designation of operators that have "significant market power" is also permissibly subject to full jurisdiction review before the Administrative Court of Appeal.[152] Even though this series of cases helpfully clarified matters, the abstractness of the jurisdictional criteria in StE 3919/2010 contributed to the ambiguity regarding the respective jurisdictions of the Council of State and the Administrative Court of Appeal. In turn, this legal uncertainty often prompted operators to "flout legal obligations until final decisions were taken."[153]

Law 4070/2012 sought to address these issues and offer clarity by codifying the recent Council of State jurisprudence. More specifically, Article 78 provides that EETT's regulatory acts are challenged by petition for annulment before the Council of State. Decisions that impose sanctions are reviewable as full jurisdiction disputes before the Administrative Court of Appeal. Every other individual decision is challenged by petition for annulment before the Administrative Court of Appeal. This may be a welcome step toward clarification and legal certainty, which is particularly important in a crucial and fast-evolving telecommunications sector. At the same, this new provision, and the previous judgments of the Council of State, seem to roll back judicial review in a way that may raise concerns. Our starting point should be Article 4 of the Framework Directive. As a reminder, the pertinent part reads:

> Member States shall ensure that effective mechanisms exist at national level under which any user or undertaking providing electronic communications networks and/or services who is affected by a decision of a national regulatory authority has the right of appeal against the decision to an appeal body that is independent of the parties involved. *This body, which may be a court, shall have the appropriate expertise available to it to enable it to carry out its functions.* Member States shall ensure that the *merits of the case are duly taken into account* and that there is an effective appeal mechanism.

The form of review (full jurisdiction before the Administrative Court of Appeal) that Law 4070/2012 provides for administrative sanctions meets the EU requirement that the merits of the case be "duly taken into account." This is harder to argue in the case of review in annulment before either the Council of State or the Administrative Court of Appeal. One scholar has argued that annulment review does not meet the EU requirements under Article 4 of the Framework Directive.[154] I would suggest that the position is not so clear-cut. As was mentioned in Part II.A., a recent move toward "substantialization" of annulment review allows for more flexibility and broader judicial scrutiny primarily on the grounds of review of the agency's reasoning. Therefore, this form of review could still formally meet the standard that the "merits of the case are duly taken into account." In practice, this might be even more the case when annulment review occurs before the Administrative Court of Appeal that hears mostly substantive disputes and is accustomed to reviewing the merits of the cases before it.

The most perplexing case pertains to review of rulemaking. A full merits review of regulatory acts runs into constitutional obstacles that the Council of State enunciated unequivocally in its 3919/2010 judgment. It also finds little support in the literature. In one exception, George Dellis, writing before the 2010 judgment, argued that the power of the administrative judge to revise a regulatory act in full jurisdiction cases might indeed lead to impermissible judicial rulemaking. Nonetheless, a limited review of legality in annulment cases seems inadequate. Instead, Dellis proposed a "limited substantive review." This form of review is similar to review in annulment in that the judge may not substitute her own substantive judgment for that of the administration. At the same time, it has substantive content as it allows the judge to review with evidence both the factual basis of the contested act and its efficiency. From this standpoint, Dellis was sympathetic to the judicial review provisions of Law 3431/2006.[155]

Law 3431/2006, however, is no longer good law. Yet the EU requirements under Article 4 of the Framework Directive still stand. As already noted, this does not necessarily mean that review in annulment infringes Greece's EU obligations. Nonetheless, the introduction of a mechanism of "fuller" merits review might be more consistent with the spirit of Article 4 of the Framework Directive. It would also meet the preferences of stakeholders who in interviews expressed support for in-depth judicial review that annulment proceedings cannot meet easily.[156] One relevant suggestion in the literature has been the establishment of a hybrid appellate body[157] akin to the Competition Appeal Tribunal in the United Kingdom, which will be examined in some detail in chapter 5. This specialist institution would not be able to substitute the judiciary since the Greek Constitution stipulates that the institutions exclusively empowered with providing judicial protection are the ordinary courts (Articles 87ff.). It could, however, be set up as an administrative organ whose decisions would then be appealed before the ordinary administrative courts. This institutional arrangement could alter significantly the nature of appellate review. As the UK experience suggests, it could also feed back into EETT's decision-making processes. At the same time, this additional layer of review would come with challenges of its own. These will similarly become apparent in the next chapter which discusses the operation of such a specialist regulatory court in the United Kingdom.

Where does this leave us? In the absence of a specialist appellate body and with review in annulment still being the norm, how can public consultations figure in judicial review while respecting the doctrinal framework that the Council of State has set up? As in the other two country cases, courts must review whether the Greek regulator has carried out a public consultation when this process is mandatory. This is what was called in chapter 3 the "checklist obligation" and is the bare minimum that courts should review. On the contrary, Greek courts do not routinely assess the adequacy of the consultation process.[158] In the words of EETT's legal adviser, "there have never been cases of judicial invalidation because we follow the public consultation requirements religiously."[159] This statement correctly captures the agency's commitment to launching a public consultation. Nevertheless, it should not overshadow the courts' deferential approach, albeit tacit, with respect to the adequacy of the consultation processes and the agency's compliance with its own Regulation of Public Consultations.

At any rate, reviewing public consultations in this checklist fashion potentially deprives this participatory process of its full potential. The narrow confinement of judicial review (bolstered by the restrictive choice as to judicial oversight in Law 4070/2012 discussed just above) may ultimately weaken the democratic accountability and policy effectiveness of EETT's decisions. By contrast, I would propose a more capacious reading of existing judicial standards that would accommodate and tap into the public consultation file. Proportionality analysis, which courts employ even in reviewing regulatory acts,[160] would be the primary candidate for developing this function. This test could serve as a good avenue through which to incorporate the results of the public consultation as the judge examines, for instance, whether the agency was remiss in considering (and dismissing) a less restrictive measure that a stakeholder had brought to its attention.[161]

IV. Looking to the future

A. Reform proposals for the electronic communications sector

In the process of presenting EETT's accountability practices, Part III identified weaknesses and gaps. For instance, despite the fact that EETT's Regulation of Public Consultations mandates that the agency publish its conclusions at the end of the consultation process, this happened in only 57% of the cases in the period between 2000 and 2010. In a similar vein, even though the same Regulation requires that all stakeholder submissions be publicized, EETT has not consistently complied with this obligation. In other words, the deficiencies observed are not at the level of legislative provisions but, consistently with an earlier theme discussed in Part II, in their implementation.

A way of remedying this problem would be through the more active involvement of courts in policing EETT's self-imposed accountability requirements. The latter are already included in the binding Regulation of Public Consultations (2006), so courts would only need to be less deferential on the specifics of the consultation process in addition to reviewing the "checklist obligation." Another idea to nudge EETT into full compliance with its own Regulation would be to impose an obligation to add a new section in its Annual Report presented to Parliament and the Minister of Infrastructure, Transports and Networks. This additional section would address specifically the agency's compliance with the Regulation, and therefore highlight any weaknesses that might have otherwise fallen through the cracks. Moreover, EETT might consider designating a specific staff member that would be responsible for drafting this section of the Annual Report and therefore monitor the agency's record. Chapters 5 and 6 will return to this idea when discussing the position of the "consultation champion" in the UK.

Part III.D.4. examined the role of judicial review for the proper functioning of public consultations. It further explored alternative institutional arrangements that would foster the agency's accountability practices. Last, it proposed a mechanism of building a more searching scrutiny that incorporates public consultations into current doctrine. A related aspect is the capacity of administrative courts to review highly complex regulatory decisions. According to one account, the administrative judge is currently not assisted in this job: the tool of expert testimony is rarely employed in practice, while written expert opinions are not particularly valuable.[162] Instead, Dellis's proposal is to create a permanent service of experts in the fields of competition, telecommunications and energy that would assist the special sections of the Administrative Court of Appeal with highly technical cases.[163] This proposal may not be feasible currently due to important resource constraints afflicting the judicial system. However, it does highlight the importance of the judge's tapping into the public consultation record which is already available to her and may contain a wealth of information that could help guide the judicial enterprise.

These targeted approaches could enhance the democratic accountability of EETT's operations. However, the greatest challenge identified from the very beginning of this chapter is a deeper, structural one. That is to say, the supply of participatory processes is a necessary but, as the Greek case study has shown, not sufficient condition to correct the structural pathologies noted in Part II.B. and ensure public engagement. Figure 4.3 in Part III.D.1. depicted the stark imbalance between industry and civil society involvement in regulatory decision making. Addressing this problem necessitates broader initiatives that should also aim at what Part II termed the "background conditions," and potentially include positive interventions.[164]

As a preliminary matter, it should be clarified that the weakness of the civil society in Greece is not a matter of legal rules.[165] Setting up an association is fairly easy.[166] In fact, one of the problems may be the high fragmentation of the civil society landscape; this might lead to the dilution of the voice of citizens organized in diffuse, small groups that are poorly funded. However, even larger associations—for instance, in the telecommunications case, the biggest consumer groups—face organizational and resource challenges that prevent them from effectively and consistently participating in policymaking.[167] Building civil society capacity in an environment with a long legacy of an underdeveloped third sector would require a multi-pronged approach that could, for example, include an educational component. However, the Greek state could also consider more concrete steps.

The first obvious one would be to increase state funding. Public funds are currently not the most significant part of the associations' budget—nor should they be. For instance, in the case of KEPKA, one of the biggest consumer groups for which financial data is available, in 2011 domestic funds amounted to 8.8% of its total inflows; domestic projects represented 10%; European and international projects 16%; and, importantly, membership fees 65%. In 2012, the respective percentages were: 76% from membership fees; 18.5% from domestic grants and projects; 5% from European and international projects. In other words, public subsidies represented less than 10% of the group's income; taking into account national projects and the total of funds from domestic sources, the percentage is still below 20%. This should not be considered particularly high for a country with a statist tradition. In absolute numbers, public subsidies are in the range of 11,500 euros per year for the three major consumer groups, and no more than 5,000 euros per year for smaller associations.[168] Therefore, there is room for more state support.

Several objections could be raised against this suggestion. First, there is the point of resource constraints for the government itself. Even though this is a valid concern, a small increase in state subsidies would have a small impact on the national budget (in light of the figures quoted above)[169] but a significant effect on the groups' ability to be more involved in policymaking. Besides, funds could also come from the EU in an effort to enhance domestic civil society capacity. Furthermore, the concern about preserving the associations' autonomy and independent voice in the policymaking process is not as acute in this context: this increased funding would come from the central government, while EETT is an independent agency. Nonetheless, it is still a valid concern. Therefore, the literature has called attention to the need for public subsidies to be designed in a way that does not undermine the groups' independence. These accounts have proposed options such as matching funds based on membership numbers or private gifts, and tax checkoffs.[170]

Moreover, it is not clear that these proposals would necessarily have the unequivocal support of all civil society groups. For instance, in an interview the President of a major consumer group appeared skeptical toward increased state involvement.[171] Instead, he stressed the importance of the credibility of consumer associations and recommended the strict enforcement of relatively recent accreditation rules applying to consumer associations. More specifically, Article 13 of Law 3587/2007 introduced a series of requirements pertaining to consumer groups. These include among others an obligation to be transparent about their finances, hold board and general assembly meetings, and not provide any compensation to board members (other than for certified expenses incurred to promote the groups' aims). Accreditation is recalled if a consumer association does not abide by certain of these requirements or does not carry out any activities for two consecutive years. However, the law does not tie public funding to all the requirements listed above; only "inactive" groups are ineligible for state subsidies. There are currently 42 accredited consumer associations even though it is doubtful that the number would be so high had the accreditation requirements been enforced strictly. This statute raises a broader point, that is, the tradeoff between excessive fragmentation of the third sector on the one hand, and the introduction of specific rules for consumer groups deviating from the general provisions on associations on the other. A possible middle ground would be to make additional state funding (in the form, for instance, of competitive extra grants) dependent on these accreditation requirements. This would create an important incentive for consumer groups to merge and become more active. Relatedly, with respect to the "activeness" prong, the law should consider adding participation in public consultations as an express metric for ascertaining whether groups are "active" and for allocating subsidies accordingly.

One last suggestion would be for Greece to consider setting up a body similar to the UK Communications Consumer Panel, which chapter 5 will present. This would be a public body with expertise in the sector that would sit outside EETT as an independent partner in the agency's policymaking and contribute to public consultations. This would be a more reliable way of including the citizens' voice in the policymaking process as opposed to the current situation in which generalist consumer groups may be reluctant to participate because none of their staff members has a particular specialization in telecoms. Resource constraints could again be an obstacle to the creation of this body. However, it could be funded partly by government and partly by industry contributions, as a fraction of the fees and fines that they pay every year. Another way of rendering this proposal more feasible would be to build this unit into the existing Consumer Ombudsman. The latter is an independent body, established by Law 3297/2004, which currently assists consumers with individual disputes and has not developed, to date, a role in policy formation. Furthermore, the Greek Communications Panel could potentially cover both electronic communications and broadcasting, and therefore it could develop synergies in citizen representation vis-à-vis two independent agencies, EETT and the National Radio and Television Council.

These reform proposals reflect an important point raised earlier: in the absence of fertile background conditions, the EU-mandated consultation processes may not develop their full deliberative-participatory potential. This, however, should not cast doubt on the importance of these participatory mandates in the first place. Simply put, this discussion about reform might not have been possible if these mandates had not opened up these participatory avenues and consequently highlighted remaining weaknesses in the Greek administrative state and civil society. In fact, as the last section will discuss, these participatory requirements may have set in motion a process that will ultimately result in the generalization of such accountability tools across the administration.

B. Generalizing public participation in policymaking

Recent legislative initiatives indicate that Greece may be moving toward a more general framework on administrative procedure that will increase policymaking accountability across the board. These reforms are indeed promising but their scope and, more importantly, their implementation signal that generalization of a deliberative-participatory model is still very much a work in progress.

More specifically, George Papandreou's government, which was formed after the election of October 2009, declared its commitment to "open government." A new program, called "Transparency" (*Diavgeia*), was adopted as a first important part of this agenda: Law 3861/2010 mandates the online publication of all decisions taken by the central government, local government and public administration bodies, including commitments of funds and financial decisions. According to the same law, these public decisions are applicable only after the publication requirement has been fulfilled.[172]

A second step, with potentially broader and more significant implications for the nature of governance in Greece, was the enactment of a law on better regulation (Law 4048/2012) in February 2012. This statute, entitled "Regulatory Governance: Principles, Procedures and Tools for Better Lawmaking," enunciates the principles of better regulation that should govern the elaboration and assessment of statutes and regulatory acts: necessity, proportionality, clarity and simplicity, avoidance of conflicting provisions, effectiveness and efficiency, transparency, accountability, electronic accessibility, legal certainty, democratic legitimacy (Article 2). Importantly for present purposes, this statute lists consultation, regulatory impact assessment, and statements of reasons among the "tools for better regulation" (Article 5).

More specifically, Article 6 now places on a statutory basis the requirement that consultation on draft bills take place through the www.opengov.gr website,[173] a practice that was followed before 2012 as well. Article 6 provides for a two-stage public consultation process. The goal of the first phase, lasting at least two weeks, is to inform the public and invite comments on the objectives of the planned measure, including its potential costs and benefits. The second stage lasts at least three weeks; it covers the actual draft of the measure and allows for comments on each individual provision. These two stages may take place in parallel. If the text of the bill is ready, the first stage may be omitted altogether, in which case the second stage is prolonged by a week—this is common practice. Ministers may also interrupt, abbreviate or extend the consultation process but must provide "adequate reasons" in the public consultation report accompanying the regulation. The Bureau of Legislative Initiative of the relevant Ministry prepares a "public consultation report." This document groups and presents the interested parties' submissions, and justifies the decision to incorporate or not these proposals into the final text. This report is submitted to Parliament together with the bill and is also published online and emailed to all participants in the consultation process.

Furthermore, the 2012 law on better regulation formalizes the obligation of administrative authorities to conduct Regulatory Impact Assessments (RIAs) on all bills as well as regulations of "major economic or social importance."[174] The RIA is submitted together with the draft measure to the Better Regulation Office. The latter, the Greek Ombudsman, and the Bureaus of Legislative Initiative in the pertinent ministries "collaborate on improving the quality of the RIA," as the statutory text describes this process. With respect to bills, in particular, the RIA and the "remarks" of the Better Regulation Office are also submitted to Parliament and published on the Parliament's website. In addition to this ex ante impact assessment, the 2012 law also introduced an ex post evaluation of implementation that covers only statutes. The latter must take place after three years and no later than five years subsequent to the enactment of every statute, and shall examine the cost, benefits, and impact of the statute. The Bureaus of Legislative Initiative are responsible for carrying out this process, during which they must consult with stakeholders and the Economic and Social Committee. Their conclusions and reform proposals must then be submitted to the Better Regulation Office.

Last, Article 8 introduces an express requirement that a "statement of reasons" accompany every bill or statutory amendment tabled in Parliament. This statement must detail the necessity and objectives of the new provisions and describe their compliance with the better regulation principles set out in Article 2. These procedural requirements should be considered together with institutional reforms aimed at supporting better regulation across the board. For example, in June 2011 a cabinet reshuffle created the new Ministry of Administrative Reform and E-Government (MAREG), moving this portfolio from the former Ministry of Interior, Decentralization and E-Government and placing it in a specialized Ministry. Moreover, a new position of deputy minister for e-Government was created to oversee the establishment of ICT within the administration.[175] In addition, as already noted, the 2012 law on better regulation introduced supporting structures at a central and line ministry level to help embed better regulation: the Better Regulation Office—formerly, the Office for the Support of Better Regulation—is based in the General Secretariat to the Government and oversees, supports, and coordinates the operation of the Bureaus of Legislative Initiative in all ministries.[176]

This cluster of legislative provisions reflects a stronger commitment on the part of the Greek administration to institutionalize better regulation principles and implement them across the administration. Nonetheless, these initiatives still face important limitations, both formal and operational. The first set of limitations concerns the scope of coverage of the law on better regulation. For instance, with respect to public consultations, it is not entirely clear that administrative regulations fall within the ambit of Article 6 of Law 4048/2012. Paragraph 1 of the article refers to "regulation." According to its definition in Article 1(2), this term covers bills and legislative amendments as well as general administrative rules "of major importance." Nevertheless, Article 6(1) stipulates that the minister who has the "legislative initiative" is responsible for launching the public consultation, thus excluding at least the regulatory acts issued by administrative authorities. Furthermore, the two-stage consultation process through www.opengov.gr expressly pertains to legislative bills exclusively. Similarly, the public consultation report must be submitted to Parliament, which indicates that this is again part of the legislative process. Other provisions of the Law 4048/2012 are even clearer. Both the requirement for a "statement of reasons" under Article 8 and the ex post impact assessment under Article 9 concern bills and statutes but not administrative regulatory acts.

However, even in cases that do not focus on statutes explicitly, the requirement that the regulatory act be "of major importance" means that the minister has some leeway to define an act as not being "of major importance," thus precluding the application of the better regulation processes that she may consider too cumbersome. Courts would be unlikely to interfere and invalidate this characterization considering that in analogous cases they have abstained from reviewing the existence of "extraordinary circumstances of an urgent and unforeseeable need" that justify the issuance of "acts of legislative content" under Article 44(1) of the Constitution.[177]

These ambiguities may account for the inconsistent implementation of public consultation by ministries in practice. Different departments seem to accord varying degrees of importance to public consultations.[178] Drafts of important ministerial decisions are put up for public consultation—indeed, some times through the central www.opengov.gr platform that is generally reserved for bills. Nonetheless, even though there are no precise data available, at present it seems that only a small fraction of executive rulemaking goes through the public consultation process. In a related vein, public consultation reports are often not published (especially when it comes to administrative rules) or are not as detailed as Law 4048/2012 mandates. As to the "Transparency" (*Diavgeia*) program, a mapping exercise showed that the information provided online can be "inaccurate or out of date."[179]

An additional challenge, which may also underlie the weak implementation of better regulation policy, is structural. As the OECD noted, even after the enactment of Law 4048/2012 fragmentation of responsibilities regarding better regulation continues to be an issue: the Ministry of Administrative Reform and E-Government, the General Secretariat to the Government through the Better Regulation Office (BRO), the Ministry of Finance, and individual ministries have responsibilities in this area. It was hoped that the establishment of the BRO would raise the profile of better regulation and improve implementation of various reform efforts. However, the BRO has been significantly under-resourced and lacks real powers to compel other ministries to implement these better regulation principles.[180] The MAREG was merged back into the "Ministry of Interior and Administrative Restructuring" in January 2015 but this could be seen more as a cost-cutting attempt, which might even reduce the salience of administrative reform, and less as a rationalization exercise.

The example of regulatory impact assessment showcases weaknesses both in the drafting of Law 4048/2012 and in the organizational and structural preconditions for its effective implementation. A RIA requirement was first introduced in a "soft law" instrument, a Prime Minister's Circular entitled "Regulatory Policy and the Assessment of Quality and Effectiveness of Legislation and Regulation."[181] The circular did not create a binding legal obligation on administrative authorities. Therefore, compliance was variable, and the quality of the RIAs, when public authorities chose to conduct them, was in general not particularly high.[182] With the enactment of Law 4048/2012, RIA is now given a "harder edge."[183] Nonetheless, the statutory drafting does not ensure effective compliance with this now legally binding procedural requirement. We saw earlier that the BRO, which has general oversight responsibility, collaborates with the Greek Ombudsman and the Bureaus of Legislative Initiative "on improving the quality of the RIA" and offers "remarks." Importantly, Article 7 is "toothless" in that it provides no enforcement mechanism. The BRO has no power to decline a regulatory proposal that is accompanied by no RIA, or by a sub-standard or poorly developed RIA.[184] Furthermore, the formal transition from a circular to a statute does not mean that the administration has built the in-house capacity to carry out this type of expert policy analysis effectively. Indeed, as the OECD noted, improvements have been made in the number of RIAs produced, but neither the MAREG nor the BRO has the resources to assess the quality or consistency of the substantive content of these RIAs.[185]

These are important qualifications that showcase the limits of this ambitious regulatory reform agenda. The success of this agenda will ultimately hinge on the background conditions and structural challenges facing the Greek administrative state that were discussed earlier in this chapter. Nonetheless, an important contribution of these recent initiatives is that they provide a framework that invites administrative authorities to reflect and build on their accountability practices. The telecommunications sector tells a relatively optimistic story in this regard. Despite the persistent implementation challenges, a binding legal framework (deriving from the EU) prompted EETT to gradually gain a comfort level with the new accountability mechanisms. So, too, can the broader Greek administration.

Notes

1. *See* VIVIEN A. SCHMIDT, DEMOCRACY IN EUROPE: THE EU AND NATIONAL POLITIES 108 (2006) (placing Greece next to France on the statist end of a continuum from statist to corporatist processes).

2. Greece was the final EU member state to fully liberalize its market (Ian Walden, *European Union Communications Law, in* TELECOMMUNICATIONS LAW AND REGULATION 143, 163 (Ian Walden ed., 2012)).

3. The Constitution of 1975 as amended in 1986, 2001, and 2008.

4. This is not to detract from the political and symbolic significance of the earlier revolutionary Constitutions. See Constitutional History of Greece http://www.hellenicparliament.gr/en/Vouli-ton-Ellinon/To-Politevma/Syntagmatiki-Istoria/ (providing a brief overview of the constitutional history of Greece, on which I draw in the text).

5. It was absent from the Constitution of 1844, which marked a period of constitutional monarchy (1844-1862).

6. *See* ANTONIS MANITAKIS, KRATOS DIKAIOU KAI DIKASTIKOS ELEGXOS TIS SYNTAGMATIKOTITAS (RULE OF LAW AND JUDICIAL REVIEW OF CONSTITUTIONALITY) 81–87 (1994) (reviewing the French version of the rule of law and referring to the endorsement of some of those aspects in Greece); IFIGENEIA KAMTSIDOU, I EPIYLAKSI YPER TOU NOMOU, OS PERIORISMOS, EGGYISI KAI DIAMESOS TON ELEFTHERION (THE RESERVATION OF LAW, AS RESTRICTION, GUARANTEE, AND MEDIATION OF LIBERTIES) 70*ff*., 39*ff*. (2001).

7. KAMTSIDOU, *supra* note 6, at 258–61, 288, 348. According to the telling description of N.I. Saripolos, the so-called father of Greek constitutional law and theory, "these rights inherent to man . . . are placed, so to speak, under the aegis of the general will" (quoted in ANTONIS M. PANTELIS, STEFANOS I. KOUTSOUMPINAS & TRIANTAFYLLOS A. GEROZISIS, KEIMENA SYNTAGMATIKIS ISTORIAS (TEXTS OF CONSTITUTIONAL HISTORY) 301 (1993)).

8. YIANIS Z. DROSSOS, DOKIMIO ELLINIKIS SYNTAGMATIKIS THEORIAS (AN ESSAY ON GREEK CONSTITUTIONAL THEORY) 180–81 (1996). *See also* N.I. SARIPOLOS, PRAGMATEIA TOU SYNTAGMATIKOU DIKAIOU, TOMOS C (TREATISE ON CONSTITUTIONAL LAW, VOL. C) 157 (2nd ed., 1874) ("the judge is subservient to the statute, rendering it the dominant ruler in the polity").

9. Areios Pagos [AP] 198/1847. For an analysis of the case, *see* DROSSOS, *supra* note 8, at 84–94; Epaminondas Spiliotopoulos, *Judicial Review of Legislative Acts in Greece*, 56 TEMPLE L. QUART. 463, 471 (1983).

10. See the concise formulation of the foundational case AP 23/1897: "when a statutory provision is contrary to the Constitution, because it alters by a simple legislative act one of its fundamental provisions, the court has the power to not apply it in the case before it." *See also* Akis Psygkas, *Anichnevontas kai Epananoimatodotontas ti "Theoria ton Politikon Zitimaton" stin Elliniki Ennomi Taksi (Tracing and Redefining the "Political Question Doctrine" in Greece)*, 47 DIKAIOMATA TOU ANTHROPOU (REVIEW OF HUMAN RIGHTS) 743, 759–64 (2010) (outlining the development of judicial review of constitutionality and the judicialization of politics in the late 20th century).

11. Judges would frequently and tacitly resort to a presumption of constitutionality of statutes to justify their reluctance to oppose the "political powers" and strike down legislative choices (ANTONIS MANITAKIS, I IDRYSI SYNTAGMATIKOU DIKASTIRIOU (THE ESTABLISHMENT OF A CONSTITUTIONAL COURT) 84 (2008)). In fact, it has been suggested in the constitutional law literature that the statute "retains the weight of its history" until today, and in expressing the "general interest" and the priorities of the democratically constituted polity it may on some occasions come into tension with constitutional choices (KAMTSIDOU, *supra* note 6, at 263).

12. Quoted in DROSSOS, *supra* note 8, at 330, 486.

13. *See* MANITAKIS, *supra* note 6, at 87–88.

14. *See* THEODORA TH. ZIAMOU, RULEMAKING, PARTICIPATION AND THE LIMITS OF PUBLIC LAW IN THE USA AND EUROPE 32 (2001).

15. *See* P. Nikiforos Diamandouros, *Transition to, and consolidation of, democratic politics in Greece, 1974–1983: A tentative assessment*, 7 WEST EUROPEAN POLITICS 50, 63–64 (1984).

16. Constitutional History of Greece, available at http://www.hellenicparliament.gr/en/Vouliton-Ellinon/To-Politevma/Syntagmatiki-Istoria/.

17. *See* Georgios Trantas, Paraskevi Zagoriti, Torbjörn Bergman, Wolfgang C. Müller & Kaare Strøm, *Greece: "Rationalizing" Constitutional Powers in a Post-dictatorial Country*, in DELEGATION AND ACCOUNTABILITY IN PARLIAMENTARY DEMOCRACIES 376, 396 (Kaare Strøm, Wolfgang C. Müller & Torbjörn Bergman eds., 2003) (noting that the Greek process of delegation is highly institutionalized and exhaustively regulated in the Constitution). As Theodora Ziamou explains (*supra* note 14, at 60–61), before the Constitution of 1952, the government produced autonomous legislation that would never pass through Parliament or be based on statutory authorization. The courts justified this irregularity by describing the practice as a "constitutional custom." After the enactment of the Constitution of 1952, governments used the method of legislative delegation, which was not directly provided for by the Constitution but was still made possible by the courts on the basis of an interpretation *a contrario* of Article 59(2). The latter expressly forbade the use of delegated legislation on matters of tax imposition.

18. Article 35(2) provides for a narrow set of five types of presidential acts that do not require countersignature.

19. ZIAMOU, *supra* note 14, at 62.

20. Trantas et al., *supra* note 17, at 379.

21. ZIAMOU, *supra* note 14, at 64; Trantas et al., *supra* note 17, at 379–80.

22. *See also* Trantas et al., *supra* note 17, at 392 (noting that instances of this type of legislative delegation—e.g., in environmental protection—are of great practical importance).

23. Council of State [StE] Decision 3596/1991. *See also* MANITAKIS, *supra* note 6, at 343–45.

24. *See* Panayiotis Pikrammenos, *To Elliniko Symvouleio tis Epikrateias kai oi Gnomodotikes Armodiotites tou (The Greek Council of State and its Advisory Competences)*, (2011) THEORIA KAI PRAKSI DIOIKITIKOU DIKAIOU (THEORY AND PRACTICE OF ADMINISTRATIVE LAW) 361, 361–63. The first Council of State was introduced in 1833 under the regime of absolute monarchy, and served as the "King's Council." It was subsequently abolished by an express provision of the Constitution of 1844 because it was considered as an organ associated with absolute monarchy. It was reestablished by the Constitution of 1864 and assigned a consultative function in the lawmaking process. Nevertheless, this second Council was also short-lived; it was abolished nine months after its creation. A brief discussion of the Council of State's history is available on the Council's website at http://www.ste.gr.

25. Pikrammenos, *supra* note 24, at 362.

26. *Id.*, at 366.

27. EPAMINONDAS SPILIOTOPOULOS, GREEK ADMINISTRATIVE LAW 189 (2004); Pikrammenos, *supra* note 24, at 366.

28. *See* OECD, Regulatory Reform in Greece: Government Capacity to Assure High Quality Regulation in Greece (2001), at 19.

29. The Council of State remains the course of last instance in these cases [Article 95(1)(b) of the Constitution].

30. *See* OECD, Better Regulation in Europe: Greece 2012 (2012), at 96.

31. SPILIOTOPOULOS, *supra* note 27, at 308–309. See also, more recently, StE 189/2007 of the Plenary of the Council of State (noting that the transfer of cases from the Council of State to the ordinary administrative courts may not result in the abrogation or absorption of the general jurisdiction in annulment of the Council of State).

32. This constitutional provision reads: "Every person shall be entitled to receive legal protection by the courts and may plead before them his views concerning his rights or interests, as specified by law."

33. *See* Arend Lijphart, Thomas C. Bruneau, P. Nikiforos Diamandouros & Richard Gunther, *A Mediterranean model of democracy? The Southern European democracies in comparative perspective*, 11 WEST EUROPEAN POLITICS 7, 19–21 (1988). With two very brief exceptions in 1989, the formation of coalition governments is a recent phenomenon in Greece: in 2011

under Prime Minister Lucas Papademos (a government that lasted for six months), since June 2012 under Prime Minister Antonis Samaras, and since January 2015 under Prime Minister Alexis Tsipras.

34. *See* Prodromos D. Dagtoglou, *Constitutional and Administrative Law, in* INTRODUCTION TO GREEK LAW 23, 27 (Konstantinos D. Kerameus & Phaedon J. Kozyris eds., 3rd ed., 2008) (noting that the amended Constitution weakened not only the President but also Parliament by creating a very strong government under a particularly powerful Prime Minister).

35. KAMTSIDOU, *supra* note 6, at 266–67, 349.

36. *See* OECD, *supra* note 28, at 10 (citing estimates from the Ministry of the Interior, Public Administration, and Decentralization that each new statute "produces on average six new presidential decrees and 63 ministerial decisions. That is, between 1987 and 1998, there was an average of 450 new presidential decrees and over 5,200 new ministerial decisions every year"). *See also* SPILIOTOPOULOS, *supra* note 27, at 41 (noting the extensive regulatory power by virtue of legislative delegation, and explaining that this is mainly due to the very broad involvement of the administration in the social, cultural, and economic life).

37. *See* ZIAMOU, *supra* note 14, at 64.

38. Trantas et al., *supra* note 17, at 379–80.

39. MANITAKIS, *supra* note 6, at 342–43.

40. On this trend, *see* Eugenia V. Prevedourou, *O Akyrotikos Elegxos ton Dioikitikon Prakseon ypo to Prisma tis Europaikis Symvaseos ton Dikaiomaton tou Anthropou (Annulment Review of Administrative Acts Through the Lens of the European Convention on Human Rights)*, 2010 THEORIA KAI PRAKSI DIOIKITIKOU DIKAIOU (THEORY AND PRACTICE OF ADMINISTRATIVE LAW) 858, 893.

41. SPILIOTOPOULOS, *supra* note 27, at 338–56.

42. *Id.*, at 351.

43. *Id.*, at 355–56. *See also* ZIAMOU, *supra* note 14, at 208–209 (explaining that the Council has long been of the opinion that it would be contrary to logic to suggest that the executive could use its rulemaking power for purposes other than those for which it was statutorily granted. Such an attempt would constitute action contrary to law because the executive would be effectively going beyond the limits of its statutory authorization but it would not constitute abuse of power).

44. *See* Prevedourou, *supra* note 40, at 893–94.

45. StE 3919/2010, discussed later in this chapter.

46. SPILIOTOPOULOS, *supra* note 27, at 348–49.

47. *See* Calliope Spanou & Dimitri A. Sotiropoulos, *The Odyssey of Administrative Reforms in Greece, 1981–2009*, 89 PUBLIC ADMINISTRATION 723, 728 (2011).

48. These are the Hellenic Data Protection Authority, the National Radio and Television Council, the Hellenic Authority for Communications Security and Privacy, the Supreme Council for Civil Personnel Selection (ASEP), and the Ombudsman.

49. GEORGE DELLIS, KOINI OFELEIA KAI AGORA. TOMOS B. TO DIMOSIO DIKAIO TON YPO APELEFTHEROSI KOINOFELON YPIRESION (ILEKTRONIKES EPIKOINONIES, ENERGEIA, TACHIDROMEIO, METAFORES, RADIOTILEORASI) (PUBLIC UTILITIES AND THE MARKET. VOL. II. LIBERALIZED UTILITIES LAW (ELECTRONIC COMMUNICATIONS, ENERGY, POST, TRANSPORT, BROADCASTING)) 61–62 (2008).

50. *See* Antoni S. Kechri, *Skepseis epi tis ennoias "Aneksartiti Dioikitiki Archi" (Thoughts on the notion of of "Independent Administrative Authority")*, 2007 EFIMERIDA DIMOSIOU DIKAIOU (JOURNAL OF PUBLIC LAW) 353, 359; Charalambos G. Chrysanthakis, *I Leitourgia ton Aneksartiton Archon stin Chora mas: Mia Apotimisi (The Operation of Independent Authorities in our Country: An Assessment)*, 2009 THEORIA KAI PRAKSI DIOIKITIKOU DIKAIOU (THEORY AND PRACTICE OF ADMINISTRATIVE LAW) 5, 7–8; Alexis P. Pararas, *Oi Aneksartites Dioikitikes Arches Simera (The Independent Administrative Authorities Today)*, 2006 EFIMERIDA DIMOSIOU DIKAIOU (JOURNAL OF PUBLIC LAW) 123, 130.

51. *See* Foivou I. Botsi, *O Koinovouleutikos Elegxos ton Syntagmatopoiimenon Aneksartiton Archon (Parliamentary Control of the Constitutionalized Independent Authorities)*, 2007 EFIMERIDA DIMOSIOU DIKAIOU (JOURNAL OF PUBLIC LAW) 361, 362; Giorgos Kaminis, *Oi Aneksartites*

Arches Metaksy Aneksartisias kai Koinovouleutikou Elegxou (The Independent Authorities Between Independence and Parliamentary Control), 50 NOMIKON VEMA (LEGAL TRIBUNE) 95, 99 (2002).

52. Botsi, *supra* note 51, at 363–64.
53. Kaminis, *supra* note 51, at 102.
54. Botsi, *supra* note 51, at 363–64 (noting that it has been described as "symbolic").
55. DELLIS, *supra* note 49, at 9. *See also* Vassilios Kondylis, *The creation of an Independent Authority as a measure of compliance with European Law and balancing between Independence and Accountability: The case of the Hellenic National Telecommunications' and Post Commission (EETT)*, presented at Workshop "Public Administration in the Balkans—from Weberian bureaucracy to New Public Management" (5–6 February 2010 in Athens, Greece), at 15 (noting that between 1998 and January 2010, over 350 regulatory decisions had been issued in the sectors regulated by EETT).
56. Kondylis, *supra* note 55, at 15.
57. *See also* ZIAMOU, *supra* note 14, at 251 ("Courts and theory have not really been concerned with rulemaking procedures, because rulemaking itself has been considered of secondary importance in comparison to the legislation produced by Parliament. But as the administration makes more and more use of rules with a decisive influence on private conduct, often without the possibility of any substantial, political or legal control, the need to seek an additional form of legitimation becomes imperative").
58. Spanou & Sotiropoulos, *supra* note 47, at 723.
59. Calliope Spanou, *European integration in administrative terms: a framework for analysis and the Greek case*, 5 JOURNAL OF EUROPEAN PUBLIC POLICY 467, 474 (1998) (emphasis added).
60. OECD, Regulatory Reform in Greece: Enhancing Market Openness through Regulatory Reform (2001), at 10.
61. GEORGE PAGOULATOS, GREECE'S NEW POLITICAL ECONOMY: STATE, FINANCE AND GROWTH FROM POSTWAR TO EMU 20–47 (2003).
62. *See* P.C. Ioakimidis, *The Europeanization of Greece: An Overall Assessment, in* EUROPEANI-ZATION AND THE SOUTHERN PERIPHERY 73, 76–77 (Kevin Featherstone & George Kazamias eds., 2001) (noting that "[o]ne of the striking features of the state morphology at the time of Greece's accession [to the EU] was the gigantic size of the state apparatus and the over-centralized nature of the state and the political system in general. The state occupied a hegemonic position in practically every aspect of Greek society. The gigantism of the state was exemplified in (1) the over-employment in the public sector; (2) the high amount of public expenditure as a share of GNP; and (3) the extensive regulatory role performed by the state and the latter's overwhelming participation in economic activities").
63. *See* Dimitri A. Sotiropoulos, *A Colossus with Feet of Clay: The State in Post-Authoritarian Greece, in* GREECE, THE NEW EUROPE, AND THE CHANGING INTERNATIONAL ORDER 43, 46–51 (Harry J. Psomiades & Stavros Thomadakis eds., 1993) (citing Nicos P. Mouzelis).
64. Christos Lyrintzis, *Political parties in post-junta Greece: A case of 'bureaucratic clientelism'?*, 7 WEST EUROPEAN POLITICS 99, 103–104 (1984/). *See also* Euripidis Loukis, Ann Macintosh & Yannis Charalabidis, *Editorial*, 13 JOURNAL OF BALKAN AND NEAR EASTERN STUDIES 1, 8 (2011) (listing among the distinct characteristics of the Greek state as to its relation with society "political clientelism 'at the top' (extensive politicization of the higher civil service) and 'at the bottom' (parties offering to their voters jobs in the public sector)").
65. *See* Spanou, *supra* note 59, at 474.
66. Dimitri A Sotiropoulos, *Southern European Public Bureaucracies in Comparative Perspective*, 27 WEST EUROPEAN POLITICS 405, 415 (2004); Calliope Spanou, *On the Regulatory Capacity of the Hellenic State: A Tentative Approach Based on a Case Study*, 62 INTERNATIONAL REVIEW OF ADMINISTRATIVE SCIENCES 219, 230 (1996).
67. Sotiropoulos, *supra* note 63, at 52 ("The French state, resting on a long tradition of interventionism, is managed by the powerful grand corps of graduates of the Ecole National d'Administration").
68. Sotiropoulos, *supra* note 66, at 416.
69. More information is available on the Council's website at http://www.asep.gr/.

70. Spanou & Sotiropoulos, *supra* note 47, at 729. *See also* the Center's website at http://www. ekdd.gr/ekdda/index.php/en/2012-06-29-09-59-33.

71. Spanou & Sotiropoulos, *supra* note 47, at 729.

72. *See* KEVIN FEATHERSTONE & DIMITRIS PAPADIMITRIOU, THE LIMITS OF EUROPEANIZATION: REFORM CAPACITY AND POLICY CONFLICT IN GREECE 57 (2008) (citing the relevant data).

73. *See* Ioakimidis, *supra* note 62, at 79. *See also* FEATHERSTONE & PAPADIMITRIOU, *supra* note 72, at 41 (noting that until around the 1990s, "the Anglo-Saxon notion of freedom from the state, of liberty resulting from anti-statism, has been an alien notion. The state was to dominate an underdeveloped economy and society").

74. Sotiropoulos, *supra* note 63, at 47. *See also* OECD, *supra* note 60, at 12 ("As they were able to obtain information or advance their interests through informal avenues, the most influential civil society groups did not feel compelled to push the State for greater transparency and accountability").

75. Kevin Featherstone, *Introduction: 'Modernisation' and the Structural Constraints of Greek Politics*, 28 WEST EUROPEAN POLITICS 223, 229 (2005).

76. *See* GIORGOS TH. MAVROGORDATOS, BETWEEN PITYOKAMPTIS AND PROCROUSTIS: PROFESSIONAL ASSOCIATIONS IN TODAY'S GREECE (METAKSY PITYOKAMPTI KAI PROCROUSTI: OI EPAGGELMATIKES ORGANOSEIS STI SIMERINI ELLADA) 49–57, 202–203 (2nd ed. 1998).

77. PAGOULATOS, *supra* note 61, at 161, 162.

78. Kostas A. Lavdas, *Interest Groups in Disjointed Corporatism: Social Dialogue in Greece and European 'Competitive Corporatism'*, 28 WEST EUROPEAN POLITICS 297, 306 (2005) (noting that "the absence of concertationist traditions combined with fragmentation in interest intermediation and political regime discontinuities result, after 1974, in a corporatist (tripartite-based) system, which can be described as being neither authoritarian corporatist nor liberal corporatist in Schmitter's sense. Its fragmentation constrained the liberal elements in the economic system while at the same time finding it difficult to broker social pacts and intersectoral agreements beyond wage negotiation"). In his earlier work Lavdas defined "disjointed corporatism" as "the combination of a set of corporatist organizational features and a prevailing political modality that lacks diffuse reciprocity and remains incapable of brokering social pacts" (KOSTAS A. LAVDAS, THE EUROPEANIZATION OF GREECE: INTEREST POLITICS AND THE CRISES OF INTEGRATION 17 (1997)).

79. Trantas et al., *supra* note 17, at 395.

80. Lavdas, *supra* note 78, at 307.

81. *Id.*, at 302.

82. *See* Sotiropoulos, *supra* note 66, at 407 (noting that in the South European version of "assisted capitalism," corporate governance was characterized by close personal relationships, developed by membership in closed elites. The principal benefactors of this role of the state in society . . . became accustomed to depend on the state for their enrichment and for the reproduction of their power position in society).

83. *See, e.g.*, Sotiropoulos, *supra* note 63, at 51 ("voluntary associations are sparse and social service organizations are sanctioned by the state; gender groupings, peace movements, and environmental groups do not enjoy a long life, and they usually fall under the tutelage of one of the political parties . . . . Big business . . . have benefited from preferential treatment by the postwar Greek state . . . . Other strong interest groups, such as the professional associations of lawyers and physicians, have become the arena of party struggles . . . . In a nutshell, Greek civil society is weak because it has itself been permeated by party politics and, as a result, the state cannot count on civil society to fend off political parties").

84. Lavdas, *supra* note 78, at 298.

85. *Id. See also* FEATHERSTONE & PAPADIMITRIOU, *supra* note 72 at 41 ("Over the last decade or more, it is claimed that civil society has been strengthened with activity expressed on various social issues, such as the environment. Greek society has undergone significant change—it has become a country of immigration; a cultural 'Europeanism' has affected attitudes; and a new weight has been given to civil liberties").

86. OECD, *supra* note 60, at 12.

87. Ioakimidis, *supra* note 62, at 89, 91 (noting that statistical data show that the number of social associations financed by the European Commission quadrupled between 1996 and 1998).

88. *See* MICHEL STASSINOPOULOS, LE DROIT DE LA DÉFENSE DEVANT LES AUTORITÉS ADMINIS-TRATIVES 33 (1976). Article 20(2) of the Constitution reads: "The right of a person to a prior hearing also applies in any administrative action or measure adopted at the expense of his rights or interests."

89. *See* SPILIOTOPOULOS, *supra* note 27, at 335. In fact, courts have been quite adamant in supporting the contrary view. *See* ZIAMOU, *supra* note 14, at 209; StE 2040/1977; StE 6/1993; StE 251/1995; AP 1141/1980.

90. *See* DIMITRA KONTOGIORGA-THEOCHAROPOULOU, I DIOIKITIKI ORGANOSI TOU KRATOUS (APO APOPSIS DIOIKITIKOU DIKAIOU KAI DIOIKITIKIS EPISTIKIS) [THE ADMINISTRATIVE ORGANIZATION OF THE STATE (FROM THE PERSPECTIVE OF ADMINISTRATIVE LAW AND ADMINISTRATIVE SCIENCE)] 56 (2002). *See also* Dimitra Kontogiorga-Theocharopoulou, *To "Meteoro Vima" tou Management ston Dimosio Tomea (The "Suspended Step" of Management in the Public Sector)*, 2011 THEORIA KAI PRAKSI DIOIKITIKOU DIKAIOU (THEORY AND PRACTICE OF ADMINISTRATIVE LAW) 372, 375 (2011) (also pointing to the risks to administrative efficiency posed by the extensive involvement of syndicates).

91. *See* Lavdas, *supra* note 78, at 309.

92. According to OECD data (http://stats.oecd.org/Index.aspx?QueryId=20167), trade union density in Greece is around 25%. One scholar has further noted that unionization in the private sector is much lower than suggested by the average figure. "Less than 50% of the Greek labour force comprises employees. This, and the relatively high percentage of self-employed, constitutes the framework within which we can assess strengths and weaknesses of unions" (Lavdas, *supra* note 78, at 302).

93. OECD, *supra* note 28, at 24.

94. *See* OECD, *supra* note 60, at 14. Further information on the operation of the ESC is available in a more recent OECD Report, *supra* note 30, at 64–66, and the Committee's website (http://www.oke.gr/index_en.html).

95. Evaggelos Venizelos, *Poiotita Nomothesias, Koinoniki Synainesi kai Antagonistikotita tis Ellinikis Nomothesias (Legislative Quality, Social Consensus and Competitiveness of the Greek Legislation)*, 2006 EFIMERIDA DIMOSIOU DIKAIOU (JOURNAL OF PUBLIC LAW) 374, 377 (2006).

96. OECD, *supra* note 28, at 25.

97. Interview n. 41002.

98. VASILEIOS SKOURIS, CHOROTAKSIKO KAI POLEODOMIKO DIKAIO (PLANNING LAW) 140 (1997). *See also* APOSTOLOS GERONTAS, I SYMMETOCHI TON POLITON KAI TON KOINONIKON FOREON STI DIADIKASIA LIPSIS DIOIKITIKON APOFASEON (THE PARTICIPATION OF CITIZENS AND CIVIL SOCIETY ACTORS IN ADMINISTRATIVE DECISIONMAKING) 231 (1986).

99. *See* OECD, *supra* note 60, at 23.

100. OECD, *supra* note 30, at 53 (noting the examples of the National Council for Agricultural Policy and the National Council for Education which act as autonomous advisory bodies).

101. *See* OECD, *supra* note 28, at 39 ("Currently, public consultation of legal and regulatory proposals is done informally. Formal consultation is based on a corporatist approach. Consultation is not carried out for legislative amendments or subordinate regulations") and 26 ("Greece has lagged other OECD countries in creating public consultation mechanisms. This weakens the accountability of the ministries, and reduces their ability to assess impacts, reactions, and compliance issues for new regulations. A government-wide policy on the use of consultation in making and amending regulations is key to improving regulatory quality . . . . Notice and comment processes are the most open form of consultation, and should be implemented as a complement to other forms of consultation").

102. StE 1451/1957. *See also* GEORGE DELLIS, KOINI OFELEIA KAI AGORA. TOMOS A. TO TELOS TONN DIACHORISTIKON GRAMMON: I "AGORAKENTRIKI" DIMOSIA RYTHMISI TON KOINOFELON DRASTIRIOTITON (PUBLIC UTILITIES AND THE MARKET. VOL. I. "MARKET-ORIENTED" REGULATION FOR PUBLIC UTILITIES) 172 n. 162 (2008).

103. StE (PE) 158/1992. On telecoms, in particular, see StE (PE) 385/1995 (describing it as "goods of vital importance to the public").

104. *See also* FEATHERSTONE & PAPADIMITRIOU, *supra* note 72, at 19 ("the EU's instruments are too weak to overcome the inertial tendencies. To explain the latter, the particularities of the Greek 'model' must be brought into the picture. The Greek model—the political system, the economy, and the 'welfare' system—displays both tension and inertia. These are the result of a complex pattern of embedded and conflicting interests and, to some extent, identities").

105. This timeline is drawn from OECD, *supra* note 60, at 37.

106. OECD, Regulatory Reform in Greece: Regulatory Reform in the Telecommunications Industry (2001), at 9–10. *See also* Paul Mylonas & Isabelle Joumard, Greek Public Enterprises: Challenges for Reform. Economics Department Working Papers No. 214 (1999), at 20.

107. OECD, *supra* note 106, at 25 (questioning the derogation "on the basis of experience in other EU countries that opened their markets to full competition even before full re-balancing had been achieved").

108. ECJ, Judgment of 16 October 2001, Joined Cases C-396/99 and C-397/99—*Commission v Hellenic Republic.*

109. ECJ, Judgments of 15 December 2005 in cases C-250/04, C-252/04, C-253/04, C-254/04— *Commission v. Hellenic Republic.*

110. George Pagoulatos, *The Politics of Privatisation: Redrawing the Public–Private Boundary*, 28 WEST EUROPEAN POLITICS 358, 361–62 (2005).

111. OECD, *supra* note 60, at 10.

112. *See* Pagoulatos, *supra* note 110, at 364 (noting that the Simitis governments after 1996 implemented a privatization program which was "distinctly pragmatic in its reasoning, gradualist in its pace, and non-conflictual in its implementation [and] emphasised the retention of public control over major public utilities"); Mylonas & Joumard, *supra* note 106, at 20 (noting that OTE was the most profitable enterprise in the country in absolute terms).

113. Featherstone, *supra* note 75, at 232.

114. Hellenic Telecommunications and Post Commission, Annual Report 2009 (2010), at 10.

115. DELLIS, *supra* note 49, at 52.

116. The agency's resources may come from: 1. Fees and charges for general authorization procedures; 2. Fees and charges for granting rights to the use of radio frequencies and numbers; 3. Fees for services to operators; 4. Fines imposed as penalties for breaches of legislation on electronic communications, postal services and the protection of free competition; 5. Other monies collected in the course of an administrative or judicial procedure (Kondylis, *supra* note 55, at 12).

117. Furthermore, they could determine through a joint decision that any unspent funds held by EETT should pass on to the General Secretariat of Communications of the Ministry to fund its operations, as well as to fund universal service objectives, or relevant studies for the sector (OECD, *supra* note 106, at 20).

118. *Id.*, at 20–21.

119. Law 3431/2006 provided for a total of 220 staff members, and Law 4070/2012 raised this number to 247.

120. *See* Kondylis, *supra* note 55, at 11.

121. OECD, *supra* note 106, at 21.

122. *Id.*, at 20.

123. *See* Anna Tzimapiti, *Oi Kanonistikes kai Apofasistikes Armodiotites ton Aneksartiton Dioikitikon Archon: Symperasmata apo tin Elliniki Pragmatikotita (Rulemaking and Decisionmaking Competences of Independent Administrative Authorities: Conclusions from the Greek Reality)*, 2009 THEORIA KAI PRAKSI DIOIKITIKOU DIKAIOU (THEORY AND PRACTICE OF ADMINISTRATIVE LAW) 1166, 1181 (noting that EETT stands out for the breadth of its regulatory powers and mentioning a similar residual provision under the prior Law 3431/2006 as an example of this).

124. *Cf.* Sotiropoulos, *supra* note 66, at 418–19 ("in contrast to South European states, other Western states had adequate time to become democratic, to build modern and account-able bureaucracies, and to transform them in the direction of public management and European integration at successive stages over the span of the previous two centuries. This was not the case, for instance, with Greece . . . where the transition from authori-tarianism was made in the mid-1970s. South European bureaucracies did not have the time to proceed in a stepwise fashion. They were simultaneously confronted with all the above challenges in the last quarter of the twentieth century, i.e., in a condensed time period").

125. *See* interview n. 40002: "We are now obliged under Law 3431/2006 to carry out public consultations. Before that, we launched public consultations for practical purposes, to get a sense of the market. However, even before 2002 we knew that we were heading toward the institutionalization of public consultations. We had followed the relevant discussions at the EU level and then saw the directives as well." *See also* EETT, Annual Report 2001, at 35 ("Towards achieving this goal, the European Parliament and the Council were working towards the adoption of the New Regulatory Framework for electronic communications, which is specially designed to meet the needs of increasingly competitive and converging markets").

126. Decision 515/2001 of the Undersecretary of Transports and Communications regarding the process of public consultation on the award of special licenses under conditions of lim-ited number.

127. My archival research has found that this was the case for the consultations on the limitation and award of special licenses of stable wireless access; on the award of Licenses for Public Telecommunications Networks DECT; and two consultations on the allocation of radiofre-quency spectrum for mobile services. Further information on one of these consultations is available in an OECD report as well (OECD, *supra* note 60, at 38: "EETT entrusted the organ-isation of the consultation to a team of scholars from the National Technical University of Athens, who addressed to all parties active in the field of telecommunications and computer sciences in Greece, including businesses and academics").

128. EETT Decision 375/10/14.2.2006 "Regulation of the Public Consultation Process" (Gazette 314/B´/16.3.2006).

129. EETT Regulation of Public Consultations (2006), Article 2.

130. These usually included formulations, such as "care for the consumer" or "the consumer at the center of developments."

131. Annual Report 2008, at 73–74.

132. Interviews n. 41001 and 41002: "EETT has not asked us to participate in policy discussion meetings since 2009"; "We are not invited to speak at conferences or we are only given little time at the end."

133. Interview n. 45001.

134. StE 602/2003.

135. StE 2217/1963; StE 2506/1982. *See also* GRIGORIOS G. LAZARAKOS, TO DIKAIOMA PROSVASIS STI DIMOSIA PLIROFORIA. ANOIKTI DIOIKISI KAI KOINONIA TIS PLIROFORIAS (THE RIGHT OF ACCESS TO PUBLIC INFORMATION. OPEN ADMINISTRATION AND INFORMATION SOCIETY) 63 (2006).

136. These exceptions cover cases involving the private or family life of a third person; confiden-tial information under other legislative provisions; cabinet discussions; or cases in which disclosure would considerably hinder the investigations of judicial, administrative, police or military authorities.

137. ZIAMOU, *supra* note 14, at 80.

138. SPILIOTOPOULOS, *supra* note 27, at 109. They are, however, notified to their specific addressee but do not become ipso facto readily available to the public.

139. *See also* Kondylis, *supra* note 55, at 16 (noting that "[a] significant institutional feature that demonstrates the correct transposition of the 2002 directives into the Greek legal order is the publicizing of EETT regulatory decisions").

140. This is the reason why these submissions are shown as confidential in Figure 4.2 as we cannot ascribe submissions to their authors and thus trace the impact of specific stakeholders even if we can deduce some information about the content of submissions.
141. Interview n. 45003.
142. SPILIOTOPOULOS, *supra* note 33, at 112; PRODROMOS D. DAGTOGLOU, GENIKO DOIKITIKO DIKAIO (GENERAL ADMINISTRATIVE LAW) 117 (2004); ZIAMOU, *supra* note 14, at 210. By contrast, the Council of State has insisted on the requirement that individual administrative acts affecting the interests of their addressees must state their reasons (Dagtoglou, *supra* note 34, at 50) The latter requirement was codified in Article 19 of the Administrative Procedure Code of 1999 stipulating that every individual administrative act should include clear, specific, and adequate reasoning.
143. Interview n. 45004 (mentioning a specific example regarding the auction of spectrum at 1800MHz. More specifically, Cosmote had raised with EETT the question of the commencement date for the use of the new part of the spectrum to be allocated. Nevertheless, EETT did not reply to that point. Eventually, the agency decided that commencement date of the new license would be six months after the conclusion of the auction, which Cosmote's technicians noted was later than necessary) and interview n. 41002.
144. There are examples in which some aspects of the public consultation seem to resemble a head-counting exercise. *See, e.g.,* National Telecommunications and Post Commission, Annual Report 2004 (2005), at 97 ("Issues of the specific market and the proposed obligations were posed in a Public Consultation during the period from 11 February to 18 March 2004. Thirteen (13) telecommunications providers participated in this Consultation and 75% of them agreed with the views of EETT. EETT, taking into account the results of the Consultation, announced its final position in relation to the imposed regulatory obligations").
145. Interview n. 40002.
146. StE 3919/2010 (Plenary).
147. Kondylis, *supra* note 55, at 22.
148. As a reminder, Article 43 of the Constitution provides the rules of delegation that Part I discussed in further detail.
149. *See, e.g.,* ZIAMOU, *supra* note 14, at 204 (noting that direct challenge of regulatory acts is not permitted by way of petition of full jurisdiction before the ordinary administrative courts. Since the latter have the power not only to set aside but also to revise the administrative acts before them, this type of review would "interfere with lawmaking discretion and violate the principle of separation of powers").
150. StE 3604/2011, 4032/2011, 617/2013, 618/2013.
151. StE 616/2013, 619/2013.
152. StE 620/2013, 621/2013, 622/2013.
153. European Commission, 15th Progress Report on the Single European Electronic Communications Market—2009 (COM(2010)253 final/3–25 August 2010), at 209.
154. DELLIS, *supra* note 49, at 422.
155. *Id.,* at 461–63.
156. Interview n. 45002.
157. DELLIS, *supra* note 49, at 428.
158. *See* DELLIS, *supra* note 49, at 188 and n.185 ("The agency's omission to conduct a statutorily mandated public consultation will result in the judicial invalidation of its decision. On the contrary, the lack of strict adherence to specific procedural provisions relating to consultation should not be deemed to constitute ipso facto a violation of a substantial formality").
159. Interview n. 40002.
160. For a recent example from the electronic communications sector, see StE 3604/2011.
161. *See also* DELLIS, *supra* note 49, at 188.
162. *Id.,* at 472.
163. *Id.,* at 473. Consider the French example as well: As was mentioned in chapter 3, decisions concerning dispute settlements fall under the jurisdiction of the Paris Court of Appeal,

which has an economic regulation division specializing in regulation and competition disputes (ARCEP, Annual Report 2011 (2012), at 44).

164. *See also* William E. Forbath, *Habermas's Constitution: A History, Guide, and Critique*, 23 LAW & SOC. INQUIRY 969, 1000–1001 (1998) (noting, more generally, that forging and sustaining an institutional role for civil society frequently requires affirmative state intervention. In fact, "the broader, more diffuse, or more subjugated the potential 'publics,' the more pressing the need for state support," *id.*, at 1001).

165. *See* SUSAN ROSE-ACKERMAN, FROM ELECTIONS TO DEMOCRACY: BUILDING ACCOUNTABLE GOVERNMENT IN HUNGARY AND POLAND 237 (2005) (noting that "[t]he registration of nonprofit advocacy groups should be a simple and inexpensive process that concentrates on avoiding the fraudulent use of the nonprofit form for personal financial gain").

166. The main requirement under the Greek Civil Code is that 20 people sign the bylaws, and register the association with the local court of first instance—currently, the local court of peace.

167. *See* ROSE-ACKERMAN, *supra* note 165, at 172 (noting that "[t]o have staying power, advocacy organizations need professional staff and a budget with some stability").

168. *See, e.g.*, Decision Z1- 658/ 19-12-2011 of the General Secretariat for Consumers for 2011.

169. The total expenditure for 2011 was 136,500 euros.

170. *See* ROSE-ACKERMAN, *supra* note 165, at 237 (also noting, however, that the example of Hungary, where only one-half of the taxpayers took advantage of a law that permits them to earmark 1% of their taxes for charity, suggests that simply lowering the costs of giving is insufficient).

171. Interview n. 41002.

172. *See* OECD, Greece: Review of the Central Administration (2011), at 23.

173. OECD, *supra* note 30, at 65.

174. The RIA must include the following: a description of the problem requiring regulation and of existing related provisions; an assessment of the negative effects that the absence of a regulation would have; an analysis of alternative options and their relative capacity to achieve the desired objectives; a cost-benefit analysis.

175. OECD, *supra* note 30, at 44.

176. *Id.*, at 15, 40.

177. *See* the judgments of the Plenary of the Council of State, StE 1250/2003; StE 3636/1989.

178. *See also* OECD, *supra* note 30, at 65 ("The importance and benefits of consultation with key stakeholder groups throughout the policy development cycle is not well embedded or consistently applied across the administration").

179. OECD, Greece: Review of the Central Administration (2011), at 63.

180. OECD, *supra* note 30, at 17. The OECD report further noted that "there is as yet no strategic basis for a whole-of-government policy on BR in the Greek administration . . . . Developing an overarching administrative unit such as the BRO/OSBR and an action plan on BR will not on its own be sufficient to guarantee implementation or success. High level political support and leadership is essential. BR needs a political champion who will provide a voice at Cabinet meetings, who can follow up with other ministers or regulatory bodies on BR issues and who will support the administrative structures . . . in fulfilling their mandates."

181. Circular Y190/2006.

182. *See* OECD, *supra* note 30, at 39; George Dellis, *Can You Teach an Old Public Law System New Tricks? The Greek Experience on Good Regulation: From Parody to Tragedy without (Yet) a Deus Ex Machina* (2013) (available at http://papers.ssrn.com/sol3/papers.cfm?abstract_id=2220636).

183. I borrow the phrase from CAROL HARLOW & RICHARD RAWLINGS, LAW AND ADMINISTRATION 258 (3rd ed., 2009), who use it to describe how earlier "soft law" statements of better regulation were given a harder edge across the LRRA 2006, a statute that is discussed in more detail in chapter 5.

184. OECD, *supra* note 30, at 19.

185. *Id.*, at 17.

5

The United Kingdom

At first glance, the United Kingdom (UK) would appear to be a more challenging case for the argument that EU law has had an accountability-enhancing effect at the member-state level. One could even go so far as to argue that the British example might constitute a negative case study: The UK was at the forefront of the privatization revolution. Concomitantly, it was a pioneer in the EU in the development of institutional structures in the aftermath of this privatization wave.[1] The 1980s and 1990s saw the creation and reorganization of a set of regulatory agencies that were entrusted with regulation and the promotion of competition in the new privatized environment. Even though, in Tony Prosser's words, "the first characteristic of the approach adopted was that regulatory institutions were improvised, almost as afterthoughts to the main aim of successful privatization,"[2] the importance of institutional innovation in the succeeding decades should not be underestimated.

The first phase of institutional development began with the ascent of Margaret Thatcher's "New Right" administration. In a series of reforms, which could fall under the general heading of "New Public Management," Thatcher's government sought to bring private-sector managerial ideals of efficiency and performance measurement into public service delivery to the benefit of citizens/users of these services. The Citizen's Charter, launched by John Major during the first year of his premiership, continued on the path of emphasizing the importance of high standards in public service provision.[3] The then Prime Minister explained the intention of the Charter in the following way: "It will work for quality across the whole range of public services. It will give support to those who use services in seeking better standards."[4] The Charter highlighted the idea of choice: "The public sector should provide choice wherever practicable. The people affected by services should be consulted. Their views about the services they use should be sought regularly and systematically to inform decisions about what services should be provided."[5] The idea of government reform continued under New Labour beginning in 1997. Nevertheless, "where Thatcher's keywords had been choice, management, regulation, contract and audit, Tony Blair's were modernization, reform, responsiveness, accessibility and voice, inclusion and equality."[6] Importantly for our purposes, the emphasis was on responsiveness and empowerment, or, in the language of New Labour, creating a "stakeholder society."[7] This new "stakeholder style" emerged as a key feature of policy for public service delivery under Gordon Brown as well.[8] David Cameron's coalition government, which took office in May 2010, demonstrated a renewed emphasis on openness and transparency, marking it as one of the new cabinet's priorities.[9] At the time of this writing, Theresa May's government has not been in power long enough for an adequate assessment. Some indications are that May might want to continue in this general direction.[10] However, with Brexit requiring vast amounts of civil service resources, it remains to be seen how up on the agenda regulatory reform could be. The preparation for Brexit itself has so far gone against the direction of openness and stakeholder involvement.

This summary cannot and does not intend to do justice to the decades of regulatory reform and institutional developments in the UK. These will be discussed in more detail in the following pages. However, it serves the preliminary purpose of suggesting that the influence EU law has had on member-state participatory processes of regulation is different from the one we traced in France and Greece. Britain had liberalized the telecommunications sector prior to the European Commission initiatives in this area; in fact, in significant part it inspired them.[11] When it comes to participatory practices specifically, again Britain was there before the EU. In the telecommunications sector in particular, as this chapter will show, Britain had been following a practice of consultation long before the EU Framework Directive mandating these participatory practices at the member-state level was passed in 2002.

Nonetheless, the different institutional realities in the UK before the advent of EU law should not be taken to suggest that the latter was inconsequential. Indeed, the brief story presented in this introduction should not give rise to an understanding that regulatory innovation and, in particular, participatory practices were an organic (or even significant) element in the development of the British administrative state. This chapter puts forward a different narrative to shed light on the extent of change in institutional structures and practices brought about by EU law in the area of electronic communications. According to this narrative, public participation in administrative policymaking—especially the deliberative-participatory model sketched in chapter 1—was inconsistent with the prevailing perception of the British state in the 19th and early 20th centuries. This is because that perception, dominated by the thought and legacy of Albert Venn Dicey and the foundational concepts of parliamentary sovereignty and the rule of law, viewed the very idea of administrative policymaking as problematic in the first place.

Even as the idea of a British administrative law evolved, open public participation was still not considered as an effective mechanism for binding the administration. Instead, the system was dominated by business elites and professions either enjoying a significant degree of self-regulation and autonomy or privileged access to a closed system of informal interactions with the Ministries, what was called a "club government." This system was disrupted under Margaret Thatcher's premiership beginning in 1979 and during the eighteen years of Conservative rule. However, the new institutional arrangements under the New Public Management program, the rise of the ideal of efficiency in public service delivery, and, more importantly, the idea of the citizen-consumer cannot be described as a manifestation of a deliberative-participatory model. In fact, even though the first years of the New Labour administration continued the process of formalization and enhanced the idea of inclusiveness and stakeholder empowerment, one could still notice the persistence of institutionally and culturally embedded features, notably the voluntary and informal nature of participatory regulatory processes.[12]

The last sections of the chapter situate the case study of the regulation of the electronic communications sector against this historical and institutional backdrop. The institutional features of this example and its operational realities reflect both the entrenched nature of some of the historical characteristics of the British regulatory model as well as the nature of changes brought about by the 2002 EU regulatory framework. As we will see, in the British case it would seem more difficult to argue that the advent of EU mandates initiated a paradigm shift in the way previous chapters suggested was the case in France and Greece. It did, however, push significantly in the direction of formalized and institutionalized open public participation, adding impetus to and concluding the shift that domestic regulatory reforms had set in motion over the previous decades.

I. The rise of the British administrative state and Dicey's legacy

A. "In England we know nothing of administrative law; and we wish to know nothing"

M. Barthélemy, the Dean of the Faculty of Law at the University of Paris, recounted in the turn of the 20th century a conversation with Albert Venn Dicey, a key figure in British public law, during which Dean Barthélemy asked a question about administrative law in England. Dicey's response was: "In England we know nothing of administrative law; and we wish to know nothing."[13] Any reference to British administrative history can hardly ignore the writings of A. V. Dicey. His textbook on *the Law of the Constitution*, first published in 1885,[14] has been described as "the most influential constitutional textbook of the [19th] century";[15] at the same time, it has been subject to the criticism that "many of the problems in twentieth century administrative law scholarship have arisen because of what might be called the Diceyan inheritance."[16]

Dicey drew a sharp distinction between the British system of the rule of law and the intentionally untranslated French system of *droit administratif*: "*Droit administratif* is a term . . . for which English legal phraseology supplies no proper equivalent . . . . This absence from our language of any satisfactory equivalent for the expression *droit administratif* is significant; the want of a name arises at bottom from our non-recognition of the thing itself."[17] This section on *droit administratif*, which was originally part of Lecture Five ("The Rule of Law: Its Nature"), was expanded into a separate full chapter in the third and subsequent editions of the book; this chapter was—perhaps tellingly—the longest. According to the British jurist,

> Any one who considers with care the nature of the *droit administratif* of France, or the topics to which it applies, will soon discover that it rests, and always has rested, at bottom on two leading ideas alien to the conceptions of modern Englishmen. The first of these ideas is that the government, and every servant of the government, possesses, as representative of the nation, a whole body of special rights, privileges, or prerogatives as against private citizens, and that the extent of these rights, privileges, or prerogatives is to be determined on principles different from the considerations which fix the legal rights and duties of one citizen towards another . . . The second of these general ideas is the necessity of maintaining the so-called 'separation of powers' (*separation des pouvoirs*), or, in other words, of preventing the government, the legislature, and the courts from encroaching upon one another's province. The expression, however, separation of powers, as applied by Frenchmen to the relations of the executive and the courts [means] something different from what we mean in England by the 'independence of the judges' . . . [It means] the maintenance of the principle that while the ordinary judges ought to be irremovable and thus independent of the executive, the government and its officials ought (whilst acting officially) to be independent of and to a great extent free from the jurisdiction of the ordinary courts.[18]

In other words, on Dicey's account, one could not talk of a British administrative law for two essential reasons: first, British law lacked a special body of principles, separate from ordinary private law, that would apply specifically to the relations of individuals to the state. Second, British officials were subject to the jurisdiction of the ordinary courts, and not to a separate system of administrative courts (*tribunaux administratifs*) at the apex of which stood the Conseil d'État as in France.

Notwithstanding this vehement opposition to a British administrative law, Dicey was, of course, not oblivious to the ongoing rise of the administrative state in England. This process had not occurred overnight; rather, the history of delegating legislative and judicial power to the departments in England was concisely described in an account of the time as "a long period of imperceptible growth, a quickening to meet the felt needs of the new Social State, a sudden flowering during the War, and after the War the full fruition."[19] Up until the first decades of the 19th century, there had been a strong tradition of local government in England; this had prohibited the "formation of a singular notion of administration" and might explain why the concept of administrative law did not become embedded in the British system.[20] However, the 19th century has been described as a "revolution in government" that marked a considerable expansion in central regulation, particularly in four main areas: factories, the Poor Law, railways, and public health.[21] Delegated legislation continued to expand later in the century. In 1891, for instance, the *Statutory Rules and Orders*, the uniform series in which delegated legislation was published, were more than twice as long as the statutes enacted by Parliament.[22] The beginning of the 20th century witnessed the introduction of a range of measures often regarded as the "basis for the welfare state," the most significant of which in the long term being the National Insurance Act 1911.[23] The growth of delegated legislation was fuelled by the two world wars and developments in the welfare state that occurred in the aftermath of the Second World War.[24]

As noted earlier, the reality of the growth of the administrative state was not lost on Dicey, who called the years 1865 to 1900 the "Period of Collectivism" precisely for this reason.[25] In a similar vein, writing in 1915, he remarked that "since the beginning of the twentieth century, the nation as represented in Parliament has undertaken to perform a large number of duties . . . The imposition upon the Government of new duties inevitably necessitates the acquisition by the Government of extended authority."[26] However, it was these "collectivist connotations" of extensive government discretion that led Dicey to condemn wide administrative powers.[27] As Jennings wrote in a critical article, albeit entitled "In Praise of Dicey," the Constitution was for Dicey "an instrument for protecting the fundamental rights of the citizen, and not an instrument for enabling the community to provide services for the benefit of its citizens."[28] The rise of administrative power caused uneasiness and made Dicey himself qualify his absolute position about administrative law being inconsistent with the British system, without, however, altogether abandoning it.[29]

Dicey's major themes and concerns about widening administrative discretion were echoed in other writings during the first decades of the 20th century. In a 1929 book entitled *The New Despotism*, Lord Hewart, the Lord Chief Justice, dramatized the issue by warning of the risk of "administrative lawlessness."[30] The language of the book had distinctively Diceyan tones. He wrote for instance: "Between the rule of law and what is called 'administrative law' (happily there is no English name for it) there is the sharpest possible contrast. One is substantially the opposite of the other."[31] In that same year, the government appointed a committee "to consider the powers exercised by or under the direction of (or by persons or bodies appointed specially by) Ministers of the Crown by way of (a) delegated legislation and (b) judicial or quasi-judicial decision, and to report what safeguards are desirable or necessary to secure the constitutional principles of the sovereignty of Parliament and the supremacy of the Law."[32] The terms of the appointment reflect, both in their concern with the growth of the administrative state and in their emphasis on parliamentary sovereignty and the rule of law, the ideas of Dicey and Hewart.[33]

The reason an examination of Dicey's writings should inform works on the development of British administrative law is his "immense influence upon the development of public law in England"[34] that dominated not only the thinking of his contemporaries but also reverberated well into the second half of the 20th century. Similarly, the reason to consider his work is not only for what it included—for example, an exposition of the two leading principles of the British constitution, that is, parliamentary sovereignty and the rule of law. It is also for what Dicey left out. It was argued that "[i]n exorcising from the British Constitution all doctrines having even the most remote connection with the hated *droit administratif*, he at the same time excommunicated from the field of his vision a series of administrative institutions."[35] Importantly for our purposes, Dicey dealt almost exclusively with administrative adjudication rather than rulemaking, or what is more frequently described in the United Kingdom as delegated or secondary legislation.[36] In other words, the rejection of the notion of administrative law in the first place coupled with the refusal to accept the reality of a growing practice of administrative policymaking and the general mistrust of the executive left a "gaping hole" in Dicey's account: the issue of the democratic accountability of the rising administrative state.[37]

The types of control deriving from and reasserting Dicey's two pillars of the British constitutional system did not envisage an open participatory system. With respect to the rule of law prong, the emphasis on control by the ordinary courts of law focused on public officials' liability for tort and breach of the law. With respect to parliamentary sovereignty, Lord Hewart's suggestions, for instance, aimed at enhancing the supervisory role of Parliament.[38] Notable exceptions to this description were two recommendations included, not saliently, in the 1932 Report of the Committee on Ministers' Powers encouraging consultation with affected interests and a reason-giving practice.[39] However, neither the whole Report nor these specific recommendations attracted significant attention or exerted noticeable influence on the development of administrative procedures.[40] The following section looks more closely at the principles of parliamentary sovereignty and the rule of law and their lasting import in the British system.

B. The fundamental principles of parliamentary sovereignty and the rule of law and their judicial reflection

Books have been written about each of these principles. As Dicey, one of their classic and influential exponents, wrote, these are "the two principles which pervade the whole of the English constitution."[41] Their history and content has been contested, and a section of a chapter could not do them justice. Therefore, the focus here will not be on a detailed outline of their development; rather, I will examine what their status as cornerstone tenets of the British system might suggest in setting up an accountability regime for administrative action.

According to Dicey's oft-cited description of the principle of parliamentary sovereignty, Parliament has "the right to make or unmake any law whatever," and "no person or body is recognised by the law of England as having a right to override or set aside the legislation of Parliament."[42] In other words, the British jurist identified as the two main prongs of this precept the unlimited legislative authority of Parliament and the absence of any competing legislative power.[43] The principle of parliamentary sovereignty has deep historical roots, although this is not an incontestable assertion.[44] A modern elaborate account demonstrates that the principle had been accepted by a large majority of English lawyers since the 1640s at the latest, and by the central institutions of English government since the Henrician Reformation of the 1530s.[45] Similarly, it has been noted that the factor that definitely established the principle of parliamentary sovereignty was the political conflict of the 17th century between the Crown and Parliament that destroyed the "old despotism" culminating in the Revolution of 1688.[46]

Recent developments have tested the limits of the Diceyan conception of parliamentary sovereignty. The Human Rights Act ("HRA"), introduced in 1998 to "bring rights home" by giving effect within the UK to rights guaranteed under the European Convention on Human Rights, is one such example. Under section 4 HRA, if a court is convinced that a statute is incompatible with a Convention right and cannot be read in a way compatible with the Convention (section 3 HRA), it can issue a declaration of incompatibility. However, pursuant to section 4(6) HRA, this declaration: (a) does not affect the validity, continuing operation, or enforcement of the provision in respect of which it is given; and (b) is not binding on the parties to the proceedings in which it is made. Therefore, from a formal point of view, the principle of parliamentary sovereignty is not upset.[47] Two other developments were perceived as challenges to the traditional understanding of the doctrine: the European Communities Act 1972 providing for the incorporation and supremacy of EU law, and the devolution of powers to Wales, Scotland, and Northern Ireland. In both cases, an argument can be made that the Westminster Parliament retains the ultimate legislative competence; hence, the principle of parliamentary sovereignty is not unraveled.[48]

For present purposes a key component of the principle of parliamentary sovereignty is its implications for and focus on the control of the executive, in particular the relation between Parliament and statute, on the one hand, and administrative action, on the other. Dicey referred to the non-sovereign or subordinate law-making bodies whose authority is "clearly delegated and subject to the obvious control of a superior legislature."[49] A means of ensuring this parliamentary scrutiny is the requirement that secondary legislation be laid before Parliament.[50] In assessing the effectiveness of this type of control, one should keep in mind the limited time for debate on the floor of the House and the high number of annullable regulations laid before it. Furthermore, under both mechanisms, the regulations are either approved or disapproved. Parliament cannot itself amend them. Last, occasionally regulations are not subject to any laying procedure whatsoever, because Parliament has omitted to make any provision and there is no general statute mandating that all statutory instruments be laid.[51]

The aim here, however, is not to provide a detailed outline of all the mechanisms of parliamentary supervision, but to point to a more general idea: the principle of parliamentary sovereignty contains a structural mandate for the distribution of institutional power between Parliament and the executive in favor of the former. The previous examples of parliamentary supervision are one manifestation of this idea. The history of the prerogative powers of the Crown—or, since the mid-19th century, the executive—is another.[52] In Lord Browne-Wilkinson's words, "[t]he constitutional history of this country is the history of the prerogative powers of the Crown being made subject to the overriding powers of the democratically elected legislature as the sovereign body."[53] This was reflected in the case law of the early 20th century affirming the primacy of the statute over the Crown's prerogative power.[54] The principle of parliamentary sovereignty also helps to explain the problematic status of the so-called Henry VIII clauses. These are provisions included in a bill that enable primary legislation to be amended or repealed by subordinate legislation, with or without further parliamentary scrutiny.[55] This reverses the hierarchy stemming from the principle of parliamentary sovereignty even if, from a formalistic point of view, it is still a statute that provides this power. Consequently, these clauses have met a hostile reception.[56]

So far the focus has been on political controls of administrative action by means of parliamentary scrutiny as an expression of the principle of parliamentary sovereignty. However, beginning in the late 17th century the idea developed of double control of governmental activity comprising two elements: political control in Parliament but also control of legality in the courts.[57] There is here, too, a connection with the principle of parliamentary sovereignty. In Dicey's terms, this principle "looked at from its negative side" meant that there is "no person or body of persons who can make rules which override or derogate from an Act of Parliament, or which will be enforced by the courts in contravention of an Act of Parliament."[58] Seen in this light, the principle of parliamentary sovereignty underlies the doctrine of ultra vires.[59] If parliamentary sovereignty provides the justification for the invalidity of administrative action in breach of an Act of Parliament, it is the second major feature that Dicey identified, i.e., the rule or supremacy of law that empowers the courts of law to strike down this administrative action.

The rule of law, which has been statutorily recognized as a constitutional principle,[60] has given rise to multiple interpretations as to its content. The goal of this section is not to revisit these different accounts. Rather, it is to briefly trace the influence of this principle on the distribution of power between the executive, Parliament, and courts, its relationship with the principle of parliamentary sovereignty, and ultimately the room the latter interaction leaves for the introduction of a system of deliberative-participatory governance. A preliminary distinction that can help organize the different definitions of the principle is between formal and substantive accounts of the rule of law. As Paul Craig explains and the terms suggest, formal conceptions of the rule of law look to the form and objective attributes of the law, that is to say, the manner in which the law was promulgated, the clarity and temporal dimension of the norm. Substantive conceptions move beyond that in that they also assess the actual content of the norm and evaluate it based on substantive criteria, such as fundamental rights.[61] On the basis of this distinction, Dicey's account would be qualified as formalist and rather limited.[62]

The discussion so far should suffice to bring to the fore the key issue, namely, the relationship between the principles of parliamentary sovereignty and the rule of law. This relationship has been much debated in the literature, which has often described these two principles as being in tension. However, I will submit that this tension is not salient when it comes to judicial review of administrative action. Dicey had suggested that "[t]he sovereignty of Parliament is (from a legal point of view) the dominant characteristic of our political institutions."[63] This formulation could be fairly assumed as a signal that the principle of parliamentary sovereignty outweighs any other principles of the British constitution, including the rule of law. Dicey acknowledged that the two principles "may appear to stand in opposition to each other, or to be at best only counterbalancing forces." However, he was quick to add that "this appearance is delusive," as parliamentary sovereignty favors the supremacy of the law, which is enhanced by the "predominance of rigid legality."[64] Nevertheless, there are indications alluding to potential limits to parliamentary sovereignty if Parliament were to override the fundamental tenets of the rule of law.[65]

This debate is far from settled and my aim here is not to elaborate on its details but to point to the dynamic relationship between Parliament and the judiciary. An example in which this relationship manifests itself in harmonious terms is judicial review of administrative action. In this context, parliamentary sovereignty and the rule of law work in tandem in providing the basis for the ultra vires doctrine. This idea was described in the following terms: "The principle of parliamentary sovereignty . . . *enables* powers to be exercised by government and specifies how it is to be exercised. The Rule of Law however *disables* government from abusing its power."[66] In other words, the primacy of the statute, which is the logical outgrowth of parliamentary sovereignty, sets the boundaries for the executive and under the rule of law courts are entrusted with policing those boundaries and ensuring that administrative action stay intra vires.[67]

To recap, Dicey's account of the two fundamental principles of the British system is important not only because of its historical significance but also, and crucially, because even in the 20th century it steered attention toward two types of control of administrative action examined in this section: political control through parliamentary scrutiny and legal control in courts. These forms of control reflected a model of administrative accountability that could not incorporate open citizen participation. Political control through parliamentary scrutiny faces limitations that were described both in this section and in chapter 1, which pointed out the deficiencies of the "transmission belt" and "chain of legitimacy" ideas. Lloyd George, who had a long experience both in the legislative and the executive branches during the late 19th and early 20th centuries, quite likely exaggerated this idea when he said: "Parliament has really no control over the Executive; it is a pure fiction."[68] However, there is a valid concern in that statement, especially considering the increase in administrative policymaking, in a system where the same party controls both the legislature and the executive. Therefore, if parliamentary scrutiny is insufficient, the argument would go, judicial review becomes all the more important. The question then arising is whether the legal control of administrative action could incorporate requirements of democratic accountability, such as those described in chapter 1.

To answer this question we need an account of the competing models of judicial review. Paul Craig proposes a useful tripartite categorization among the traditional ultra vires, the modified ultra vires, and the common law models.[69] According to the traditional ultra vires model or specific legislative intent model, Parliament expressly states its will in the language of the enabling statute. In the context of democratic accountability through open participatory processes, this would mean that Parliament has inserted into the statute specific procedures aiming at enhancing the accountability of administrative action. Should the agency fail to follow these expressly prescribed procedures, its action would be invalidated as ultra vires. This would be an obvious case of inconsistency with the statute.[70] But the crucial distinguishing feature here is that the requirement that the agency follow an open participatory process does not *flow* from the idea of the rule of law. The source is instead a prior political decision to incorporate this form of democratic accountability into the statute, thus rendering it mandatory for the administrative authority and enforceable in court.

The interesting question that would logically come next is: in the event of legislative silence could the courts—on the basis of a model other than the traditional ultra vires doctrine—hold that a failure to hold an open public consultation before reaching an administrative decision constitute a "procedural impropriety," which constitutes a main ground of judicial review?[71] This is where the intertwined ideas of natural justice and procedural fairness come in. In administrative law there is a widely shared understanding that natural justice comprises two fundamental rules: that no one may be a judge in her or his own cause (*nemo judex in causa sua*) and that she or he must be given an adequate hearing (*audi alteram partem*).[72] The idea of procedural fairness raises two questions: first, what is the justification for courts to undertake this inquiry when the sovereign Parliament has not expressly incorporated it into the statute? Second, assuming that the courts do, in fact, possess this power, does the notion of procedural fairness include a public consultation requirement?

As to the first and logically prior question, natural justice has been "claimed" by both the modified ultra vires and the common law camps. Representing the former, Wade and Forsyth argued that the principles of natural justice are "based upon implied statutory conditions: it is assumed that Parliament, when conferring power, intends that power to be used fairly and with due consideration of rights and interests adversely affected." However, even in this view, treating a breach of natural justice as a violation of an implied term or condition and hence ultra vires has been described as a "bed of Procrustes" albeit a "necessary artificiality."[73] This judicial creativity prompted other scholars to put forth the common law model, whereby these principles are judicial creations.[74] Acknowledging the validity of certain points of the common law model, Mark Elliott proceeded to offer another strand of the modified ultra vires doctrine; the interesting feature of this account, which is particularly relevant here, is that the rule of law takes center stage again:

> [t]he rule of law, which is a fundamental of the British constitution, clearly favours the exercise of public power in a manner that is fair and rational. It is entirely reasonable to assume that, in the absence of clear contrary enactment, Parliament intends to legislate in conformity with the rule of law . . . . While the details of the principles of review are not attributed to parliamentary intention, the judicially-created rules of good administration should nevertheless be viewed as having been made pursuant to a constitutional warrant granted by Parliament.[75]

Irrespective of which of these two models one espouses, the second question is common: in enforcing principles of good administration under the rule of law, can courts read into those requirements a duty to consult? The courts answered that there is no such duty when it comes to administrative rulemaking. In *Ridge v. Baldwin*,[76] a leading case on natural justice, the House of Lords held that the dismissal of a Chief Constable was void on the grounds that he had been dismissed without notice of the charge and a proper opportunity to be heard in his own defense. This case expanded process rights but should be distinguished from the focus of the inquiry here, which is open public consultations in the exercise of administrative policymaking. In *Ridge v. Baldwin* the context was different as it involved *individualized* decisionmaking/adjudication, or in the lingo of the courts the exercise of administrative or executive functions. In contrast, British courts have rejected requests to expand this participatory obligation to cover the exercise of rulemaking powers, or again in the lingo of the courts the exercise of a legislative function under delegated powers.[77] Part II.C will examine these cases in more detail. The brief point to be made here is that the UK approach was that process rights in relation to rulemaking should in general be available only when provided by specific legislation.[78] In the words of Justice Sedley in *BAPIO*, "Parliament has the option, which the courts do not have, of extending and configuring an obligation to consult function by function. It can also abandon or modify obligations to consult which experience shows to be unnecessary or unworkable and extend those which seem to work well. The courts, which act on larger principles, can do none of these things,"[79] even when they act, I would add, on such "larger [constitutional] principles" as the rule of law. In other words, judicial review under any of the three competing models and the criteria imposed by the rule of law does not create a duty on the part of administrative agencies to hold public consultations absent a statutory provision to this effect.

In conclusion, both of the fundamental constitutional principles of parliamentary sovereignty and the rule of law, as developed by their most influential exponent, A.V. Dicey, were not meant to and did not accommodate in practice a system of participatory administrative governance. It is with this in mind that one should read Jowell's description of the rule of law: "Its promotion of the core institutional values of legality, certainty, consistency, due process, and access to justice do not merely, as Jennings would have it, further the aims of free trade and the market economy. They also promote respect for the dignity of the individual and *enhance democratic accountability*."[80] This section would challenge the validity of this claim as to democratic accountability of administrative rulemaking if the focus is narrowly on judicial review on the basis of rule of law criteria. However, its validity at the political level will be assessed in the following Part. As Conservative and Labour governments infused market economy values into public service delivery, the question will be whether this development went together with an enhancement of democratic accountability. Before we turn to these developments, we need to add a missing piece: the state-society relations during the rise of the British regulatory state; this constitutes the backdrop against which the transformation brought about by New Public Management can be evaluated in its proper dimensions.

C. The rise of club government

The previous section argued that the adequacy of political controls of the executive through parliamentary action should be and were viewed with skepticism. Dicey himself voiced his concerns regarding this type of control.[81] His disillusionment with Parliament and in particular the rise of party dominance explains his early support for the referendum, which he viewed as "an institution which would be strong enough to curb the absolutism of a party possessed of a parliamentary majority" and as bringing "some considerable diminution in the most patent defects of party government."[82] Notably, Dicey believed that the referendum offered certain advantages over elections, one of which was that it allowed people to focus on a specific issue while elections involved a range of issues making it more difficult to discern the people's opinion on a given topic.[83]

This is an argument that chapter 1 employed in discussing the limitations of the "transmission belt" idea, which, in turn, favored a more direct citizen involvement in administrative policymaking. Could this then mark an interesting twist? While the previous section explained that Dicey did not focus on the control of administrative policymaking, could we read into his support for the device of the referendum an implicit support for direct public participation in administrative rulemaking? The answer is, again, negative. Dicey's concerns, and the privileged domain he singled out for referendums, pertained to the larger questions of constitutional change, not administrative matters.[84] Besides, Dicey envisaged the referendum primarily as a "conservative weapon" operating as a veto power on legislation passed by Parliament.[85] In other words, citizen involvement was perceived as a negative check on government, which is far from the affirmative and empowering role that a system of open participatory governance ascribes to citizens.

There is a double historical irony here. The first was that the very democratization of Britain through the extension of the franchise, notably by means of the Reform Acts of 1867 and 1884, contributed to the growth of the party system and the faults that urged Dicey to advocate for the referendum; at the same time, the considerations underpinning the enfranchisement of the people supported the introduction of the referendum as well.[86] The second irony is that the same historical event, i.e., the expansion of the suffrage, created a backlash that insulated regulation and embedded a system of "club government," the origins of which dated in the Victorian era, well into the 20th century. This system, finally disrupted by the Thatcher administration, was antithetical to the fundamental tenets of an open participatory model in administrative regulation. It is this second irony that the last part of this section addresses.

Michael Moran presents an excellent account of the rise (and fall) of the club government in his book, *The British Regulatory State*.[87] As the name suggests, the main features of the club system were that it was informal, secretive, insulated from political controls, and open only to a small elite of privileged insiders. Writing about the Victorian era in which this system emerged, David Marquand described the atmosphere of British government as "that of a club, whose members trusted each other to observe the spirit of the club rules; the notion that the principles underlying the rules should be clearly defined and publicly proclaimed was profoundly alien."[88] A driving factor for the development of the British regulatory state, especially in the second half of the 19th century, was industrialization. A consequence of this key historical event was the rise of a new working class, which, in turn, brought with it stronger democratic pressures.[89] Moran explains that in the face of these threats powerful elites developed a system of club regulation to protect their interests and preserve control of their "own affairs." Interestingly, the same forces of resistance against rising "threats" of popular rule, fuelled by the extension of the franchise by successive Reform Acts in 1867, 1884 and notably the Representation of the People Act 1918, were responsible for "embedding" the system of club government into the 20th century.[90]

The features of the club model of government were reflected in the "administrative technology" of the time.[91] Perhaps the most salient example of this culture was the emergence and prevalence of the system of self-regulation. Britain was described as "something of a haven for self-regulation"[92] and the characteristic embodiment of that was the self-regulation of the professions and the City of London.[93] The emphasis on self-regulation was to be expected because it presented one "undeniable attraction to both politicians and businessmen of the period: state intervention with its unpalatable ideological implications, its potential bureaucratic costs, and its unpredictable demands for new standards of behaviour was rendered unnecessary."[94] Furthermore, the reliance of self-regulation on gentlemen's agreements, trust and self-discipline fit well with the features of the British elite that had been "fairly small, close-knit, and socially exclusive."[95] Another interesting feature of this arrangement was that while these professional bodies were, for the most part, insulated from external control, they imposed self-restraints through the development of codes that helped "foster trust among potential consumers and delimit areas of legitimate and illegitimate competition."[96] In the context of industrial regulation and inspection, the effects of the club culture, with its emphasis on trust and cooperation, were also apparent.[97] Across different sectors, experience would commonly reveal the "relatively limited contribution of formal law and legal institutions, and the creative potential of non-coercive administrative intervention."[98] This reflected a traditional perception in Britain that "business was expected to lead and government to facilitate this."[99]

After the Second World War, bureaucrats consulted with associations outside Whitehall, but again that style of consultation was another instantiation of the informal, closed style of the club system observed elsewhere. According to a telling description,

> [t]he official guide to civil servants' duties came to include a section on their obligation to consult all *recognised interest groups*. The criteria by which a group became accepted and put on the list of bodies to be consulted were fairly simple. The group had to represent the bulk of persons or companies or organisations in the area of activity and had to accept that *all negotiations were to be confidential, even from its own members*. In return, the leaders of these groups were consulted before any government plans were published and they could thus make their representation at a formative stage when plans were still open to argument and when no loss of face were involved in making changes.[100]

I added emphasis to the two key elements in this description: bureaucrats would choose whom to consult and the process would happen behind closed doors on the basis of trust that excluded not only the general public but even the members of the organizations being consulted. Therefore, even though British higher civil servants stood out compared to their counterparts in other European countries in their being comfortable with or even favoring the idea of consulting with interest groups,[101] the picture was not one of open participatory governance but rather one of "inner-circle negotiation"[102] reminiscent of the prewar "gentlemanly" style.

The operation of the nationalized public utilities sector, which is of particular relevance to this study, followed a similar pattern until the premiership of Margaret Thatcher. As an illustrating account suggests, "[t]he operation of the regulatory regime in practice was a 'game' largely played between the utility suppliers, large manufacturers firms that depended on utility orders, and ministers and their civil servants. The 'game' was highly closed; occasionally outsiders such as trade unions penetrated it, but even so, mostly on employment-related matters. Users played little role. The decision-making processes were informal and involved discussions and negotiations conducted in private."[103] In a similar vein, Moran describes that "[b]ehind a public language of ownership and accountability, the reality was a sustained history of evasion of public accountability, behind the scenes intervention by Ministers to shape business plans around short-term political pressures, and lack of transparency about institutional arrangements."[104] Part II will suggest that Margaret Thatcher's administration unraveled this club system. While up until then business enjoyed relations with

Whitehall that could be consistently characterized as "close and consensus-seeking," Thatcher's approach altered these traditional relations.[105]

In conclusion, Part I aimed to show that the development of the British administrative state, mostly in the 19th and early 20th centuries, neither intended nor in practice accommodated elements akin to an open participatory model of administrative governance. Dicey's early rejection of the notion of a British administrative law might have partly obscured the realities of the rise of the British administrative state and did not facilitate the development of a sustained debate on the features that a new model should possess. His influential account of parliamentary sovereignty and the rule of law, in large part, set the tone of the conversation as to the appropriate controls of administrative action with an overwhelming stress on parliamentary scrutiny and the jurisdiction of the ordinary courts. However, as this Part argued, neither of these elements incorporated the requirements of an open participatory model of democratic accountability. Indeed, at that same time, the state-society relations on the ground demonstrated quite the opposite features, i.e., a club system of government marked by informality, secrecy, flexibility, "gentlemanly" relations, and privileged access for a small elite. Dicey's influence was not limited to his time but extended well thereafter. As Harlow and Rawlings have suggested, his mistrust of discretionary power became a theme "dominating administrative law in the second half of the 20th century." According to the same account, "[i]t is not surprising, therefore, to find many authors believing that the primary function of administrative law should be to *control* excesses of state power and, more precisely, subject it to the rule of the law courts. Light-heartedly, we have called this conception of administrative law 'red light theory' because of its emphasis on control."[106]

This description has interesting reflections in the major books on general administrative law. The late Sir H. W. R. Wade, described as "perhaps Dicey's greatest and certainly his most influential heir,"[107] in the first edition of his *Administrative Law* highlighted the notion of control in his definition of administrative law as "concerned with the operation and control of the powers of administrative authorities."[108] While red light theory prioritizes courts, green light theory focuses on alternatives to courts with a preference for democratic or political forms of accountability.[109] This explains Harlow and Rawlings's emphasis on "process," "legitimacy," "effectiveness and efficiency," and "accountability." In response, Wade and Forsyth clarified that "the essence of administrative law lies in judge-made doctrines." Green-light objectives, such as more effective consultation, "whether or not desirable, are of a different order from those of this book."[110] Probably unsurprisingly, the later edition of their *Administrative Law* dedicates two pages to public consultations. Paul Craig's *Administrative Law* seems to aim for middle ground: while two of the three major parts of the book pertain to judicial review and remedies, at various points throughout the book there are discussions of accountability and public consultations.

This description is much more than a mere methodological debate. It raises a key question with important implications for the discussion of the development of British administrative law in which we can situate the impact of EU law: would the realities of the administrative state in the second half of the 20th century justify an emphasis on participatory administrative governance in a book with the declared purpose to focus on the operating paradigm and the actual law? If the answer to this question is negative—as some of the preceding references suggest—then it becomes clear that the deliberative-participatory model designed in chapter 1 was not only far from the Diceyan influential paradigm but also not ingrained into the administrative law system of the second half of the 20th century. This chapter opened with Dicey's remark in the turn of the 20th century that "in England we know nothing of administrative law." A few decades later Lord Denning stated that "it may truly now be said that we have a developed system of administrative law."[111] A question for the following Parts is the extent to which this developed system of British administrative law incorporated elements of open participatory governance. Against this backdrop, we will then assess whether these early features of administrative development are reflected in the case study of electronic communications and consequently the EU influence in this respect.

II. From the New Right to New Labour to a new model of administrative governance?

A. The New Right and New Public Management: The idea of "citizen-consumer" as a new building block and its strained relationship with administrative democracy

The previous section described the environment in response to which certain key aspects of Thatcher's policy innovations—most relevant for our purposes, privatization—were developed: an environment "where the prevailing theory of private corporate regulation, and the prevailing practice of public ownership, marginalized public accountability and transparency."[112] Privatization might have been the watershed, but it was accompanied by a range of other market-oriented policies falling under the umbrella of "New Public Management": contracting out, partnerships between the public and private sectors, and market-mimicking experiments in the retained public sector.[113] Thatcher's New Right administration moved from the prior consensual style of governing, which would often occur, as Part I.C. suggested, in an informal, "gentlemanly" fashion behind closed doors, to more conflictual politics privatizing and deregulating business.[114] Opening up markets and privatizing previously publicly owned companies created and empowered new actors that would participate and compete in these new markets.

These deregulatory policies signaled in effect the official dismantlement of older, informal structures that had already been under pressure;[115] at the same time, they were accompanied by re-regulatory policies setting up new, "more explicit regulatory structures" in the place of the previous regime to organize and facilitate the transition to competition.[116] When the Conservative government came to power, there existed more than 2,000 non-departmental public bodies (NDPBs), otherwise known as "quangos," that is, public bodies that were not government departments or part of a government department.[117] The election of a government committed to the retrenchment of quangos created an expectation of a "quangocide"[118]; some public bodies were indeed wound up in the aftermath of the 1980 review of non-departmental bodies but the curbing effort certainly did not rise to the level of a massacre of quangos.[119] In fact, Margaret Thatcher's own reform program led to the creation a new type of regulatory agency, the "Ofdogs."[120] These were originally established in the liberalized utility sectors to develop competitive markets in the public interest and "draw a line between the governmental and the regulatory role" as well as between the government and the formerly state-run public services now transferred to the private sector.[121] Part III.A. will return to these agencies in the electronic communications sector. The interesting observation here is that these re-regulatory initiatives represented a formalization of regulation that developed in response to "an erosion of trust in the ability of informal regulatory institutions to provide public assurance."[122]

Therefore, in challenging the old regulatory culture and necessitating some other mechanism in its place, privatization led to a more legalistic and "juridified relationship" between the state and the private sector.[123] Liberalization multiplied the number of participants in each sector; in turn, increasingly these actors were seeking to "test their rights and obligations against the legal frameworks of each sector."[124] Writing in 1997, Mark Thatcher succinctly summarized the change that had occurred in the policymaking processes: "the closed regulatory game of the pre-privatization era has given way to a more open and public one, with more participants, a higher degree of formalization of decision-making processes, greater public availability of information, more open conflict and complex manoeuvres involving ministers, the DGs, former monopolists, new entrants, consumer bodies and the MMC [Monopolies and Mergers Commission]."[125] A related development beginning in the 1980s was that pure self-regulation lost is prominence on the institutional stage.[126]

As the "tilt to the market" resulted in the breakdown of the traditional consensual informal structures of the old club system, a new era of intensified competition emerged; this prompted the rise of public relations/lobbying activity targeted at government.[127] However, the intentions of the New Public Management initiatives, at least in the rhetoric, were not just an expansion of the consultancy sector. Instead, the New Right governments brought to the fore a new actor, the citizen-consumer. This hyphenated term might sound odd, for its two components seem to be pulling in different directions: "In the public realm, people as citizens fulfil their obligations to one another, engage in mutual deliberation and exercise thought and choice in the definition and pursuit of the 'public interest.' By contrast, the consumer is a figure motivated by personal desires, pursuing their own interests through anonymous transactions."[128] But it was precisely the spread of market-like practices and expectations to the public realm that gave birth to this hybrid figure.[129] The citizen was redefined as an economic actor, a customer.[130] The driving idea was that citizens should be viewed not just as users of public services but as active consumers empowered to exercise choice,[131] have access to information about those services, request high-quality standards, and have avenues for complaint and redress in case of failure. Differently put, in this construction, the categories of "citizen, user of public services, and private sector consumer" were elided; the notion of choice, expressing the "ruling political sentiment" of the time, was particularly highlighted in the figure of the citizen-consumer and linked to the idea of responsiveness in public service delivery.[132]

Britain has been described as unique in advocating a consumerist approach to politics over the last decades.[133] A testament to this observation is that the theme of citizen-consumer was not simply carried forward but put to the center of John Major's agenda and enshrined in a key initiative of the first year of his premiership, the Citizen's Charter. This was signaled as his distinctive "big idea" on public service reform.[134] The ideas of choice and empowerment were central.[135]

To sum up, the New Right's institutional reform initiatives created a new liberalized environment, empowered a larger number of entrants in those markets, encouraged citizens to behave as active economic participants requiring higher standards of performance in public services, broke the old pattern of consensual secretive arrangements, and in so doing moved more in the direction of transparency, formalization, and juridification. Michael Moran maintains more emphatically that "the evolution of the system did indeed displace some of the more pathological features of club government. In particular, it broke open closed policy communities, enforced more transparency in both institutional relationships and in commercial transactions . . . . By any of the standards by which we might expect to judge economic government in a liberal democracy—accountability, transparency, plurality of representation—it was immensely superior to the way the nationalized sector had been governed."[136]

However, what drives these observations is the benchmark we employ, namely, the previous regime. The preceding paragraphs showed that the New Right administration unraveled the old club system, but the next question is whether it built a new regime that would fit the description of the deliberative-participatory model of governance. The answer is no. Whereas the New Right introduced new institutional structures, it crucially entrusted discretionary functions to individual persons, the Directors-General; whereas some degree of formalization and juridification was introduced, this was neither a self-conscious attempt nor the whole story; whereas new actors were empowered, consultation retained its preexisting characteristics; last, among those new actors rose the figure of the citizen-consumer. However, the conflation of the two components of the hyphenated term may suggest that this creation did not necessarily further administrative democracy but in essence pertained to managerial efficiency.

Let me take up these four points in turn. First, under Thatcher, the British system, unlike others, opted to vest legal powers for each liberalized sector directly in Directors-General (DGs) rather than in commissions.[137] Of course, as noted above, these DGs headed and were assisted by regulatory offices, the "Ofdogs." The key feature, however, was that the central figure in this new institutional environment was the DG as an individual with the Secretary of State retaining important formal powers, such as licensing.[138] In fact, this institutional choice in favor of DGs constituted a conscious departure from the American pattern of vesting authority in a regulatory board, where decisions were taken collectively.[139] This regulatory design in conjunction with a statutory framework leaving a wide range of discretion to the DGs resulted in a "highly personalized model of regulation": this characteristic was described as probably the most criticized one in the post-privatization UK regulatory system.[140] In December 1996, a report on the regulation of utilities discussed the merits of a system of individual DGs compared with regulatory boards. As with other questions, the report considered submissions from organizations and individuals concerned with utility regulation. A majority of respondents favored a move to a regulatory board. Criticisms leveled against the institutional design of the time included the excessive reliance on individuals and the danger of "personal agendas." In contrast, it was suggested that a regulatory board would achieve greater continuity, consistency, transparency, and formality, and would depersonalize regulation.[141] As the next Part will examine in more detail in the example of telecommunications, the move was indeed from the DG model to the regulatory commission model, a move, however, that occurred only in 2003.

These findings illustrate a point that should allow readers to evaluate the degree of the New Right's institutional reforms with respect to both the prior club system and my model of open participatory governance. Even though in practice the system of individual DGs seems to have worked well[142] while it lasted, this personalized system of regulation reflecting the highly personalized tradition of UK government[143] and the concomitant lower degree of formality tell a slightly modified story; one in which what was initially described as the transformative impact of the New Right's regulatory initiatives did not extinguish all aspects of the former club system and culture.

This brings us to the second and related point concerning the actual degree of formalization and juridification. In the debates about the shape of the regulatory regime for the new privatized environment, the question of US-style regulatory commissions, as opposed to individual DGs, was not the only comparative inquiry. Moran observes that in those debates two important American features, the democratic doctrines of accountability and a highly juridified constitutionalism, were pictured as "undesirable signs of inflexibility and legalism in the regulatory process."[144] As to transparency, in a similar vein, a 1990 book with the characteristic title *Government by Moonlight* lamented that "the flexible and informal networks of British government, with its 'off the record' concordats, its failure to adopt freedom of information (FOI) legislation, help the associations of mutual accommodation to develop behind a veil of confidentiality."[145] Formalization was intertwined with juridification, and again the assessment is that the New Right reforms moved more toward that direction compared to the old regime but not much. Our starting point should be that in the British tradition we observe a "largely non-juridified structure of administrative law."[146] Not only did the Thatcher government not wish to challenge that tradition but, in fact, one of the aims of the regulatory design, as Prosser observed, was to avoid judicial involvement in regulatory decisionmaking.[147] According to Harlow and Rawlings's interesting description of this,

> [t]he determinedly subjective and permissive language of the privatization statutes locked up together with a continued use of informal techniques of regulatory bargaining and the technical complexity of much of the subject matter to reduce its potency. A decade of operations saw only a handful of cases. In the event, far from the so-called 'hard look' doctrine of judicial examination of the basis of regulatory decisions once fashionable in America, the judges stressed the breadth of the statutory discretion, declining to become involved in detailed questions of fact.[148]

A striking example, given the importance of the statutory procedures for modification of license conditions by the regulators, is that the first litigation to challenge a regulator's actions occurred only in 1996.[149] Subsequent sections will return to questions of judicial review. What is noteworthy here is that even though the New Right reforms created certain conditions potentially favoring formalization and juridification, the process was not completed. In fact, through the 1980s and1990s the default judicial position seemed to be mostly one of deference to the regulator.[150]

The third point is that even though the New Public Management initiatives created and empowered new actors, this move was not accompanied by an increase in consultation or a general change in the mode of consultation. In fact, under Margaret Thatcher, there was a "perceived decline in consultation and in publication of preliminary Green and White Papers."[151] An explanation offered for this was that Thatcher's impositional style ran counter to the idea of consensus that was the cultural norm underlying the practice of consultation.[152] The formalization process under the New Right did not include a general legal obligation to consult, and the range of consultative practices existing instead were described as "on average highly unsatisfactory."[153] This resulted in the critique that the British legal order "has long been behind the times" especially "in terms of its failure to lend democratic help to the policy-making process, which is notoriously elitist."[154] The same account rebutted the argument, "seemingly [made] since time immemorial[,] that the British practice of consultation is in reality quite as effective as in other countries where distinct legal requirements exist" on the grounds that: "First, a mere practice of consultation allows government to decide when and if to consult. Secondly, it allows governments to determine the quality of consultation without there being any check on the openness of the process, its inherent rationality or the level of information made available to allow an informed assessment."[155] A similar kind of criticism applied to cases in which there was a statutory requirement of consultation.[156] These remarks suggest that the practice of consultation under Thatcher did not alter fundamentally the paradigm of consultation that had predominated in the decades preceding her reforms.[157] This should not come as a big surprise, however. The main drivers of New Public Management reforms were not ideas of democratic accountability but rather those of managerial competence and efficiency.[158] Understandably then, the focus was not on administrative processes furthering open democratic controls but on efficient outcomes. In this sense, the requirements flowing from managerialism do not map perfectly onto the demands of democratic administrative governance and their reflection in administrative law.[159]

These ideas of democratization and managerialism are the underpinnings of the notions of citizen and consumer, respectively, which brings us to our fourth and last point. One could say that the hybrid concept of the citizen-consumer harmoniously bridges those two underpinnings. In fact, it is their differences that help explain why the prominence of the citizen-consumer may not promote administrative democracy. Chapter 1 touched on this question in the discussion of the open access prong of the deliberative-participatory model, but the UK experience provides an excellent opportunity to examine the relationship of market citizenship with administrative democracy. A first strand of criticism points to the deficiencies of the construct of Citizen's Charters itself. It was argued that "[t]he shift to contract was largely a deception. The charters, left unenforceable, were not true contracts and, as public lawyers noted, classical public law protections and direct citizen participation in the making of policies and rules might be seriously curtailed."[160]

However, substantive concerns lie deeper than just matters of legal form. For instance, the Charter did not contain any new measures to promote the democratization of government institutions, such as a general right of access to official information.[161] As pointed out earlier, one of the themes of the 1991 Citizen's Charter was "choice and consultation." A report that Prime Minister Major presented to Parliament four years later elaborated on what this meant: "The Charter aims to give members of the public a greater say in the way their public services are run. Most public services now consult their users, both to gauge customer satisfaction and to identify areas of service delivery that are a priority to customers. Many services have targets for levels of customer satisfaction."[162] This language reveals the limitations of the citizen-consumer model: in the context of the Citizen's Charter, consultation aims at customer satisfaction and not at public involvement in the policymaking process. This gave rise to stark criticism. It was noted, for instance, that the emphasis on consumerism "has profound implications for the relationship between government and citizen. It restricts citizens to a passive consumption of politics, excluding them from playing a creative and productive role in civic life."[163] Similar concerns were voiced in multiple accounts of the citizen-consumer idea.[164]

Even if one does not subscribe to this very skeptical approach, the shift toward the notion of "market citizenship"[165] does come with the risk of obfuscating the distinction between individual consumer satisfaction and citizen participation in administrative policymaking as a collective project. The latter reaffirms a renewed concept of active citizenship in an environment in which regulatory agency action is increasingly important; the former is mostly preoccupied with efficient and responsive delivery of high-quality services in markets. Therefore, the figure of the citizen-consumer neither supports nor fits nicely into a model of open participatory governance.

The above should not be taken to question the importance of the regulatory reforms that the Thatcher government undertook. The aim of this section was to demonstrate that the New Right had the transformative effect of unraveling the club system and bringing to the fore new actors in a more formalized environment. For this reason, it constituted a necessary but not sufficient condition in moving toward an open participatory model of accountability. Whether New Labour completed this process will be examined in the following pages.

B. The New Labour reforms and the persistence of informality and discretion

New Labour's rise to power translated, in effect, into both continuity of certain major themes of the Thatcher era[166] as well as a move toward greater openness and participation. According to an interesting depiction of this idea: "As the old saw has it: we can turn an aquarium into fish soup, but we cannot turn the fish soup back into an aquarium. The Thacherites made fish soup of the old club system. The first Blair administration, if anything, drove the high modernist revolution even harder."[167] More specifically, New Labour pushed marketization and privatization forward "at least as zealously as the Conservatives did."[168] Similarly, the figure of the consumer of public services continued to take center stage.[169] However, the "visible sense of continuity did not mean that New Labour lacked ideas for the reform of government institutions: very much the reverse."[170] According to Anthony Giddens's prominent account of "third way" politics, the aim of the third way was neither to shrink the state (as the neoliberals would wish to do) nor to expand it (as the social democrats, historically, have been keen to do) but rather to reconstruct it. A key component of this process was an emphasis on deepening and widening of democracy, "democratizing democracy." The third way acknowledged the need "to combat the culture of secrecy that has pervaded the higher levels of British institutions, [that t]he executive holds too much power and the existing forms of accountability are weak." Consequently, it pointed to the importance of transparency, forms of democracy other than the "orthodox voting process" and the introduction of more direct contact between citizens and the government.[171]

The previous section described certain aspects of Thatcher's reforms as a necessary but not sufficient condition in moving toward an open participatory model of accountability. This section presents the New Labour themes of both continuity and change with the latter pushing further the need for openness and citizen empowerment.[172] Therefore, the question posed previously reemerges here: Did the reforms introduced by the Blair administration amount to a paradigm shift in administrative governance? Again, my answer is that that they moved the system closer to a deliberative-participatory model but the entrenched nature of discretionary and informal arrangements would prevent us from talking about a complete shift. Since the two key features of third way politics in our field of interest were transparency and public involvement,[173] two examples that illuminate my claim are two initiatives of the Blair government: the introduction of freedom of information legislation and the Code of practice on written consultation.

The British system had been characterized by a long-standing culture of secrecy and confidentiality, supported by legislation such as the Official Secrets Act of 1911.[174] The Major government had taken an important, albeit limited, step toward more open government by drawing up the Code of Practice on Access to Government Information in 1994.[175] Although the Code created a presumption of disclosure thus reversing the long-standing default position, this was a non-statutory and essentially non-enforceable duty consistent with the tradition of informality and discretion. In other words, in the absence of a legal statutory right to official information, publication of this information was still in essence—as had been the case in the past—under the control of government and on its terms.[176] New Labour had taken issue with the lack of legislative teeth with regard to freedom of information, and included in its manifesto for the 1997 election a commitment to enact freedom of information legislation.[177] Indeed, within six months after it had come to power, the New Labour government published a "hugely encouraging" White Paper proposing the introduction of such legislation.[178]

Nonetheless, the actual legislation that was passed and is currently still in effect with some amendments, namely the Freedom of Information Act 2000 ("UK FOIA"), was far less ambitious. In this sense, it constitutes a useful case to evaluate the transformative impact of the New Labour reforms. A detailed examination of this piece of legislation is beyond the scope of this section.[179] However, certain examples should clarify the delicate balance between formalization and discretion. On the one hand, the Act introduced a higher degree of formalization by enacting a statutory legal right of access to government information[180] and a rule of disclosure that credibly promoted more openness and accountability (s. 1(1)). The enforcement provisions had more teeth as well.[181]

On the other hand, the Act maintained a noteworthy degree of governmental discretion as reflected in several provisions. For instance, the UK FOIA contained twenty-three exemptions, eight of which were absolute; the range of these exemptions has resulted in strong criticism.[182] Another extraordinary provision of the UK FOIA is s. 53, the "ministerial veto." This provision allows an "accountable person," i.e., a Cabinet minister or the Attorney General, to issue a veto overriding the decision of the Commissioner or Tribunal to allow disclosure if she has "on reasonable grounds formed the opinion" that there has been no failure to comply with the duty to disclose. This clause was described as leaving an excessive scope of discretion, thus undermining "any credibility to the claim that the Act creates a legally enforceable individual right of access."[183] The reality is, however, more nuanced than this: there were seven vetoes until March 2014, so this is not widespread practice, and courts may review the lawfulness of these decisions.[184] A third example relates to the "duty" of public authorities to draw up publications schemes (ss. 19-20). However, these provisions are rather weak: there is no mandatory specification of the categories of information that must be included, and therefore they leave a high level of discretion to public authorities; while schemes are to be approved by the Commissioner, the latter is not given any power to compel the inclusion of specific items.[185]

All these discretionary features help explain why the UK FOIA was originally met with skepticism, occasionally couched in very strong terms: "The Freedom of Information Act 2000 is not only a sheep in wolf's clothing but a fraud on democratic accountability."[186] Nevertheless, again the picture is more nuanced than this quote. The operation of the UK FOIA, in practice, has contributed to transparency and is changing the culture of secrecy; therefore, it has gained support among the press, the public, and academics.[187] In fact, writing three years after that first quote, Rodney Austin qualified his position in noting that "[t]he Freedom of Information Act 2000 remains a sheep in wolf's clothing but its operation may, despite its limitations, save it from becoming a fraud on democratic accountability."[188] The fact that the UK FOIA took full effect only on January 1, 2005, five years after its adoption, and the discretion built into several provisions of the Act reflect a degree of uneasiness in fully transforming entrenched features of the British system. In this sense, the UK FOIA represents an example of the point made earlier: New Labour's ascent to power pushed the British system further in the direction of an open participatory model of administrative governance,[189] albeit without fully completing the process.

A key factor in encouraging the move just described was the formalization enshrined in the UK FOIA. This feature was, however, conspicuously absent in New Labour's approach to public consultation. The Blair government opted for the soft law method by first promulgating a Code of Practice on Written Consultation in 2000. The Code put forth seven consultation criteria to be reproduced in all consultation documents, including:

- Timing of consultation should be built into the planning process for a policy from the start.
- It should be clear who is being consulted, about what questions, in what timescale and for what purpose.
- A consultation document should be as simple and concise as possible. It should include a summary, in two pages at most, of the main questions it seeks views on.
- Documents should be made widely available, with the fullest use of electronic means.
- Sufficient time should be allowed for considered responses from all groups with an interest. Twelve weeks should be the standard minimum period for a consultation.
- Responses should be carefully and open-mindedly analysed, and the results made widely available, with an account of the views expressed, and reasons for decisions finally taken.
- Departments should monitor and evaluate consultations, designating a consultation co-ordinator who will ensure the lessons are disseminated.[190]

These criteria are indeed important and conducive to a meaningful consultation. However, the Code constituted only Cabinet Office guidelines; it did not create binding legal duties and vested significant amount of discretion with administrators concerning when and how to consult.[191] NDPBs were "encouraged" and devolved administrations were "free" to adopt the Code. The following language might, but should not, create any misunderstandings as to the nature of the Code: "Though [the criteria in this code] have no legal force, and cannot prevail over statutory or other mandatory external requirements (eg under European Community law), they should otherwise generally be regarded as binding on UK departments and their agencies, unless Ministers conclude that exceptional circumstances require a departure."[192] The Code did not create *ex nihilo* any duty to consult. The text itself suggested as much when it referred not only to the lack of legal force but also to the fact that those criteria "apply to all UK national public consultations on the basis of a document in electronic or printed form."[193] In other words they *applied* to consultations but did not mandate one in the first place.[194] This was made even clearer at multiple points in the third version of the Code published in 2008: "The Government has had a Code of Practice on Consultation since 2000 setting out how consultation exercises are best run and what people can expect from the Government *when* it has *decided* to run a formal consultation exercise"; "When developing a new policy or considering a change to existing policies, processes or practices, it will often be *desirable* to carry out a formal, time-bound, public, written consultation exercise"; "This Code is not intended to create a commitment to consult on anything, to give rise to a duty to consult, or to be relied on as creating expectations that the Government will consult in any particular case."[195]

Following a review of the 2000 Code, a new Code of Practice on Consultation was published in January 2004.[196] This second, shorter version of the Code did not revise fundamentally the consultation criteria included in the 2000 version. It reiterated the importance of allowing a minimum of twelve weeks for written consultation. This continued in the 2008 version. The scope of the Code was restricted considerably when the Coalition government replaced the 2008 Code with new Consultation Principles in 2012, which were amended further in 2016.[197] Under the 2012 Principles, departments could follow a range of timescales (typically between two to twelve weeks) rather than defaulting to a 12-week period. The 2016 Principles state that consultations should last for a "proportionate amount of time." Both the 2012 and 2016 Consultation Principles reiterate that "this document does not have legal force and is subject to statutory and other legal requirements." Interestingly, the 2016 Principles added clear guidance to the government departments to "not consult for the sake of it. Ask departmental lawyers whether you have a legal duty to consult."

The key point remains unaltered: In contrast with its policy on access to governmental information, with respect to public participation New Labour adopted a Code promoting good administrative practice but not a legally enforceable general mandate. In the familiar fashion this section described above, this important initiative of the first Blair administration continued along the path toward a model of open participatory governance but did not quite reach it. This is also mirrored in the Code's introduction by the Prime Minister: "We have worked hard since this Government came to power in May 1997 to make the administration of the country more open and responsive: giving more information about

Table 5.1 **National public consultations (2001-2004)**[1]

Year	Number of national public consultations	Percentage of consultations lasting 12 weeks or more
2001	396	80%
2002	621	71%
2003	622	77%
2004	621	76%

[1]Compiled with data drawn from the annual reports on consultation ("Assessment of Performance") available at: http://webarchive.nationalarchives.gov.uk/20060213205513/cabinetoffice.gov.uk/regulation/consultation/index.asp.

the way departments and services are operating, taking more account of people's views of policy, and of what they want from public services . . . . But we still have more to do, and this Code is another major step along the road, and a real contribution to modernising the way the country is governed."[198] In terms of the impact of the Code, Tony Blair noted in his Foreword to the revised 2004 Code that the 2000 Code "has been effective in raising both the quality and quantity of consultation carried out by government. We consult more extensively now than ever before. And, in the vast majority of cases, consultation periods are now at least 12 weeks long, enabling more time for responses and more people to be involved." Table 5.1 lists some of those figures.

Paul Craig invites us to place these numbers, and the impact of the Code, in perspective. For instance, the figure of 571 public consultations carried out in 2006 should be viewed against the volume of legislation enacted during that year: 55 Acts of Parliament and 1,777 statutory instruments.[199]

But beyond numbers, the broader and focal point of the preceding discussion is that public consultation under the Code retained a high degree of discretion and did not translate into a legally enforceable duty.[200] As the following section will show, what soft law could not provide, common law did not deliver either.

C. Judicial review of public consultations

1. *The sources of the duty to consult*

As was noted earlier, courts did not step in to fill the gap left by the absence of a general statutory duty to consult, and impose such a requirement on the basis of the common law.[201] The landmark *Ridge v. Baldwin* case[202] affirmed the right to a fair hearing stemming from the principle of natural justice. Citations included in that judgment referring to a rule of "universal application" did not obscure the fact that this right pertained to acts determining the status and the rights of an individual: *Ridge* concerned the dismissal of a Chief Constable, that is, it had nothing to do with administrative policymaking.

This distinction played itself out in *Bates*.[203] The court held that a statutory committee's delegated power to make general orders regulating the remuneration of solicitors was of a legislative and not an administrative, executive or quasi-judicial nature, and thus not bound by rules of natural justice or by any general duty of fairness to consult all bodies that would be affected by the order. Megarry J. added: "Many of those affected by delegated legislation, and affected very substantially, are never consulted in the process of enacting that legislation; and yet they have no remedy. Of course, the informal consultation of representative bodies by the legislative authority is a commonplace; but although a few statutes have specifically provided for a general process of publishing draft delegated legislation and considering objections . . . I do not know of any implied right to be consulted."[204] Interestingly, in this case the existence of a specific procedural requirement, i.e., the statutorily mandated consultation with the Law Society, served as an additional ground for the court's refusal to imply any further consultative requirements based on the principle that "what is expressed renders what is implied silent."[205]

A later case, *BAPIO*,[206] had interesting pronouncements to add. The case concerned the lawfulness of two government measures: importantly in this context, the alteration without consultation by the Home Secretary of the Immigration Rules so as to abolish permit-free training for doctors who lacked a right of abode in the United Kingdom. No transitional provision was made for international medical graduates ("IMGs") who were lawfully in the UK on visitor visas and, though unemployed, had passed a specific language test (PLAB test) and were seeking traineeships. The appellants' main argument was that IMGs, including importantly the members of the British Association of Physicians of Indian Origin (BAPIO), and BAPIO itself had a "legitimate expectation not that the Immigration Rules would not be changed to their detriment, but that no such change would be undertaken without consulting them about it." In this case, consultation was not required by law; the appellants therefore sought to establish a consultation requirement on the basis of legitimate expectations (a doctrine to which this section will return). Lord Justice Sedley held that there had not been a consistent practice of consultation on the part of the Home Secretary and appeared reluctant to find a duty to consult on this basis alone.

The most interesting parts of the judgment pertain to the relationship between consultation and the role of Parliament and the courts. One of the government's arguments for there being no duty to consult relied on the presumed parliamentary intent: Parliament could not have intended, when it gave the Home Secretary power to make and alter the Immigration Rules, that he should consult, in view of the fact that such procedural requirements are expressly included in other statutes and absent in the statute at hand. Lord Justice Sedley rejected this argument:

> express provision for consultation in other statutes cannot by itself impliedly exclude consultation from the implementation of s. 3 of the Immigration Act 1971. There is, if I may say so, a touch of innocence about the submission that Parliament was well aware by 1971 of the 'technique', as the respondents call it, of prescribing consultation, so that the non-use of it proves a contrary intent. Such reasoning would bring down the entire body of adjectival common law constraints on the use of statutory powers. Given . . . the fact that Home Secretaries have more than once elected to consult about changes to them, it is quite impossible to extract from the statute's silence about consultation an intent that there should be none.[207]

The real question for Lord Justice Sedley, however, lay elsewhere. It is instructive to quote him directly in some length:

> The real obstacle which I think stands in the appellants' way is the difficulty of propounding a principle which reconciles fairness to an adversely affected class with the principles of public administration that are also part of the common law . . . . It is not unthinkable that the common law could recognise a general duty of consultation in relation to proposed measures which are going to adversely affect an identifiable interest group or sector of society.
>
> But what are its implications? *The appellants have not been able to propose any limit to the generality of the duty.* Their case must hold good for all such measures, of which the state at national and local level introduces certainly hundreds, possibly thousands, every year. If made good, such a duty would bring a host of litigable issues in its train: is the measure one which is actually going to injure particular interests sufficiently for fairness to require consultation? If so, who is entitled to be consulted? Are there interests which ought not to be consulted? How is the exercise to be publicised and conducted? Are the questions fairly framed? Have the responses been conscientiously taken into account? *The consequent industry of legal challenges would generate in its turn defensive forms of public administration.* All of this, I accept, will have to be lived with if the obligation exists; but it is at least a reason for being cautious.
>
> The proposed duty is, as I have said, not unthinkable – indeed many people might consider it very desirable - but thinking about it makes it rapidly plain that *if it is to be introduced it should be by Parliament and*

not by the courts. Parliament has the option, which the courts do not have, of extending and configuring an obligation to consult function by function. It can also abandon or modify obligations to consult which experience shows to be unnecessary or unworkable and extend those which seem to work well. The courts, which act on larger principles, can do none of these things.[208]

These thoughts on the institutional competence of courts relative to Parliament and on the complex practicalities of recognizing by judicial fiat a duty to consult led the court to reiterate the earlier position that there is no such general common law duty.[209] However, what stands out in the excerpt is the cautious approach highlighting both the dangers of over-juridification and the limits of informal, discretionary practice. Both these points reflect traits that are seemingly still entrenched in the 2007 jurisprudence. It is almost as if we could hear voices from several decades before that were mentioned earlier in this chapter and cautioning against an overly litigious culture (like the American one?) not befitting the British tradition. A crucial distinguishing factor was, of course, that litigation revolving around stakeholder participation in the United States had a statutory hook, the APA, which several cases expanded. Here the court refrained from imposing a duty to consult in the absence of statutory support, but the emphasis on the potential perils of excessive litigation is in any event telling.

Interesting issues of institutional balance between the different branches of government also arose from the two concurring opinions in this case. Lord Justice Kays, with Lord Justice Rimer agreeing in his own concurrence, shifted the emphasis on two other accountability mechanisms, which, in his view, further counseled against a judicial decision implying a duty to consult:

I doubt that, as a matter of principle, a duty to consult can generally be superimposed on a statutory rule-making procedure which requires the intended rules to be laid before Parliament and subjected to the negative resolution procedure. I tend to the view that, in these circumstances, primary legislation has prescribed a well-worn, albeit often criticised, procedure and I attach some significance to the fact that it has not provided an express duty of prior consultation, as it has on many other occasions. The negative resolution procedure enables interested parties to press their case through Parliament, although I acknowledge that their prospects of success are historically and realistically low. They also retain the possibility of challenge by way of judicial review . . . [A]s a matter of principle, I consider that where Parliament has conferred a rulemaking power on a Minister of the Crown, without including an express duty to consult, but subject to a Parliamentary control

mechanism such as the negative resolution procedure, it is not generally for the courts to superimpose additional <u>procedural</u> safeguards.[210]

Lord Justice Kays's discussion is another interesting depiction of ideas examined in Part I and still informing judicial opinions; namely, that parliamentary
scrutiny—in this case, the negative resolution procedure also described in Part
I—and substantive judicial review establish sufficient controls on administrative action. This recalls our treatment of the limitations of the traditional parliamentary safeguards; Lord Justice Kays acknowledges these limitations as well
but does not shy away from drawing the inference that the existence of these
traditional safeguards precludes the necessity of public consultation. Therefore,
even though in all three opinions in *BAPIO*, functional considerations come into
play in determining whether there is a common law duty to consult, in the two
concurring opinions consultation is not viewed as complementary to, but rather
as displaced by parliamentary processes. Interestingly, this position does not
find support in a House of Lords case that included a reference to the inadequacy
of the process of "laying before Parliament" in representing all interests in the
immigration context.[211]

The discussion so far has established that a general duty of fairness based on
common law does not constitute a sufficient ground on which to establish a duty
of public authorities to consult when they make public policy. Nevertheless, consultation rights have been accorded by case law in certain instances involving
the protection of legitimate expectations.[212] The latter may arise either from a
representation on the part of a public authority that there will be consultation
prior to the adoption (or a change in) policy or from consistent past practice.
One of the earliest cases in this context was *R v. Liverpool Corporation, ex parte
Liverpool Taxi Fleet Operators Association*.[213] In *Council of Civil Service Unions*[214]
a trade union was found to have a legitimate expectation of being consulted
before policy change based on a long prior practice of consultation, although
this did not lead to the invalidation of the government action in question due to
national security reasons. Likewise, in *Dredger*, stall-holders were found to have
a legitimate expectation of being consulted about a major change in the basis of
computation of rent for market stalls where there had been a practice giving rise
to a legitimate expectation of consultation on the level of rents.[215]

Even though this series of judgments expanded the scope of judicially enforceable consultation beyond the cases in which such participatory processes were
statutorily mandated, the ambit of this case law should not be overestimated.
Before courts recognized a legitimate expectation of prior consultation, they
required clear evidence of either consistent agency practice or express representations and clear assurances on the part of public authorities that they would
consult prior to adopting or changing a particular policy.[216] In other words, a
general ambiguous promise or practice of prior consultation that would not

cover agency decisions germane to the one a court is considering in a particular case may not suffice.[217]

2. *The content of the duty to consult*

Whether consultation is a legal requirement (which, in turn, might derive from a statute or legitimate expectations) or undertaken voluntarily, UK courts have held that once "embarked upon it must be carried out properly."[218] There are four factors against which courts assess whether a public authority has adequately carried out its obligation to consult, known as the *Gunning* criteria or the Sedley requirements (named after Sedley QC who was counsel for the applicants in the 1986 *Gunning* case). These criteria, which Lord Woolf set out clearly in *Coughlan* as well,[219] are:

a. consultation must be at a time when proposals are still at a formative stage,
b. the proposing authority must give sufficient reasons for any proposal to per-mit of intelligent consideration and response,
c. adequate time must be given for consideration and response,
d. the product of the consultation must be conscientiously taken into account in finalizing any statutory proposals.

The Supreme Court finally endorsed the Sedley criteria in a 2014 case, *Moseley*, describing them as "a prescription for fairness."[220] Lord Reed wrote a separate judgment (with which Baroness Hale and Lord Clarke agreed) distinguishing between different purposes of consultation. In Lord Reed's opinion, the wide-ranging consultation at issue in *Moseley*, which pertained to a local authority's exercise of a general power in relation to finance, was "far removed in context and scope from the situations in which the common law has recognized a duty of procedural fairness." The purpose of public consultation in *Moseley* was "not to ensure procedural fairness in the treatment of persons whose legally protected interests may be adversely affected, as the common law seeks to do." Instead, the particular statutory duty to consult was to "ensure public participation in the local authority's decision-making process."[221]

Whether the Sedley criteria are satisfied is context-specific but courts have held that agencies have "an obligation to give a real and not an illusory oppor-tunity to make representations."[222] In this case, involving the reorganization of local schools upon a comprehensive basis, the court stated that a consultation period of four weeks would be reasonable but any substantially shorter period—in the case at hand, less than five days—would not. Relatedly, in *Gunning* itself, a case pertaining to school closures, the court held that the consultation period was wholly inadequate for a fundamental change in policy. More specifically, in this case copies of the consultation document had been given to each student to take home before school breaks for the mid-term holiday. Hodgson J held that it was unrealistic to expect the "pigeon post" method of distribution to be effective before half term as the vast majority of parents had only received the document about ten days before the closing date for written responses and three days before the public meetings. He also found that the consultation document was wholly inadequate and even positively misleading with respect to the existence of information as to the cost of maintaining the whole school stock.

That last point brings to the fore questions regarding the relevant information that public authorities may need to provide to consultees. According to a useful summary of the pertinent case law,[223] this information includes the following:

- the proposed action and the factual information upon which it is based;
- in some situations, sufficient reasons for what is proposed and any assumptions underlying the proposals;
- in some circumstances relevant documentary advice, or possibly a summary of that advice, may need to be disclosed to consultees;
- sufficient information as to the basis or criteria by which the proposal will be considered;
- there is support for the view that the public body should indicate possible alternatives to the proposal. For instance, *Moseley* held that sometimes, particularly when statute does not limit the subject of the requisite consultation to the preferred option, fairness will require that interested persons be also consulted upon arguable yet discarded alternative options. Meaningful public participation in a context with which the general public cannot be expected to be familiar requires that the consultees should be provided not only with information about the draft, but also with an outline of the realistic alternatives, and an indication of the main reasons for the public authority's adoption of the draft. [224]

However, courts have also employed restrictive language. In *Coughlan*, for instance, the Court of Appeal underscored:

> It has to be remembered that *consultation is not litigation: the consulting authority is not required to publicise every submission it receives or (absent some statutory obligation) to disclose all its advice.* Its obligation is to let those who have a potential interest in the subject matter know in clear terms what the proposal is and exactly why it is under positive consideration, telling them enough (which may be a good deal) to enable them to make an intelligent response. The obligation, although it may be quite onerous, goes no further than this.[225]

Since these criteria are capacious and abstract enough to accommodate both higher and lower demands for agency disclosure, and their application is context-specific, not surprisingly cases have come out in both ways. In *Coughlan* itself, the court held that there was no need to disclose to the applicant both a paper and a report that the public committee had commissioned from a third party in response to the consultation exercise. Due to time limitations, the public authority had not afforded the consultees an opportunity to comment on them. The court did not consider this a fatal defect. With respect to the report, it held that this was external advice and constituted itself a response to the consultation (hence, not necessarily disclosable), albeit one solicited by the health authority. It continued by noting that both documents were not a part of the agency's proposal and not necessary to explain the proposal, and added that "[t]he risk an authority takes by not disclosing such documents is not that the consultation process will be insufficient but that it may turn out to have taken into account incorrect or irrelevant matters which, had there been an opportunity to comment, could have been corrected. That, however, is not this case."[226] In other words, the court seemed to look favorably to the idea that some procedural flaws may be overcome on substantive grounds, but also importantly for present purposes, was quite lenient in recognizing that the public authority need not publicize any submission or advice it receives. This runs counter to the approach proposed under the transparency prong of the deliberative-participatory model of chapter 1. As the following Part will describe, in the telecommunications domain the regulatory agency on multiple occasions allowed a second round of comments responding to submissions regarding the original consultation document.

However, there have been cases in which courts imposed a higher burden on the public authority. *Eisai*[227] is one such example. The National Institute for Health and Clinical Excellence ("NICE") is responsible for appraising the clinical benefits and cost effectiveness of particular treatments, and for making recommendations as to their use in the UK healthcare system (the National Health Service, "NHS"). NICE's system of technology appraisals is quite complex and entails multiple stages of consultations. This case involved specific drugs for the treatment of Alzheimer's disease ("AD"); these had previously been recommended for use in the treatment of NHS patients with mild to moderately severe AD. In 2006, however, NICE issued fresh guidance recommending their use only for patients with moderately severe AD. The claimant ("Eisai") was a pharmaceutical company holding the UK marketing authorization for one of the drugs. It challenged this fresh guidance on the ground that the consultation process had been unfair because NICE had not provided in the public consultation a fully executable version of the economic model that was central to the appraisal of the cost-effectiveness of the drugs. Instead, the pharmaceutical companies had received only a "read-only" version of the model that had not allowed it to be re-run with alternative assumptions and inputs; this meant that Eisai was unable to test the reliability of the model by running sensitivity analyses. The Court of Appeal unanimously accepted this argument:

procedural fairness does require release of the fully executable version
of the model. It is true that there is already a remarkable degree of disclosure and of transparency in the consultation process; but that cuts
both ways, because it also serves to underline the nature and importance of the exercise being carried out. The refusal to release the fully
executable version of the model stands out as the one exception to the
principle of openness and transparency that NICE has acknowledged as
appropriate in this context. It does place consultees . . . at a significant
disadvantage in challenging the reliability of the model. In that respect
it limits their ability to make an intelligent response on something that
is central to the appraisal process.[228]

The court was not convinced by the reasons that NICE put forward for its refusal
to release the fully executable version. The first pertained to confidentiality.
The second, and more interesting for present purposes, was that provision of
the fully executable model would have profoundly counterproductive practical
consequences: NICE would have to devote a great deal of time and resources to
understanding the various amendments made to its model. The court disagreed:

it would be open to NICE to impose reasonable conditions on the release
of the fully executable version, for example by requiring sensitivity test
results to be presented in a specified manner or limiting the scale of
submissions or laying down an appropriate time limit. But even if one
accepts the possibility that release of the fully executable version would
add 2 to 3 months to the appraisal process, that has to be viewed in the
context of an already lengthy process (this one took almost 2½ years in
total). I do not think that either the additional time or the additional
cost to NICE should weigh heavily in the balance in deciding whether
fairness requires release of the fully executable version.[229]

So what changed in the intervening time between the 2001 *Coughlan* court pro-
claiming that "consultation is not litigation" and the 2007 *Eisai* court overlook-
ing administrative considerations of cost and delay in the interests of fairness
that mandated full disclosure? We could say that in the latter case the background assumptions had started to change as the Freedom of Information Act
had already been in full effect for two years, and that might have created a culture
of increased transparency. At any rate, these judgments may not be as inconsistent as a first reading might suggest. After all, both applied the same legal framework, that is, the Sedley criteria, and it may simply be the different sets of facts
that account for the different disclosure requirements.[230] In *Coughlan*, the undis-
closed documents might have been less material than the economic model in
Eisai. Therefore, *Eisai* must not necessarily be read as reflecting a higher degree

of comfort on the part of courts with the judicialization of the consultation process. It is also true that in terms of practical outcomes for the claimants—namely, the relief granted—there was not much difference either. In fact, in *Coughlan* the court concluded that the decision of the public authority was unlawful on other grounds. In *Eisai*, on the other hand, the issue of relief was deferred until the parties had had an opportunity to consider the judgment.[231] In any event, the combined reading of these two cases helpfully reiterates a concern that readers will recall other UK actors (judicial and otherwise) had expressed in the past: that is, the appropriate degree of formalization of the regulatory process and courts as the appropriate forum for strictly policing, or even imposing, procedural requirements on agencies. The last case of this section, *Greenpeace*,[232] returns to this question.

3. *A useful recap:* Greenpeace *and the role of judicial review of participatory processes*

In *Greenpeace*, the preliminary question of establishing an obligation to consult and the subsequent issue of properly carrying out the consultation were intertwined. Greenpeace applied to quash a government decision, announced in "The Energy Challenge Energy Review Report 2006" ("Energy Review 2006"), to support nuclear new build as part of the UK's future electricity generating mix. The quashing order was sought on the ground that the consultation process leading to the decision had been procedurally flawed and therefore the decision was unlawful. In 2003 the government had published a White Paper (the "2003 White Paper") that did not contain proposals for building new nuclear power stations. However, it did not rule out the possibility that in the future new nuclear build might be necessary but emphasized, in bold fonts, that "before any decision to proceed with the building of new nuclear power stations, there would need to be the fullest public consultation and the publication of a white paper setting out the Government's proposals." The consultation document at the basis of the challenge was issued on January 23, 2006 ("the 2006 Consultation Document"), together with a summary consultation paper for members of the general public. On July 11, 2006, the Industry Secretary published the "Energy Review 2006," which stated that "the Government believes that nuclear has a role to play in the future UK generating mix alongside other low carbon generation options." Having reached this position, this document also set out how the government intended to create a policy framework under which developers would be able to make proposals for new nuclear build that would be published in a forthcoming Energy White Paper. The Energy Review 2006 also sought views on the proposal.

The claimant argued that the government, having promised in the 2003 White Paper that there would be "the fullest public consultation" before it reached any decision to change its policy "not . . . to support new nuclear build now," failed to live up to that promise before deciding in the Energy Review "that nuclear has a role to play in the future UK generating mix." Two broad criticisms were made of the 2006 Consultation Document: First, it either was or appeared to be in the nature of an "issues paper," seeking consultees' views as to which issues should be examined by government rather than the consultation paper on the substantive issue itself: should the new nuclear build option be taken up? Second, if it was intended to be a consultation paper on the substantive issue, it was inadequate.

The court agreed on both counts. As to the first, it pointed to a number of features of the 2006 Consultation Document suggesting that it was an issues paper to be followed by "policy proposals," on which there would be further consultation. There were no such proposals in relation to nuclear power in the 2006 Consultation Document. In this sense, there was no public consultation, let alone "the fullest possible consultation," that would afford the general public an opportunity to comment on the substantive issue of whether the government should support nuclear new build;[233] this constituted a breach of the public's legitimate expectations that were well founded on the clear promise of consultation that the government had made in the 2003 White Paper. Turning to the claimants' second main claim, the court found that there had been no proper consultation:

> As an issues paper [the consultation exercise] was perfectly adequate. As the consultation paper on an issue of such importance and complexity it was manifestly inadequate. It contained no proposals as such, and even if it had, the information given to consultees was wholly insufficient to enable them to make "an intelligent response." The 2006 Consultation Document contained no information of any substance on the two issues which had been identified in the 2003 White Paper as being of critical importance: the economics of new nuclear build and the disposal of nuclear waste. When dealing with the issue of waste, the information given in the 2006 Consultation Document was not merely wholly inadequate, it was also seriously misleading . . . On both the economics and the waste issues all, or virtually all, the information of any substance . . . emerged only after the consultation period had concluded.[234]

All in all, *Greenpeace* would be a good textbook example combining all the steps of the judicial reasoning in consultation cases discussed in previous sub-sections: if the consultation document was only an issues paper, the decision to support nuclear new build had not been preceded by any consultation in violation of the principle of legitimate expectations based, in this case, on a clear prior promise on the part of the government. If, on the other hand, the consultation document *was* the key document purporting to support the government's decision, the consultation had not been properly carried out on the basis of the *Gunning/Coughlan* criteria.

However, another noteworthy facet of this case is that it could serve as a springboard to revisit the interesting interplay between formalization and judicialization of consultation processes. As has been correctly noted, this judgment "takes consultation seriously, seeing it as making a real contribution to rational risk assessment and decision-making."[235] The question of the appropriate degree of judicial intervention was brought up in the case. The defendant (the Secretary of State for Trade and Industry) submitted that the court should be very slow to intervene in respect of such a "high-level, strategic policy document" as the Energy Review; the defendant would be accountable to Parliament for the policies contained in a forthcoming White Paper. Parliament would be entitled to consider both the merits of the policies themselves and the fairness of the process by which they have been arrived at. In these circumstances it was contended that the court should interfere with the process "only if something has gone clearly and radically wrong."[236]

The court adopted this test and recognized that "a decision-maker will usually have a broad discretion as to how a consultation exercise should be carried out. This applies with particular force to a consultation with the whole of the adult population of the United Kingdom."[237] It was on the application of this test that the decision in the Energy Review 2006 was found unlawful. In addition to the 2006 Consultation Document and the Summary Document, stakeholder seminars, conferences, receptions, and other meetings had been held. Harlow and Rawlings suggest that because the decision was ruled unlawful, all these procedures would have to be replayed; this provided an incentive for public authorities to "draw back, for fear of litigation, from more generous consultation practices."[238] But even if not all participatory processes were "poisoned," still the uncertainty on the part of public authorities as to which innovative participatory processes courts would invalidate when evaluating consultation exercises might have a chilling effect on the adoption of such practices. Drawing on this, a critic of formalization and judicialization might say that even my suggestion in chapter 1 that it may be helpful analytically to unbundle judicial review from consultation[239] did not go far enough: not only does judicialization's potentially deterrent effect, the same argument would go, not support the other prongs of the "deliberative-participatory model," it may actually undermine participatory processes.

I do not agree. The "problem of excessive judicialization," which had been, as shown at multiple previous points, associated with formalization, was in this case in fact the outgrowth of the *lack* of formalization. The court had to operate on the basis of a clear, and expansive, promise of "the fullest possible consultation" on the part of the public authority, but with no signposts. Formalization would reduce uncertainty and the chilling effect that this case might have; for this to be the case, however, we would need a kind of formalization that would acknowledge the importance of flexibility and build it into a formal roadmap. This framework would provide for a phased consultation: the first stage would be a softer form of consultation on green and white papers, whereby agencies would be allowed to test the waters and solicit input on a wide range of broader, "strategic" substantive issues while experimenting with forms of consultation; courts at this stage should be more deferential. The second stage would be statutorily prescribed in more details, as it would pertain to specific proposals; courts would be more actively policing these processes. This phased approach would have positive implications for the further development of techniques of participation in an incremental way. Agencies would have incentives to move beyond the floor and adopt more elaborate participatory process without the fear of extensive litigation and delay at the first "issues stage." This experience would allow some of those procedures to be then potentially incorporated into the more stringent second stage.

Chapter 6 will return to questions of institutional design. The key conclusion of this section is that the case law provided no autonomous trigger of a duty to consult. If there was an external source of this obligation (statutory or on the basis of legitimate expectations narrowly defined), then the adequacy of the process was examined. However, the latter was not interpreted expansively, for instance, there was no general duty to disclose the submissions of other consultees. In cases that are not flagrant, judges have tended to show some leniency in interpreting statutory consultation requirements as "directory," rather than "mandatory."[240] Sections A and B argued that neither the New Right nor New Labour completed a paradigm shift in the model of administrative governance; Section C showed that the operation of judicial review followed along the same path.[241]

Parts I and II set up the historical and institutional framework in which we may now situate the example of telecommunications regulation.

III. The case study: Public participation in telecommunications regulation

This chapter began by noting the leading role that the UK played in the liberalization of the telecommunications sector in Europe. In fact, scholars writing in the 1980s stressed the contrast between those developments in the UK and the emphasis on the role of the state in France.[242] While the UK was at the forefront of the world privatization revolution and has had an impact on telecommunications regulation both in individual European countries and at the

EU level,[243] within the country the regulatory initiatives in the telecommunications area became the standard model that applied across the public utilities.[244] Interestingly, the divergence with the French model began in the 1970s and particularly in the 1980s with the privatization of British Telecommunications and the creation of Oftel. Before 1969, there were commonalities between the institutional arrangements in the two countries: telecommunications services (together with postal services) were supplied by a government department, with the employees of the monopoly operator being civil servants.[245] The institutional gap was partly bridged with the post-1996 institutional reforms in France and the creation of the ART/ARCEP, which chapter 3 described in more detail, and even more so after 2004. The description of institutional developments in the following pages will showcase the different path that the UK followed in contrast with the French and the Greek accounts in the previous two chapters.

Section A provides a brief overview of the history of telecommunications regulation in the UK. It focuses on the establishment of regulatory bodies to prepare the transition to competition in this sector. Section B then moves from the institutional structure of the regulators themselves to the policymaking processes they employed. Particular emphasis is given to the impact that EU law has had on the domestic regulatory framework adopted in 2003, as well as on Ofcom's policymaking practices. Section C reviews Ofcom's decision-making processes on the basis of the criteria of the deliberative participatory-model.

A. Telecommunications regulation from the Director General of Telecommunications to Ofcom

1. *Liberalization of the telecommunications sector in the UK: A brief overview*

The period between the invention of the telephone in 1876 up to 1912 saw the establishment of a public monopoly over telecommunications. The General Post Office, a government department headed by the Postmaster General, was the monopoly supplier of telephone services throughout most of Britain.[246] In October 1969, the Post Office Act 1969 established the Post Office as a public corporation with the exclusive privilege of running telecommunications systems and the newly created Ministry for Post and Telecommunications as its "sponsoring ministry."[247] Powers were largely confined to the Minister of Post and Telecommunications, the Treasury, and the Post Office. Other possible participants, such as users and Parliament, were given almost no role.[248] Public sector accounting rules meant that the Post Office spending continued to count toward total public expenditure, and extra-budgetary means of borrowing were not created for it.[249] Partially because of these rules and sparse funding, the Post Office "was not doing its job" so Parliament passed the British Telecommunications Act 1981, opening the equipment and the value-added services market to competition. The Post Office's functions in telecommunications were transferred to British Telecom (BT).[250] At that time, the first steps were taken to introduce competition into the UK telecommunications industry. In February 1982, Mercury Communications Limited was granted a license to supply telecommunications network services in competition with BT.[251]

The next step came with the Telecommunications Act 1984.[252] The main provisions pertained to: the transfer of BT into private ownership; the appointment and functions of the Director General of Telecommunications who was head of and supported by the Office of Telecommunications (Oftel); requiring licenses for all private telecommunications operators, including BT, which would no longer have the exclusive right to provide services; and stipulating the process for the modification of licenses.[253]

The new legislation provided the framework for the government's duopoly policy in the fixed market: Mercury was allowed to provide generally the same services as BT with the assurance that the government would not authorize any further entry for a period of seven years.[254] The results of the duopoly policy during that seven-year period (1984–1991) were not satisfactory.[255] In March 1991, following the duopoly review, the Department of Trade and Industry issued a White Paper effectively ending the duopoly and abolishing any limits on the number of competitors domestically.[256] The period after the duopoly review (1992–2003) was one of increasing liberalization, particularly during the second half of the decade.[257] Service competition was further facilitated in December 2000 when BT offered local loop unbundling to other telecommunications operators.

One of the defining features of that time, however, was the rapidly emerging convergence in the communications sector. The advent of digital broadcasting and the widespread takeup of the Internet undermined conventional boundaries between telecommunications, broadcasting, and other media.[258] Appreciating these trends and following EU moves for reform,[259] which resulted in the 2002 regulatory package outlined in chapter 2, in December 2000 the Department of Trade and Industry and the Department for Culture, Media and Sport published a White Paper entitled "A New Future for Communications."[260] The White Paper set out the government's proposals for "a new framework for communications regulation in the 21st century." As part of the preparation for that White Paper, the government had sought views from interested individuals and organizations as well as of a group of experts, and published 159 responses on its website.[261] The centerpiece of the White Paper was the creation of a unified regulator that would replace the five bodies or officeholders who exercised regulatory responsibilities in the communications sector.[262] The White Paper made express reference to the EC legislation under consideration that was proposing a common regulatory framework for electronic communications networks and services in the European Community and was later adopted as the 2002 regulatory package. The White Paper further explained that the new UK regulatory framework would be consistent with the proposed EC Directives. To give effect to the government's proposals, Parliament passed the Office of Communications Act 2002 and the Communications Act 2003.

The Office of Communications Act 2002 was quite brief. Its main aim was to enable the government to establish Ofcom, so that practical steps could be taken to get the regulator ready to receive the functions that the Communications Bill would confer upon it the following year. The 2002 Act sought to facilitate an orderly transition by giving Ofcom a preparatory function and placing the existing regulators under a duty to assist Ofcom to prepare.[263] The more detailed Communications Act 2003 provided for:

- the transfer of functions to Ofcom from the bodies and officeholders which up until regulated the communications sector;
- Ofcom's general duties in carrying out its functions;
- the replacement of the previous system of licensing for telecommunications systems by a general authorization regime with "specific conditions" applying only to certain communications providers in specific instances;
- the power to develop new mechanisms to enable spectrum to be traded in accordance with regulations made by Ofcom, and a scheme of recognized spectrum access;
- procedures for appealing decisions relating to networks and services and rights of use for spectrum.[264]

Importantly for our purposes, the 2003 Act implemented the 2002 EU regulatory package that had been adopted the year before.[265] This new legislation brought about significant changes in terms of both institutional structures and policymaking processes. The following pages examine these two prongs and their evolution in further detail.

2. The Regulators: The Director General of Telecommunications and Oftel (1984–2003)

I noted earlier that the operation of the nationalized public utilities sector prior to the liberalization initiatives of the Thatcher administration had followed the pattern of the club system, with ministerial decisions taken behind closed doors as the key driver of telecommunications policy. When BT was privatized, a political decision was taken that it should not be regulated by ministers.[266] The government had sounded out City institutions on the conditions for a successful sale of BT shares, and the main one was "predictable regulation by a body independent of the government."[267] However, the government "did not want to hand over all control of telecoms policy to a strong independent agency at the outset."[268] Instead, it opted to establish the position of Director General of Telecommunications (DGT), which would be assisted by Oftel.[269]

Oftel was described as a "semi-independent regulator" and a "non-ministerial department within the ambit of the Department of Trade and Industry."[270] The fact that the new regulatory institutions put in place (DGT and Oftel) were not accorded full independence should not downplay the importance of their role. Besides, the same authors describe the evolution of Oftel from its "complicated birth" through a "repressed adolescence" to a "confident youth as a maturing organization."[271] Indeed, both the new regulatory framework and the actual evolution of the telecommunications market suggest that Oftel and particularly its Director wielded increasingly important power—in fact, according to some accounts, excessively so.[272] To assess these claims we need to review the statutory status of the new regulator, its mandate, and the interface of its statutory powers with the regulatory realities on the ground.

The DGT was appointed by the Secretary of State for Trade and Industry for a term of five years.[273] He[274] chose his staff, subject to Treasury approval over numbers as well as terms and conditions of service. Funding for the DGT and Oftel was provided by Parliament. The Secretary of State could remove the DGT "on the ground of incapacity or misbehaviour."[275] Spiller and Vogelsang observed that while clashes between the Secretary of State and the DGT could lead to reductions in the agency's budget or a decision not to reappoint the DGT, firing the DGT was not an easy matter.[276] The Secretary of State for Trade and Industry and the DGT were the two key actors in policymaking. The Secretary retained the formal licensing power. The DGT, in turn, was responsible notably for the enforcement of licenses (ss. 16-19), the investigation of complaints (s. 49), the publication of information and advice (s. 48), and had an important role in the process of license modification. In other words, the Telecommunications Act 1984 set out a "relatively clear division of functions and powers" between those two actors, with each "enjoying considerable autonomy in his sphere of activity."[277] The Secretary of State, however, retained control of strategic-level decision making both by effectively determining the number of new entrants through licensing as well as by the, less important in practice, formal power to give general directions to the DGT under s. 47 (3) of the Telecommunications Act 1984.[278]

At the same time, the statutory framework provided the Director with discretionary power that was "unusually wide" for a non-ministerial office.[279] Section 3(1) of the Telecommunications Act 1984 imposed on the DGT the duties to secure the provision of "such telecommunication services as satisfy all reasonable demands for them," and that any person providing any such services is able to finance the provision of those. Section 3(2) of the Act stipulated additional, secondary duties, including the duty to:

(a) promote the interests of consumers, purchasers and other users in the United Kingdom (including, in particular, those who are disabled or of pensionable age) . . .

(b) maintain and promote effective competition . . .

(c) promote efficiency and economy . . .

(e) encourage major users of telecommunication services whose places of business are outside the United Kingdom to establish places of business in the United Kingdom.

These duties reflected broad principles, often in tension with each other, without a clear prioritization.[280] For instance, the financing duty might conflict with the principle of satisfying all reasonable demands for access.[281] Therefore, this general, broad language allowed significant scope for choice and discretion to the DGT.[282] The same duties were placed on the Secretary of State; this does not refute the point about the DGT's wide discretion. As noted earlier, both these policymaking actors enjoyed discretion in their spheres of activity, even in cases of overlap.[283] The wide range of the DGT's discretionary powers, which became increasingly important in the 1990s when more actors entered the stage at the end of the duopoly period,[284] further highlighted what was likely the most salient feature of the new institutional regime to begin with: the single-person regulator. As explained earlier in this chapter, this institutional choice was a conscious departure from the US model of regulatory commissions. The aim of the government was to develop a "quicker and less bureaucratic system" centered on a single Director General "operating without undue bureaucracy and supported by a small staff."[285] The emphasis on the individual DGTs was also a "conscious PR device" to build them up as a force that could drive the liberalization process even against high-profile, powerful actors, such as BT.[286]

As a consequence of this personalization, the DGTs left their imprimatur on the regulatory regime. This was concisely captured in a quote about the first DGT, Sir Bryan Carsberg, by his acting successor: "During the eight years that he led OFTEL, Sir Bryan was the embodiment of the regulatory regime; and he created a model for others to follow in the UK and internationally."[287] Bryan Carsberg, the first and influential DGT from 1984 until 1992, adopted a strong pro-competition approach that he clearly enunciated in his first Annual Report.[288] At multiple points in his Annual Reports, he stressed that competition is often the best means of promoting consumer interests.[289] In 1992 Bryan Carsberg went on to head the Office of Fair Trading, and Bill Wigglesworth took over the duties of DGT until April 1993, when he was succeeded by Don Cruickshank. During Cruickshank's tenure (1993–1998), the language of competition as the most effective means of promoting consumer welfare did not change.[290] Importantly for present purposes, Don Cruickshank introduced procedural reforms in the agency's operations to which Section B will return.[291] David Edmonds was installed as the fourth and last DGT in April 1998, at a time of huge growth in the use of mobile phones and the introduction of subscription-free access to the Internet.[292]

The "cult of the individual regulator" was not only a function of the DGTs's substantive discretionary powers or the regulatory issues that they chose to prioritize and articulate in their Annual Reports. It was also reinforced by their public salience, especially in the media.[293] Bryan Carsberg was perceived, as noted earlier, as the embodiment of the regulatory regime; Don Cruickshank's tenure saw telecoms regulation achieve "an unparalleled public awareness" with frequent newspaper reports[294]; David Edmonds, who took over "with the intention of building bridges with BT and the DTI after his predecessor's stormy reign," was himself ferociously criticized in the press over his handling of local loop unbundling.[295]

The central position of the DGT, however, was not only a PR strategy or a statutory happenstance. The roots were deeper, as this personalized model of regulation reflected characteristics of the club culture (described in earlier parts of this chapter) that had rolled over into the new regulatory regime.[296] This strong reliance on individuals was described as one of the most heavily criticized features of the system[297]–and not without reason. Drawing an analogy between the position of the independent regulator and that of the ruler as described in Plato, a commentator observed that only the "select and most enlightened individuals" can be entrusted with such discretion.[298] Concerns about the risk of "personal agendas" were raised, however, even though in practice the system of individual DGs was working well, and the individuals selected were knowledgeable, competent, and not party partisan.[299] Personalization did not result in partisanship, but—as the history showed in the example of controversial DGTs—it did not prevent polarization.

Two major solutions were proposed in the literature to address the problem of excessive discretion and the "cult of the individual regulator."[300] One was to change the personalized nature of the office by moving to the model of regulatory commissions; the sub-section immediately following describes this new institutional structure. The other strand of proposed reforms was the introduction of policymaking processes that would constrain and structure the discretion of the regulator; Section B discusses these. In both cases, EU law has had a role to play.

3. The Regulators: Ofcom (2003–)

Writing in 1997, Tony Prosser correctly predicted that "the effect of the developing law of utility liberalization in the EU is to bring regulatory matters into the open much more clearly, and the stress on the requirements of independence in regulation are, in the long term, likely to result in further use of the independent commission model."[301] Indeed, as described earlier, the increasing convergence in the UK communications sector in conjunction with the EU regulatory developments[302] led the government to establish Ofcom, the regulatory body that took on the new regulatory tasks across the communications sector.

The institutional choice for the new unified regulator marked a departure from the past. Ofcom was set up as an independent statutory corporation rather than a government department or non-departmental public body. In other words, its governance structure is based upon a model that is familiar to the commercial sector. Therefore, its staff are not civil servants, and it is easier to attract staff from industry.[303] Reflecting this hybrid institutional structure, section 3 of the Office of Communications Act 2002 places Ofcom under a duty to have regard to general guidance concerning the management of public bodies and to generally accepted principles of good corporate governance insofar as they are applicable to OFCOM. Ofcom's main decision-making body is the Board, which provides strategic direction for the organization.[304] The Board currently comprises six non-executive members and three executive members. The Chairman and non-executive members are appointed jointly by the Secretaries of State for Trade and Industry (now Secretary of State for Business, Innovation and Skills) and for Culture, Media and Sport for a period of between three and five years. The Chief Executive is appointed by the Chairman and the independent non-executive members with the approval of the State Secretaries; the other executive members are appointed by the Board on the recommendation of the Chief Executive.[305] The Board meets at least once a month (with the exception of August). Agendas as well as brief minutes and notes of Board meetings are published regularly on the website of Ofcom.

Even though Ofcom is an independent statutory corporation and decisions are now taken collectively by a Board, thus breaking with the prior highly personalized model of the Director General, an external observer might still express some skepticism as to the independence of this new regulatory body. She could, for instance, point to the fact that the majority of the Board is appointed by the government; additionally, that the appointment of the inaugural Chairman, an expert economist with a long academic career, was not treated as non-political in the press.[306] While this is true, one should also consider that appointments to the Ofcom Board fall within the remit of the Commissioner for Public Appointments and therefore need to comply with the regulatory framework for public appointments processes.[307] Furthermore, the Board comprises both executive and non-executive members. Its decisions will be made by consensus rather than by formal vote unless it is not possible to reach a shared decision, in which case a vote will be taken and recorded in the minutes.[308] Moreover, because of the different terms of appointment, not all members of the Board are appointed at the same time and can therefore be selected by different governments. In addition, the Chairman or another non-executive member may be removed only for specific causes.[309]

With respect to Ofcom's relationship with the government in the exercise of the agency's functions, there is no general power of ministerial direction over Ofcom.[310] Nonetheless, specific provisions of the Communications Act 2003 provide for the power of the Secretary of State to issue directions to Ofcom in designated areas of activity. For instance, in regard to networks and spectrum functions, the Secretary of State may give directions but only in the interests of national security, relations with foreign governments, to secure compliance with international obligations, or in the interests of public safety or health (section 5). Similarly, Ofcom must act in accordance with ministerial directions as may be given to it when it represents the government on international bodies (section 22). Moreover, the Secretary of State has the power to issue directions regarding radio spectrum management (section 156).

With respect to funding, Ofcom is required to balance its expenditure with its income in each financial year.[311] The organization raises its funds from specific sources.[312] These guarantees are coupled with provisions aiming at ensuring the Board's impartiality and independence from the industry. Both at the appointment stage and during the tenure of the Chairman and non-executive members, the Secretary of State "shall satisfy himself that [these persons] have no such financial or other interest as is likely to affect prejudicially the carrying out [of their] functions."[313] Ofcom has also put in place a detailed policy on conflicts of interest. Furthermore, the agency maintains a publicly available register of disclosable interests.

The move away from the single-person regulator model to a larger, independent organization deciding collectively was also necessary because of the magnitude of the tasks the new legislative framework assigned to Ofcom. As already noted, the Communications Act 2003 transferred to Ofcom the functions of five pre-commencement regulators as well as many of the functions of the Secretary of State, effectively rendering it a "super-regulator." In fact, the Communications Act 2003 mandated 263 separate statutory duties for the new regulator, that is, more than double the total number of duties inherited from the five regulators that Ofcom replaced.[314] Furthermore, in October 2011, Ofcom officially took over regulation of the UK's postal services from the previous regulator, Postcomm. Ofcom's principal duties under section 3(1) of the Communications Act 2003 are: "(a) to further the interests of citizens in relation to communications matters; and (b) to further the interests of consumers in relevant markets, where appropriate by promoting competition." Section 3(2) further stipulates specific duties in six areas. Even without going into specifics, the range of these statutory duties suggests that they may come into conflict.[315] There is a recurring theme here that we also encountered in the discussion of the DGT in the previous sub-section; namely, the possibility of conflicts between statutory duties and the discretion that the need to resolve them accords to the regulators.[316] The situation under the DGT/Oftel and Ofcom differs in two important respects, though: the imposition of statutory procedural requirements and the obligation to comply with EU duties.

More specifically, where OFCOM needs to resolve a conflict between its duties, under the Communications Act 2003 it now has to publish a statement setting out the nature of the conflict, the manner in which it has decided to resolve it, and the reasons for this decision (section 3(8)). These reason-giving and transparency requirements attending what was formerly perceived as a highly discretionary function raise a broader point, one that the following section will discuss. That is, the choice of the new legislative framework to structure discretion through formally binding procedural requirements, including notably requirements for open, participatory policymaking processes. The 2000 White Paper preceding the Communications Act 2003 had explicitly acknowledged the link between increased regulatory powers and enhanced accountability requirements: "Rather than having detailed rules set out in primary legislation, the regulator will have the responsibility to develop and maintain the necessary rules within the statutory framework. OFCOM will be required to do this in full consultation with industry and with citizen and consumer groups, within a clear statutory framework of guiding principles."[317]

The second point raised by Ofcom's conflicting statutory duties pertains to the primacy of EU mandates. In the case of conflict, the agency is under a statutory obligation to give priority to duties deriving from EU law (sections 3(6) and 4). Again, this is an opportunity to highlight the bigger point of the effect of EU mandates on the UK regulator. Certainly, these specific provisions do not capture fully either the formal changes in the UK legislation in response to the developing EU regulatory framework or the indirect effect of EU law that translated into changes in agency practices. The following section addresses these broader questions. We can better appreciate these changes under Ofcom against the benchmark of the policymaking process its predecessor, Oftel, had been employing.

B. From structure to process: Participatory processes under Oftel and Ofcom

1. *Oftel's policymaking processes*

As noted earlier in this chapter, during the pre-privatization period, the utilities sector was governed almost exclusively by informal bureaucratic methods.[318] Policymaking was largely a closed process involving only the Post Office and the government, and the role of other actors was minor.[319] The previous section also argued that the privatization revolution and the creation of a new regulatory institution, i.e., the DGT and Oftel, constituted a significant departure from the previous regime. It did not, however, eradicate fully all the features of the club culture.

The same description of "considerable change without complete reversal" applies not only to the structure of the new regulator but also to the policymaking processes that this new regulatory institution employed. As one scholar has observed, the new regulatory regime had a "contradictory parentage":[320] One of its parents was Professor Stephen Littlechild, the author of a 1983 report that was "enormously influential in shaping the design of the British utility regulators."[321] Littlechild expressed the concern that a discretionary regulatory scheme would increase the risk of capture of the DGT by the incumbent operator.[322] His position was consequently described as "a distinctly modernist attempt . . . to create an open, transparent world of non-discretionary regulatory decision guided by fixed rules." In contrast, the Conservatives in Whitehall wanted to design a regulatory regime that retained the informality and closed character of the system.[323] The mistrust of American-style legalism, perceived as excessively rigid and cumbersome,[324] resulted in a formal institutional framework that has been described as reflecting "an old domestic style, so facilitating a closed, bipolar dialogue between regulators and regulated, devoid of hearings."[325]

The formal statutory mandates providing for participatory processes in the Telecommunications Act 1984 are a good example of this.[326] Indeed, the Act stipulated mandatory consultations in a very limited set of cases, most notably as part of the license modification process (section 12).[327] Furthermore, there was no general duty for reason giving or transparency. The limited number of such procedural requirements prompted scholars to describe the UK understanding of due process as "highly impoverished."[328] Perhaps recognizing the narrow scope of the formal statutory mandates, the first DGT, Sir Bryan Carsberg, seemed committed to going further in his first Annual Report: "I have made a commitment, in public statements, to be as open as possible in the discussion of issues arising out of my functions and duties. I intend to make public statements about major issues under review and to invite representations from any interested parties; I intend to establish contact with individuals, companies and representative bodies with interests in telecommunications so that I may become fully aware of their views on important issues; and I intend to give the fullest possible explanation of the basis for my conclusions, subject only to the need to respect commercial confidentiality."[329]

This statement of intent was important but could neither fill the statutory gaps in itself nor meet the criteria described in Part II.C.1. so as to give rise to a legitimate expectation of prior public consultation. Oftel did indeed carry out some public consultations during Carsberg's tenure.[330] However, this was a highly discretionary, personal decision, nothing close to a formal duty. Similarly, the commitment to provide reasons was not always followed consistently.[331] Moreover, the first DGT availed himself of other opportunities to hear the voice of the players in the telecommunications sector, but not through a public consultation process. These included, for instance, the establishment of a new advisory body, the Telecommunications Forum, which Bryan Carsberg described as "a vehicle for regular contact with a number of organisations, including the public telecommunications operators, associations representing user and industry interests, the trade union and others."[332] In addition, the DGT would seek the advice of the statutory advisory committees that were set up for each country within the UK (England, Scotland, Wales, and Northern Ireland) under section 54 of the Telecommunications Act 1984. Nonetheless, the decision to refer an issue to these advisory bodies was again up to the discretion of the DGT. While during that stage the effort to introduce participatory, transparency and reason-giving features into the decision-making process was entirely discretionary, it did create some momentum. In his last Annual Report as DGT, Bryan Carsberg noted a greater interest, expressed in the media and in comments to Oftel, in the provision of additional financial information about BT that would facilitate public participation, as well as in greater transparency of regulatory decisions.[333]

Don Cruickshank, the DGT between 1993 and 1998, built on that momentum. Cruickshank defended publicly the statutory grant of discretionary powers to the DGT.[334] Nevertheless, since the beginning of his tenure, he also opted to use this discretion in order to develop more transparent and participatory policymaking processes to structure these discretionary powers.[335] In his first Annual Report he articulated his goal of making Oftel more transparent and open-minded and his commitment to ensuring that the regulation process "is conducted as far as possible in public."[336] Consultation thenceforth played a central part in formulating changes to the regulatory regime. For major changes, Oftel had a policy of putting submissions by interested parties on the public record, thus affording other market actors the opportunity to respond to them, often during a second consultation round.[337] After a review of Oftel's policymaking processes, in March 1995 the DGT announced Oftel's new approach to public consultations, which aimed at increasing the transparency of these processes: Oftel would generally make all responses to both statutory and informal public consultations available in its library unless consultees requested confidentiality. The agency, however, urged that such requests be kept to an absolute minimum, and suggested that in some circumstances the DGT might consider using his statutory powers to publish such confidential information in the public interest or decide to give that material less weight. To promote discussion among interested parties, Oftel would usually include a second consultation stage of 14 days to allow parties to consider the responses made by others during the first stage and to comment on them. Finally, Oftel expressed its commitment to explaining the basis of its decisions, often by reference to representations made in the consultation.[338] The emphasis on transparency and consultation was a recurring theme in Don Cruickshank's public statements.[339]

Oftel was also committed to updating its consultation processes.[340] In July 1997, Oftel published a consultative document entitled "Improving

Accountability: Oftel's Procedures and Processes."[341] The document sought the views of consumers, consumer organizations, industry, and other actors on nine proposed actions to improve accountability. Transparency and consultation figured prominently among the plans to give telecoms users and companies a more effective voice in shaping policy.[342] Oftel's procedural reforms were lauded as "nothing less than revolutionary for British public administration."[343] According to a similar account, the use of novel and transparent policymaking processes "effectively broke with the Whitehall culture of secrecy."[344] In fact, Oftel's practice was influential in Whitehall because it put pressure on other departments to explain why they were less transparent.[345]

The increasing emphasis on public consultations in Annual Reports and other public statements was also reflected in practice in the number of consultation exercises that Oftel carried out during this period, as Figure 5.1, in sub-section 2b later in the chapter, demonstrates.

The spike beginning in 1993 reflects Don Cruickshank's establishment of participatory mechanisms and his commitment to use the tool of public consultations increasingly thereafter. This practice was continued under his successor, David Edmonds. This new consultative approach coincided with, and arguably was encouraged by, developments in the telecommunications market during the 1990s. As Section A.1 outlined, that decade saw an ever-increasing number of players enter the telecommunications markets; during Richmond's directorship (1998–2003), this dynamism was enhanced by developments in a rapidly growing mobile sector and local loop unbundling.

By now it probably wouldn't even take a skeptical reader to think: therein lies difficulty for the claim that EU law has had a noticeable impact on the UK model of policymaking processes. Figure 5.1 shows a long practice of consultation *before* the advent of the 2002 EU law. Don Cruickshank was not overstating the claim that openness in regulation was one area where they had well exceeded their target.[346] The discussion in this section confirms the DGT's characterization of their work as having gone "much further on consultation than is formally required."[347] So was there any room left for EU procedural mandates? Might the actual value of the British example be that it constitutes a negative case study?

This sub-section discussed Oftel's policymaking processes and stopped at the year 2002, which is when the EU regulatory package was adopted but also the year of the Office of Communications Act that paved the way for the new domestic regulatory framework, which has already been presented. Sub-section 2 will tell the post-2002 story and thus provide a more detailed answer to the previous two questions. Nonetheless, part of the answer can be found in the question itself as posed in the previous paragraph: the novel open participatory processes constituted a policy decision that was *taken by the Director General* and went much further than what was *formally* required. Just as the regulatory structure of a DGT with considerable discretionary powers reflected a highly personalized model of regulation, so too the decision to put in place those policymaking processes looked more like a matter of personal choice in keeping with the British tradition of personalized, informal, and discretionary decision making. The importance of personality was obvious in that observers associated those processes with a single individual and gave credit to him for going beyond the statutory requirements. The statute itself was not amended to accommodate those practices until after almost twenty years—and that was in response to the new EU legislation.

In fact, the limitations pertained not only to the form of the decision initiating those participatory processes but also to the way these were carried out. My archival research suggests that for most of the period under examination, the common practice was for Oftel to send out the consultation document to selected actors—admittedly, a great number of them—and then they would choose whether to respond to this invitation. Even though the agency's website went online in June 1995,[348] consultation responses were normally publicly available in Oftel's library but often not online. The whole consultation process migrated online to a greater extent around 1999. Nonetheless, even in 2001 there were cases in which the website would state only that "the following responses are available to view/copy from R&I," that is, Oftel's Research and Information Unit. In another case in 2002, there were three "No comment" responses sent to the agency; this was an indication that the practice of sending individualized invitations to designated actors had not fully subsided.

These remarks should in no way be taken to detract from the importance of the participatory processes that the DGT introduced, which was highlighted from the very beginning of this section. Oftel was the leader in developing open procedures not only within the British public administration but also beyond national borders. Nevertheless, in applauding those efforts we should not lose sight of an important missing piece that was ultimately contributed primarily by EU law: formality. As we read enthusiastic accounts about the "procedural developments championed by Don Cruikshank at OFTEL [that] are very close to the model of rule-making under the Administrative Procedure Act and the Telecommunications Act in the United States," we should not overlook that "the difference is, however, the greater rigour imposed by the structure of rules creating rule-making procedures, rules which have no formal legal counterpart in the United Kingdom."[349] Oftel itself acknowledged this. In a statement issued in August 2001 after a consultation on Oftel's use of consultation process, the agency referred to the EU Framework Directive and the Universal Service Directive, which had been adopted by the Council of Ministers in June 2001, would come into force in the spring of 2002 and provided for a "general obligation to consult." Oftel explained: "While it is Oftel's current practice to engage in public consultation and, in some limited cases, the Telecommunications Act 1984 and the licences granted under that Act require consultation, the

Framework Directive and Universal Service Directive will *formalise a wider obligation to consult* interested parties."[350]

The following section will elaborate on this point. Before that, a related aspect of the informality of the accountability mechanisms under Oftel worth noting was the lack of robust judicial review. The earlier discussion of the New Right reforms suggested that one of the government's aims in designing the privatization regulatory regime was to avoid the excessive judicialization often associated with the US model.[351] In the telecommunications sector, this goal was, for the most part, achieved. My research did not find any instances of judicial review of the DGT's decisions in which the court assessed the adequacy of the public consultation. This should not be particularly surprising, as—with the exception of the limited number of mandatory consultations under the Telecommunications Act 1984—all the other public consultations were informal.

In one case before the High Court, a public consultation was used in the assessment of the rationality of the DGT's decision in the context of substantive review, to which I shall return in the immediately following paragraph. The case involved a license modification process, namely, a process for which section 12 of the Telecommunications Act 1984 provided a mandatory consultation. Justice Lightman held that the evidence established that the DGT's decision had been reached "after a protracted consultation period, full regard to the responses received . . . and full consideration of the interests of everyone effected." The case included another interesting pronouncement from a procedural point of view: "A party can in judicial review proceedings adduce evidence to show what material was before the decision-maker, but not fresh material not available to the decision-maker designed to persuade the court that the decision-maker's decision was wrong. *This must a fortiori be the case where (as here) there was a statutory consultation period before the decision was made and the fresh evidence could and should have been put before the decision-maker during that period*."[352] This formulation may recall a line of court judgments examined in the French case, in which I described a court-imposed implicit obligation on market actors to avail themselves of the consultation process and be consistent. Nonetheless, the High Court did not elaborate on this point, as it found that "it is common ground that the greater part of the evidence originally served in support of [the application for judicial review] did no more than inform the court of the material before the Director."[353]

In general, judicial review was relatively uncommon during this period, and courts adopted a deferential approach toward the regulator.[354] For instance, in a 1992 case the court stressed the breadth of the statutory discretion, declining to become involved in detailed questions of fact.[355] The standard for substantive review of a discretionary decision was a reasonableness one. This is known as the *Wednesdury* test, from the oft-cited *Wednesbury* case,[356] in which Lord Greene, speaking for the court, stated:

if a decision on a competent matter is so unreasonable that no reasonable authority could ever have come to it, then the courts can interfere.
[B]ut to prove a case of that kind would require something overwhelming . . . It is not what the court considers unreasonable, a different thing
altogether. If it is what the court considers unreasonable, the court may
very well have different views to that of a local authority on matters of
high public policy . . . The effect of the legislation is not to set up the
court as an arbiter of the correctness of one view over another. It is the
local authority that are set in that position.

Wednesbury advocated judicial self-restraint, and this guiding principle was
taken by some to apply with particular force in the commercial context, in which
courts are called upon to review decisions by expert regulators.[357] More specifically, in the telecommunications area, in a case regarding a license modification,
the Queen's Bench Division applied this test. Justice Lightman said:

Where the Act has conferred the decision-making function on the
Director, it is for him, and him alone, to consider the economic arguments, weigh the compelling considerations and arrive at a judgment.
The applicants have no right of appeal: in these judicial review proceedings so long as he directs himself correctly in law, his decision can only
be challenged on *Wednesbury* grounds. The court must be astute to
avoid the danger of substituting its views for the decision-maker and
of contradicting (as in this case) a conscientious decision-maker acting
in good faith with knowledge of all the facts . . . . *If (as I have stated)
the court should be very slow to impugn decisions of fact made by an expert
and experienced decision-maker, it must surely be even slower to impugn his
educated prophesies and predictions for the future* . . . . The resolution
of disputed questions of fact is for the decision-maker, and *the court
can only interfere if his decision is perverse, e.g. if his reasoning is logically
unsound*.[358]

This deferential approach to a technical decision by the "expert and experienced"
regulator was consistent with *Wednesbury*. In this case, however, the court's
conclusion that the DGT's decision was not irrational was further supported
by the preceding consultation, which had lasted for approximately two years.
It was also consistent with an earlier case in which BT had brought a judicial
review action following a consensual modification to its license conditions. The
"implicit assumption" in that case, which involved again the DGT's discretionary
powers, was that the court was unlikely to intervene "provided that procedural
requirements [were] met and [the DGT's] powers were used to advance the purposes of the statute."[359]

Another decision of the House of Lords, however, was taken to indicate a more "interventionist approach" to substantive review.[360] The case pertained primarily to a procedural issue (abuse of the process of the court), but the court's pronouncements were interesting for our purposes with respect to the substantive question of the interpretation of a license condition. More specifically, Lord Slynn, with whom the other Lords agreed, said that if the DGT misinterprets conditions in a license and makes a determination on the basis of an incorrect interpretation, "he does not do what he was asked to do," and his interpretation could be reviewed by courts.[361] Scholars read that case as suggesting a greater willingness to overturn substantive decisions, for license interpretation appeared to be treated as "a question defining the jurisdiction of the regulator, and not as something in relation to which he had discretion, and thus subject to a lower standard of review."[362] That was the first time that the courts were prepared in principle to examine a substantive decision of a utility regulator.[363] At the end, Mercury did not pursue the substantive issue further, and no outburst of challenges followed the case.[364] Nevertheless, it was reported that Oftel doubled its legal staff in response to the decision.[365]

A last example of a non-deferential approach comes from a 2000 decision by the Queen's Bench Division.[366] In this case, Justice Moses reviewed the regulator's decision on several grounds, including the proportionality principle. The proportionality test is more demanding than *Wednesbury* unreasonableness.[367] Nevertheless, the standard of review in this case was not judicially created. Rather, it was in application of a specific statutory mandate, the new section 46B(2) of the Telecommunications Act 1984, which had come into force in December 1999, explicitly referred to lack of proportionality as one of the grounds of appeal, and covered the DGT's decision before the court. This judgment does not cut against my main argument that the period under consideration did not see many instances of robust substantive judicial review. In fact, it serves as a bridge to a point that the following section will make regarding the indirect effect of EU law on the formalization of the regulatory process.

Some useful context to understanding this 2000 decision and its difference from earlier cases applying the *Wednesbury* test is the difference between an "appeal" and review on a "conventional judicial review" basis. The former allows the reviewing body to apply a more searching degree of scrutiny, which may include the facts of the case and grounds such as proportionality, as in the 2000 judgment; the latter type of review is usually narrower in scope. In an earlier case, I highlighted the part of the judgment explaining that the applicants had "no right of appeal," and so long as the DGT had directed himself correctly in law, his decision could be challenged only on *Wednesbury* grounds.[368] By contrast, in the 2000 judgment considered here, the course of action was a statutory appeal on grounds that expressly allowed for heightened scrutiny. The most interesting feature for present purposes is that, as the court itself noted, this statutory appeals procedure under section 46B was inserted into the Telecommunications Act (by the Telecommunications (Appeals) Regulations 1999) in order to meet the United Kingdom's obligations *under EC Directives*.[369] The following sub-section will show that an indirect effect of EU law was the provision for an appeals mechanism in the Communications Act 2003, which in turn fed back into Ofcom's policymaking processes.

Nevertheless, this 2000 judgment should not divert our attention from the main point in this sub-section. That is to say, during Oftel's period—especially during the first decade of its operations—the informal nature of policymaking was further encouraged by the lack of searching substantive judicial review or an appeals mechanism that was just described. Indeed, when the Trade and Industry Select Committee during an inquiry raised the point with the DGT that he would have powers "to become prosecutor, judge and jury," Don Cruickshank, fresh from a Divisional Court victory over BT, replied: "The people who matter, the judges, have denied all of that, so it is not a matter of what I think or that the *Daily Telegraph* thinks, it is a matter of what the courts of the land have decided about what the Telecommunications Act means, how I should exercise the discretion and how I should pursue my duties under that Act. That issue is now resolved, and I hope that some of that language that you quote will go away."[370]

Having reviewed Oftel's policymaking processes, we can now appreciate better the changes in the statutory framework and practices under Ofcom.

2. Ofcom's policymaking processes

Section A.3. described the breadth of the new agency's regulatory tasks across the communications sector, which effectively rendered it a "super-regulator." The Communications Act 2003 stipulates that in performing its duties, OFCOM must have regard to: "(a) the principles under which regulatory activities should be transparent, accountable, proportionate, consistent and targeted only at cases in which action is needed; and (b) any other principles appearing to OFCOM to represent the best regulatory practice." Furthermore, under section 3(4)(k) of the same statute, the agency must have regard, to the extent it appears relevant in the circumstances, to "the opinions of consumers in relevant markets and of members of the public generally." Ofcom itself has adopted a set of regulatory principles, including notably that:

- It will strive to ensure its interventions will be evidence-based, proportionate, consistent, accountable and transparent in both deliberation and outcome.
- It will consult widely with all relevant stakeholders and assess the impact of regulatory action before imposing regulation upon a market.[371]

In other words, transparency and consultation have a prominent place among the principles guiding the agency's decision-making processes. In this respect, one could say that Ofcom continues on the path of Oftel. An important difference, however, lies in the source of these obligations. This section will focus on two major driving forces that account for Ofcom's more open and participatory processes: (a) direct statutory mandates, and (b) the indirect effect of the appeals mechanism for review of agency action. It will argue that EU law played a role as to both of these prongs.

a. Consultation under statutory mandates

The main provision implementing Article 6 of the Framework Directive (on consultation and transparency) is section 403 of the Communications Act 2003, whereby

(4) Before making any regulations or order under a power to which this section applies, OFCOM must—
   (a) give a notice of their proposal to do so to such persons representative of the persons appearing to OFCOM to be likely to be affected by the implementation of the proposal as OFCOM think fit;
   (b) publish notice of their proposal in such manner as they consider appropriate for bringing it to the attention of the persons who, in their opinion, are likely to be affected by it and are not given notice by virtue of paragraph (a); and
   (c) consider any representations that are made to OFCOM, before the time specified in the notice.
(5) A notice for the purposes of subsection (4) must—
   (a) state that OFCOM propose to make the regulations or order in question;
   (b) set out the general effect of the regulations or order;
   (c) specify an address from which a copy of the proposed regulations or order may be obtained; and
   (d) specify a time before which any representations with respect to the proposal must be made to OFCOM.

These procedural requirements apply when another provision expressly refers to section 403. The Communications Act 2003 includes more than a dozen provisions, excluding broadcasting, that incorporate section 403[372] and pertain to significant powers, for instance, powers related to universal service and spectrum access. Furthermore, a series of other provisions mandate a public consultation before the exercise of powers of practical significance that affect consumers and the overall operation of the market. For example, section 16(1) of the Communications Act 2003, which transposes Article 33 ("consultation with interested parties") of the Universal Service Directive

(Directive 2002/22/EC), establishes Ofcom's duty to "establish and maintain effective arrangements for consultation about the carrying out of its functions" with consumers in various markets. Section 48 stipulates that Ofcom follow a similar open consultation procedure before setting, modifying, or revoking conditions of entitlement to provide network or services. Last and very important in terms of practical impact, a prior consultation is required on Ofcom's proposals for identifying markets and for market power determinations (section 80).

Public consultation is also required as part of another accountability mechanism, Impact Assessments. Under section 7(2) of the Communications Act 2003, Ofcom has a duty to carry out an Impact Assessment when it proposes to do anything for the purposes of, or in connection with, the carrying out of its functions, and it appears to the agency that the proposal is important. When Ofcom decides to proceed to an Impact Assessment, section 7(7) states:

(a) Ofcom must provide an opportunity of making representations to it about its proposal to members of the public and other persons who, in the agency's opinion, are likely to be affected to a significant extent by its implementation;

(b) the published assessment must be accompanied by a statement setting out how representations may be made; and

(c) Ofcom is not to implement its proposal unless the period for making representations about it has expired and the agency has considered all the representations made in that period.

The Communications Act 2003 does not provide detailed directions on how an Impact Assessment must be conducted, other than it must set out how, in Ofcom's opinion, the performance of its general duties is secured or furthered by what it proposes [section 7(4)]. Other questions are left up to the agency to decide [section 7(5)]. In July 2005, subsequent to a public consultation, Ofcom issued its Impact Assessment guidelines. The agency describes Impact Assessments as a key part of best practice policy-making, and concludes that it therefore expects Impact Assessments to be carried out in relation to the great majority of its policy decisions.[373] The precise details of the guidelines are beyond the scope of this study.[374] It is useful to point out that, in addition to the consultation component of the process, Impact Assessments increase the transparency and reason-giving prongs of Ofcom's regulatory process: the agency is in essence required to spell out its assumptions, alternatives considered, and reasons for opting for one of those.[375] The language of the statutory mandate is rather permissive. The duty to carry out an Impact Assessment does not apply "if it appears to OFCOM that the urgency of the matter makes it impracticable or inappropriate" [section 7(1)]. In a similar vein, the Impact Assessment guidelines state that they "do not have binding legal effect."[376] Notwithstanding this discretionary nature of the decision to follow the guidelines and carry out an Impact Assessment, the general conclusion is that for significant proposals the agency is expected to conduct an Impact Assessment *and* consult on it.

Mapping the express (specific or general) mandates for participatory processes in the new statutory framework for electronic communications highlights the first important difference between the new and the prior regulatory regime; under the latter, consultation was mostly a good-will practice on the basis of DGT decisions, and statutory mandates were scarce. Even though the exact language of Article 6 of the Framework Directive is not per se replicated in the Communications Act 2003, as was the case with the French and Greek legislation, the extensive cluster of procedural provisions—most of which can be traced back to EU obligations[377]—in the 2003 Act covers the range of activities for which public consultation is required under EU law.

Even though a consultation requirement has been formalized in the statute for a very wide ambit of agency functions, including the most influential policy measures, Ofcom did not limit itself to simply carrying out these statutory mandates. In the words of the Chief Executive in Ofcom's first Annual Report: "Why consult? The law requires Ofcom to consult ahead of many of its decisions. This legal obligation is entirely appropriate; even if consultation was not mandated by the statute, our own belief is that our decisions must be informed by the views of people and organisations with an interest in the outcome. Stakeholder consultation is an important aspect of our commitment to transparency."[378] The agency carried this commitment through by going beyond the statutory requirements,[379] and launching public consultations on issues (often termed "discussion papers") for which consultation would not be strictly mandated by the statute.[380] In some cases, consultation is supplemented by public meetings.[381] For example, since its inception, Ofcom has been holding a series of public meetings across the UK to hear people's views on its draft Annual Plan every year.[382] The meetings include a panel of Ofcom experts; they begin with a brief presentation, after which there is an opportunity to comment and ask questions.

In light of the importance of public consultation in Ofcom's policymaking processes, as early as 2003 the agency developed a formal consultation strategy. That was led by a consultation champion (the first one was Philip Rutnam), whose role was to ensure that the organization adheres to its stated principles.[383] I had the opportunity to interview the third and fourth[384] consultation champions in London, who added further detail to the history of the position of the consultation champion. While the new agency was being set up, it became clear that consultation would be a key part of its activities. In addition to the publication of its consultation guidelines, Ofcom decided that it needed a central focal point, a consultation champion who would advise the Chief Executive and agency staff on issues that would come out of the consultation process. The consultation champion would act as an internal source of advice and ensure that all staff followed the same practice consistently with the guidelines; she would also be an external contact and receive queries from stakeholders regarding the consultation process. Even though quite often those external questions or objections would be policy- and not process-oriented, namely, they raised concerns pertaining to the substantive issue under consultation, there were examples of responses that targeted the consultation process itself.[385]

When Vicki Nash took over as the third consultation champion, she undertook a comprehensive review of Ofcom's consultation guidelines.[386] That review process entailed both internal and external consultation. Internally, she had three roundtable discussions with 16 colleagues from various groups who were used to applying the principles; externally, she contacted 73 external stakeholders across broadcasting and telecoms, and invited them to submit their views. Not many (around ten) responses were received externally, as the majority of stakeholders did not express disappointment with the processes. Some responses suggested a dropping satisfaction with the timeliness of Ofcom's decision making, a finding congruent with the results of other research that the agency had carried out. The review led to minor changes to the consultation guidelines that were published in November 2007 and are still in force.[387] A noteworthy modification was the introduction of a three-tier system to determine the duration of three different types of consultation:

Category 1: Consultations that "contain major policy initiatives and/or of interest to a wide range of stakeholders (especially those who may need a longer time to response)"; Ofcom will consult for 10 weeks.

Category 2: Consultations that, whilst containing important policy proposals, "will be of interest to a limited number of stakeholders who will be aware of the issues"; Ofcom will consult for 6 weeks.

Category 3: Ofcom will consult for one month when those consultations fall within one or more of the following: detailed technical issues; where there is a need to complete the project in a specified timetable because of market developments or other factors; the issue has already been the subject of a consultation; a proposal will have a limited effect on a market; a proposal is only a limited amendment to existing policy or regulation.

This system was different from the default 12-week consultation period pursuant to the government's Code of Practice on Consultation, although this general default rule has since been abolished under the Consultation Principles 2012 and 2016 described in Part II.B. Ofcom was not listed among the public sector organizations that had signed up to the Code of Practice on Consultation. This meant that Ofcom could adopt different criteria, as it did with respect to the duration of the consultation exercise. However, in general its consultation principles were consistent with the suggestions of the general Code of Practice on Consultation. More specifically, according to Ofcom's consultation guidelines, the seven principles that the agency will normally follow for each written consultation, and which are reproduced in every consultation document, are as follows:

Before the consultation
- Where possible, we will hold informal talks with people and organisations before announcing a big consultation to find out whether we are thinking in the right direction. If we do not have enough time to do this, we will usually hold an open meeting to explain our proposals shortly after announcing the consultation.

During the consultation
- We will be clear about who we are consulting, why, on what questions and for how long.
- We will make the consultation document as short and simple as possible with a summary in plain English. We will try to make it as easy as possible to give us a written response. If the consultation is complicated, we may provide a shortened plain English Guide for smaller organisations or individuals who would otherwise not be able to spare the time to share their views.
- We will consult for up to ten weeks depending on the potential impact of our proposals.
- A person within Ofcom will be in charge of making sure we follow our own guidelines and reach out to the largest number of people and organisations interested in the outcome of our decisions. Ofcom's Consultation Champion will also be the main person to contact with views on the way we run our consultations.
- If we are not able to follow one of these principles, we will explain why.

After the consultation
- We think it is important for everyone interested in an issue to see the views of others during a consultation. We would usually publish all the responses we have received on our website.

Beyond these principles, the guidelines explain that at the end of the process the team in charge of the consultation will review all the submitted responses. They will then prepare a summary for the Board or another decision-making unit. Ofcom usually aims to produce this summary within two weeks of the consultation closing. The summary will also include other important and relevant information. This might include the results of market research, the views given in seminars and meetings, and the outcome of informal talks with interested stakeholders. It will also identify any issues that might merit further analysis.

Although the guidelines state explicitly that they only set out the approach Ofcom expects to take and do not have binding legal effect, my own research confirmed that the agency rarely departs from its own principles.

The existence of a consultation champion monitoring and facilitating compliance may account for this observation. Indeed, the position of a consultation champion is specific to the United Kingdom; neither the French nor the Greek telecommunications agencies provide for a similar position. This was not an institutional innovation that began at Ofcom. As noted in Part II.B., one of the consultation criteria in the Cabinet Office's Code of Practice on Written Consultation issued in November 2000 was that "departments should monitor and evaluate consultations, designating a consultation co-ordinator who will ensure the lessons are disseminated."[388] Furthermore, the functions of the consultation champion are not the exclusive, or even the main, duty of the officer who has been designated to serve in that role.[389] Nevertheless, the existence of a specialized position that deals specifically with consultation matters contributes both to a more effective and consistent enforcement of existing participatory requirements (statutory and otherwise) as well as to the development of better practice.

In conclusion, Ofcom's extensive use of public consultations is primarily the result of a set of formal provisions in the Communications Act 2003 that cover a wide range of agency functions. It is also attributable to the agency's commitment to follow its own consultation principles, a commitment that is policed by the consultation champion. Nevertheless, the decision to consult in a consistent and structured way was not only statutorily mandated. The following pages will demonstrate that it was further encouraged, albeit in an indirect and thus potentially not always readily appreciable fashion, by the introduction of a more robust review of Ofcom's decisions in the 2003 statutory framework. Again, the role of EU law in the creation of this appeals mechanism was crucial.

b. The indirect effect of review on appeal

The increased emphasis on public consultations and reasoned consideration of their outcome stemmed not only from formalization by means of explicit statutory mandates but also from the establishment of more robust substantive review on appeal; EU law was the motivating force behind the latter development as well. I shall call this the "formalization breeds formalization" thesis. The gist of the claim is that enhancing review on appeal (the first formalization, or maybe more precisely "juridification") fed back into Ofcom's policymaking processes, thus encouraging further formalization. This argument finds support in interviews with key actors, but it may not seem straightforward. It would therefore be analytically useful to break it down into these three steps: EU law mandates providing for a right of appeal → Domestic transposition of rigorous substantive review (before the Competition Appeal Tribunal or by way of judicial review) → Increased attention on the part of Ofcom and stakeholders to the agency's policymaking processes.

EU law is, again, the place to begin. Indeed, as described in chapter 2, the right of appeal was introduced at the EU level; it was the 2002 Framework Directive (Directive 2002/21/EC) that elaborated on and strengthened this mechanism in Article 4, entitled "Right of appeal." As a reminder, this provision (before its slight amendment in 2009 discussed in chapter 2) read:

1. Member States shall ensure that effective mechanisms exist at national level under which any user or undertaking providing electronic communications networks and/or services who is affected by a decision of a national regulatory authority has the right of appeal against the decision to an appeal body that is independent of the parties involved. *This body, which may be a court, shall have the appropriate expertise available to it to enable it to carry out its functions. Member States shall ensure that the merits of the case are duly taken into account and that there is an effective appeal mechanism.* Pending the outcome of any such appeal, the decision of the national regulatory authority shall stand, unless the appeal body decides otherwise.

2. Where the appeal body referred to in paragraph 1 is not judicial in character, written reasons for its decision shall always be given. Furthermore, in such a case, its decision shall be subject to review by a court or tribunal within the meaning of Article 234 of the Treaty. (emphasis added)

At the second step, sections 192 to 196 and Schedule 8 of the Communications Act 2003 implemented these EU requirements in the domestic legal context by providing a right of appeal on the merits to the Competition Appeal Tribunal (CAT). More specifically, under section 192(1), an affected person may appeal to the CAT against:

- decisions made by OFCOM under Part 2 of the Act (which covers electronic communications networks and services as well as spectrum use) and the Wireless Telegraphy Acts 1949 and 1998 (governing the use of the radio spectrum);
- decisions made further to a condition of entitlement to provide network or services set under section 45 of the 2003 Act;
- certain decisions made by the Secretary of State.

Decisions that may not be appealed to the CAT are specified in Schedule 8 to the Communications Act 2003. They are either decisions that do not have an immediate effect on a person, but are of a legislative or quasi-legislative nature that require a further act or decision to be given effect, or decisions on matters falling outside the scope of the EU Communications Directives.[390] The grounds of appeal must be set out in sufficient detail to indicate: (a) to what extent (if any) the appellant contends that the decision appealed against was based on an error of fact or was wrong in law or both; and (b) to what extent (if any) the appellant is appealing against the exercise of a discretion by OFCOM, by the Secretary of State, or by another person (section 192(6)). The CAT must decide the appeal on the merits (section 195(2)). Its decisions may be appealed only on a point of law, with the permission of the CAT or the appellate court, to the Court of Appeal or to the Court of Session (section 196).

The CAT was created by section 12 and Schedule 2 to the Enterprise Act 2002 that came into force on April 1, 2003. It is a specialist judicial body with cross-disciplinary expertise in law, economics, business, and accountancy the function of which is to hear and decide cases involving competition or economic regulatory issues.[391] The CAT is headed by the President. The membership consists of two panels: a panel of chairmen and a panel of ordinary members. The President must be a lawyer qualified in any part of the UK and of at least ten years standing. She is appointed by the Lord Chancellor (upon the recommendation of the Judicial Appointments Commission) and must appear to the Lord Chancellor to have appropriate experience and knowledge of competition law and practice. The majority on the panel of chairmen are judges of the Chancery Division of the High Court. Some chairmen and all the other members come from academia, private practice, the civil service, business, and industry.[392] As Sir Christopher Bellamy, the President of the CAT until February 2007, noted, the procedure of the Tribunal is essentially based on that of the Court of First Instance, now the General Court, of the European Union.[393]

The cross-disciplinary nature of the Tribunal is described as the CAT's great strength as a "specialist regulatory court"; the expertise of its members translates into heightened scrutiny akin to a "hard look" review.[394] In the words of a practitioner, "review of experts by generalists - wide margin of appreciation; review of experts by other experts (potentially even 'more expert experts') - narrow margin."[395] An assessment of the validity of this claim should begin by noting that the more searching standard of review is the corollary of full merits review. There are numerous CAT cases that demonstrate this intensive standard. For instance, in a 2008 judgment ("H3G case") the Tribunal stated:

> this is an appeal on the merits and the Tribunal is not concerned solely with whether the 2007 Statement is adequately reasoned but also with whether those reasons are correct. The Tribunal accepts . . . that *it is a specialist court* designed to be able to scrutinise the detail of regulatory decisions in a *profound and rigorous* manner. The question for the Tribunal is not whether the decision to impose a price control was within the range of reasonable responses but whether the decision was the right one.[396]

A formulation in another judgment handed down that same day seemed to cabin the extent of the Tribunal's interference with the exercise of Ofcom's discretion:

> It is also common ground that there may, in relation to any particular dispute, be a number of different approaches which OFCOM could reasonably adopt in arriving at its determination. There may well be no single "right answer" to the dispute. To that extent, the Tribunal may, whilst still conducting a merits review of the decision, be slow to overturn a decision which is arrived at by an appropriate methodology even if the dissatisfied party can suggest other ways of approaching the case which would also have been reasonable and which might have resulted in a resolution more favourable to its cause.[397]

However, this more deferential approach did not have a particular impact in that case, as the Tribunal found that the challenges raised by the appellants were more fundamental and went far beyond alleging errors of appreciation.[398] In another case later that year, the CAT, citing those earlier judgments, held:

> What the above judgments clearly demonstrate is that the Tribunal may, depending on particular circumstances, be slower to overturn certain decisions where, as here, there may be a number of different approaches which OFCOM could reasonably adopt . . . . However it is still incumbent on OFCOM, in light of their obligations under section 3 of the CA [Communications Act] 2003, to conduct their assessment with appropriate care, attention and accuracy so that their results are soundly based and can withstand the profound and rigorous scrutiny that the Tribunal will apply on an appeal on the merits under section 192.[399]

The more searching scrutiny following a full merits review distinguishes the latter from conventional judicial review. The conclusion of the previous section on Oftel's policymaking processes touched on these differences; nonetheless, a more recent CAT case helpfully summarized this: "[A]ppeals to the Tribunal under section 192 of the 2003 Act are not dealt with on a judicial review standard, but 'on the merits'. The Tribunal is <u>obliged</u>, by statute, to take the 'substitutionary approach' that is not permitted in judicial review cases. In this respect, appeals to the Tribunal under section 192 are more intrusive than a judicial review would be: the Tribunal is concerned with whether OFCOM's decision was <u>correct</u>."[400]

The practical significance of a specialist regulatory court becomes apparent when one also considers the criteria against which the CAT will examine the regulator's decision. These were set out in the first CAT case in the telecommunications sector; the Tribunal explained that it needs to be persuaded that the regulatory decision is "incorrect or, at the least, insufficient, from the point of view of (i) the reasons given; (ii) *the facts and analysis relied on*; (iii) the law applied; (iv) the investigation undertaken; or (v) the procedure followed."[401] This fact-intensive review requires adjudicators conversant in the highly technical questions involved in the assessment of regulatory analysis. The CAT itself alluded to this point in the *H3G* case cited earlier, in which it agreed that it is a specialist court designed to be able to scrutinize the detail of regulatory decisions in a profound and rigorous manner.

Interestingly, the standard of review on appeal does not change even if the appeal is brought before an ordinary court. An example of this would be a challenge against a regulatory decision for which there is a right of appeal under EU law, but which may fall under an exception under Schedule 8 to the Communications Act 2003, therefore the CAT would lack jurisdiction. The Court of Appeal dealt with one such case in 2008. Lord Justice Jacob, writing for a unanimous court, agreed with the CAT's earlier determination that, as matter of statutory construction, that particular challenge was excluded from CAT appeal jurisdiction. Thus, the appellants' route of redress would be via judicial review. The court, however, did accept—indeed, as "common ground"—that the challenge before it constituted an "appeal" within the meaning of Article 4(1) of the EC Framework Directive. The Court of Appeal also recognized that EU law imposed an obligation on a national court to adapt its procedures as far as possible to ensure EU rights are protected. In this respect, it noted that the common law in the area of judicial review "is adaptable so that the rules as to [judicial review] jurisdiction are flexible enough to accommodate whatever standard is required by Art. 4 [of the 2002 Framework Directive]." The court concluded that "EU law is completely neutral about the question we have to decide. It points neither to the CAT nor [judicial review]. Given that one route or the other complies with Art. 4, EU law stands aside because its requirements are met either way."[402]

In other words, the heightened standard of scrutiny applies under EU law requirements before either the CAT or ordinary courts. At this point, a reader might respond: "Surely the forum matters. Same standards will be applied in different ways by appellate bodies whose members have different backgrounds and expertise." Lord Pannick, representing the appellants, raised this point. Lord Justice Jacob was not convinced:

> Lord Pannick referred to the "appropriate expertise" requirement, using it to suggest a JR [judicial review] court would not comply with it. But since the Chairman of the CAT is a Chancery Judge and all Chancery Judges can sit in the CAT and, by arrangement, in the Administrative Court there was nothing in this. Lord Pannick emphasised that the CAT has lay members whereas the JR court does not. But the CAT's lay members may well not have any experience of the particular subject-matter,

so that point goes nowhere. And besides the JR court itself, if it felt expertise were necessary (which would be a rare case) could sit with assessors – see s.70 Supreme Court Act 1981 and CPR Part 35 r.15. Also, Lord Pannick did not identify with particularity any expertise which would be unavailable to a JR court so far as this case is concerned.

We do not need a definite answer to this question, although arguably a combination of full merits review with a specialist regulatory court[403] may facilitate more searching scrutiny of the agency's regulatory analysis even on the application of the same intensive standard of review. My broader point is that the introduction of this intensive standard was driven by EU requirements and had a clearly noticeable impact, as two further pieces of evidence suggest.

First, in matters falling outside the scope of the EU requirements for a right of appeal, the conventional, and deferential, judicial review standard of *Wednesbury* reasonableness still applied. Indeed, in *Wildman v. Ofcom*, a case about the award of an independent radio license, the Queen's Bench Division expressly endorsed the *Wednesbury* language. The court stated that "Ofcom is an expert body, and it, and not the Court, has been given the responsibility for making the evaluations and exercising the discretions inherent in a licensing process."[404] This approach is in clear contrast with the language of "profound and rigorous" scrutiny we saw in appeal cases. Lest there be any doubt, the court concluded: "this is not an appeal on fact. This is an area in which . . . . the Court allows the decision maker a wide measure of discretion and width of decision."[405]

A second piece of evidence demonstrating the intensity of full merits review is that in August 2011 the government proposed amendments to the appeals process. More specifically, the government argued that "the current standard of review leads to unnecessary lengthy and expensive appeals of the regulator's decisions. These delays in the implementation of remedies and decisions are bad for market certainty and ultimately bad for consumers." For this reason, the Department proposed that section 195(2) of the Communications Act 2003 be amended to read as follows: "In deciding the appeal the Tribunal must apply the same principles as would be applied by a court on an application for judicial review, ensuring that the merits of the case are duly taken into account." It further explained that importing verbatim the requirement to take due account of the merits according to Article 4 of the Framework Directive would "result in appeals which are more focussed on material points, with a corresponding reduction in the need for and/ or scope of oral examination and cross examination of factual and expert witnesses, leading to shorter hearings and more focussed pleadings than is presently the case."[406] These proposals raised concerns among stakeholders and did not lead to any statutory amendments on that occasion. Nevertheless, the government's intention to roll back CAT review, which was reiterated in a 2013 consultation document and a 2016 impact assessment,[407] is an indication that the introduction of sections 192-196 of the Communications Act 2003 (under EU impetus) has had a clear impact on policymaking in the electronic communications sector.

This brings us to the last step of the reasoning that opened this section, which has probably become clear by now. The existence of a credible "threat" that Ofcom's decisions are appealable,[408] that the appellate body (primarily the CAT) will examine the agency's analysis in a rigorous manner and may ultimately overturn it, feeds back into Ofcom's policymaking processes and imposes stricter discipline on them. The agency's methodology, the facts it has considered or dismissed in order to reach its decision are now under profound scrutiny that goes far beyond the unreasonableness test employed in conventional judicial review proceedings. Representatives of both sides of the table pointed to this fact in interviews. A senior Ofcom official mentioned that an effective way to reduce the likelihood that a decision will be overturned is to show that the agency made that decision after having consulted widely and considered evidence, and, if it discarded some of the responses, to provide reasons for doing so.[409] Similarly, the Regulatory Strategy and Planning Manager at the BT Group suggested that one of Ofcom's concerns is to ensure that the evidence it has and the process it went through to reach its decisions can stand up in appellate review.[410] The Tribunal's jurisprudence also confirms the understanding that review on appeal reflects on the agency's policymaking processes. Section C.4. will elaborate on how consultation figured in specific instances of CAT review, but a brief excerpt from one case is instructive for present purposes: "the Common Regulatory Framework [i.e., the 2002 EC directives] makes very clear the importance of consultation, so as (amongst other things) to ensure that the least intrusive form of regulation is imposed in a market where SMP exists . . . . As a general proposition, *a failure by a regulator to consult is likely to result in poor decisions.*"[411]

Formalization breeds formalization. Irrespective of the source of this formalization (direct effect of explicit statutory mandates, indirect effect of full merits review), the data also seem consistent with this thesis. Figure 5.1[412] shows a steady increase in the number of public consultations during the second half of the 1990s. This period coincides with the tenure of Don Cruickshank, who, as we saw, expressed publicly his commitment to a practice of public consultation. The momentum continued during the last years of Oftel, particularly after 2000. During that time, the direction in which the new EU regulatory framework would go (including in terms of mandatory public consultation) was apparent and acknowledged, as Section B.2. showed, in Oftel and government documents. The number of consultations peaked in 2003, as the new super-regulator assumed a greater number of functions, and remained high thereafter.

The number of comments received and published in the same 1984-2010 period (Figure 5.2) reveals a similar trend as the market became increasingly dynamic in the late 1990s and the 21st century. With the markets becoming

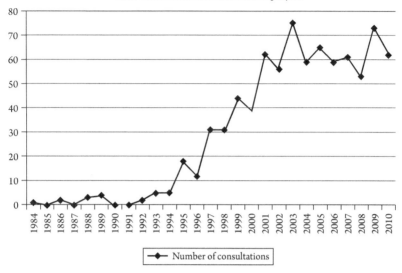

Figure 5.1 Oftel/Ofcom: Number of public consultations per year (1984–2010)

Source: Own elaboration with data drawn from Oftel's archives and Ofcom's website

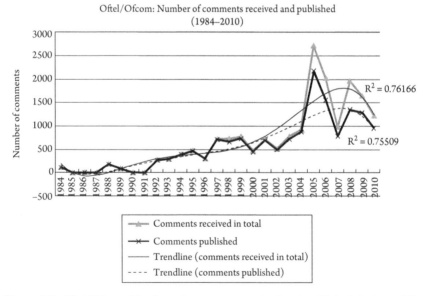

Figure 5.2 Oftel/Ofcom: Number of comments received and published during public consultations in the telecommunications sector (1984–2010)

Source: Own elaboration with data drawn from Oftel's archives and Ofcom's website

increasingly open, the regulator resorting more frequently to the tool of public consultation and stakeholders becoming accustomed to these participatory processes, the curve of the trendlines is not surprising. The year 2005 stands out for the number of responses submitted. Public consultation on high-salience issues accounts for this spike: Ofcom received 1,308 responses to its consultation on Number Translation Services in the fall of 2005.[413]

In conclusion, formalization had a noticeable impact on the practices of the agency and the perceptions of key actors in the electronic communications sector. Having focused on the role of EU law in driving this formalization process, let us now take a step back to consider Ofcom's regulatory processes on the basis of the four prongs of the deliberative-participatory model.

C. Evaluating Ofcom's regulatory processes against the fundamental operative elements of the deliberative-participatory model

1. Open access

Ofcom's open consultations are publicly available on the agency's website, and every interested stakeholder or citizen may submit a response. The system of specific invitations sent to designated market actors, which Oftel used when it first started to consult, has been replaced by this more open process. Nevertheless, the policy teams at Ofcom know who the key stakeholders are, and, especially in highly technical cases, they are likely to contact specifically that defined set of potential respondents. There is also an alert system on which interested parties can register to receive updates about new documents that Ofcom has published.

A common question in the three cases is who participates in these public consultations in practice. Figure 5.3 provides an answer for a recent five-year period.

A number that immediately stands out is the high percentage of individuals submitting responses to consultations. To put this 38% of individual participation into perspective, a useful reminder is that the corresponding numbers of individual citizen responses in France and Greece were 7% and 2%, respectively. What accounts for this stark variation in the UK case?

I submit that a major explanatory factor for this 38% is the persistence of the traditional idea of citizen-consumer, this time reflected in the context of public policymaking in telecommunications. Part II.A. introduced the hybrid notion of citizen-consumer and examined its strained relationship with administrative democracy. Both the hyphenated term and its individual components appear with high frequency and relevance in the electronic communications framework, and they have an interesting pedigree. The 2000 White Paper "A New Future for Communications,"[414] which had set out the government's proposals that ultimately resulted in the Communications Act 2003, devoted a section to each

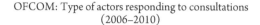

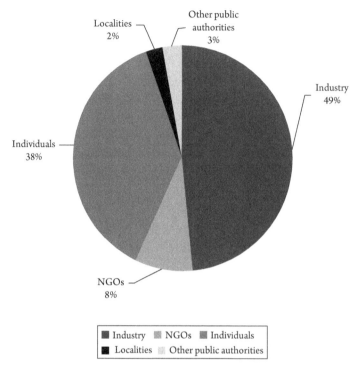

Figure 5.3 Ofcom: Type of actors responding to consultations (2006–2010)

Source: Own elaboration with data from the website of Ofcom

component: section 6 on safeguarding the interests of citizens and section 7 on protecting the interests of consumers. The former pertained mostly to content (broadcasting), while the latter focused on competition. Nevertheless, the reference to citizens had not been included in the Draft Communications Bill 2002. This omission was noted during the scrutiny of the bill by a joint committee of both Houses of Parliament, which was chaired by Lord Puttnam, a renowned former filmmaker.[415] The Puttnam Report stated:

> we are also persuaded that there are public interests relating to the regulatory framework that are not encompassed in a consumer-driven objective and are not properly reflected in OFCOM's general duties as presently drafted. The concept of citizens' interests was to the fore in the White Paper and is referred to in the Policy document accompanying the draft Bill, but fails to feature in the duties set out in the draft Bill itself . . . . [T]his is more than a matter of semantics. Evidence we received reflected genuine concern that the democratic, social and cultural interests of

citizens, most notably in relation to broadcast content, were not given due weight in the formulation of OFCOM's general duties . . . . Broadcast content is not the only area where it will be the duty of OFCOM to serve a wider public interest beyond that of consumers . . . . We recommend that it be the principal duty of OFCOM, in carrying out its functions - (a) to further the long-term interests of all citizens . . . and (b) to further the long-term interests of consumers by promoting the efficiency of electronic communications networks and services, and broadcasting.[416]

A dual duty toward citizens and consumers was introduced into the bill in the House of Lords through an amendment proposed by Lord Puttnam.[417] As a result, Ofcom has a statutory duty to further these two distinct sets of interests under section 3(1) of the Communications Act 2003. In the words of Lord Currie, its first Chairman, "Ofcom is statutorily responsible both to individual members of the public, both in their capacity as *homo economicus* and as *homo civicus*, as well as to the public at large."[418] During its first year, Ofcom was using the hyphenated term "citizen-consumer" in various documents. For example, its mission statement, unveiled when the organization began its operation, stated: "Ofcom exists to further the interests of citizen-consumers, through a regulatory regime which, where appropriate, promotes competition." Similar references were included in the agency's first Annual Report. Ofcom's use of this phrase attempted to capture both the citizen and the consumer perspectives and reflect their connection. However, as the agency recognized, critics viewed the hyphen as a means of reasserting the primacy of economic regulation, with "citizen" being subsumed into "consumer." Therefore, it moved away from referring to citizen-consumers and began to distinguish more clearly between citizens' and consumers' interests.[419] This dual language was reproduced in the Annual Reports beginning in 2004–2005.[420]

It is true that the emphasis on citizen interests is particularly fitting in the broadcasting area, which falls within the remit of Ofcom but outside the scope of this study. Nevertheless, as Tony Prosser has correctly observed, the division between Ofcom's dual duty is much more complex, "with the competition duty applying right across the Ofcom's responsibilities, and the same being also true of the duty to further citizens' interests."[421] Ofcom itself was clear on this: "Of course, the interests of citizens stretch significantly beyond broadcasting. All our work is relevant to citizens' interests and we recognised this in our review of consumer policy . . . which reiterated the distinction between the individual interests of consumers and the shared interests of citizens . . . . [I]t may be necessary to address tensions between the interests of consumers and the interests of citizens. For example, making services available more widely for the benefit of society as a whole may mean that some consumers have to pay more for those services than might otherwise have been the case."[422]

An example in which both consumer and citizen interests are implicated is the net neutrality debate. Ofcom dealt with each separately in its discussion paper[423] in a specific section entitled "How could traffic management affect citizens and consumers?" For instance, the agency explained that no traffic management would, in principle, allow *consumers* to enjoy open access to all content and services on the Internet; in practice, however, it might come with a risk of their bandwidth becoming congested at peak times with the result that certain applications are slowed down or degraded. On the other hand, network operators and ISPs might be able to offer consumer benefits through traffic management, perhaps promising to deliver their own services at a certain level of quality, for example offering high definition video without interruption (paras. 2.10-2.13). At the same time, the agency expressed "no doubt that in principle, the 'citizenship' aspect of our primary duty could come into play as a result of the deployment of traffic management," and referred to the argument that traffic management may lead "to a closing down of the 'open' internet as we know it today in favour of a series of closed platforms tightly controlled by telecoms operators" (para. 2.22). Furthermore, it pointed out that "an increasing number of Government departments and agencies are putting forms and information online . . . . Access to broadband is therefore becoming an important way to access public services and traffic management could potentially have an impact on how citizens might access these services in the future." Last, it reiterated the importance of the Internet as a powerful communication tool that facilitates full participation in a modern democratic society (paras 2.14-2.15).

Even though Ofcom treated the two sets of interests separately, the response of the Communications Consumer Panel highlighted the differences and potential tensions between them in a starker way. The Panel suggested that "in the short term consumers' interests are likely to be met through a solution that delivers a range of different services with different approaches to traffic management, and potentially including prioritised services or applications paid for by the content provider, the consumer, or both." On the other hand, the Panel pointed to ways in which online public services could be negatively affected by traffic management, and urged Ofcom to assess more thoroughly the citizen impact of net neutrality and traffic management.[424] In other words, the net neutrality debate usefully demonstrates the limits of the consumerist approach: one could argue consumers' interests could be furthered if they made an informed choice to pay for higher quality service in a regime of more extensive traffic management. In contrast, an approach focusing on citizen empowerment would stress the importance of having enough bandwidth for public service content that would be open to all, and ensuring that willingness to pay is not tantamount to equal participation.

It is not necessary to exhaust the discussion about terminology and its implications to suggest that the idea of citizen-consumer, first brought to the fore by the New Right administrations, remained very much present even after the creation of Ofcom. The most interesting question in this context is how the formalized participatory processes mapped onto the cultural background of long commitment to consumer choice and voice. As Part II noted, the driving idea behind the notion of the "citizen-consumer" was that citizens should be viewed not just as users of public services but as active consumers empowered to exercise choice, have access to information about these services, request high quality standards, and have avenues for complaint and redress in case of failure. The formalization and generalization of public consultation processes in the electronic communications sector provided an additional outlet for individuals to express their voice. And having been socialized in a public environment with an individualistic emphasis on the consumer,[425] they did so massively (compared to other countries) but individually.

This explanation offers support for the high percentage of participation by individuals but may also account for the type of responses. Public consultation processes constitute an avenue for civic participation. Nonetheless, when mapped onto embedded perceptions of the citizen-consumer demanding high quality and complaining when they do not receive it, these processes may also transform into a platform for the expression of consumer discontent or frustration, thereby not fulfilling their full deliberative potential. Ofcom seemed aware of this potential tension in its document discussing consumers' and citizens' interests: "We are committed to carrying out research to understand people's views, but it is important that this reflects not only their views and expectations as consumers but also what they share as citizens, such as common values, culture and national identity. In some cases, it can be useful to carry out deliberative research. This means involving people in thinking about an issue as citizens, rather than as self-interested consumers, and considering the trade-offs between alternative policy options."[426]

Reading through hundreds of comments from individuals revealed interesting responses that reflect this concern: one-line comments calling Ofcom's proposals "a disgrace" or simply stating "I wish the end of 0870." On the opposite side, comments suggesting that "whoever came up with this idea should have a beer." Another comment raised procedural concerns: "you consult and consult until you find support for predetermined outcomes." In a different case, an individual sounded rather apprehensive about potential agency capture ("you were bought out by the industry")!

This selection was deliberately provocative to fuel the skepticism of readers who are inclined to dismiss the significance of the 38% of individual participation. A partial response would be that I left out examples of other comments coming from individuals that were more elaborate, offering facts and figures and reasoned analysis. Even though these highly sophisticated comments were not in abundant supply, my broader point regarding the high percentage of citizen responses goes back to the discussion about mass comments campaigns in chapter 1. The argument made there was that comments expressing preferences or discontent may be useful in flagging issues that the agency should consider in more detail or in which it should engage stakeholders via different methods (e.g., focus groups). In any event, the high percentage of individual participation (regardless of the sophistication of specific comments) contrasts sharply with the French and Greek cases and is significant from a comparative perspective: it reflects how embedded cultural characteristics survive in new forms in the face of external pressures, as are the EU mandates for public consultation. These persistent features account for variations we see in the three country cases when we quantify public participation, even though the telecoms agencies in all these countries implement the same core of procedural requirements.

This sociological background was coupled with Ofcom's own efforts to encourage consumer involvement in its policymaking processes. As the Chief Executive explained in Ofcom's first Annual Report, "[o]ur major consultation documents are made available to a broad range of stakeholders; wherever an issue is likely to be of direct interest to citizen-consumers we also produce a summary granted a Crystal Mark by the Plain English Campaign."[427] Indeed, for consultations on questions that the agency thought concerned consumers primarily,[428] Ofcom often made available a "plain English summary." Per its consultation guidelines, Ofcom also runs "a consultation helpdesk to help organisations such as small businesses and consumer and community groups make their views heard in response to [its] consultations."

The second mechanism for consumer engagement is a bulky governance structure involving a set of advisory bodies, the most important of which is the Communications Consumer Panel ("CCP"). The CCP is an independent group of experts established under sections 16-19 of the Communications Act 2003. Its role is to provide advice to Ofcom to ensure that the interests of consumers are central to regulatory decisions. Panel members are appointed by Ofcom, subject to ministerial approval. Their number has varied between six and ten over the years, but, as a general matter, they have experience in different fields, such as consumer advocacy, dispute resolution, the telecoms and content industries, regulation, the non-profit sector, trade unions, and market research. There are four members of the Panel who represent the interests of consumers in England, Northern Ireland, Scotland, and Wales (section 17(3)). They liaise with the key stakeholders around the UK to understand the concerns of consumers and bring these perspectives into the Panel's consideration of issues.[429] The CCP is often described as a "critical friend" to Ofcom,[430] and this was my own experience after my visit to the CCP and Ofcom, both based in the same building in London. Ofcom funds the CCP and provides an executive team to support it in its work. An interesting example of these ties is that Colette Bowe, the Chair of Ofcom since March 2009, had chaired the Consumer Panel from its inception in 2003 to December 2007. The Panel interacts with Ofcom in three main ways:

- by responding to formal consultations;
- perhaps more importantly, through informal consultations, through the informal relationship it has with Ofcom, at the point when the agency is considering a change in policy or at the preparation stage of a consultation document. The Panel has placed particular emphasis on its proactive work.[431] Similarly, Ofcom has committed to consulting "the Panel throughout in its deliberations on policies and practices with particular consumer or citizen impact well in advance of the final stage of Ofcom's policy-making processes";[432]
- at the post-consultation stage, the Panel can issue a formal advice note to the Ofcom Board if it feels that something material has not been properly reflected in the public consultation process. In that case, Ofcom has to formally respond to this advice. Nevertheless, the CCP has used this device very sparingly.

Furthermore, in fulfillment of its statutory duties, Ofcom has set up five advisory committees and may seek their input on the whole breadth of its communications responsibilities. More specifically, under section 20 of the Communications Act 2003, Ofcom has established separate advisory committees for the Nations (England, Scotland, Wales, Northern Ireland), and, under section 21, an Advisory Committee on Older and Disabled People.[433] It has been suggested that these advisory committees (unlike the CCP) are not influential within Ofcom, although the agency is attempting to improve their role,[434] and their contributions are often acknowledged in its Annual Reports.

Notwithstanding the high number of comments from individuals, the structures that are in place to provide consumer input, and the lack of major complaints against the public consultation processes, Ofcom officials still acknowledged the challenge of reaching out to individual members of the public. As they explained, when they put up a consultation document (often with a press release), they cannot be sure how it will be picked up by the media. If it is a very technical question, there will likely be little interest in the media; it will thus be more difficult to reach beyond the usual stakeholders who know what the agency is doing and have an ongoing dialogue with it. A way to remedy this is through roundtables around the country, which, however, are not always well attended. As already noted, Ofcom holds public meetings to discuss its Annual Plans. An experienced stakeholder who has participated in such meetings commended the agency on its efforts to reach out to citizens; at the same time, he noted that because of the nature of these meetings and the limited time available, the discussion would not involve careful consideration of evidence but provide an opportunity to raise issues of concern to stakeholders ranging, for example, from digital TV switchover, mobile coverage to why local radio stations were being closed down. He concluded, therefore, that written responses remain the most effective way of creating a public record and encouraging the agency to examine all the evidence.[435]

This discussion raises the last point to consider under the open access prong; that is, the role of stakeholder meetings in addition to the formal consultation process. According to Ofcom's consultation guidelines:

> We will speak regularly to a number of different people and organisa-tions in an informal way to help us understand their concerns. We may have a period of pre-consultation in some circumstances with stake-holders who might potentially be particularly affected so that we can understand the issue better. Any stakeholders views gathered during pre-consultation may help inform Ofcom's initial thinking but will not be treated as formal consultation responses, as these informal discus-sions will apply as well as not instead of the formal consultation proc-ess. We undertake pre-consultation through a mixture of informal meetings and seminars.

In a similar vein, Ofcom's Impact Assessment guidelines clarify that "[p]rior to stakeholders being consulted formally on the options, more detailed work may need to be carried out to identify the impacts . . . . In presenting this work, we will generally show how we have taken account of the information obtained from stakeholders, subject to the need to preserve any requirements of confidentiality."[436] Representatives from both the industry and consumer groups confirmed that informal meetings do occur.[437] Nonetheless, even though the agency may informally sound out options in the buildup to the consultation, the same interviews suggested that the time to put evidence forward is during the public consultation phase.[438] This is consistent with the formulation in Ofcom's consultation guidelines that views submitted during informal discussions will not be treated as formal consultation responses. Besides, a decision based on informal meetings (especially if these were with specific stakeholders to the exclusion of others) could be considered proce-durally tainted and thus struck down on review. Therefore, formal public consultations that are open to everyone remain a key phase in Ofcom's poli-cymaking processes.

2. Transparency

A scholar of regulation remarked that Ofcom differs from other regulators in that its board meetings are not held in public, though brief agendas and minutes are published. He further pointed to recommendations that meetings should be held in public, but noted that the Ofcom board has to handle much confidential information and regulates a particularly litigious industry.[439] When it comes to public consultations, however, the level of transparency is higher. Ofcom's consultation guidelines state:

> We believe it is important for everyone interested in an issue to see the views expressed by consultation respondents. We therefore usually publish all responses on our website, www.ofcom.org.uk, ideally on receipt. If you think your response should be kept confidential, you should specify what part or whether all of your response should be kept confidential, and specify why. Please place confidential parts in a separate annex. If someone asks us to keep part or all of a response confidential, we will treat that request seriously and try to respect it. But sometimes we will have to publish all responses, including those that are marked as confidential, in order to meet legal obligations.

In compliance with these principles, information about ongoing and past consultations as well as the stakeholders' submissions are, as a general matter, readily and consistently available on the agency's website. It is not unusual, however, for comments to be kept confidential. In fact, the data I have collected suggest that, between 2003 and 2010, 21% of the responses submitted during public consultations were confidential. This percentage may seem high partly because of my methodology: I have counted as non-published comments the content of which was available but their author was not disclosed. The idea underlying this choice is that if external observers cannot attribute specific responses to identifiable stakeholders and therefore appreciate the influence of other market actors, the goal of transparency is not fully served even if the substantive arguments in the comments are publicly available. Interestingly, in a 2004 consultation in which no submissions were published, Ofcom explained in its Statement that it had made that decision due to the confidential nature of many of the responses provided, without it being clear whether the stakeholders themselves had requested confidentiality.

Furthermore, a closer look at Figure 5.2 earlier in this chapter reveals that the percentage of confidential responses seems to be higher under Ofcom than it was under Oftel. This should not mislead us into thinking that more information was available before 2003. Indeed, quite the opposite is true. As we saw, for most of the 1990s, consultation responses were not available online but only at the agency's library in London. The fact that information is now much more readily available online may have prompted stakeholders to be more cautious and request confidentiality more frequently. Moreover, Ofcom now issues more detailed statements at the end of the consultation process that address issues raised in comments regardless of their confidentiality status. In any event, Ofcom's transparency practices go beyond the common law requirements when there is an obligation to consult. As Part II.C.2. examined in further detail, the UK courts did not recognize a general duty to disclose the representations of other consultees.[440] Nevertheless, this should not be taken to suggest that Ofcom should not consider ways of encouraging stakeholders to only request confidentiality when absolutely necessary.

Another consultation guideline that Ofcom has not followed is that responses would be published on receipt. As chapter 1 explained, this practice would be conducive to a more deliberative exchange of views among stakeholders. Admittedly, the guidelines themselves only describe this as an *ideal* practice. Relatedly, however, Ofcom did not engage in another practice that could have an equivalent deliberation-enhancing effect, i.e., the two-stage consultation. This was a practice that Oftel had followed on several occasions, whereby it would set aside a formal 14-day period for respondents to comment on the views expressed by others (also known as "comment-on-comments") during the first consultation round. In fairness to Ofcom, it was Oftel that had decided to cease that practice as of 2001,[441] and Ofcom merely did not reinitiate it. Last, Ofcom is covered by the Freedom of Information Act 2000. The agency website[442] provides information on how to make a FOIA request as well as a list of responses since 2011. Furthermore, Ofcom's Annual Reports address how the agency has responded to FOIA requests.[443]

3. Reason giving

UK law imposes no general duty on public authorities to give reasons in the absence of a clear statutory provision to this effect.[444] The majority of statutory tribunals are required by the Tribunals and Inquiries Act 1992 to give reasons for their decisions on request. This Act also applies to ministerial decisions subsequent to statutory inquiries.[445] This reason-giving requirement is expressly excluded, however, in the case of rules, orders, or schemes "of a legislative and not executive character" (section 10(5)(b)).

The Communications Act 2003 includes several provisions that impose an obligation on Ofcom to give reasons for its decisions. These decisions include penalties and enforcement notifications directed at specific companies; more interesting for present purposes, however, are reason-giving mandates that cover decisions with broader implications. For instance, we have already seen that, under section 3(8), when Ofcom needs to resolve a conflict between its duties, it must publish a statement setting out the reasons for its decision. There are various other such provisions, including notably an obligation for Ofcom to give reasons before setting, modifying, or revoking a condition of entitlement to provide network or service (section 48(2)) or when it proposes to identify a market or make a market power determination (section 80(3)).

Nevertheless, even in the absence of express reason-giving obligations, Ofcom generally justifies its decisions by issuing a statement at the conclusion of the public consultation. This is in accordance with the agency's consultation guidelines, whereby the statement shall "give reasons for [Ofcom's] decisions and . . . an account of how the views of those concerned helped shape those decisions." Indeed, one issue that external stakeholders raised when Ofcom was reviewing its consultation processes was how the agency weighs up conflicting evidence provided by consultation responses.[446] Therefore, the statement will normally list (or group) the views of stakeholders and set out Ofcom's thinking and reasons for taking some comments into account while dismissing others. In practice, Ofcom almost always issues such statements; the limited number of instances in which it did not commonly involved cases where it had received no representations. Ofcom's attention to these statements and the explanation of its decisions, even when it is not statutorily obliged to provide them, is attributable to the risk of having these decisions overturned on appeal if they are not reasoned.[447] This brings us to the last prong of the model, judicial review.

4. Judicial review

Even though one could perhaps imagine a judicial review challenge against an Ofcom decision on a telecommunications matter on the single ground of procedural irregularities involving the public consultation process, in practice allegations of this type have been incorporated into appeals before the CAT pursuant to sections 192-196 of the Communications Act 2003. Therefore, the title of this section should be read to include review on appeal.

The first puzzle about the connection between review on appeal and the public consultation process is that the former is, as we saw in Part III.B.2b, a full merits review, whereas the latter is definitionally a procedural question, thus, *in principle*, falling outside the scope of CAT review. In fact, however, in several CAT cases, procedural and merits review were intertwined. The Tribunal considered the interplay between procedural and substantive points in a 2012 judgment.[448] The main issues in this case were TalkTalk's contentions that Ofcom had erred procedurally in failing to take proper steps to satisfy itself that there had been a material change within the meaning of section 86(1)(b) of the Communications Act 2003 (Ground A); and that Ofcom's decision that there had been no material change within the meaning of section 86(1)(b) was, in substance, wrong (Ground B). The Tribunal first noted that in the context of an appeal, its role is to "assess the <u>correctness</u> of OFCOM's decision, and <u>not</u> to apply a judicial review standard (by, for example, seeking to determine whether OFCOM has taken into account immaterial factors or failed properly to consult)."[449] Nevertheless, it went on to explain that consideration of Ofcom's decision-making process is not necessarily irrelevant, and parties are not precluded from raising such matters in an appeal. The Tribunal accepted TalkTalk's argument that Ofcom must be able to justify its decision as being "adequately and soundly reasoned and supported in fact" and added:

> Without adequate consultation, it may be <u>unclear</u> whether there has been a material change or not. To take a hypothetical example, suppose a case where OFCOM simply fails to consider or consult upon the question of material change <u>at all</u>. In such a case, it may be that it is impossible – without the benefit of a proper consultation – for either OFCOM or, on appeal, the Tribunal to determine whether there has, or has not, been a material change. In such a case, on an appeal, it may be that the proper course would be for the Tribunal to remit the matter to OFCOM with a direction that a proper consultation be carried out.[450]

The CAT, therefore, enunciated the idea of consultation as a "checklist obligation" also discussed in the other country cases of this book. The absence of consultation would be reviewable, but the specifics of the process are not. In the Tribunal's words, "what constitutes a proper consultation is coloured by the facts of the given case. We consider that it would be wrong, in cases where OFCOM is considering whether there has been a material change for the purposes of section 86 of the 2003 Act, to lay down strict rules as to how OFCOM should go about this process."[451]

The interesting twist, however, is that this seemingly deferential approach stems not from restraint but the opposite, that is, the *intrusive* nature of merits review. The CAT stated that in cases where it has concluded that the regulator's decision was correct on the merits, it does not consider that it is its function "<u>also</u> to review OFCOM's decision by reference to the judicial review standard . . . . It is clear law that where a decision of an administrative body, such as OFCOM, is subject to a full, on the merits appeal, such an appeal is capable of making good any deficiency in the procedure of the administrative body taking the original decision. In other words, a procedural failure at the level of the first instance administrative body can be remedied by a wide, on the merits, appeal."[452] Conversely, "even if OFCOM's consultation process has been unimpeachably conducted, the Tribunal may nevertheless conclude that OFCOM's decision was wrong."[453] The Tribunal's approach, however, is not as simple as a scheme like "deference on process, heightened scrutiny on merits" might suggest. As the CAT explained,

> It may be that there are cases where OFCOM's approach in reaching its decision was <u>so</u> defective as to preclude the Tribunal from reaching an "on the merits" conclusion. In paragraph 76 above, we considered

the case where OFCOM reached a decision regarding "material change" without any consultation at all. It may be that, in such a case, the procedural deficiency on the part of OFCOM is so serious as to render it unsafe for the Tribunal to conclude that, "on the merits", OFCOM reached the correct decision. In such a case . . . it may be that the only appropriate course is to remit the matter back to OFCOM for OFCOM to carry out its decision-making process again.[454]

The absence of any consultation whatsoever would be a clear case of procedural deficiency precluding review on the merits. The Tribunal's formulation, however, could also accommodate less clear-cut cases. We will indeed return to instances in which the adequacy of the policymaking process was at stake. On the merits, the Tribunal in this case held that Ofcom had reached the correct substantive decision, and therefore rejected TalkTalk's Ground B. The CAT further explained that "this case does not disclose the sort of procedural deficiencies which cause us in any way to doubt the soundness of the conclusion we have reached on Ground B."[455] As to TalkTalk's Ground A, the Tribunal's short answer was that where, as in this case, "there is a full rehearing by the Tribunal of an issue initially determined by OFCOM and the appellant's case has received 'overall, full and fair consideration' . . . that will, in general, dispose of a challenge based upon deficiencies or alleged deficiencies in OFCOM's procedure."[456]

Nevertheless, the Tribunal went on to consider Ground A in a series of obiter dicta.[457] More specifically, it noted that Ofcom had given third parties "every opportunity" to participate in its decision-making process; and, second, that although TalkTalk was entitled to rely upon any procedural failure on the part of Ofcom, whether this directly affected TalkTalk or not, no stakeholder, other than the appellant, had made any complaint regarding the consultation process. The CAT went on to reject TalkTalk's suggestion that consideration of whether there had been a material change for the purposes of section 86(1)(b) of the 2003 Act required, in all cases, detailed and extensive consultation. The CAT held, instead, that the extent of the consultation required turns on the facts of any given case, and it is, in the first instance, for Ofcom, as the decision-maker, "to decide upon the manner and intensity of the enquiry to be undertaken." In the case before it, the Tribunal "would have rejected TalkTalk's Ground A on basis that Ofcom did properly satisfy itself that there had been no 'material change'" subject to one qualification.[458] Namely, the CAT recognized that the summary description of Market 1 contained in Ofcom's Wholesale Broadband Access [WBA] Market Power Determination was "obviously wrong" and amounted to an inaccurate statement of how OFCOM had defined its markets. For the Tribunal, this was "an important point."

> For a consultation exercise to be meaningful, the consultation must be adequate. It must, amongst other things, contain sufficient information

> so as to enable potential consultees to make a proper and informed
> response . . . . Here, persons interested in the WBA Market might
> well not have understood exactly how OFCOM had defined Market 1
> in the WBA Market Power Determination, and this might well have
> coloured submissions made in response to the [public] consultation.
> To this extent only, would we have been minded to accept TalkTalk's
> contentions as regards the adequacy of OFCOM's consultation process.
> However, for the reasons we have given, we consider that this deficiency
> of process was cured by the full rehearing that has now taken place.[459]

In other words, the Tribunal did assess the adequacy of Ofcom's policymaking processes, albeit in obiter dicta, and found a procedural deficiency; yet, that deficiency would not have been so grave as to not be cured by the full rehearing before it.

In earlier cases, the CAT had examined the propriety of regulatory processes against the Sedley/*Gunning* (and now *Moseley*) criteria, which apply to consultations in general and were discussed in Part II.C.2. More specifically, the Tribunal endorsed these criteria in a 2009 judgment on the disposal of an appeal by H3G and BT.[460] The case did not pertain to Ofcom's processes per se, yet it shows the Tribunal's approach to stakeholder participation. H3G and BT had appealed against the price control conditions contained in a Statement by Ofcom on mobile call termination rates. The price control matters raised in the appeal were referred to the Competition Commission ("CC") pursuant to section 193 of the Communications Act. The CC notified the Tribunal of their determination, which, broadly, rejected H3G's appeal; as to BT's appeal, it determined that Ofcom had erred in two respects. According to section 193(6)-(7) of the Communications Act 2003, the CAT had to decide the price control matters in accordance with the determination of the CC except to the extent that "the Tribunal decides, applying the principles applicable on an application for judicial review, that the determination of the [CC] is a determination that would fall to be set aside on such an application." Three Interveners, Orange, T-Mobile, and Vodafone, argued that certain parts of the determination should be set aside. Their pertinent challenge for present purposes was procedural: the Interveners alleged that the CC had not provided a fair and adequate opportunity for the parties to comment on its methodology. The Tribunal invoked the Sedley/*Gunning* criteria, and noted that the Court of Appeal in *Coughlan* had taken into account the "prehistory" of the consultation, that is to say, the fact that the consultation period that was under attack in those proceedings was not the first time that the applicant had had an opportunity to make representations. In the case before it, the CAT held, based on a chronology set out in annex, that the Interveners had had ample opportunity to make their submissions and made extensive use of that opportunity.

A CAT case decided the year before involved the policymaking processes of Ofcom itself, and it had a different outcome.[461] Vodafone brought an appeal against a decision by Ofcom to modify the system of telephone number portability ("the Decision"). The Decision was the result of consultations that had begun under Oftel and continued under Ofcom. Vodafone alleged that Ofcom had breached several of its obligations, including notably: the obligation to correctly evaluate the likely benefits and detriments arising from the implementation of its proposed Decision, via an appropriate impact assessment, under section 7 of the Communications Act 2003; the obligation to consult with all interested parties and, in order to allow such consultation to be undertaken effectively, to act transparently, by publishing full details of the evidence and reasoning on which its proposed Decision was to be based. In the appellant's view, each of these breaches individually, and some or all of them collectively, amounted to serious procedural and/or substantive errors, as a result of which it was likely that, or there was a serious risk that, the conclusions that Ofcom had drawn from its cost-benefit analyses were wrong. Narrowing in on the procedural irregularities of the public consultation, Vodafone submitted that the point of consultation

> is that people affected by a potential decision should have an opportunity to be heard . . . . Consultees should also expect that the decision maker will listen to the responses received, even if the decision maker is not required to adopt every suggestion put forth by consultees. This requires consultation at an appropriate level of specificity and detail. It is not supposed to be an empty exercise. [OFCOM] did not disclose sufficient inputs and Vodafone was required to backsolve figures in order to understand the inputs adopted . . . . [C]ertain inputs were only provided to [mobile network operators] after the publication of the Decision, and then only following a request by Vodafone. The lack of detail in the consultation paper affected the detail of the consultation responses, which in turn affected the quality of OFCOM's reasoning.[462]

Relying on *Coughlan* and *Greenpeace*, Ofcom responded that Vodafone had been able to make detailed submissions, both to Ofcom during the consultation process and later to the CAT. Therefore, Vodafone had had adequate disclosure of inputs and, in any event, further information had been supplied once asked for. The CAT noted that the Decision had followed a lengthy process, including two consultation documents and two notices issued under section 135 of the Communications Act 2003.[463] It could hardly be suggested, therefore, that, at least in form, the consultation process had been inadequate. The Tribunal added, however, that "mere consultation and transparency alone are not sufficient grounds to save a decision which is in itself flawed as a substantive matter to the extent we find in this case. The purpose of consultation is to seek the informed views of, and best available information from, industry and, with the benefit of the expertise inherent in a specialised regulatory body, apply those views and information to the perceived industry failings." Citing *Coughlan*, the Tribunal found unanimously that, in the absence of a provisional technical specification on which consultees could provide useful data, the process undertaken by Ofcom had not fully allowed stakeholders to provide "intelligent and realistic responses" as to the likely costs of adopting the proposed measures.[464]

The remedy that the Tribunal chose in view of its findings is also noteworthy from a procedural point of view. The CAT remitted the whole matter to Ofcom for reconsideration, directing the agency to "seek the fresh views of the industry on the issue of altering the current arrangements in the UK for fixed and mobile porting, on the basis of appropriate evidence and analysis in light of the findings set out in this judgment."[465] Interestingly, the Tribunal went further in suggesting that "a staged approach to decision making in a matter of such complexity may be advantageous. Such an approach would enable information gathered from earlier stages to provide the basis for CBA-based decisions upon whether to proceed to the next stage(s)."[466] Even though this formulation suggests that the proposal for a "staged approach to decision making" is not a binding direction but rather a recommendation, one reading could see this as a signal for the future: when it comes to questions of high complexity—and practical significance, such as number portability—the agency should seriously consider multiple stages in its policymaking process to better insulate its decisions from reversal on appeal. Even though the Tribunal does not elaborate on the proposed "advantageous approach" and does not limit it to public consultation, the language is capacious enough to be consistent with my proposal at the end of Part II.C.3. I suggested there that, in the absence of a formal roadmap (which did exist in the *Vodafone* case given the procedural requirements of the Communications Act 2003), public authorities could consider a phased consultation.

In conclusion, CAT review on appeal may give the impression of turning conventional judicial review[467] on its head: in principle, the Tribunal exercises profound and rigorous scrutiny of the substance of the regulatory decisions, but is deferential on the process preceding those decisions. Nevertheless, this section explained how procedural review has been integrated into full merits review, thus prompting Ofcom to pay special attention to its consultation processes and its regulatory analysis. In this respect, CAT review contributes to the better functioning of Ofcom's deliberative-participatory processes. And it does so both directly through remand to the agency when there have been significant procedural flaws and indirectly through the prospect of review feeding back into Ofcom's processes, as Part III.B.2b demonstrated.

IV. Looking to the future

Part III described the development of deliberative-participatory policymaking processes which went way beyond the Diceyan paradigm of controls on administrative action examined in Part I. Part II told a story of increasing, yet incomplete, formalization. The case study of regulatory institutions and processes in the telecommunications sector mirrored the description of gradual evolution presented in Part II, but took it one step further: this time, formalization (and juridification) had a much more prominent role to play, and EU law—especially the 2002 regulatory package—was a key driving force behind this development. This concluding part seeks to broaden the scope of inquiry by looking beyond the telecommunications sector (Section A), and beyond national borders (Section B).

A. Generalizing public participation in administrative policymaking

Previous parts showed that the original design of regulatory institutions and processes in the telecommunications sector was consciously different from the US model in order to avoid what was perceived as excessive formalization and judicialization. This reflected a broader regulatory pattern that emphasized flexibility and informality. However, the shift away from legalized administrative procedures in the model of the US Administrative Procedure Act of 1946 ("APA") also had its critics. One account described British law as "less than a world leader" when it came to ex ante accountability, and emphasized that "it is the policy process which now constitutes the most important area for constitutional concern, where there exists a clear need for 'due process writ large.' "[468] Other scholars described the US APA as a statute that "successfully regularized the administrative process" and noted, in comparison, that the British understanding of "due process and procedures is highly impoverished."[469] Writing in 1997 and taking into account Oftel's participatory practices championed by Don Cruickshank, Tony Prosser described the Oftel pattern as very close to the US APA model of rulemaking. He did, however, point to an important difference, i.e., "the greater rigour imposed by the structure of rules creating rulemaking procedures [in the US], rules which have no formal legal counterpart in the United Kingdom."[470] Part III showed that under EU impetus, Ofcom's policymaking processes have now moved even closer to the US formal model. The question then is: can this formalized model spread from the electronic communications sector across the board?

In March 2006, the House of Lords Select Committee on the Merits of Statutory Instruments lauded the government's commitment to improving regulatory processes, but criticized "failures to engage in 'grass roots' consultation where regulations are being made which will affect the lives of ordinary citizens."[471] A step toward generalizing accountability processes was taken with the adoption of the Legislative and Regulatory Reform Act 2006 ("LRRA"). Section 2 of the Act ("Power to promote regulatory principles") empowers a minister to make provision by order that she considers would serve the purpose of ensuring that regulatory functions are exercised so as to comply with five principles of good regulation. These principles are that regulatory activities should be carried out in a way that is transparent, accountable, proportionate, consistent, and should be targeted only at cases in which action is needed. The Explanatory Notes to the LRRA provide two examples that section 2 could cover: The ministerial powers under this section could impose a requirement on a regulator to have regard to views of a body representing consumers in that area; or to exercise its regulatory functions on the basis of risk assessment.[472] Therefore, section 2 could similarly provide the basis for a public consultation requirement.

Part 2 of the LRRA focuses on regulators; it stipulates that they must have regard to the same principles of good regulation (section 21). The minister may also issue, after consultation, a code of practice in relation to the exercise of regulatory functions to which regulators must have regard (sections 22-23). However, public utilities regulators are excluded from the scope of these provisions (section 24(5)). This is to "preserve their independence and to reflect the fact that they are all committed to such regulatory principles anyway,"[473] which Part III demonstrated in the example of Ofcom.

Following a lengthy consultation process and approval by both Houses of Parliament, the Regulators' Compliance Code[474] was issued under section 22(1) of the LLRA, and came into force in April 2008. The Regulators' Compliance Code explains:

> The duty on a regulator to "have regard to" the Code means that the regulator must take into account the Code's provisions and give them due weight in developing their policies or principles or in setting standards or giving guidance. The regulator is not bound to follow a provision of the Code if they properly conclude that the provision is either not relevant or is outweighed by another relevant consideration. They should ensure that any decision to depart from any provision of the Code is properly reasoned and based on material evidence.[475]

The Code outlines the Hampton Principles[476] and sets out the specific provisions that elaborate these principles. The Hampton Principles and the italicized statement at the start of each numbered section do not form part of the Code's requirements, but they set the context in which the specific obligations set out in the numbered paragraphs should be interpreted.[477] For our purposes, the more relevant part of the Code is section 9 ("Accountability"), which reads:

Hampton Principle: Regulators should be accountable for the efficiency and effectiveness of their activities, while remaining independent in the decisions they take....

9.1 Regulators should create effective consultation and feedback opportunities to enable continuing cooperative relationships with regulated entities and other interested parties.

9.2 Regulators should identify and explain the principal risks against which they are acting. They should, in consultation with regulated entities and other interested parties, set and publish clear standards and targets for their service and performance.

Therefore, consultation is included among the principles to which regulators must have regard. This brings us back to the opening question: does the recognition of regulatory principles, such as transparency, accountability, and proportionality, in the LRRA, as further specified in the Regulators' Compliance Code, mean that the United Kingdom is moving toward APA-like requirements for accountable policymaking? My answer is negative. Even the most laudatory account, offered by Professors Harlow and Rawlings, would not go so far. According to this account, the LRRA, which they liken to a miniature "Regulatory Procedures Act," is "breaking new ground" in the British administrative law system as "earlier 'soft law' statements of better regulation are given a harder edge." Furthermore, they describe the Regulators' Compliance Code as "a milestone in the ongoing juridification of UK regulatory policy and practice."[478] Nevertheless, even in this account we can see the limits of the LRRA and the Code: "As so often with tertiary legislation [as is the Regulators' Compliance Code] the precise legal effects are hard to pin down however. In principle, judicial review is a possibility (failure to give specific obligations due weight). Any decision to depart from the Code would need to be carefully reasoned and based on material evidence."[479] Even if abstractly or in principle we could envisage that the Regulators' Compliance Code might potentially be judicially enforceable, about which other scholars are not confident either,[480] the participatory requirements in particular seem to lack the specificity required for judicial implementation. In this respect, the UK version of a "miniature Regulatory Procedures Act" is not akin to the US Administrative Procedure Act.

This is not to say that the LRRA and the Regulators' Compliance Code are not important developments toward the generalization of participatory regulatory processes. Quite the contrary. They push further in this direction and recognize ministerial powers that could formalize general binding consultation requirements. The experience of the telecommunications sector could be very useful for UK policymakers to tap into. Just like regulatory processes in this sector went from informal practices and soft law to statutory mandates and a formal, juridified model, so, too, we could witness a similar path toward formalization in the context of the general administration.

B. Lessons from the British experience

This chapter began with a quote attributed to A. V. Dicey: "In England we know nothing of administrative law; and we wish to know nothing." It concludes now by reversing this remark, and examining what England (the United Kingdom) could share with Europe with respect to regulatory processes. As noted in the beginning, the UK was at the forefront of the privatization revolution in Europe and a pioneer in the development of regulatory structures to implement the post-liberalization regime. Indeed, the literature suggests that "other national governments and agencies engaged in telecoms privatization and re-regulation actively sought to draw on the knowledge and experience Oftel had gained as an international pioneer in that field."[481] My emphasis here, however, is not on substantive regulation but rather on decision-making processes, and whether the UK regulatory model could offer insights to other national regulators. Three examples, listed from the least to most controversial, should be examined.

The first, and probably least controversial, lesson that the UK model could offer is the importance of the office of consultation champion within a national regulatory authority. The British experience suggests that the existence of a specialized position that deals specifically with consultation matters contributes both to a more effective and consistent enforcement of existing participatory requirements as well as to the development of better practice. It offers the agency an opportunity to reflect on ways of effectively receiving stakeholder input internally but also to demonstrate a commitment to public engagement externally. Furthermore, the establishment of this position is minimally disruptive, as the person who is designated to serve as the consultation champion can have further duties. Other countries would be well advised to consider replicating this practice. In fact, the suggestion in chapter 6 will be that this requirement be included in future reforms of the EU regulatory regime in the electronic communications sector.

The second example is the "comment-on-comments" practice. As we saw, Oftel would often engage in two rounds of consultation. This allowed market actors to comment on other stakeholders' submissions, thus facilitating a more deliberative exchange of views. This practice was not specific to the UK. Chapter 3 referred to instances in which ARCEP similarly launched two-staged consultations. A likely reason for which Ofcom abandoned this practice, and why other NRAs may not be inclined to adopt it, is that it introduces delay into the process. Nevertheless, the second round could be brief (e.g., Oftel usually allocated 14 days for that purpose) and used only in cases of high complexity and significance.

The third, and most controversial yet still worth considering, aspect of the UK model is review on appeal by the Competition Appeal Tribunal, that is, a specialist regulatory court. This chapter demonstrated how the assessment of policymaking processes was integrated into full merits review. The question of comparative interest here is whether procedural review by an ordinary court or a specialist body makes any difference. After all, an argument could go, Article 4 of the Framework Directive specifically states that appeals can be examined by a court, and ordinary courts have traditionally reviewed administrative action on the basis of procedural requirements. I would suggest that procedural review incorporated into merits review is not a one-way street. Conversely, an appellate body, some members of which have backgrounds relevant to the regulated sector, may be better situated to appreciate what kind of process was required to reach the substantive regulatory decision under review. When process is necessary to get the substance right, as is often the case in highly technical fields such as telecoms regulation, it is increasingly difficult to disentangle procedural and merits review and be clear about what the law requires under either prong.[482] Of course, the risk of intensive review on both counts (which could arguably be higher when the appellate body is a specialist regulatory court) is a potential duplication of the regulatory process and the introduction of further delays—we can call this "ossification squared." There are complicated trade-offs associated with one or the other institutional choice. This is why, as described in Part III, the UK government sought to amend the appeals process, and why each member state needs to consider this policy question individually. It would, therefore, be imprudent to introduce further requirements on this matter at the EU level. In fact, doing so might infringe impermissibly on the institutional and procedural autonomy of the member states.

The referendum of June 23, 2016, which resulted in 51.9% of the electorate voting in favor of the UK leaving the EU, may complicate the picture. At the time of this writing, there are not enough details on the kind of deal that the United Kingdom will seek with the 27 other member states of the EU—other than the tautological "Brexit means Brexit" and signs that curbing immigration will be high on the agenda, thus rendering single marker membership unlikely. It is also not clear whether these negotiations will result in a transitional agreement during which EU law may continue to apply in the United Kingdom. However, even on the assumption of a "hard Brexit," it is unlikely that the regulatory regime for electronic communications will change drastically or swiftly. This is both because important aspects of telecommunications regulation had been under the control of NRAs anyway and because, more generally, the stated government intention is to convert the *acquis* into domestic law through the so-called Great Repeal Bill with the UK Parliament then free to amend or repeal legislation later.[483] Indeed, regulatory coordination after the United Kingdom has exited the EU is likely considering the salient transborder elements of electronic communications and the size and global operations of the UK's £57-billion communications sector.[484]

Furthermore, it is unlikely to see any fundamental changes with respect to participatory regulatory processes even when the UK is no longer bound by the

EU public consultation mandates. As this chapter has documented, these processes have been formalized and in continuous operation since 2003. All the stakeholders are both familiar with these mechanisms and cognizant of their significance, and Ofcom may well continue building on the "EU floor." In the same vein, the EU should not shy away from continuing to draw on the British experience. As Ofcom's Chief Executive explained in an article, Ofcom has contributed to EU policy in this sector and wishes to remain a constructive and influential player in these debates.[485] Both sides will gain from sustaining a productive dialogue on future regulatory reforms. Chapter 6 returns to issues of reform at the EU level; the inquiry concludes by revisiting questions of institutional design based on the experience drawn from the operation of the regulatory system and the implementation of EU mandates in the three country cases.

Notes

1. *See* MICHAEL MORAN, THE BRITISH REGULATORY STATE: HIGH MODERNISM AND HYPER-INNOVATION 2 (2007); Pablo T. Spiller & Ingo Vogelsang, *The United Kingdom: A Pacesetter in Regulatory Incentives, in* REGULATIONS, INSTITUTIONS, AND COMMITMENT: COMPARATIVE STUDIES OF TELECOMMUNICATIONS 79, 79 (Brian Levy & Pablo T. Spiller eds., 1996).
2. TONY PROSSER, LAW AND THE REGULATORS 45 (1997).
3. The Citizen's Charter: Raising the Standard, Cm 1599 (July 1991).
4. Speech by Rt Hon John Major MP to Conservative Central Council annual meeting, 23 March 1991, cited in House of Commons Public Administration Select Committee, *From Citizen's Charter to Public Service Guarantees: Entitlements to Public Services*, Twelfth Report of Session 2007–08, HC 411 (2008), p. 6.
5. Citizen's Charter, *supra* note 3, at 5. *See also* David Faulkner, *Public Services, Citizenship and the State-the British Experience 1967-97, in* PUBLIC SERVICES AND CITIZENSHIP IN EUROPEAN LAW. PUBLIC AND LABOUR LAW PERSPECTIVES 35, 42–43 (Mark Freedland & Silvana Sciarra eds., 1998) (noting that "[t]he Citizen's Charter and the charters associated with it have encouraged greater sensitivity to the views and feelings of the public, and have provided avenues for explanation and, if necessary, apology or compensation for those not satisfied with the service they have received").
6. CAROL HARLOW & RICHARD RAWLINGS, LAW AND ADMINISTRATION 71 (3rd ed. 2009).
7. *See also* ANTHONY GIDDENS, THE THIRD WAY: THE RENEWAL OF SOCIAL DEMOCRACY 69–86 (1998) (describing the need to "democratize democracy" by means of a constitutional reform directed toward greater transparency and openness and government reestablishing more direct contact with citizens).
8. HARLOW & RAWLINGS, *supra* note 6, at 73 (further noting that "[t]alk of efficient service provision gave way before a rhetoric of concern for the needs of users and user satisfaction. Information, consultation and involvement became the watchwords of . . . government").
9. *See*, e.g., http://www.cabinetoffice.gov.uk/content/transparency-overview.
10. *See* Ben Worthy, "Brexit and Open Government" (July 2016), available at http://www.open-government.org.uk/2016/07/14/brexit-and-open-government/.
11. PROSSER, *supra* note 2, at 27: "in many ways [the developments in the liberalization of telecommunications, posts, and energy markets within the Community] reflect the model adopted in the United Kingdom in terms of opening up access to competing suppliers and separating regulation from the supply of services." *See also* MARK THATCHER, THE POLITICS OF TELECOMMUNICATIONS: NATIONAL INSTITUTIONS, CONVERGENCE, AND CHANGE IN BRITAIN AND FRANCE 212 (1999) (noting that the UK government and Oftel supported

liberalization by the EC and the World Trade Organization, believing that British companies would be "well placed to gain market share").

12. *See*, e.g., LARRY SIEDENTOP, DEMOCRACY IN EUROPE 106 (2001) (noting that the hallmark of the British model is its informality).

13. Quoted by William A. Robson, *The Report of the Committee on Ministers' Powers*, 3 THE POLITICAL QUARTERLY 346 (1932).

14. The last (eighth) edition by Dicey himself was published in 1915. There was a ninth edition in 1939 and a tenth in 1959, both with an introduction by E. C. S. Wade.

15. RICHARD A. COSGROVE, THE RULE OF LAW: ALBERT VENN DICEY, VICTORIAN JURIST 113 (1980).

16. Martin Loughlin, *Why the History of English Administrative Law Is Not Written*, in A SIMPLE COMMON LAWYER: ESSAYS IN HONOUR OF MICHAEL TAGGART 151, 152–53 (David Dyzenhaus, Murray Hunt & Grant Huscroft eds., 2009). The fact that this criticism persisted also attests to the lasting influence of Dicey's ideas despite earlier forceful critical formulations, such as that by Justice, then Professor, Frankfurter; *see* Felix Frankfurter, *Foreword*, 47 YALE L.J. 515, 517 (1938) ("Few law books in modern times have had an influence comparable to that produced by the brilliant obfuscation of Dicey's The Law of the Constitution . . . . Generations of judges and lawyers were brought up in the mental climate of Dicey. Judgments, speeches in the House of Commons, letters to *The Times*, reflected and perpetuated Dicey's misconceptions and myopia. The persistence of the misdirection that Dicey had given to the development of administrative law strikingly proves the elder Huxley's observation that many a theory survives long after its brains are knocked out").

17. A. V. DICEY, LECTURES INTRODUCTORY TO THE STUDY OF THE LAW OF THE CONSTITUTION 180 (1885). *See also* J. W. F. ALLISON, A CONTINENTAL DISTINCTION IN THE COMMON LAW: A HISTORICAL AND COMPARATIVE PERSPECTIVE ON ENGLISH PUBLIC LAW 19 (2000) (noting that Dicey's original antagonism to French administrative law is evidenced by the repeated of use phrases like "foreign," "totally different," "radically opposed," "absolutely inconsistent," "despotic," "utterly unknown," and "fundamentally inconsistent").

18. A. V. DICEY, INTRODUCTION TO THE STUDY OF THE LAW OF THE CONSTITUTION 336–37 (10th ed., 1959).

19. JOHN WILLIS, THE PARLIAMENTARY POWERS OF ENGLISH GOVERNMENT DEPARTMENTS 5 (1933, repr. Lawbook Exchange, 2003).

20. Loughlin, *supra* note 16, at 156–57. The history of the structure and functions of the forms of local government from the 17th to the 19th centuries—in some cases from the 14th to the 20th centuries has been extensively documented in the multivolume work of Sidney and Beatrice Webb on ENGLISH LOCAL GOVERNMENT: THE PARISH AND THE COUNTY (1906), THE MANOR AND THE BOROUGH (1908), STATUTORY AUTHORITIES FOR SPECIAL PURPOSES (1922), THE STORY OF THE KING'S HIGHWAY (1913), ENGLISH PRISONS UNDER LOCAL GOVERNMENT (WITH PREFACE BY BERNARD SHAW) (1922), ENGLISH POOR LAW HISTORY: PART. I: THE OLD POOR LAW (1927), ENGLISH POOR LAW HISTORY: PART II: THE LAST HUNDRED YEARS (1929). *See also* PAUL CRAIG, ADMINISTRATIVE LAW 48 (6th ed., 2008) (noting that "[t]he limited size and scope of central government in the 19th century must be kept very much in the forefront of one's mind"). During the 18th century in particular, the central government deliberately abstained from any consideration of local authorities (SIDNEY & BEATRICE WEBB, ENGLISH LOCAL GOVERNMENT: STATUTORY AUTHORITIES FOR SPECIAL PURPOSES 352–53 (1922) [hereinafter WEBB, STATUTORY AUTHORITIES].

21. Oliver MacDonagh, *The Nineteenth-Century Revolution in Government: A Reappraisal*, 1 THE HISTORICAL JOURNAL 52 (1958); HENRY PARRIS, CONSTITUTIONAL BUREAUCRACY: THE DEVELOPMENT OF BRITISH CENTRAL ADMINISTRATION SINCE THE EIGHTEENTH CENTURY 281 (1969); PAUL CRAIG, ADMINISTRATIVE LAW 38 (7th ed., 2012). The Poor Law Amendment Act of 1834, in particular, was a landmark reform establishing the first central government department enjoying rulemaking powers and deliberately created for the purpose of controlling and directing local authorities (WEBB, STATUTORY AUTHORITIES, *supra* note 20, at 466–67, 465; NORMAN CHESTER, THE ENGLISH ADMINISTRATIVE SYSTEM 1780–1870, at 259–65 (1981)).

22. WILLIAM WADE & CHRISTOPHER FORSYTH, ADMINISTRATIVE LAW 733 (10th ed., 2009). On the growth of delegation, see "Report of the Committee on Ministers' Powers" (presented by the Lord High Chancellor to Parliament), Cmd. 4060 (1932), p. 21–24 [hereinafter "Report on Ministers' Powers"].

23. See CRAIG, supra note 21, at 49–51.

24. WADE & FORSYTH, supra note 22, at 733.

25. A. V. DICEY, LECTURES ON THE RELATION BETWEEN LAW AND PUBLIC OPINION IN ENGLAND DURING THE NINETEENTH CENTURY 259 (Macmillan and Co., 2nd ed., 1914). However, Dicey's treatment of legislation in the middle decades of the 19th century and his characterization of the period 1825 to 1870 as the "Period of Benthamism and Individualism" was criticized in the literature, see Henry Parris, The Nineteenth-Century Revolution in Government: A Reappraisal Reappraised, 3 THE HISTORICAL JOURNAL 17, 26 (1960).

26. A. V. Dicey, The Development of Administrative Law in England, 31 THE LAW QUARTERLY REVIEW 148, 149 (1915).

27. HARLOW & RAWLINGS, supra note 6, at 17. Chantal Stebbings notes that Dicey reflected the orthodox views of his contemporaries. Although the popular and political consensus throughout most of the 19th century favored an ideology of individualism, laissez-faire, and localism, in the end "pragmatism won over." The emergence of pressing social problems due to industrialization and urbanization, and the realization that they could be addressed only through central intervention resulted gradually in a "noisily unwilling" public acceptance of centralist and collectivist legislation (CHANTAL STEBBINGS, LEGAL FOUNDATIONS OF TRIBUNALS IN NINETEENTH-CENTURY ENGLAND 75–109 (2006).

28. W. Ivor Jennings, In Praise of Dicey: 1885–1935, 13 PUBLIC ADMINISTRATION 123, 132 (1935).

29. Dicey, supra note 26, at 152 ("Modem legislation . . . has undoubtedly conferred upon the Cabinet . . . a considerable amount of judicial or quasi-judicial authority. This is a considerable step towards the introduction among us of something like the droit administratif of France, but the fact that the ordinary law courts can deal with any actual and provable breach of the law committed by any servant of the Crown still preserves that rule of law which is fatal to the existence of true droit administratif").

30. See John M. Gaus, The Report of the British Committee on Ministers' Powers, 26 THE AMERICAN POLITICAL SCIENCE REVIEW 1142 (1932).

31. LORD HEWART OF BURY, THE NEW DESPOTISM 35 (1929).

32. "Report on Ministers' Powers," supra note 22, at v.

33. As was more poignantly observed, "[h]ere we have the curious spectacle of the conclusions at which the Committee is expected to arrive being embodied in its terms of reference. The Committee started life with the dead hand of Dicey lying frozen on its neck" (Robson, supra note 13, at 351).

34. Jennings, supra note 28, at 133.

35. Robson, supra note 13, at 347.

36. John A. Rohr, Dicey's Ghost and Administrative Law, 34 ADMINISTRATION & SOCIETY 8, 18 (2002).

37. Cf. HARLOW & RAWLINGS, supra note 6, at 16 ("A far stronger criticism of Dicey is that he left English administrative law with a great mistrust of executive or administrative action but without any theoretical basis for its control"). But see Carol Harlow & Richard Rawlings, Administrative Law in Context: Restoring a Lost Connection, 2014 PUBLIC LAW 28, 30–31 (noting that "Dicey, collective bête noire and pantomime villain, is routinely blamed for the Whiggish tendencies and chauvinism that had seen him deny and so hamper an informed engagement with administrative law" but that this is not enough in itself to explain the strong "anathema to administrative law" of the time). See also Colin Scott, Accountability in the Regulatory State, 27 JOURNAL OF LAW AND SOCIETY 38, 43 (2000) ("In its narrowest form, an adequate accountability system would ensure that all public bodies act in ways which correspond with the core juridical value of legality, and thus correspond with the democratic will. Such a Diceyan conception of accountability was already in severe difficulty within Dicey's lifetime as discretionary authority was more widely dispersed with the growth of the welfare state").

38. HEWART, *supra* note 31, at 149–59.
39. *See* "Report on Ministers' Powers," *supra* note 22, at 66 ("X. The system of Department consulting particular interests specially affected by a proposed exercise of law-making power should be extended so as to ensure that such consultation takes place whenever practicable. XI. The Departmental practice of appending to a regulation or a rule in certain cases a note explaining the changes made thereby in the law etc., should be extended").
40. *See* G. W. KEETON, THE PASSING OF PARLIAMENT 1-2 (1952) ("few reports have assembled so much wisdom whilst proving so completely useless, as the Report of the Committee on Ministers' Powers. Except amongst students of administrative law (one is tempted to say historians of administrative law) its recommendations are forgotten, even by lawyers and administrators, and in no important respect did the report influence, much less delay, the onrush of administrative power"); *see also* WADE & FORSYTH, *supra* note 22, at 13 (noting that the Report's recommendations "proved unacceptable to the strongly entrenched administration. In most respects it was little more than an academic exercise").
41. DICEY, *supra* note 18, at 406.
42. *Id.*, at 39–40.
43. *Id.*, at 65. *See also* Michael Gordon, *The Conceptual Foundations of Parliamentary Sovereignty: Reconsidering Jennings and Wade*, 2009 PUBLIC LAW 519, 520.
44. Dicey maintained that the principle "lies deep in the history of the English people and in the peculiar development of the English constitution" (DICEY, *supra* note 18, at 68–70n.1). *But see* GEOFFREY DE Q. WALKER, THE RULE OF LAW: FOUNDATION OF CONSTITUTIONAL DEMOCRACY 149 (1988) ("the omnipotence idea toyed with by Blackstone and made absolute by Dicey became the orthodoxy that was absorbed by law students and later carried by them to the bench"); Geoffrey de Q. Walker, *Dicey's Dubious Dogma of Parliamentary Sovereignty: A Recent Fray with Freedom of Religion*, 59 AUSTRALIAN LAW JOURNAL 276, 283–84 (1985) ("It seems that Dicey's theory is like some huge, ugly Victorian monument that dominates the legal and constitutional landscape and exerts a hypnotic effect on legal perception"); *see also* T. R. S. ALLAN, LAW, LIBERTY, AND JUSTICE: THE LEGAL FOUNDATIONS OF BRITISH CONSTITUTIONALISM 269 (1993) ("modern assertions of unlimited sovereignty rest on a misunderstanding of constitutional history").
45. JEFFREY GOLDSWORTHY, THE SOVEREIGNTY OF PARLIAMENT: HISTORY AND PHILOSOPHY 7 and passim (1999).
46. Peter Lindseth, *"Always Embedded" Administration: The Historical Evolution of Administrative Justice as an Aspect of Modern Governance*, in THE ECONOMY AS A POLITY: THE POLITICAL CONSTITUTION OF CONTEMPORARY CAPITALISM 117, 124 (Christian Joerges, Bo Stråth and Peter Wagner, eds., 2005).
47. In the words of Lord Hoffmann, what the court does is draw the infringement to the attention of Parliament. It is then "for the sovereign Parliament to decide whether or not to remove the incompatibility" (*Regina v. Secretary of State for the Home Department Ex Parte Simms (A.P.)* [2000] 2 AC 115).
48. For a presentation of the long debates on these questions, which move beyond the scope of this chapter, see Anthony Bradley, *The Sovereignty of Parliament—Form or Substance?*, in THE CHANGING CONSTITUTION 35 (Jeffrey Jowell & Dawn Oliver eds., 7th ed. 2011); JEFFREY GOLDSWORTHY, PARLIAMENTARY SOVEREIGNTY: CONTEMPORARY DEBATES 280–304 (2010); Gordon, *supra* note 43, at 519; Mark Elliott, *The Principle of Parliamentary Sovereignty in Legal, Constitutional and Political Perspective*, in THE CHANGING CONSTITUTION 38–66 (Jeffrey Jowell, Dawn Oliver and Colm O'Cinneide eds., 2015). The conclusion of Brexit will result in the repeal of the European Communities Act 1972; this development itself can be described as an exercise of parliamentary sovereignty.
49. DICEY, *supra* note 18, at 91*ff.*
50. There are three types of laying procedures. First, the empowering legislation may merely require the subordinate legislation to be laid. Second, the rules or regulations may be subject to the so-called affirmative resolution procedure, whereby they will be of no effect unless confirmed by resolution of each House. This offers more opportunity for parliamentary control. Third, secondary legislation may be subject to the so-called negative resolution

procedure, whereby it will take effect without further formality in Parliament but subject to annulment by resolution of either House (CRAIG, *supra* note 21, at 440–41).

51. Laying before Parliament has a long history in the United Kingdom extending back into the 19th century (JOHN E. KERSELL, PARLIAMENTARY SUPERVISION OF DELEGATED LEGISLATION: THE UNITED KINGDOM, AUSTRALIA, NEW ZEALAND AND CANADA 158–60, 14–21 (1960)). For more information on these procedures, see CRAIG, *supra* note 21, at 440–42; WADE & FORSYTH, *supra* note 22, at 762–63, 765–66, from which the presentation in the text and previous note has drawn extensively.

52. *See* Paul Craig, *Prerogative, Precedent and Power, in* THE GOLDEN METWAND AND THE CROOKED CORD. ESSAYS ON PUBLIC LAW IN HONOUR OF SIR WILLIAM WADE QC 65, 65 (Christopher Forsyth & Ivan Hare eds., 1998) (arguing that "the legal history of the prerogative is best understood in terms of structural constitutional review," in which what was at stake were the "boundaries of institutional competence" of the different arms of government).

53. *R v. Secretary of State for the Home Department, ex p Fire Brigades Union*, [1995] UKHL 3, 9 (Lord Browne-Wilkinson).

54. *See Attorney General v. De Keyser's Royal Hotel Ltd*, [1920] AC 508 (Lord Atkinson); *see also* Craig, *supra* note 52, at 78.

55. Definition drawn from the UK Parliament's Glossary (available at http://www.parliament. uk/site-information/glossary/henry-viii-clauses/). The clauses received this name from the Statute of Proclamations 1539 that gave King Henry VIII power to legislate by proclamation.

56. *See* HARLOW & RAWLINGS, *supra* note 6, at 167. Lord Judge, the Lord Chief Justice, speaking extra-judicially has expressed serious concerns about Henry VIII clauses (House of Lords Select Committee on the Constitution, 9th Report of Session 2010–11, Meetings with the Lord Chief Justice and the Lord Chancellor [HL Paper 89], p. 5). Courts have responded by insisting upon a narrow and strict construction of these clauses (WADE & FORSYTH, *supra* note 22, at 737–38).

57. *See* J. D. B. Mitchell, *The Causes and Effects of the Absence of a System of Public Law in the United Kingdom*, 1965 PUBLIC LAW 95, 98.

58. DICEY, *supra* note 18, at 40.

59. WADE & FORSYTH, *supra* note 22, at 21.

60. Constitutional Reform Act 2005, s.1: "This Act does not adversely affect—(a) the *existing constitutional principle* of the rule of law" (emphasis added).

61. *See* Paul P. Craig, *Formal and Substantive Conceptions of the Rule of Law: An Analytical Framework*, 1997 PUBLIC LAW 467.

62. *Id.*, at 470–74. *But see* Geoffrey Marshall, *The Constitution: Its Theory and Interpretation, in* THE BRITISH CONSTITUTION IN THE TWENTIETH CENTURY 29, 58 (Vernon Bogdanor ed., 2003) (noting that "although Dicey's initial discussion of the rule of law refers to a number of formal or procedural matters, chapter 5 to 12 of *The Law of the Constitution*, which deal with [rights] are all placed within part II of the book, which is entitled 'The Rule of Law' the reader could be forgiven for thinking that Dicey intended them to form part of an account of what the rule of law meant for Englishmen").

63. DICEY, *supra* note 18, at 39.

64. *Id.*, at 406.

65. See the dicta by Lord Steyn, Lord Hope and Lady Hale in the famous case *Jackson v. Her Majesty's Attorney General*, [2005] UKHL 56. Writing extra-judicially, Lord Bingham disagreed with his colleagues' observations (TOM BINGHAM, THE RULE OF LAW 167 (2010)).

66. Jeffrey Jowell, *The Rule of Law and Its Underlying Values, in* THE CHANGING CONSTITUTION 11, 24–25 (Jeffrey Jowell & Dawn Oliver eds., 7th ed. 2011). This formulation reflects Dicey's description: "Powers, however extraordinary, which are conferred [to the executive] or sanctioned by statute, are never really unlimited, for they are confined by the words of the Act itself, and, what is more, by the interpretation put upon the statute by the judges" (DICEY, *supra* note 18, at 413).

67. The sixth component of the rule of law in Lord Bingham's famous account seems also to square well with our description: "My sixth sub-rule expresses what many would, with reason, regard as the core of the rule of law principle. It is that ministers and public officers

at all levels must exercise the powers conferred on them reasonably, in good faith, for the purpose for which the powers were conferred and without exceeding the limits of such powers. This sub-rule reflects the well-established and familiar grounds of judicial review. It is indeed fundamental" (Lord Bingham, *The Rule of Law*, 66 CAMBRIDGE L.J. 67, 78 (2007).

68. Quoted by SIR CARLETON KEMP ALLEN, LAW AND ORDERS: AN INQUIRY INTO THE NATURE AND SCOPE OF DELEGATED LEGISLATION AND EXECUTIVE POWERS IN ENGLAND 161 (3rd ed., 1965).

69. Paul Craig, *Competing Models of Judicial Review*, 1999 PUBLIC LAW 428 (Craig's discussion pertains to the foundation of judicial review itself, but it is helpful for our purposes as well).

70. WADE & FORSYTH, *supra* note 22, at 31.

71. *Council of Civil Service Unions v. Minister for the Civil Service* [1984] 3 All ER 935, at 951 (per Lord Diplock): "I have described the third head as 'procedural impropriety' rather than failure to observe basic rules of natural justice or failure to act with procedural fairness towards the person who will be affected by the decision."

72. WADE & FORSYTH, *supra* note 22, at 372; CRAIG, *supra* note 21, at 339; HARLOW & RAWLINGS, *supra* note 6, at 616

73. WADE & FORSYTH, *supra* note 22, at 30; see also *id.*, at 372–73.

74. John Laws, *Law and Democracy*, 1995 PUBLIC LAW 72, 79. See also DAWN OLIVER, COMMON VALUES AND THE PUBLIC-PRIVATE DIVIDE 257 (1999).

75. Mark Elliott, *The Ultra Vires Doctrine in a Constitutional Setting: Still the Central Principle of Administrative Law*, 58 CAMBRIDGE L.J. 129, 143 (1999).

76. [1964] AC 40.

77. *See Bates v. Lord Hailsham*, [1972] 1 W.L.R. 1373 [hereinafter *Bates*] and *R (Bapio Action Limited) v. Secretary of State for the Home Department*, [2007] EWCA Civ 1139 [Court of Appeal] [hereafter *BAPIO*].

78. Paul Craig, *Perspectives on Process: Common Law, Statutory and Political*, 2010 PUBLIC LAW 275, 279–80.

79. *BAPIO, supra* note 77, at para. 45.

80. Jowell, *supra* note 66, at 30 (emphasis added).

81. Dicey, *supra* note 26, at 152 ("any man who will look plain facts in the face will see in a moment that ministerial liability to the censure not in fact by Parliament, nor even by the House of Commons, but by the party majority who keep the Government in office, is a very feeble guarantee indeed against action which evades the authority of the law courts"). See also A. V. Dicey, *Will the Form of Parliamentary Government Be Permanent?*, 13 HARV. L. REV. 67, 74 (1899) (noting the "widespread distrust of representative systems under which it, occasionally at least, may happen that an elected Parliament represents only the worst side of a great nation").

82. ROBERT S. RAIT, MEMORIALS OF ALBERT VENN DICEY: BEING CHIEFLY LETTERS AND DIARIES 121–22 (1925).

83. Rivka Weill, *Dicey Was Not Diceyan*, 62 CAMBRIDGE L.J. 474, 488–89 (2003).

84. *See* Dicey's letter to Leo Maxse quoted in COSGROVE, *supra* note 15, at 161 ("In Executive matters I hold that the Government of the day ought even though put into office by but a small majority, to be whilst it continues the Government, in general supported by good citizens. My reason is this, viz:-that in Executive matters the majority must of necessity be treated as the organ of the nation, otherwise the action of the nation is at every turn weakened . . . . On the other hand on matters of constitutional change I do not think a small majority has any moral right to act with vigour").

85. *See* Lord Bingham of Cornhill, *Dicey Revisited*, 2002 PUBLIC LAW 39, 49–50.

86. Weill, *supra* note 83, at 485–86 and n. 42.

87. MORAN, *supra* note 1.

88. DAVID MARQUAND, THE UNPRINCIPLED SOCIETY: NEW DEMANDS AND OLD POLITICS 178 (1988).

89. *See* GODFREY HUGH LANCELOT LE MAY, THE VICTORIAN CONSTITUTION: CONVENTIONS, USAGES, AND CONTINGENCIES 145–51, 181–88 (1979).

90. MORAN, *supra* note 1, at 41, 55–56, 4.

91. I borrow the term from H. W. ARTHURS, "WITHOUT THE LAW": ADMINISTRATIVE JUSTICE AND LEGAL PLURALISM IN NINETEENTH-CENTURY ENGLAND 96 (1985).

92. Rob Baggott, *Regulatory Reform in Britain: The Changing Face of Self-Regulation*, 67 PUBLIC ADMINISTRATION 435, 438 (1989). *See also* ROBERT E. CUSHMAN, THE INDEPENDENT REGULATORY COMMISSIONS 550–51 (1941) (noting that "British tradition and practice have long looked with favor upon giving important legal powers of self-regulation to organized groups . . . . [I]t is somewhat reminiscent of the type of authority exercised for so long by the medieval guilds").

93. MORAN, *supra* note 1, at 47–55, 60.

94. ARTHURS, *supra* note 91, at 96–97.

95. Baggott, *supra* note 92, at 442–43.

96. MORAN, *supra* note 1, at 48.

97. *Id.*, at 42.

98. ARTHURS, *supra* note 91, at 109.

99. VIVIEN A. SCHMIDT, DEMOCRACY IN EUROPE: THE EU AND NATIONAL POLITIES 133 (2006); *see also* ANDREW SHONFIELD, MODERN CAPITALISM: THE CHANGING BALANCE OF PUBLIC AND PRIVATE POWER 386 (1965) (noting the "abiding prejudice which sees it as the natural business of government to react-not to act").

100. Political and Economic Planning: The Social Science Institute, Reshaping Britain: A Programme of Economic and Social Reform, Vol.XL Broadsheet No. 548, pp. 79–80 (1974) (emphasis added).

101. *See* Samuel Eldersveld, Sonja Hubée-Boonzaaijer & Jan Kooiman, *Elite Perceptions of the Political Process in the Netherlands, Looked at in Comparative Perspective*, *in* THE MANDARINS OF WESTERN EUROPE: THE POLITICAL ROLE OF TOP CIVIL SERVANTS 129, 149–50 (Mattei Dogan ed., 1975) (reporting that only 4% of the British civil servants interviewed described "relations of close collaboration between a ministry and the groups or sectors most affected by its activity [as] improper and unnecessary" and a relatively low 21% indicated that the "general welfare of the country is seriously endangered by the continual clash of particularistic interest groups").

102. *See* Grant Jordan & Jeremy Richardson, *The British Policy Style or the Logic of Negotiation?*, *in* POLICY STYLES IN WESTERN EUROPE 80, 91 (Jeremy Richardson ed., 1982).

103. Mark Thatcher, *Institutions, Regulation and Change: New Regulatory Agencies in the British Privatised Utilities*, 21 WEST EUROPEAN POLITICS 120, 123 (1998).

104. MORAN, *supra* note 1, at 100.

105. SCHMIDT, *supra* note 99, at 134–35.

106. HARLOW & RAWLINGS, *supra* note 6, at 18, 23.

107. *Id.*, at 24.

108. H.W. R. WADE, ADMINISTRATIVE LAW 2 (1st ed. 1961).

109. HARLOW & RAWLINGS, *supra* note 6, at 36–38; *see also* Adam Tomkins, *In Defence of the Political Constitution*, 22 OXFORD JOURNAL OF LEGAL STUDIES 157, 159 (2002) (noting that green-light theorists believe, among other things, that the objective of administrative law "to encourage and facilitate good administrative practices-to control administration by channelling and guiding").

110. WADE & FORSYTH, *supra* note 22, at 5–6.

111. *Breen v. Amalgamated Engineering Union* [1971] 2 QB 175, at 189.

112. MORAN, *supra* note 1, at 100.

113. NORMAN D. LEWIS, CHOICE AND THE LEGAL ORDER: RISING ABOVE POLITICS (1996); Christopher Hood, *A Public Management for All Seasons?*, 69 PUBLIC ADMINISTRATION 3, 4–5 (1991).

114. SCHMIDT, *supra* note 99, at 135.

115. John Kay & John Vickers, *Regulatory Reform: An Appraisal*, *in* DEREGULATION OR RE-REGULATION? REGULATORY REFORM IN EUROPE AND THE UNITED STATES 223, 223 (Giandomenico Majone ed., 1990); *see also* MORAN, *supra* note 1, at 109–10 ("by the time privatization regulation appeared in the 1980s that club world was itself in decay. But, of course, what was going on involved a complex interaction between these wider processes of decay and the forces shaping the world of privatisation more directly").

116. Kay & Vickers, *supra* note 115, at 223.

117. *See* the "Report on Non-Departmental Public Bodies," Cmnd. 7797 (1980) (providing the total numbers of executive and advisory bodies, and of tribunal systems that were 489, 1,561, and 67, respectively).

118. Christopher Hood, *The Politics of Quangocide*, 8 POLICY AND POLITICS 247, 248 (1980).

119. *Id.*, at 248–49 and 264.

120. HARLOW & RAWLINGS, *supra* note 6, at 67.

121. COSMO GRAHAM, REGULATING PUBLIC UTILITIES: A CONSTITUTIONAL APPROACH 45 (2000). For a description of the duties and powers of the regulators, see *id.*, at 23–44.

122. David Levi-Faur & Sharon Gilad, *The Rise of the British Regulatory State: Transcending the Privatization Debate*, 37 COMPARATIVE POLITICS 105, 115 (2004).

123. HARLOW & RAWLINGS, *supra* note 6, at 236.

124. Colin Scott, *The Juridification of Regulatory Relations in the UK Utilities Sector*, *in* COMMERCIAL REGULATION AND JUDICIAL REVIEW 19, 20 (Julia Black, Peter Muchlinski and Paul Walker eds., 1998).

125. Thatcher, *supra* note 103, at 139.

126. Self-regulation was either replaced by independent statutory regulation or split between independent and self-regulatory bodies or shared in "co-regulation" arrangements (Dawn Oliver, *Regulation, Democracy, and Democratic Oversight in the UK*, *in* THE REGULATORY STATE: CONSTITUTIONAL IMPLICATIONS 243, 246 (Dawn Oliver, Tony Prosser & Richard Rawlings eds., 2010)).

127. David Miller & William Dinan, *The Rise of the PR Industry in Britain, 1979-98*, 15 EUROPEAN JOURNAL OF COMMUNICATION 5, 12–13 (2000).

128. JOHN CLARKE, JANET NEWMAN, NICK SMITH, ELIZABETH VIDLER & LOUISE WESTMARLAND, CREATING CITIZEN-CONSUMERS: CHANGING PUBLICS AND CHANGING PUBLIC SERVICES 2 (2007).

129. *Id.*, at 4

130. Anne Barron & Colin Scott, *The Citizen's Charter Programme*, 55 MOD. L. REV. 526, 527 (1992).

131. *See* John Clarke, Morag McDermont & Janet Newman, *Delivering Choice and Administering Justice: Contested Logics of Public Services*, *in* ADMINISTRATIVE JUSTICE IN CONTEXT 25, 33 (Michael Adler ed., 2010) (noting that "[t]he consumer-choice link was a potent feature of several aspects of Thatcherism's remaking of the welfare state and public services").

132. Barron & Scott, *supra* note 130, at 537; LEWIS, *supra* note 113, at xi.

133. Florence Faucher-King Political Participation in the Age of the "Citizen-Consumer," Paper presented at the Centre d'études européennes (10 February 2011), at 2 (on file with author).

134. Gavin Drewry, *Citizen's Charters*, 7 PUBLIC MANAGEMENT REVIEW 321, 328 (2005).

135. Citizen's Charter, *supra* note 3, at 2 ("The Citizen's Charter is about giving more power to the citizen . . . . [It] is not a recipe for more state action; it is a testament of our belief in people's right to be informed and choose for themselves").

136. MORAN, *supra* note 1, at 115–16.

137. Tony Prosser, *Public Service Law: Privatization's Unexpected Offspring*, 63 LAW & CONTEMP. PROBS. 63, 66 (2000).

138. Bryan Carsberg, the first Director General of Telecommunications who held that position for eight years before becoming Director General of Fair Trading, described this as the "uniqueness of the British system" and went on to point out the benefits of this system: "Oftel's enabling act gives the Director General regulatory powers, with the Office to assist him or her. I think that this has worked well. But of course I would, wouldn't I! It enables us to take fast action in many circumstances. It avoids some of the high costs associated with the long, drawn-out procedures that may be inevitable within commissions, although other factors are involved in that. Perhaps most important, it makes it easier to establish a clear policy line" (Sir Bryan Carsberg, *Telecommunications Competition in the United Kingdom: A Regulatory Perspective*, 37 N. Y. L. SCH. L. REV. 285, 298 (1992)).

139. *See* MORAN, *supra* note 1, at 106.

140. PROSSER, *supra* note 2, at 9. *See also* HARLOW & RAWLINGS, *supra* note 6, at 67 (noting that the fact that the "first Ofdogs were highly individual with a single regulator at the helm . . . also led to complaints that relationships with ministers by whom the regulator was appointed were too cosy and lacked transparency").

141. The Hansard Society & European Policy Forum, "The Report of the Commission on the Regulation of Privatised Utilities (1996)," at 47.

142. See PROSSER, *supra* note 2, at 9 ("The Government may have been fortunate in that it has appointed individuals of high quality, and personalized regulation may have had advantages in facilitating a strong and single-minded approach in each sector from the outset"); see also Thatcher, *supra* note 103, at 130 ("appointments have not been party partisan: although the DGs have been sympathetic to government policy of extending competition among private suppliers, they have also been strong-minded capable individuals with expertise rather than mere party supporters").

143. PROSSER, *supra* note 2, at 9.

144. MORAN, *supra* note 1, at 105–106.

145. PATRICK BIRKINSHAW, IAN HARDEN & NORMAN LEWIS, GOVERNMENT BY MOONLIGHT: THE HYBRID PARTS OF THE STATE 11 (1990) (further noting that "[t]he political rhetoric may undergo profound changes, the details of policy options will change markedly, but the practice of informal government displays a remarkable durability. Although allegiances will differ over time, secreted processes have remained," *id.*, at 12).

146. MARTIN LOUGHLIN, LEGALITY AND LOCALITY: THE ROLE OF LAW IN CENTRAL-LOCAL GOVERNMENT RELATIONS 379 (1996).

147. PROSSER, *supra* note 2, at 53 (attributing this both to antipathy toward the U.S. model of regulation and to other reasons for finding judicial involvement unhelpful).

148. HARLOW & RAWLINGS, *supra* note 6, at 311 (internal citations omitted).

149. Scott, *supra* note 124, at 29 (further explaining that it is "less surprising when we notice that the statutory regimes were established in such a way as to encourage consensual bargaining between licensees and regulators").

150. *See* JAIME ARANCIBIA, JUDICIAL REVIEW OF COMMERCIAL REGULATION 15–57 (2011) (describing the "orthodox deferential approach").

151. HARLOW & RAWLINGS, *supra* note 6, at 170.

152. *See* SCHMIDT, *supra* note 99, at 135; Jordan & Richardson, *supra* note 102, at 85.

153. BIRKINSHAW, HARDEN & LEWIS, *supra* note 145, at 261.

154. LEWIS, *supra* note 113, at xiii.

155. *Id.*, at 150. Interestingly, at another point Lewis makes a recommendation that does come with a cautious note when he advocates the "need to adopt broader consultation practices, ultimately enforceable by law *if need be*. In this respect, there is a great deal to be learnt from the administrative law of the USA although it is important to guard against the excesses of an overly-litigious culture" *id.* at 147 (emphasis added).

156. *See* BIRKINSHAW, HARDEN & LEWIS, *supra* note 145, at 261 ("Many statutes do of course require the minister or agency to consult, but in most cases the requirement gives enormous discretion to the policy-maker over who is consulted and what form it takes").

157. Certain characteristic aspects of which were described in Political and Economic Planning, *supra* note 100. Compare also, e.g., the role of the general public and the members of associations vis-à-vis those consulted associations as described in that 1974 report with the observation that "[a]s to the forms of ex ante accountability which exist in relation to organized private, business and voluntary interests, we can only say here that they vary enormously. No corpus of legal theory has been developed to address the issue as to the generic rights of either members of such organized interests or the general public where such groups are afforded privileged status" (BIRKINSHAW, HARDEN & LEWIS, *supra* note 145, at 18).

158. Hood distinguished between sigma-type and theta-type values. The former emphasize economy and parsimony, the latter honesty and fairness: classic expression of theta-type values include "notice and comment" and "hard look" requirements. He concluded that New Public Management "can be understood as primarily an expression of sigma-type values" (Hood, *supra* note 113, at 10–12, 15).

159. *Cf.* Peter Aucoin, *Contraction, Managerialism and Decentralization in Canadian Government*, 1 GOVERNANCE 144, 152 (1988) (noting that "[ma]nagerialism, in contrast to the traditional bureaucratic ideal of 'administration,' emphasizes 'results,' 'performance' and 'outcomes' rather than the 'administration' of activities, procedures and regulations").

160. HARLOW & RAWLINGS, *supra* note 6, at 58.

161. Barron & Scott, *supra* note 130, at 533.

162. "The Citizen's Charter: The Facts and Figures, A Report to Mark Four Years of the Charter Programme," Cm 2970 (September 1995), at 37.

163. CATHERINE NEEDHAM, CITIZEN-CONSUMERS: NEW LABOUR'S MARKETPLACE DEMOCRACY 8 (2003).

164. *See, e.g.,* John Clarke, *Consumerism and the Remaking of State-Citizen Relations in the UK* ANALYSING SOCIAL POLICY: A GOVERNMENTAL APPROACH 89, 91 (Greg Marston & Catherine McDonald eds., 2006) ("the transformation of citizens into consumers diminishes the collective ethos and practices of the public domain (embodied in the figure of the citizen) and both privatizes and individualizes them (in the figure of the consumer)"); DAVID MARQUAND, DECLINE OF THE PUBLIC: THE HOLLOWING-OUT OF CITIZENSHIP 123 (2004) ("The great question is how to meet this challenge: how to preserve the values of citizenship and service in the face of consumerist pressures"); ANTHONY GIDDENS, THE THIRD WAY AND ITS CRITICS 164 (2000) ("The citizen is not the same as the consumer, and freedom is not to be equated with the freedom to buy and sell in the marketplace"); Eran Vigoda, *From Responsiveness to Collaboration: Governance, Citizens, and the Next Generation of Public Administration*, 62 PUBLIC ADMINISTRATION REVIEW 527, 528 (2002) (criticizing the "unidirectional pattern of relationships where citizens are covertly encouraged to remain passive clients of government. The role of 'customer' or 'client' denotes a passive orientation of citizens toward another party [the government and public administration], which is more active in trying to satisfy the customer/client's needs").

165. Mark Freedland, *Law, Public Services, and Citizenship-New Domains, New Regimes?*, *in* PUBLIC SERVICES AND CITIZENSHIP IN EUROPEAN LAW. PUBLIC AND LABOUR LAW PERSPECTIVES 1, 10 (Mark Freedland & Silvana Sciarra eds., 1998) (further describing the emphasis "placed on the role of the citizen as the discriminating purchaser of goods and services").

166. In Tony Blair's own words: "I knew the credibility of the whole New Labour project rested on accepting that much of what she wanted to do in the 1980s was inevitable, a consequence not of ideology but of social and economic change. The way she did it was often very ideological, sometimes unnecessarily so, but that didn't alter the basic fact: Britain needed the industrial and economic reforms of the Thatcher period" (TONY BLAIR, A JOURNEY: MY POLITICAL LIFE 101 (2010)).

167. MORAN, *supra* note 1, at 184.

168. MARQUAND, *supra* note 164, at 118.

169. *See* Clarke, *supra* note 164, at 101; FLORENCE FAUCHER-KING & PATRICK LE GALÈS, THE NEW LABOUR EXPERIMENT: CHANGE AND REFORM UNDER BLAIR AND BROWN 111 (Gregory Elliott trnsl., 2010); CATHERINE NEEDHAM, THE REFORM OF PUBLIC SERVICES UNDER NEW LABOUR: NARRATIVES OF CONSUMERISM 1–2 (2007). *See also* House of Commons— Public Administration Select Committee, From Citizen's Charter to Public Service Guarantees: Entitlements to Public Services, HC 411 (2008), p. 31 (noting the "lasting impact of the Charter programme").

170. HARLOW & RAWLINGS, *supra* note 6, at 71.

171. GIDDENS, *supra* note 7, at 69–78.

172. *Cf.* HARLOW & RAWLINGS, *supra* note 6, at 72 (depicting this theme as "New Labour aim[ing] to graft onto the managerial values of efficiency, effectiveness and customer satisfaction prioritized by previous Conservative governments the softer, more responsive and participatory values of public service").

173. *See, e.g.,* the sequel to his 1998 book that Anthony Giddens published in 2000 to discuss the criticism that *The Third Way* had attracted. In that second book Giddens reiterated that "[i]n what has become an open information society, the established democracies are

not democratic enough" and advocated for a "second wave democratization" introducing greater transparency and accountability (GIDDENS, *supra* note 164, at 61–62).

174. *See* PATRICK BIRKINSHAW, FREEDOM OF INFORMATION: THE LAW, THE PRACTICE AND THE IDEAL 69–117 (4th ed., 2010) (covering the history of national security, secrecy, and information).

175. For a presentation and evaluation of the content of the Code, see ADAM TOMKINS, THE CONSTITUTION AFTER SCOTT: GOVERNMENT UNWRAPPED 112–26 (1998).

176. Patrick Birkinshaw, *Regulating Information, in* THE CHANGING CONSTITUTION 365, 367 (Jeffrey Jowell & Dawn Oliver eds., 7th ed. 2011).

177. *See* Drewry, *supra* note 134, at 329; Rodney Austin, *The Freedom of Information Act 2000—A Sheep in Wolf's Clothing?, in* THE CHANGING CONSTITUTION 387, 391 (Jeffrey Jowell & Dawn Oliver eds., 6th ed. 2007).

178. *See* ADAM TOMKINS, OUR REPUBLICAN CONSTITUTION 135 (2005); Your Right to Know: The Government's Proposals for a Freedom of Information Act, Cm 3818 (1997). This proposed a statutory right of access to a wide range of government records or information [paras. 2.6-2.16]; strict tests would be applied to ensure that information would be released except where disclosure would cause harm to one of a limited number of specified interests (seven categories), and in that case only if the public interest in non-disclosure outweighed the public interest in the release of that information [section 3].

179. For a detailed analysis, see BIRKINSHAW, *supra* note 174, at 118–244.

180. The Information Tribunal in a 2007 decision spoke of a "new fundamental right to information held by public bodies" (*Department for Education and Skills v. Information Commissioner and the Evening Standard*, EA/2006/0006 (19 February 2007), at para. 61).

181. For example, if the Information Commissioner is satisfied that a public authority has failed to comply with its duties under the Act, she may issue an enforcement notice (s. 52). Failure to comply with a notice may be treated as a contempt of court (s. 54). Appeals against the Commissioner's notices are heard by the Information Tribunal, which is recognized as a "strongly pro-disclosure, independent adjudicator" even by strong critics of the U.K. FOIA (e.g., Austin, *supra* note 177, at 404).

182. *See* Birkinshaw, *supra* note 176, at 380, 391. See especially Austin, *supra* note 177, at 397–98 ("the range of exemptions is far wider and more extensive than in any other statutory freedom of information regime in any comparable democratic state"). The current version of the FOIA includes twenty-four exemptions, nine of which are absolute.

183. Austin, *supra* note 177, at 399.

184. Oonagh Gay and Ed Potton, *FoI and Ministerial Vetoes*, SN/PC/05007 (March 2014); *R (Evans) v. Attorney General* [2015] UKSC 21.

185. Under s. 19 (3), in adopting or reviewing a publication scheme, "a public authority shall have regard to the public interest." *See also* BIRKINSHAW, *supra* note 174, at 122–23; Austin, *supra* note 177, at 398–99.

186. Rodney Austin, *The Freedom of Information Act 2000—A Sheep in Wolf's Clothing?, in* THE CHANGING CONSTITUTION 401, 415 (Jeffrey Jowell & Dawn Oliver eds., 5th ed. 2004); *see also* TOMKINS, *supra* note 178, at 136 ("in many respects the regime under the Act allows for less openness than had been the case under the non-statutory scheme of the Code of Practice").

187. Birkinshaw, *supra* note 176, at 387–88, 391–92.

188. Austin, *supra* note 177, at 406.

189. *Cf. Dr John Pugh MP v. Information Commissioner and Ministry of Defence*, EA/2007/0055 (17 December 2007) [Information Tribunal] at para. 53 (noting "the general public interests in the promotion of transparency, accountability, public understanding and involvement in the democratic process").

190. Cabinet Office, Code of Practice on Written Consultation (November 2000), at 7–20.

191. The Cabinet Office describes a code of practice as "an authoritative statement of practice to be followed in some field. It typically differs from legislation in that it offers guidance rather than imposing requirements: its prescriptions are not hard and fast rules but guidelines which may allow considerable latitude in their practical application and may

be departed from in appropriate circumstances. The provisions of a code are not directly enforceable by legal proceedings, which is not to say that they may not have significant legal effects." (Cabinet Office, Guide to Legislative Procedures (October 2004), Appendix C, para. 2.1.). *See also* Francesca Bignami, *Creating European Rights: National Values and Supranational Interests*, 11 COLUM. J. EUR. L. 241, 317 n. 328 (2005); Craig, *supra* note 78, at 294–95.

192. Code (2000), *supra* note 190, at 3. This language was repeated in the revised 2004 version of the Code.

193. Code (2000), *supra* note 190, at 3.

194. *See also* PETER CANE, CONTROLLING ADMINISTRATIVE POWER: AN HISTORICAL COMPARISON 291 (2016) (noting that the Code is "primarily concerned with how, not when, to consult").

195. Better Regulation Executive -Department for Business, Enterprise and Regulatory Reform, Code of Practice on Consultation (July 2008), at 3, 5, 6 (emphasis added).

196. Cabinet Office—Regulatory Impact Unit, Code of Practice on Consultation (January 2004).

197. See Consultation Principles: Guidance (July 2012) and Consultation Principles 2016, available at https://www.gov.uk/government/publications/consultation-principles-guidance.

198. Code (2000), *supra* note 190, at 1.

199. CRAIG, *supra* note 21, at 455–56.

200. Other documents reflected this discretionary nature by using permissive language. *See, e.g.,* Cabinet Office, Public Bodies: A Guide for Departments, Chapter 8: Policy—Openness and Accountability (2006), para. 4.1.1 ("Departments and public bodies *should aim to* consult their users and stakeholders on a wide range of issues by means of questionnaires, public meetings or other forms of consultation to ensure that they are responsive to and meeting the needs of their customers") (emphasis added).

201. *See,* in reverse order, CRAIG, *supra* note 21, at 450 ("The absence of any common law duty to consult is matched by the lack of any such general statutory duty").

202. [1964] AC 40.

203. *Bates v. Lord Hailsham St Marylebone and others,* [1972] 1 W.L.R. 1373 [Chancery Division].

204. *Id.,* at 1378.

205. *Id.,* at 1379: "Here, Parliament has laid down the procedure to be followed. Expressum facit cessare tacitum. It is easier to imply procedural safeguards when Parliament has provided none than where Parliament has laid down a procedure, however inadequate its critics may consider it to be."

206. *R. (BAPIO Action Limited) v. Secretary of State for the Home Department,* [2007] EWCA Civ 1139 [Court of Appeal].

207. *Id.,* at para. 36.

208. *Id.,* at paras. 43–45 (emphasis added).

209. Sedley LJ added a qualification in the concluding paragraph of his opinion: "I do not seek to elevate this to a general rule that fairness can never require consultation as a condition of the exercise of a statutory function; but in the present context it seems to me that a duty to consult would require a specificity which the courts, concerned as they are with developing principles, cannot furnish without assuming the role of a legislator" (*id.,* at para. 47).

210. *Id.,* at para. 58 (emphasis in the original).

211. *Huang and Kashmiri v. Secretary of State for the Home Department* [2007] UKHL 11, at para. 17: "it was said, the appellate immigration authority should assume that the Immigration Rules and supplementary instructions, made by the responsible minister and laid before Parliament, had the imprimatur of democratic approval and should be taken to strike the right balance between the interests of the individual and those of the community. [However, these rules] are not the product of active debate in Parliament, where non-nationals seeking leave to enter or remain are not in any event represented."

212. *See* CRAIG, *supra* note 21, at 450–52.

213. [1972] 2 QB 299.

214. *Supra* note 71.

215. *R v Birmingham City Council Ex parte Dredger* [1993] C.O.D. 340, 91 LGR 532, CO/2453/90 [Queen's Bench Division].

216. *See also* CANE, *supra* note 194, at 290 (noting that the legitimate expectation cases are "mostly concerned with applying and changing soft rules rather than with hard rule-making").

217. *Kelly* is a good example of the limits of legitimate expectations. The Board of Governors of BBC decided, for practical purposes, to merge two local radio stations. The effect of this decision was that broadcasting from the applicant's locality was significantly reduced; the impact was particularly significant for Mr. Kelly, who was blind and relied heavily on local radio. Therefore, he initiated judicial review proceedings to quash the decision arguing that he had a legitimate expectation to be consulted. The court explained that in the absence of a legislative or contractual context, as was the case in the issue at hand, a legitimate expectation would arise from statements made by the BBC that there would be consultation, and not merely general consultation but consultation when significant alterations of the type in question in the present case were proposed. However, the court held that there was not sufficient evidence of appropriate promises, undertakings, or representations by the BBC that it would consult about the details of the future of local radio services of the kind arising in that case; hence, the application was not successful (*R v British Broadcasting Corporation, ex parte Kelly*, CO/1448/95 [1998] COD 58).

218. *R v. North East Devon HA ex parte Coughlan* [2001] QB 213, para. 108. *See also R (on the application of Medway Council and others) v. Secretary of State for Transport* [2002] EWHC 2516 (Admin), para. 28 ("it is axiomatic that consultation, whether it is a matter of obligation or undertaken voluntarily, requires fairness"). *Cf. R v. The London Borough of Brent ex parte Gunning* (1986) 84 LGR 168 (stating that the requirements should not differ based on a distinction between a statutory duty to consult and a duty to fulfil a legitimate expectation).

219. *Coughlan, supra* note 218, at para. 108.

220. *Regina (Moseley) v. Haringey London Borough Council* [2014] UKSC 56, at para 25.

221. *Id.*, at para. 38.

222. *Lee v. Department of Education and Science* (1967) 66 LGR 211 (Queen's Bench Division).

223. Jonathan Auburn, *Consultation*, at para. 17 (Judicial Review Conference paper, on file with author) (internal citations omitted). See also the classic HARRY WOOLF, JEFFREY JOWELL & ANDREW LE SUEUR, DE SMITH'S JUDICIAL REVIEW 385–88 (6th ed., 2007).

224. *Supra* note 220, at paras. 27 (per Lord Wilson) and 39 (per Lord Reed).

225. *Coughlan, supra* note 218, at para. 112 (emphasis added).

226. *Id.*, at paras. 115, 117.

227. *R (Eisai) v. National Institute for Health and Clinical Excellence* [2008] EWCA Civ 438 [Court of Appeal, Civil Division].

228. *Id.*, at para. 66.

229. *Id.*, at para. 65.

230. In Lord Justice Richards's words: "Overall, as it seems to me, this case depends not on the resolution of any real dispute about the legal principles, but on the application of well established principles to the particular context and particular circumstances of NICE's appraisal process" (*id.*, at para. 33).

231. Lord Justice Richards was sympathetic to Eisai's clarification that it did not seek to have the challenged guidance quashed but simply wanted the fully executable version to be released to it and to have an opportunity to make representations on it.

232. *R (on the application of Greenpeace Ltd) v. Secretary of State for Trade and Industry* [2007] EWHC 311 (Queen's Bench Division, Administrative Court).

233. *Greenpeace, id.*, at paras. 42–44, 67–68, 116. Interestingly, the emphasis on getting the general public involved, as evidenced by the publication of the summary consultation document, had considerable bearing on this particular holding. Greenpeace, and other environmental organizations, had in fact made full representations in their responses that included the issue of nuclear power. But in the court's mind this did not suffice to cure any procedural unfairness: "It is not enough that those who were thoroughly sceptical about the consultation process should have foreseen the outcome; the outcome should have been, but was not, reasonably foreseeable by any interested organisation or member of the public who took the 2006 Consultation Document and the Summary Document at face value" (*Greenpeace, id.*, at para. 88). We could read this as a welcome validation of the importance

of the openness prong which chapter 1 emphasized when it proposed the deliberative-participatory model. The fact that several repeat players–in this case, experienced environmental organizations—chose to take a more cautious approach and address broader issues should not lead to the *de facto* result of undermining the nature of the consultation as a public exercise open to all members of the public. The court was therefore correct in noting that "[i]t must also be borne in mind that it is a consultation paper, not a document produced by and for lawyers" (para. 67).

234. *Id.*, at paras. 116–17 (underlining in the original).

235. HARLOW & RAWLINGS, *supra* note 6, at 177.

236. *Greenpeace, supra* note 232, at para. 46.

237. *Id.*, at para. 62.

238. HARLOW & RAWLINGS, *supra* note 6, at 178.

239. *Supra*, chapter 1, Part IV.B.4 ("participation and judicial review should be unbundled in such a way as to accept that it is tenable that an administrative system complies with the deliberative-participatory ideal even when the three prongs of this ideal (open access, transparency, reason giving) are not judicially enforceable").

240. HARLOW & RAWLINGS, *supra* note 6, at 176.

241. *Cf.* BIRKINSHAW, HARDEN & LEWIS, *supra* note 145, at 16 (noting that "courts, operating without a tailormade Administrative Procedure Act, can provide little in the way of a developed jurisprudence of accountability for the organs of extended government").

242. *See* Kevin Morgan & Douglas Webber, *Divergent Paths: Political Strategies for Telecommunications in Britain, France and West Germany*, 9 WEST EUROPEAN POLITICS 56, (1986) ("Until recently it seemed that France had embarked on a strategy that was the antithesis of the neo-liberal path being pursued in Britain. The most conspicuous divergence lay in the emphasis that France ascribed to a *state-led* strategy in telecommunications") (emphasis in the original).

243. MORAN, *supra* note 1, at 2; Martin Cave, *The Evolution of Telecommunications Regulation in the UK*, 41 EUROPEAN ECONOMIC REVIEW 691, 692 (1997).

244. *See* David Heald, *The United Kingdom: Privatisation and its Political Context*, 11 WEST EUROPEAN POLITICS 31, 37–39 (1988) (describing the "British Telecom model").

245. *See* THATCHER, *supra* note 11, at 31–46. Thatcher's book provides an interesting story of long-standing similarities, increasing divergence until the mid-nineties, and thereafter a degree of convergence between the two countries.

246. *See* Helen Kemmitt & John Angel, *The Telecommunications Regime in the United Kingdom*, in TELECOMMUNICATIONS LAW AND REGULATION 93, 95–97 (Ian Walden ed., 2012); *see also* THATCHER, *supra* note 11, at 32–33.

247. "The Historical Development of BT," at: http://www.btplc.com/Thegroup/BTsHistory/History_of_BT.pdf.

248. THATCHER, *supra* note 11, at 94.

249. *Id.*, at 110.

250. Carsberg, *supra* note 138, at 286. This legislation was adopted in response to the findings of the 1977 Carter Committee report (Kemmitt & Angel, *supra* note 246, at 99).

251. Spiller & Vogelsang, *supra* note 1, at 96.

252. No mention of the privatization of telecommunications had been made in the Conservatives' 1979 general election manifesto. Nevertheless, in July 1982 the Government published a White Paper proposing the sale of 51% of British Telecom and the creation of Oftel as the regulatory body. The Telecommunications Act 1984 was enacted after Margaret Thatcher's reelection in 1983. THATCHER, *supra* note 11, at 145. *See* "A Brief History of Recent UK Telecoms and Oftel," available at: http://www.ofcom.org.uk/static/archive/oftel/about/history.htm#1982.

253. *See* Spiller & Vogelsang, *supra* note 1, at 85; Kemmitt & Angel, *supra* note 246, at 107–108.

254. *See* Carsberg, *supra* note 138, at 296; Kemmitt & Angel, *supra* note 246, at 101.

255. In Bryan Carsberg's words, "[a]t the end of 1990 . . . it was clear that we could not be content with that form of competition. The duopoly had been successful, but competition between two is not real competition-certainly not the kind that really makes the marketplace

dynamic" (Carsberg, *supra* note 138, at 289). Other accounts described them as "meager" (Cave, *supra* note 243, at 692) and "disappointing" (Kemmitt & Angel, *supra* note 246, at 111).

256. Competition and Choice: Telecommunications Policy for the 1990s, Cm.1461; Carsberg, *supra* note 138, at 289. On a side note, the mobile telephony sector began, in practice, as a duopoly as well between Cellnet (jointly owned by BT and Securicor) and Racal Vodafone (now Vodafone) in May 1983. In 1993 two further licenses were issued to Orange and Mercury One-2-One (now T-Mobile) to operate 2nd Generation (2G) networks. In 2000 an auction process resulted in five 3G licenses being granted to Vodafone, One2One, Orange and BT. In February 2013 Ofcom announced the winners of the 4G mobile spectrum auction (Kemmitt & Angel, *supra* note 246, at 102–103).

257. When the government decided the end of the duopoly in 1991 and the further liberalization of the market, it limited competition in the international market. In 1996 the government liberalized the market further by licensing an initial batch of 44 companies to provide international telecommunications services on any route they choose over their own facilities. By the end of September 2000, the government had received 823 applications for licenses to run new telecommunication systems in the United Kingdom; it had granted 632 licenses and 102 were under consideration (Spiller & Vogelsang, *supra* note 1, at 113; DEPARTMENT OF TRADE & INDUSTRY, COMMUNICATIONS LIBERALISATION IN THE UK: KEY ELEMENTS, HISTORY & BENEFITS 5, 20 (2001).

258. CLAIRE HALL, COLIN SCOTT & CHRISTOPHER HOOD, TELECOMMUNICATIONS REGULATION: CULTURE, CHAOS AND INTERDEPENDENCE INSIDE THE REGULATORY PROCESS 18 (2000).

259. *See* Kemmitt & Angel, *supra* note 246, at 113–14.

260. Cm 5010.

261. *Id.*, at 4, 13.

262. These were the Broadcasting Standards Commission, the Director General of Telecommunications, the Independent Television Commission, the Radio Authority and the Radiocommunications Agency.

263. *See* Explanatory Notes to the Office of Communications Act 2002 at: http://www.legislation.gov.uk/ukpga/2002/11/notes/contents.

264. *See* Explanatory Notes to the Communications Act 2003, at para. 5 (available at http://www.legislation.gov.uk/ukpga/2003/21/notes/contents).

265. *Id.*, at para. 7 (explicitly referring to the transposition); see also Kemmitt & Angel, *supra* note 246, at 114.

266. *See* C. D. FOSTER, PRIVATIZATION, PUBLIC OWNERSHIP AND THE REGULATION OF NATURAL MONOPOLY 125 (1992).

267. THATCHER, *supra* note 11, at 147 (reporting on interviews).

268. HALL, SCOTT & HOOD, *supra* note 258, at 20.

269. This system was modeled after the Office of Fair Trading. In fact, the original government inclination was to assign the regulatory responsibility to the Office of Fair Trading instead of creating a new body. However, Sir Gordon Borrie, who was director general of the OFT at that time, argued that this was too big a task for OFT (Jon Stern, *What the Littlechild Report Actually Said*, *in* THE UK MODEL OF UTILITY REGULATION: A 20TH ANNIVERSARY COLLECTION TO MARK THE "LITTLECHILD REPORT". RETROSPECT AND PROSPECT 7, 8 (Ian Bartle ed., 2003)).

270. HALL, SCOTT & HOOD, *supra* note 258, at 21.

271. *Id.*, at 19–28.

272. *See, e.g.*, Cento Veljanovksi, *The Need for a Regulatory Charter*, 1 JOURNAL OF FINANCIAL REGULATION AND COMPLIANCE 355, 356 (1993).

273. Therefore, the DGT's term in office was usually longer than the Secretary's appointing him (Spiller & Vogelsang, *supra* note 1, at 82).

274. Historically, all four DGTs were men.

275. Telecommunications Act 1984, s. 1 and Schedule 1.

276. Spiller & Vogelsang, *supra* note 1, at 99. However, a countervailing factor in appreciating the degree of independence of the new regulator at this level is that at the outset the first DGT

did not exercise in practice the power to appoint staff: a "shadow Oftel" had been established within the Department of Trade and Industry (DTI) before his appointment and the staff were simply transferred from the Department to Oftel when the latter was formally set up (HALL, SCOTT & HOOD, *supra* note 258, at 25–26).

277. THATCHER, *supra* note 11, at 148.

278. *See* HALL, SCOTT & HOOD, *supra* note 258, at 64–65.

279. *Id.*, at 24.

280. GRAHAM, *supra* note 121, at 32 (noting that the legislation sets out "a series of factors which pull in different directions. The job for the regulator, unaided by any open guidance from government, is to decide on priorities and how to balance competing interests").

281. PROSSER, *supra* note 2, at 23.

282. THATCHER, *supra* note 11, at 150; Kemmitt & Angel, *supra* note 246, at 110; COSMO GRAHAM & TONY PROSSER, PRIVATIZING PUBLIC ENTERPRISES: CONSTITUTIONS, THE STATE, AND REGULATION IN COMPARATIVE PERSPECTIVE 193 (1991).

283. The process of license modification, which recognized a role for both the Secretary and the DGT, is instructive; see sections 12–15 Telecommunications Act 1984; HALL, SCOTT & HOOD, *supra* note 258, at 23.

284. Furthermore, s. 1 of Competition and Service (Utilities) Act 1992 empowered the DGT to make regulations prescribing standards of performance and providing for compensation if the designated operator failed to meet a prescribed standard.

285. National Audit Office, "Report by the Comptroller and Auditor General: The Work of the Directors General of Telecommunications, Gas Supply, Water Services and Electricity Supply," 1995/96 HC 645, at 6 (1996).

286. *See* HALL, SCOTT & HOOD, *supra* note 258, at 61–62.

287. Report of the Director General of Telecommunications for the period 1 January to 31 December 1992 to the Secretary of State for Trade and Industry, at 1 (1993).

288. *See* Report of the Director General of Telecommunications for the period 5 August to 31 December 1984 to the Secretary of State for Trade and Industry [Annual Report 1984], at 8 (1985) ("I attach a high priority to my duty to promote effective competition and I have quickly come to believe that this is one of the most important and urgent duties laid upon me by the Act").

289. *See*, e.g., Annual Report 1984, at 7–8. *See also* Report of the Director General of Telecommunications for the period 1 January to 31 December 1985 to the Secretary of State for Trade and Industry [Annual Report 1985], at 10–11, 14 (1986).

290. *See* Report of the Director General of Telecommunications for the period 1 January to 31 December 1993 to the Secretary of State for Trade and Industry, at 1–2 (1994); Report of the Director General of Telecommunications for the period 1 January to 31 December 1994 to the Secretary of State for Trade and Industry, at 1 (1995).

291. *See* HALL, SCOTT & HOOD, *supra* note 258, at 28 (noting that Cruickshank's most distinctive contribution was perhaps not in developing substantive policy but rather regulatory processes).

292. Report of the Director General of Telecommunications for the period 1 January to 31 December 1998 to the Secretary of State for Trade and Industry (1999), p.1.

293. *See* HALL, SCOTT & HOOD, *supra* note 258, at 61 ("In contrast to the traditional anonymity of senior civil servants in Britain, the regulators made regular media appearances and their names became widely known, at least during times when the politics ran hot in their regulatory domains").

294. Oftel Review 1984–2003, Creating Competition and Choice (2003), at 12.

295. *Id.*, at 14 (with Edmonds quoted as saying: "When you find, as I did, The Economist, The Times and The Daily Telegraph all demanding your resignation in the same week, it does make you focus quite hard on what life's all about").

296. *See* MORAN, *supra* note 1, at 106 ("The practical design of the institutions also showed the continuing hold of the club culture . . . . [I]n line with the assumption that personal relations rather than formal rules were what really mattered in regulatory design, it assigned a central place to the individual figure of the Director General").

297. PROSSER, *supra* note 2, at 9. *See also* HARLOW & RAWLINGS, *supra* note 6, at 67 (noting that the fact that the "first Ofdogs were highly individual with a single regulator at the helm . . . also led to complaints that relationships with ministers by whom the regulator was appointed were too cosy and lacked transparency").

298. FOSTER, *supra* note 266, at 285–86.

299. *See* PROSSER, *supra* note 2, at 9; *see also* Thatcher, *supra* note 103, at 130.

300. *See* HALL, SCOTT & HOOD, *supra* note 258, at 62 (with further citations).

301. PROSSER, *supra* note 2, at 56.

302. *See also* MIKE FEINTUCK, "THE PUBLIC INTEREST" IN REGULATION 107–108 (2004) (noting that the need to give effect to the 2002 EU regulatory package was a significant motivating force driving the new UK legislation forward); TONY PROSSER, THE REGULATORY ENTERPRISE: GOVERNMENT, REGULATION, AND LEGITIMACY 154 (2010) (similarly observing that the EU legislation was "a further spur for UK reform, and was important in shaping the tasks of the new regulator").

303. PROSSER, *supra* note 302, at 156.

304. More information on the Board is available on the agency's website at https://www.ofcom.org.uk/about-ofcom/how-ofcom-is-run/ofcom-board.

305. *See* Office of Communications Act 2002, section 1 and Schedule, paras. 1–6.

306. *See* BBC News, Peer named media watchdog chief (July 25, 2002) [available at http://news.bbc.co.uk/2/hi/entertainment/2150739.stm] (quoting the Conservative culture spokesman as saying: "I'm sure Lord Currie will be objective. My fear is that actually he is going to have to work even harder to demonstrate that because there will be a lot of people who will see this as just another example of Labour cronyism").

307. For more information, see http://publicappointmentscommissioner.independent.gov.uk.

308. *See* Board Procedures available at https://www.ofcom.org.uk/__data/assets/pdf_file/0015/42225/board_procedures.pdf.

309. Office of Communications Act 2002, Schedule, para. 2(4).

310. PROSSER, *supra* note 302, at 157.

311. Office of Communications Act 2002, Schedule para. 8(1).

312. The main sources are: television broadcast license fees; radio broadcast license fees; administrative charges for electronic networks and services and the provision of broadcasting and associated facilities; administration charges for postal regulation; funding to cover its operating costs for spectrum management, in the form of grant-in-aid from the Department for Culture, Media and Sport (DCMS); grant-in-aid funding to cover statutory functions and duties, which Ofcom must discharge, but for which there is no matching revenue stream (The Office of Communications, Annual Report and Accounts for the period 1 April 2011 to 31 March 2012, at 70 (2012)).

313. Office of Communications Act 2002, Schedule, para. 1.

314. Chairman's Message, in Ofcom Annual Report 2003-04 (2004), at 2.

315. PROSSER, *supra* note 302, at 159

316. *Id.*, at 159 (noting that resolving such conflicts will be central to policymaking by Ofcom).

317. "A New Future for Communications" (Cm 5010) at 81.

318. *See* Scott, *supra* note 124, at 19.

319. THATCHER, *supra* note 11, at 113. *See also* Spiller & Vogelsang, *supra* note 1, at 86 (noting that most of the price-setting process was arranged informally between the government and the Post Office, and no written records were available).

320. MORAN, *supra* note 1, at 107.

321. PROSSER, *supra* note 302, at 3 n.13. The report was Stephen C. Littlechild, "Regulation of British Telecommunications' Profitability. Report to the Secretary of State" (1983).

322. Littlechild, *supra* note 321, at 8, 20–21.

323. MORAN, *supra* note 1, at 120, 107.

324. *See* PROSSER, *supra* note 2, at 35, 50; FOSTER, *supra* note 266, at 267.

325. HARLOW & RAWLINGS, *supra* note 6, at 290. See also PROSSER, *supra* note 2, at 45 (suggesting that "the Government's concern to avoid legalism in the procedures of the new regulators led to it ignoring the likelihood of other familiar problems arising").

326. *See* Heald, *supra* note 244, at 38 (describing the Oftel model as "non-participatory . . . with none of the public hearings characteristic of US regulation"). *See also* Scott, *supra* note 124, at 21 (noting the "rather limited duties in respect of consultation and transparency contained within the statutory frameworks, of which the Telecommunication Act 1984 . . . is an exemplar").

327. Other provisions, of less practical significance, that included a consultation requirement were section 8(5) [consultation before granting specific licenses to which special provisions applied], section 17(1) [consultation prior to final enforcement order] and section 22(8) [consultation for the designation of standards to which apparatus must conform if it is to be approved for connection to telecommunication systems].

328. GRAHAM & PROSSER, *supra* note 282, at 239, 256.

329. *Report of the Director General of Telecommunications for the period 5 August to 31 December 1984 to the Secretary of State for Trade and Industry*, at 14 (1985).

330. *See* Figure 5.1 later in this chapter.

331. PROSSER, *supra* note 2, at 84.

332. Report of the Director General of Telecommunications for the period 1 January to 31 December 1985 to the Secretary of State for Trade and Industry (1986), at 27.

333. Report of the Director General of Telecommunications for the period 1 January to 31 December 1991 to the Secretary of State for Trade and Industry (1992), at 9.

334. In his words, "[t]he UK framework raises arguments over the discretion of the regulator. I have found it very important for discretionary powers to be both flexible and widely drawn. The only alternative to this is, in effect, to leave this discretion in the hands of the regulated company" (OFTEL Press Release 46/95, quoted in PROSSER, *supra* note 2, at 66 n.21)

335. *See* HARLOW & RAWLINGS, *supra* note 6, at 290 (noting that Oftel was "the market leader in this exercise of agency procedural discretion inside a skeletal statutory framework").

336. Report of the Director General of Telecommunications for the period 1 January to 31 December 1993 to the Secretary of State for Trade and Industry (1994), at 3.

337. Report of the Director General of Telecommunications for the period 1 January to 31 December 1994 to the Secretary of State for Trade and Industry (1995), at 4–5. *See also* PROSSER, *supra* note 2, at 296 (highlighting the use of two rounds of notice and comment as one of the "particularly noteworthy aspects" of Oftel's consultation procedures).

338. *See* Report of the Director General of Telecommunications for the period 1 January to 31 December 1995 to the Secretary of State for Trade and Industry [Annual Report 1995], at 79–80 (1996). See also PROSSER, *supra* note 2, at 84–85.

339. *See, e.g.,* "Response from the Director General of Telecommunications," in National Audit Office, "Report by the Comptroller and Auditor General: The Work of the Directors General of Telecommunications, Gas Supply, Water Services and Electricity Supply," 1995/96 HC 645, at 64 (1996): "The transparency of the regulatory process . . . is particularly important in telecoms . . . OFTEL needs to have a clear picture of how possible changes in the regulatory regime will affect all the different players in the industry . . . It is vital, therefore, that proposals for change are fully aired and discussed with all the stakeholders in the industry . . . . OFTEL's procedures for introducing changes to the regulatory regime involve extensive consultation and have been expanded considerably beyond statutory requirements."

340. *See* Report of the Director General of Telecommunications for the period 1 January to 31 December 1996 to the Secretary of State for Trade and Industry (1997), at 13 ("We will continue to review and revise our consultation process, bearing in mind the points made in the survey of OFTEL's clients").

341. Available at http://www.ofcom.org.uk/static/archive/oftel/publications/1995_98/consumer/impacc.htm#Annex%20B. See also the statement issued at the end of the process, "Improving Accountability—Further Steps. Statement" (February 1998), available at http://www.ofcom.org.uk/static/archive/oftel/publications/1995_98/consumer/ia298.htm#Appendix%201/.

342. *See* Report of the Director General of Telecommunications for the period 1 January to 31 December 1997 to the Secretary of State for Trade and Industry (1998), at 8–9.

343. PROSSER, *supra* note 2, at 84.

344. HALL, SCOTT & HOOD, *supra* note 258, at 28.

345. *Id.*, at 95 (reporting on interviews).

346. Annual Report 1995, at 8.

347. "Response from the Director General of Telecommunications," in National Audit Office, "Report by the Comptroller and Auditor General: The Work of the Directors General of Telecommunications, Gas Supply, Water Services and Electricity Supply," 1995/96 HC 645, at 63 (1996).

348. *See* Annual Report 1995, at 88.

349. PROSSER, *supra* note 2, at 286.

350. Office of Telecommunications, *Oftel's Use of Public Consultation* (2001), at 4 (emphasis added).

351. *See also* HARLOW & RAWLINGS, *supra* note 6, at 311 ("In breeding the Ofdogs, the Thatcher government showed little appetite for judicial review); Prosser, *supra* note 137, at 65 ("At the time of privatization . . . the British Government was determined to avoid legal controls as much as possible. Some perceived law as a way to facilitate meddling by courts, as well to create an unnecessary recourse to legal rights where market solutions would be more appropriate").

352. *R v. The Director General of Telecommunications, ex parte Cellcom*, [1999] E.C.C. 314, 335, 332 (emphasis added).

353. *Id.*

354. *See, e.g.,* Julia Black & Peter Muchlinski, *Introduction, in* COMMERCIAL REGULATION AND JUDICIAL REVIEW 1, 12 (Julia Black, Peter Muchlinski and Paul Walker eds., 1998) ("commercial judicial review, although a growing area, is not an important one in numerical terms"); HALL, SCOTT & HOOD, *supra* note 258, at 101 ("litigation was a device invoked sporadically by licensees for commercial advantage"); Scott, *supra* note 124, at 27 (describing the courts' non-interventionist stance).

355. *R v. Director-General of Telecommunications, ex parte Let's Talk (UK) Ltd* (6 April 1992, unreported). *See also* HARLOW & RAWLINGS, *supra* note 6, at 311; PROSSER, *supra* note 2, at 53 (noting that there were a few judicial review cases brought, and they "did not have any great effect beyond establishing some procedural requirements to be followed in determining individual disputes," citing the same case).

356. *Associated Provincial Picture Houses Ltd v. Wednesbury Corporation*, [1948] 1 K.B. 223, described by Lord Irvine as the *locus classicus* of British administrative law (Lord Irvine, *Judges and Decision Makers: The Theory and Practice of* Wednesbury *review*, 1996 PUBLIC LAW 59, 62.

357. *See* ARANCIBIA, *supra* note 150, at 15 (explaining that the arguments in favor of the "orthodox deferential approach," which he criticizes, were primarily based on the decisionmaker's special qualities and the need to ensure regulatory effectiveness). *See also* Scott, *supra* note 124, at 24, for further citations on the view that courts took a more restrictive attitude to judicial review in cases involving commercial regulation; WADE & FORSYTH, *supra* note 22, at 134 ("Challenges based upon the irrationality of regulators' decisions have generally failed").

358. *Cellcom, supra* note 352, at 331–32 (emphasis added).

359. *R v. Director-General of Telecommunications, ex parte British Telecommunications* (20 December 1996, unreported). The case is described in Scott, *supra* note 124, at 31–35.

360. *Mercury Communications Ltd v. Director General of Telecommunications*, [1996] 1 W.L.R. 48; PROSSER, *supra* note 2, at 53.

361. *Mercury, supra* note 360, at 58–59.

362. PROSSER, *supra* note 2, at 54.

363. *See* Aileen McHarg, *Regulation as a Private Law Function?*, 1995 PUBLIC LAW 539, 539 (further noting that this was welcomed in the light of controversy over inadequate regulatory accountability. McHarg argued, however, that the decision was questionable and concluded that "[i]t would be unfortunate if this case were to signal a slide towards the sort of legalism that has bedeviled U.S. regulation" (*id.*, at 550)).

364. HALL, SCOTT & HOOD, *supra* note 258, at 101; McHarg, *supra* note 363, at 539; PROSSER, *supra* note 2, at 54.
365. McHarg, *supra* note 363, at 550. *See also* HALL, SCOTT & HOOD, *supra* note 258, at 101 (describing Oftel's robust approach to the defense of its position facing this litigation).
366. *British Telecommunications plc v. Director General of Telecommunications* (4 August 2000), 2000 WL 1213055.
367. *Id.*, at para. 126.
368. *Cellcom, supra* note 352, 331.
369. *British Telecommunications, supra* note 366, at para. 38 (emphasis added). *See also* Explanatory Note to the Telecommunications (Appeals) Regulations 1999 (explaining that "[t]hese Regulations implement provisions in Directive 97/13/EC . . . . and Directive 97/51/EC . . . which require Member States to provide an appeals procedure in relation to certain decisions of national regulatory authorities in the field of telecommunications") [available at http://www.legislation.gov.uk/uksi/1999/3180/note/made].
370. Quoted in HALL, SCOTT & HOOD, *supra* note 258, at 102.
371. The full list is available at https://www.ofcom.org.uk/about-ofcom/what-is-ofcom ("statutory duties and regulatory principles").
372. Sections 55(6) [Conditions related to consumer interests], 66(10) [Designation of universal service providers], 71(9) [Sharing of burden of universal service obligations], 117(6) [Transitional schemes on cessation of application of the electronic communications code], 122(7) [Orders by Ofcom in the absence of a code for premium rate services], 134(12) [Restrictions in leases and licenses], 159(9) [Grant of recognized spectrum access], 162(2) [Conversion into and from wireless telegraphy licenses], 164(9) [Limitations on authorized spectrum use], 168(7) [Spectrum trading], 170(5) [Wireless telegraphy register], Schedule 5.1(2) [General procedure for applications for grant of recognized spectrum access]. Schedule 17 provided for the application of section 403 to different rulemaking powers under the Wireless Telegraphy Act 1949 and the Wireless Telegraphy Act 1967.
373. Office of Communications, *Better Policy Making: Ofcom's Approach to Impact Assessment* (21 July 2005), at para. 2.3.
374. See section 5 of the guidelines (*id.*, at 12–19), including notably paragraphs 5.30-5.37 on analyzing (and quantifying) costs and benefits.
375. Paragraph 5.4 of the guidelines lists the six stages for producing an Impact Assessment.
376. "Ofcom will consider each case on its merits and will apply the guidelines where it is appropriate to do so. In the event that we decide to depart from the guidelines, we will normally set out our reasons for doing so" (*Ofcom's Approach to Impact Assessment, supra* note 373, at para. 1.17). This is not to say that these reasons have always been satisfactory to stakeholders; *See*, e.g., Cathay Pacific Airways' response to a consultation document, *Applying spectrum pricing to the Maritime and Aeronautical sectors* (July 2008), in which the company criticizes the lack of a full Impact Assessment (available at http://stakeholders.ofcom.org.uk/binaries/consultations/aip/responses/cathay.pdf).
377. *See* Explanatory Notes to the Communications Act 2003, Appendix 3, which includes four transposition tables identifying how the requirements of each of the four 2002 EU Communications Directives have been dealt with in the Communications Act.
378. *Chief Executive's Report, in* Office of Communications, Annual Report 2003–2004 (2004), at 5.
379. *See* PROSSER, *supra* note 302, at172.
380. *See*, e.g., Ofcom's consultation on a "discussion paper" on traffic management and net neutrality (June 2010) that resulted in a Statement (November 2011) broadly outlining Ofcom's approach, with the agency concluding that it will "keep under review the possibility of intervening more formally" in the future. Another example was the July 2005 consultation on *Review of Alternative Dispute Resolution Schemes*, during which Ofcom also consulted on proposed "recommendations for best practice."
381. PROSSER, *supra* note 302, at 173.
382. *See* Office of Communications, Annual Report 2003-2004 (2004), at 28 (describing the agency's "consultation tour" on its 2004-05 Annual Plan, with public meetings in Cardiff, Belfast, London, Manchester, and Glasgow).

383. *Id.*, at 6.
384. Interviews n. 50001 and 50002.
385. *See*, e.g., *Office of Communications, Statement of policy on the persistent misuse of an electronic communications network or service* (1 March 2006), at para. 2.2 ("A number of respondents complained about Ofcom's consultation processes. We have improved some aspects of these processes already, including providing an on-line response form for each consultation document. A comprehensive review of our consultation processes is underway and we are grateful to those who have contributed their views on improvements").
386. Interview n. 50001.
387. Available at http://stakeholders.ofcom.org.uk/consultations/how-will-ofcom-consult.
388. Code (2000), *supra* note 190, at 20.
389. For example, Vicki Nash, the third consultation champion, was the Director of the Ofcom Scotland Team. Graham Howell, the fourth consultation champion, was the Director of the Ofcom England Team and Secretary to the Corporation since 2003.
390. Explanatory Notes to the Communications Act 2003, at para. 416.
391. Its jurisdiction covers more than appeals under the Communications Act 2003. More information on the Tribunal's other functions is available at http://www.catribunal.org.uk/242/About-the-Tribunal.html.
392. The bios of the members of the CAT are listed on the Tribunal's website (http://www.catribunal.org.uk/246/Personnel.html).
393. Sir Christopher Bellamy, *Focusing on the European Perspective of Judicial Dialogue: Issues in the Area of Competition Law*, 39 TEX. INT'L L.J. 461, 465 (2004) (adding that this means "it is a system that is based on the exchange of written submissions, on case management by the Tribunal, and on a short oral stage. The Court takes a certain degree of initiative to see that the issues are properly stated and defined, and to see that the truth of the matter is reached, rather than sitting back and allowing the parties to argue it as they might wish. At the same time, we have retained the essential strengths of the common law system, by which, in particular, I refer to cross-examination of witnesses and discovery of documents where the facts are disputed").
394. HARLOW & RAWLINGS, *supra* note 6, at 321.
395. Thomas de la Mare, Regulatory Judicial Review (quoted in HARLOW & RAWLINGS, *supra* note 6, at 321).
396. *Hutchison 3G UK Limited v. Office of Communications*, [2008] CAT 11, at para. 164 (emphasis added).
397. *T-Mobile (UK) Limited and others v. Office of Communications*, [2008] CAT 12, at para 82.
398. *Id.*, at para. 83.
399. *Vodafone Limited v. Office of Communications*, [2008] CAT 22, at para. 46.
400. *TalkTalk Telecom Group plc v. Office of Communications*, [2012] CAT 1, at para. 124 (emphasis in the original).
401. *Freeserve.com plc v. Director General of Telecommunications*, [2003] CAT 5, at para. 114.
402. *T-Mobile (UK) Ltd & Telefónica O2 UK Ltd Appellants v. Office of Communications*, [2008] EWCA Civ 1373, at paras. 19, 43.
403. Or, as Richard Rawlings called it, a "high-powered tribunal" (Richard Rawlings, *Changed Conditions, Old Truths: Judicial Review in a Regulatory Laboratory*, *in* THE REGULATORY STATE: CONSTITUTIONAL IMPLICATIONS 283, 302 (Dawn Oliver, Tony Prosser & Richard Rawlings eds., 2010)).
404. *R. on the application of Francis Wildman v. Office of Communications*, [2005] EWHC 1573, at para. 14.
405. *Id.*, at para. 67.
406. Department for Media, Culture and Sport, "Implementing the Revised EU Electronic Communications Framework—Appeals: HMG Proposals on Reform of the Telecommunications Appeals Framework" (August 2011), at para. 7, Annex 1 and para. 45.
407. Department for Business, Innovation and Skills, *Streamlining Regulatory and Competition Appeals Consultation on Options for Reform* (June 2013). The impact assessment was published in May 2016 and is available at https://www.gov.uk/government/uploads/system/

uploads/attachment_data/file/535648/2016-05-24_Appeals_-_impact_assessment.pdf. These newer initiatives have not, as of this writing, resulted in any statutory changes to the CAT's appellate jurisdiction yet.

408. Between its inception and November 2010, Ofcom was appealed 35 times under section 192 of the Communications Act (National Audit Office, "Ofcom: The Effectiveness of Converged Regulation" [2010], at 32).

409. Interview n. 50002.

410. Interview n. 52001.

411. *TalkTalk Telecom Group plc v. Office of Communications*, [2012] CAT 1, at para. 77 (emphasis added).

412. To have a more accurate picture of the pre- and post-2003 numbers of consultations and comments in Figures 5.1 and 5.2, my methodological choice was to count in the public consultations that were carried out by the Radiocommunications Agency (excluding consultations relating to broadcasting that fall outside the scope of this study). The Radiocommunications Agency was an Executive Agency of the Department of Trade and Industry. It was responsible for the management of the non-military radio spectrum in the United Kingdom. This agency was one of the five regulatory bodies that merged to form Ofcom in December 2003.

413. A NTS call is a call to a phone number that usually begins with 08 or 09. These numbers put customers through to a range of entertainment and information services, including banks, various helplines, public and government services, and pay-as-you-go Internet services. This explains the interest from both the consumer and the industry sides. Indeed, 1,207 out of the total 1,308 responses were received from consumers and small businesses.

414. Cm 5010.

415. Report of the Joint Committee on the Draft Communications Bill, HL 169; HC 876 (Session 2001–2002) ["Puttnam Report"]. The Puttnam Report was described as "a wide-ranging, well-informed and in-depth critique of the Draft Bill as a whole: an example of pre-legislative scrutiny at its very best" (FEINTUCK, *supra* note 302, at 109), with particular influence at a late stage of the lawmaking process (PROSSER, *supra* note 302, at 154).

416. Puttnam Report, *supra* note 415, at paras. 24–26.

417. *See* Office of Communications, "Citizens, Communications and Convergence: Discussion Paper" (July 2008), at para. 2.10; PROSSER, *supra* note 302, at 155.

418. House of Lords—Select Committee on the Constitution, The Regulatory State: Ensuring Its Accountability (6th Report of Session 2003–04), HL Paper 68-I, at 20.

419. Ofcom, "Citizens, Communications and Convergence: Discussion Paper" (July 2008), at paras. 2.11, 2.13-2.15.

420. *See*, e.g., Ofcom, Annual Report 2004/5 (2005), at 3, 7; Ofcom, Annual Report 2006/7 (2007), at 5, 10.

421. PROSSER, *supra* note 302, at 160.

422. Ofcom, "Citizens, Communications and Convergence: Discussion Paper" (July 2008), at paras. 2.16, 4.4.

423. Ofcom, "Traffic Management and 'net neutrality': A Discussion Document" (June 2010).

424. Communications Consumer Panel, "Net Neutrality and 'Traffic Management': Consultation Response" (2010), at 4–5.

425. *Cf.* FEINTUCK, *supra* note 302, at 72 (noting that "in Britain, the citizenship-related interests incorporated into the regulatory agenda for utilities is often less apparent than it might be as a result of the social objectives being pursued being expressed or framed primarily in terms of *individual* rights or interests").

426. Ofcom, "Citizens, Communications and Convergence: Discussion Paper" (July 2008), at para. 2.34.

427. Annual Report 2003/4, at 6.

428. For instance, its 2004 public consultation on "Mis-selling of fixed-line telecoms"

429. Communications Consumer Panel, "Informing the Debate: The Work of the Communications Consumer Panel 2011–2012" (2012), at 4.

430. *Id.*

431. In their own words, "[we] give strategic advice on policies early on in their development—before they are consulted on—so as to build consumer interests into Ofcom's decision-making from the outset" (http://www.communicationsconsumerpanel.org.uk/smartweb/about-us/about-us).

432. Ofcom and the Communications Consumer Panel Memorandum of Understanding (available at http://www.communicationsconsumerpanel.org.uk/downloads/AboutUs/MoU/MoU.pdf).

433. More information on these committees is available at https://www.ofcom.org.uk/about-ofcom/how-ofcom-is-run/committees/nations-committee and https://www.ofcom.org.uk/about-ofcom/how-ofcom-is-run/committees/acod.

434. PROSSER, *supra* note 302, at 172.

435. Interview n. 52001.

436. Office of Communications, "Better Policy Making: Ofcom's Approach to Impact Assessment" (July 2005), at para 5.6.

437. Interviews n. 52001 and 51003.

438. Interview n. 52001.

439. PROSSER, *supra* note 302, at 171–72.

440. *See Coughlan, supra* note 218, at para. 112 ("It has to be remembered that consultation is not litigation: the consulting authority is not required to publicise every submission it receives").

441. Office of Telecommunications, "Oftel's Use of Public Consultation" (2001), at v ("in most cases, Oftel will cease to allow a further 14 days for comments to be made on the responses made by others. Where, exceptionally, an iterative approach may be productive, such as where the implications of the determination are particularly wide-ranging or stakeholders' views are particularly polarised, Oftel may specify a formal period for comments-on-comments").

442. http://stakeholders.ofcom.org.uk/freedom-of-information/

443. Ofcom's response rates to FOIA requests were as follows: 98.7% (Annual Report 2004/5); 87% (Annual Report 2005/6); 86% (Annual Report 2006/7); 77% (Annual Report 2007/8); 74% (Annual Report 2008/9); 85% (Annual Report 2009/10); 90% (Annual Report 2010/11); 96% (Annual Report 2011/12).

444. HARLOW & RAWLINGS, *supra* note 6, at 103; CRAIG, *supra* note 21, at 371–72; Patrick Neill, *The Duty to Give Reasons: The Openness of Decision-Making, in* THE GOLDEN METWAND AND THE CROOKED CORD. ESSAYS ON PUBLIC LAW IN HONOUR OF SIR WILLIAM WADE QC 161, 162 (Christopher Forsyth & Ivan Hare eds., 1998).

445. WADE & FORSYTH, *supra* note 22, at 191.

446. Interview n. 50001.

447. This may point to a general trend toward incorporating a reason-giving requirement in judicial review, which has not materialized yet (WADE & FORSYTH, *supra* note 22, at 435: "there is a strong case to be made for the giving of reasons as an essential element of administrative justice. The need for it has been sharply exposed by the expanding law of judicial review, now that so many decisions are liable to be quashed or appealed against on grounds of improper purpose, irrelevant considerations and errors of law of various kinds").

448. *TalkTalk Telecom Group plc v. Office of Communications*, [2012] CAT 1.

449. *Id.*, at para. 75 (emphasis in the original).

450. *Id.*, at para. 76 (emphasis in the original).

451. *Id.*, at para 121.

452. *Id.*, at paras. 125–26.

453. *Id.*, at para 78.

454. *Id.*, at para. 131.

455. *Id.*, at para. 132.

456. *Id.*, at para. 130.

457. *Id.*, at para 136 ("Given the conclusions we have reached, it is strictly unnecessary for us to say more about Ground A in order to resolve this appeal. However, in case this matter goes further, we make the following findings in respect of Ground A").

458. *Id.*, at para. 136f.

459. *Id.*, at para 136g(ii).
460. *British Telecommunications plc & Hutchison 3G (UK) Limited v. Office of Communications*, [2009] CAT 11.
461. *Vodafone Limited v. Office of Communications*, [2008] CAT 22.
462. *Id.*, at paras. 91–92.
463. Section 135 empowers Ofcom to require industry participants to provide the agency with "all such information as [it considers] necessary for the purpose of carrying out [its] functions."
464. *Vodafone v. Ofcom, supra* note 461, at paras. 94–95.
465. *Id.*, at para. 159.
466. *Id.*
467. FEINTUCK, *supra* note 302, at 68 ("The perceived constitutional impropriety of the British judiciary reviewing the substance of primary legislation seems to have led to a broader position, whereby the judiciary will seek at almost any cost to confine its decisions to the procedure of administrative decision-making rather than risking giving the slightest appearance of reviewing the substance of decisions").
468. BIRKINSHAW, HARDEN & LEWIS, *supra* note 145, at 259.
469. GRAHAM & PROSSER, *supra* note 282, at 239. *See also* HARLOW & RAWLINGS, *supra* note 6, at 170 (noting demands for a British equivalent to the US APA).
470. PROSSER, *supra* note 2, at 286.
471. House of Lords- Merits of Statutory Instruments Committee, The Management of Secondary Legislation, HL 149-I (29th Report of Session of 2005-06), at para. 122.
472. Explanatory Notes to the Legislative and Regulatory Reform Act 2006, at para. 44.
473. PROSSER, *supra* note 302, at 209.
474. Department for Business, Enterprise & Regulatory Reform, "Regulators' Compliance Code: Statutory Code of Practice for Regulators" (2007).
475. *Id.*, at 8.
476. HM Treasury, "Reducing Administrative Burdens: Effective Inspection and Enforcement", (March 2005) [The Hampton Review].
477. "Regulators' Compliance Code," *supra* note 474, at 11.
478. HARLOW & RAWLINGS, *supra* note 6, at 258–60. According to Tony Prosser's much more modest characterization, the Code is "probably the most important specific development" that followed the Hampton Review (PROSSER, *supra* note 302, at 212).
479. HARLOW & RAWLINGS, *supra* note 6, at 260.
480. *See* WADE & FORSYTH, *supra* note 22, at 125 (noting that "[t]he impact of these obligations is not yet clear").
481. HALL, SCOTT & HOOD, *supra* note 258, at 66. The authors further report on an interview with a senior official at the European Commission who said: "We regard Oftel as the most sophisticated of the National Regulatory Authorities and they are very helpful to us" (*id.*, at 95–96).
482. *See also* Athanasios Psygkas, *The "Double Helix" of Process and Substance Review* before the UK Competition Appeal Tribunal: A Model Case or a Cautionary Tale for Specialist Courts?, *in* COMPARATIVE ADMINISTRATIVE LAW 462 (Susan Rose-Ackerman, Peter Lindseth & Blake Emerson eds., 2d ed. 2017) (arguing that, because of its institutional design and operation in practice, the CAT has the advantages of a specialist court while mitigating the associated risks of specialization).
483. *See* Ian Walden, "Brexit and the peculiar case of the telecommunications sector" (July 2016), http://brexit.bakermckenzie.com/2016/07/18/brexit-and-the-peculiar-case-of-the-telecommunications-sector/. On the Great Repeal Bill, see House of Commons Library, "Legislating for Brexit: the Great Repeal Bill," Briefing Paper 7793 (November 2016).
484. Sharon White, "As Britain Looks for the Best EU Deal, We Must Talk about Communications," DAILY TELEGRAPH, October 4, 2016, http://www.telegraph.co.uk/business/2016/10/04/as-britain-looks-for-the-best-eu-deal-we-must-talk-about-communi/.
485. *Id.*

6

Increasing the "Democratic Surplus": What Should the Path to the Future Look Like?

The previous three chapters told the story of three national systems responding in distinctive, and similar, ways to common external pressures from the EU. These responses were assessed in the light of the conditions of implementation in the three countries against the backdrop of their public law history, administrative traditions, and state-society relations. In the course of these case studies, I also tested the hypotheses that chapter 2 had spelled out. The democratic accountability model constructed in chapter 1 aimed to help structure the extensive fieldwork and the historical institutional analysis in the subsequent chapters, and to present the analytical and empirical material in a way that encourages critical engagement. This chapter concludes by looking forward to how this comparative experience may inform future developments in the EU regulatory system and further enhance democratic accountability at both the national and the supranational levels. The aim is to offer policy proposals that are theoretically and historically informed as well as empirically grounded.

I. Stories of convergence

A. Creating and expanding the "democratic surplus" domestically

The trajectory of institutional and procedural reform in response to EU pressures was different in France, Greece, and the United Kingdom. The three country cases confirmed the hypothesis in chapter 2 that the EU requirements brought about varying degrees of change in the three jurisdictions depending on the public law traditions, administrative history and procedures that had been in place before the advent of EU law.

Contrary to conventional accounts in the media and the occasional public perceptions of an uneasy relationship between the EU and the UK, the institutional pressures on the UK with respect to participatory requirements in particular were weaker compared to those on Greece and France.[1] The institutional adjustment required in the UK was comparatively smaller; public consultation mandates were transposed into an environment that had had more than a decade of experience with similar processes, even though they had been for the most part highly discretionary. By contrast, the effect of the EU accountability mandates was more salient in France and Greece where open stakeholder participation via institutionalized avenues had been a rare occurrence, and occasionally even viewed with suspicion. The notable contrasts between the role of open participatory processes before and after the second-generation EU directives are captured in the charts showing the number of public consultations as well as comments submitted and published during those consultations over the French and the Greek regulators' life span.[2]

The descriptive statistics in the case studies may tell a story of divergence in terms of the pace of change; however, they also tell a story of convergence in terms of trends. The first peak in numbers in both France and Greece came with the transposition of the EU mandates into domestic law—in 2004 in France, in 2006 in Greece. A similar upward trend was manifest in the United Kingdom, except the increase in the number of public consultations began, as detailed in chapter 5, during the tenure of Don Cruickshank in the second half of the 1990s. This momentum continued particularly after 2000, that is, during a time at which the soon-to-be-adopted procedural EU mandates were known and acknowledged in Oftel and government documents. The number of consultations peaked in 2003 as Ofcom, the new UK super-regulator, was established as part of the transposition of the new EU regulatory framework.

Cross-national variations were not limited to the timing of institutional and procedural developments but they illustrate a broader point. That is to say, common EU mandates were mediated through embedded features of the national administrative states and traditions. This, in turn, determined not only the speed but also the forms of institutional adaptation. In a similar vein, Mark Thatcher observed in his 1999 case study of telecommunications that "differences in cross-national institutional paths of development arise from contrasts in historical experiences and inheritances, distributions of power, political leadership, propensities to import ideas, themselves intimately linked to previous institutional arrangements."[3] Daniel Kelemen's 2011 study, discussing the cases of securities regulation, competition policy, and disability rights, argued that resistance to EU pressures for regulatory reform was "generally greatest in states where national policymaking traditions differed most from the approach pursued by the EU."[4] The case studies in this book are consistent with these analyses. For instance, we saw in chapter 3 that the first post-liberalization impulse of the French legislator was to bring the industry and civil society groups into the policymaking process primarily through the establishment of consultative commissions; this reflected a long-standing pattern of *corporatisme étatique*. Chapter 3 also introduced the idea of "Tocqueville's revenge" in the French example. In Greece, "Tocqueville's revenge" came back with a vengeance: the long-standing feature of an underdeveloped civil society translated into very low participation rates in public consultations on the part of non-governmental organizations (NGOs) and individual citizens (3% and 2%, respectively). The UK represented the opposite case with a 38% of individual participation in public consultations. Chapter 5 explained how an embedded cultural characteristic that is particular to the UK, namely, the idea of citizen-consumer, may account for this high percentage.

In other words, the fieldwork and primary data presented in the case studies demonstrated national variations. The previous chapters drew primarily on a historical institutional analysis, enriched by qualitative evidence, such as interviews, as the best-suited approach to account for the empirically observed cross-national divergence. This brought to the fore the different implementation features in the three countries. For example, the Greek case illustrated how long-term patterns in the "background conditions of the state" and a tradition of slow, and occasionally inconsistent, implementation of EU law played out in the specific way in which procedural EU mandates were incorporated and implemented in the Greek legal order. The interviews informed the qualitative examination of the cases and further suggested a link between developments at the EU level and the practice of national regulatory authorities. For instance, agency officials in both Greece and the United Kingdom explained that they had been aware of the European Commission's proposals and the forthcoming introduction of the new participatory requirements. In the UK, interviews shed light on a second type of (indirect) effect that the EU mandate for review on appeal has had on the regulator's consultation practices; this effect might have been difficult to trace by legal analysis alone.[5]

Therefore, in spite of national variations, the broader point is, again, one of convergence. In all the countries studied, institutional and procedural EU provisions transformed aspects of the preexisting administrative governance,[6] and brought about accountability gains on all prongs of the deliberative-participatory model: open access, transparency, reason giving, and judicial review. This does not mean that France, Greece, and the United Kingdom have reached the ideal described in chapter 1. The book's argument is rather that EU mandates have been a crucial force in enhancing aspects of the democratic accountability of regulatory agency operations within the member states and moving them closer to the deliberative-participatory model. Importantly, by introducing or formalizing open participatory processes, many of which were novel in the member states, EU law may also turn the spotlight on persistent accountability gaps not only in the telecommunications sector but also across the board. Differently put, supply of accountability processes may generate demand from the newly empowered domestic actors.

This brings us to the last aspect of convergence. That is, convergence toward a unified accountability model that applies across the national administration—in other words, something akin to the US Administrative Procedure Act. According to one of the hypotheses in chapter 2, as national regulators become familiar with these new accountability tools and a culture of public consultation takes roots, one can expect these regulatory processes to be ultimately generalized across the spectrum of national administration. The case studies lend support to this hypothesis. The previous three chapters discussed recent domestic legislative initiatives—the "Warsmann law" in France, Law 4048/2012 in Greece, the Legislative and Regulatory Reform Act 2006 in the UK—suggesting that all three countries are moving in the direction hypothesized in chapter 2. They are doing so timidly, however. The limitations of these legislative reforms and setbacks indicate that the generalization of formal, binding participatory processes is still, to a large extent, a work in progress in the national systems, as elaborated in chapters 3, 4, and 5. Nevertheless, the broader picture is that EU mandates have created a momentum, which the member states can and are building on. The question for Part II is whether the EU may have a further role to play in strengthening administrative accountability mechanisms. The lessons from exploring the conditions of implementation of EU administrative mandates within the diverse member states will help to determine the extent of this role and the modalities of diffusion of accountability mechanisms through regulatory networks. Before proceeding to this inquiry, one last question for this Part is whether the trend toward convergence described above has transnational and cross-sectoral dimensions in the EU.

B. Transnational and cross-sectoral convergence in the EU? A research agenda

This book has as one of its aims to shed light on unexplored effects of EU law in the member states and illustrate how these mandates promote a new accountability model in the EU regulatory system. The country cases in the previous three chapters fleshed out applications of this novel framework exploring the specificities of implementation of EU mandates within the historically, linguistically, and culturally diverse member states. The three countries examined represent distinctive, and influential, administrative models. Therefore, they offer a wide range of interesting insights into how national differences translated into variations in the extent and forms of impact that EU mandates had on domestic administrative governance. A single study cannot offer in-depth cases from all the member states. Future work could employ the framework proposed in this book as a frame of reference to explore variations across additional member states.

New member states from Central and Eastern Europe could be such examples. Much of the literature on the implementation of EU law in these member states focuses on the impact of Europeanization on post-communist constitutionalism with a particular emphasis on courts.[7] A smaller section of this work has looked at administrative agencies but is predominantly concerned with the implementation of substantive EU law by national authorities rather than with administrative democracy.[8] These country cases bring to the fore the democratization opportunities that can accompany EU accession, including notably the empowerment of domestic civil society actors.[9] This book addressed these issues in discussing the Greek case, which was characterized by weak civil society capacity on the ground. In fact, the other two cases are more "difficult," or at least less intuitive. These cases represent "institutionally developed" countries with long administrative traditions; the discussion in the previous chapters illustrated the role EU mandates played in promoting new modes of regulatory governance even against this backdrop.

Germany could be another case study. This country has a long and well-developed administrative tradition. However, the German case would not counter the main conclusions in this book. Germany often relies on a corporatist model of interest representation that allows "a role for associations in influencing and exercising public authority, but only those that are believed to embody . . . categories of labor and capital, or perhaps rural interests, ethnic groups, or regional identities."[10] An important feature of this model is therefore that this "style of negotiation and consensus building" does not encompass every stakeholder but only specific groups that acquire "officially recognized status and privileged access" to decision making in specific domains.[11] In fact, when it comes to regulatory policy, "[t]he elected representatives of the people and the bureaucrats to whom they delegate power are seen as the legitimate interpreters of the public interest. Private groups that make such claims may be viewed with suspicion."[12] A recent study pertaining to executive policymaking in Germany confirms that the German Administrative Procedure Act (Verwaltungsverfahrensgesetz) does not govern rulemaking, and statutes do not impose general, detailed and coherent procedural standards on administrative rulemaking—consistent with the authors' claim that parliamentary systems are unlikely to impose such general procedural constraints on the executive. This book further explains that the German Constitutional Court still views elections as the primary route for public accountability, and it distrusts calls for more public participation in policymaking.[13]

This brief overview of certain key features of the German example demonstrates important commonalities between the French and the German systems, and indicates that a similar argument about the effect of EU law on German regulatory practices, and particularly the creation of new entry points for stakeholder participation, could be made. The German telecommunications regulator (Bundesnetzagentur) itself has explicitly acknowledged that it operates on the basis of the European legal framework.[14] In fact, a provision for consultation procedures in the electronic communications sector was included in the 2004 telecommunications law to incorporate the pertinent requirement of the 2002 Framework Directive.[15]

Future studies could further build on the framework proposed in this book to assess the impact of EU law not only in additional countries but also across sectors. The country cases in the previous chapters incorporated references to other policy domains (e.g., environmental regulation, urban planning) to contextualize the discussion of the regulatory mandates in the telecommunications sector. At the EU level, as chapter 2 explained, the telecommunications industry was the first one to which the European Commission turned its attention. It was also the first sector in which the EU's involvement included advanced institutional and procedural provisions. The EU efforts in this area set the tone for similar initiatives, at later stages, in other network industries,[16] in which competitive pressures had not been as pronounced. The earlier model of electronic communications, therefore, reflects trends that have become observable in other sectors, notably energy and rail.

For instance, none of the first- or second-generation directives in the electricity or natural gas sectors contained provisions regarding stakeholder participation in regulatory processes.[17] By contrast, the third-generation directives in both fields include consultation requirements. For example, when carrying out the duties specified in these directives, national regulatory authorities must consult transmission system operators. In a similar vein, NRAs must consult all actual or potential system users on ten-year network development plans.[18] In the field of rail, the first EU initiatives, which came later than in other sectors, did not include any public consultation requirements.[19] This changed, however, in 2004 with the second generation of directives. Notably, the Railway Safety Directive stipulated decision-making principles for the national safety authorities, which included transparency and consultation requirements.[20] A 2012 recast directive similarly provided for regular consultations with representatives of users of the rail freight and passenger transport services.[21]

The developments in these sectors reflect the Commission's increasing concern for the compliance of NRAs with good governance principles, modeled after the EU initiatives in the domain of electronic communications.[22] Further studies could explore the national reception of these new procedural mandates to demonstrate commonalities or differences from what this book has demonstrated in the case of electronic communications. The brief overview of the path followed in these additional sectors offers preliminary indications that these trends may be generalizable across several network industries at the EU level, which is consistent with research on the Europeanization of other policy domains.[23] In any case, since the electronic communications sector set the trend, developments in other policy areas highlight the importance of an in-depth study of the original model which itself is new.

II. The limits of convergence: The role of the EU in maintaining and expanding the "democratic surplus"

Part I told a story of convergence between the member states as a result of the domestic implementation of common EU law mandates. Nonetheless, the cross-national variations discussed in the case studies add important qualifications to this main narrative. Therefore, they invite us to also consider whether further EU-driven convergence across European countries may be desirable. In fact, chapter 2 showed that as European regulatory integration proceeded in the electronic communications sector, subsequent generations of directives included additional requirements. The goal of these new EU provisions was to promote vertical and horizontal coordination between the center and the periphery as well as among the NRAs, and thus encourage further convergence. There is, however, the risk of too much convergence. Section A explores the limits of this notion by discussing proposals to concentrate both the main regulatory framework and its implementation to the center through the creation of a European telecommunications regulatory agency. Section B outlines a different proposal, one that respects but also taps into the institutional autonomy of the member states. The proposed scheme maintains the decentralized EU regulatory regime and activates the feedback loops created by this decentralized structure, which chapter 2 presented in some detail. Furthermore, it acknowledges that the EU can and should self-consciously engage in supporting democratic administrative governance at the national level.

A. Centralizing regulation *and* implementation: Should this be the path to the future?

The idea of establishing an EU-level telecommunications regulator to prevent widely divergent implementation of the EU legislation at the member-state level was considered at multiple points in the course of the evolution of the EU regulatory framework. It was rejected every time, mainly on substantive and subsidiarity grounds. This section will demonstrate that rejecting this type of centralization would be the correct decision on democratic accountability grounds as well—not only at the time of the adoption of the second and third-generation EU directives but also when considering future reforms.

Before examining why a centralized EU agency would be an example of too much convergence to the detriment of stakeholder participation, we should set up the historical backdrop of these proposals. Since the mid-1990s, the Commission had considered the idea of establishing an EU-level agency (hereafter called "European Regulatory Authority") to "ensure even and effective implementation" of EU legislation. The European Parliament had also repeatedly called for "a Euro-telecoms authority or committee to prevent fifteen differing regulatory areas developing."[24] In the course of reviewing the regulatory framework and considering reforms for the time after the liberalization process would have been completed, and also as a result of a directive requirement, the European Commission commissioned two studies on this issue.[25] The purpose of these reports was to examine the level of support within the telecommunications sector for the creation of a European Regulatory Authority and the added value of this type of centralization. Neither report made a strong case in favor of a centralized agency. The 1997 study found some degree of support for a European Regulatory Authority and noted that this might grow after 1998 when practical problems might show the limits of the current framework. It observed, however, that the technical debate surrounding the creation of such a centralized agency was still very much in its infancy and that consciousness of its possible relevance varied widely. Interestingly, the report found, in particular, that national regulators and policymakers were mostly against the creation of a new European regulatory body, arguing that it would create a new layer of regulatory bureaucracy and that, if this body were given any real powers at the expense of the NRAs, it would also contravene the principle of subsidiarity. Principal telecoms operators were split in their responses, while the vast majority of competitors, users and other interviewees considered that some advantages might accrue in the creation of a new body dealing with aspects of telecommunications regulation at the EU level.[26] The 1999 study reached an even clearer conclusion that "[t]he case for a radical departure in setting up a 'hard' independent EU regulator [had] not been made out," yet a requirement for continued EU involvement was "firmly established."[27]

Consequently, the Commission noted in its 1999 Communications Review that it was not "persuaded that a regulatory body at Community level would currently add sufficient value to justify the likely costs,"[28] and decided not to pursue the idea further. Nonetheless, the Commission highlighted the "urgent" need to improve cooperation between itself and the national regulators. It therefore proposed the creation of the Communications Committee (COCOM) and the High Level Communications Group (HLCG). The former would replace two existing committees (the ONP and the Licensing committees), and the latter would be composed of the Commission and the NRAs.[29] Summarizing the results of the public consultation on the 1999 Communications Review, the Commission noted the broad support for its proposal to build on current regulatory structures,

rather than to establish a European Regulatory Authority. It added that regulators were broadly in favor of replacing the current committees with the COCOM
but were more skeptical about the HLCG. Some questioned the need for such
a group, arguing that the current Independent Regulators Group (IRG) would
be capable of carrying out the tasks set for the HLCG.[30] Notwithstanding these
concerns, the Commission went ahead with the legislative proposal to set up
the HLCG.[31] The Council, however, did not agree to the establishment of the
HLCG,[32] and this group was ultimately not included in the Framework Directive
(2002/21/EC).

Nonetheless, another structure with similar functions, the European
Regulators Group (ERG), was created as a part of the 2002 reforms.[33] As chapter 2
described, the role of the ERG was to "advise and assist the Commission in consolidating the internal market for electronic communications networks and
services" and to "provide an interface between national regulatory authorities
and the Commission in such a way as to contribute to the development of the
internal market" (Article 3). It was composed of the heads of each NRA or their
representatives. The Commission was represented "at an appropriate level" and
provided the secretariat to the Group (Article 4). The ERG, however, could not
impose any binding obligations on the NRAs. Moreover, the NRAs continued
to meet regularly within the IRG, which—unlike the ERG—afforded them the
opportunity to discuss without the Commission being present.[34]

The Eurostrategies/Cullen International 1999 Study had concluded by noting that "[t]he possibility for role of an EU Regulator is not a closed issue."[35]
And indeed it was not; the Commission reopened the question when it was considering a third generation of electronic communications directives. In a 2006
speech, Viviane Reding, the Information Society and Media Commissioner at
the time, put this idea forward in unequivocal terms:

> For me it is clear that the most effective and least bureaucratic way to
> achieve a real level playing field for telecom operators across the EU
> would be to replace the present game of "ping pong" between national
> regulators and the European Commission by an independent European
> telecom authority that would work together with national regulators in
> a system similar to the European System of Central Banks.[36]

In November 2007 the Commission presented its proposals to amend the
2002 regulatory framework. These were complemented by the proposal for
a Regulation creating a new European Electronic Communications Market
Authority (EECMA).[37] Another piece of the push for centralization was the proposal to grant the Commission veto power over remedies that NRAs intended to
adopt. The Commission also issued an accompanying Communication explaining its proposals and summarizing the results of a two-phase public consultation

on the review of the regulatory framework that it had conducted in 2005-2006. The Communication spelled out the stakes of establishing the EECMA and furthering centralization:

> Under the present set of rules, NRAs exercise considerable discretion in implementing the regulatory framework but their perspective has remained largely confined to national borders, despite the efforts made to improve coordination via the European Regulators Group . . . . This has led to regulatory inconsistency and distortions of competition, hindering the development of a single European market . . . . Many stakeholders had major concerns about the differences that exist in the way the current framework is implemented at national level. . . . Some called for more regulation at EU level. Industry in particular, but consumer associations as well, deplored the continued lack of a single market and a level playing field for businesses and users in the electronic communications sector . . . . While Member States had reservations about "ceding powers" to the Commission, several industry groups (new entrants, but also some incumbents) either favoured an institutional reform of the ERG and/or asked for a stronger role for the Commission in order to avoid a "lowest common denominator" approach, seen by some as inherent in a regulatory mechanism that essentially relies on consensus among 27 NRAs.[38]

The outcome of the 2007 reform process was that the Commission can delay the adoption of a NRA decision on remedies for three months but, crucially and contrary to the original legislative proposal, it may not veto the draft measure.[39] The Commission's proposal for the EECMA was also ultimately rejected. Instead, the Body of European Regulators for Electronic Communications (BEREC) was established to "replace the ERG and act as an exclusive forum for cooperation among NRAs, and between NRAs and the Commission."[40] Even though "BEREC has more bite" than the ERG, the Commission was "once again denied a full-fledged EU agency."[41] Its founding regulation expressly recognizes that BEREC "should neither be a Community agency nor have legal personality."[42] According to a similar description, BEREC "is not a regulatory authority in any sense; [it] has no decision-making powers per se, but simply exercises an advisory function."[43] Nina Boeger and Joseph Corkin have offered an interesting and detailed chronicle of the "protracted and at times turbulent legislative process" that resulted in watering down the Commission's original proposal in the final 2009 amendments: the conventional intergovernmental account of a "turf war" between the member states and the Commission "overlooks the critical influence" of NRAs and their networks, the IRG and the ERG, over the process. More specifically, although it was the member states in Council and members of the

European Parliament who "had to form coalitions in order to block controversial aspects of the Commission's proposed reforms, their primary advisers (particularly in Council) were NRAs."[44]

Mapping the main actors in this reform process does not alter the fact that the underlying struggle was mainly over the principle of subsidiarity; in particular, the appropriate level at which market regulation should occur in the telecommunications sector. What was absent from that debate, however, was a discussion of the implications for democratic accountability if a strong form of institutional centralization was adopted. Understandably and in its usual fashion, the Commission emphasized the market integration rationale of its proposals. It highlighted how regulatory inconsistency hinders "the development of a single European market in which undertakings can operate seamlessly across borders and where private and business consumers can profit from the availability of comparable communications services independently of geographic location."[45] However, even the European Parliament, an institution that we would expect to focus more on stakeholder engagement, did not add this dimension to the discussion. For instance, the Opinion of the Committee on Economic and Monetary Affairs read in pertinent part: "The European Electronic Communications Market Authority should be substituted by the Network of National Regulatory Authorities. The [EECMA] creates a large bureaucracy, counters the principle of subsidiarity, contradicts the long-term goal to replace ex-ante regulation by competition law and in addition shows a lack of independence."[46] Factoring in public participation would suggest that having averted further centralization of the EU regulatory structure in the direction advocated by the Commission is good news.

This discussion, however, does not belong only to the past. Indeed, as history suggests, it is likely[47] that the idea of a European Regulatory Authority will reemerge in the context of a future, fourth-generation, EU regulatory package. In fact, as discussed in chapter 2, the 2016 Commission proposal for a new European Electronic Communications Code seeks to enhance the role of BEREC by introducing a "double-lock" system for national draft remedies and by giving BEREC the power to issue binding decisions identifying transnational markets.[48] The proposal falls short of establishing a European regulator[49] and it may be further watered down during the EU legislative process. However, it brings to the fore the general point that, from the perspective of stakeholder participation, establishing a full-fledged European Regulatory Authority would not be a wise idea at this stage. As a preliminary matter, we assume for the purposes of this discussion that a new centralized EU agency would employ baseline participatory processes similar to those that EU law currently imposes on NRAs. This is a reasonable assumption: it was noted in chapter 1 that the Commission is moving in the direction of recognizing a right of public participation in European governance. Other EU agencies, such as the European Food Safety Authority, the European Chemicals Agency, and the European Medicines Agency, regularly launch public consultations. More importantly, BEREC, the closest existing approximation to a future "hard" EU regulator for electronic communications, also conducts public consultations in compliance with Article 17 of its founding Regulation.[50] In other words, in plausibly assuming that the same type of participatory mandates would apply to both the national and the EU levels, we establish that any differences in participation would not be a function of divergent procedural requirements.

Indeed, the reasons for the loss in stakeholder engagement in the event of a transition to a European Regulatory Authority would not be legal; they would be structural and sociological. Chapter 2 argued that one of the benefits of decentralization is that moving the exercise of regulatory power closer to those affected by it may facilitate participation. By contrast, aggregating all decision-making at the center can create organizational challenges that local civil society groups and individuals may experience even more acutely. The EU is a fitting illustration of this difficulty, confirmed by both the literature on European interest groups and my own interviews with national stakeholders in the telecommunications sector.

More specifically, the literature on EU lobbying indicates that access to the Commission, despite the latter's attempts at wider consultation and public interest group funding, continues to be biased toward business interests; the insider status and resource advantage of business has led several scholars to call EU interest politics an "elite pluralist environment."[51] The strong form of "elite pluralism" was challenged in another study, which found that while large firms have better access to the EU Council, they do not have more contact with Commission officials and the parliamentary committees than EU associations. Hence, this study contends, the "differences between firms and EU associations are less pronounced" than the elite pluralism story might suggest.[52] Even so, and importantly for our discussion, the same account acknowledges that "EU interest intermediation displays important imbalances: in these processes, technical expertise and the economic clout of large firms and the ability of Eurogroups to represent the Europe-wide interests of their members matter more to EU policymakers *than the representation of domestic encompassing interests by national associations*."[53] I shall return to the significance of this weak role of national associations shortly.

Further scholarship in this area has similarly argued that a shift of authority from the national to the supranational level is unlikely to empower the weak.[54] As has been correctly noted, organizing across borders entails transaction costs; the "EU multi-level system raises the need for financial, social and societal resources" on the part of less affluent actors. In the absence of access regulation for interest groups, this may "reinforce a situation in which groups possessing financial and social resources are privileged whereas the voices of small interest groups, be they general interest or small business groups, are not heard quite as loudly in the consultation process."[55] Nonetheless, even if national actors acquired increased resources to Europeanize their strategies, this would not automatically translate into a higher degree of engagement at the EU level. One account has suggested that a simple "resource-based perspective" overlooks the structural connections or ties of domestic groups to their environment, and the possibility that these actors may refrain from going beyond the national level "because they are in need of, identify with or are loyal to their local or domestic resource suppliers."[56]

This brings us to the deeper issue underlying my skepticism toward a centralized EU telecommunications agency—that is, the structural configuration of interest groups in the context of a multi-level regulatory architecture that may end up disempowering domestic stakeholders (especially the weaker ones). More specifically, the literature suggests that at the EU level the "federated format," i.e., associations of national associations, predominates throughout all interest categories, and the Commission tends to favor European (con)federations over national organizations.[57] I noted earlier that EU business associations enjoy relatively privileged access to EU institutions. The concern here, however, is not related to the nature of the specific interests that these EU groupings represent (industry, consumers, etc.) but rather their general organizational characteristics, and the challenges the latter pose to the participation of domestic actors at the EU level. The effective representation of national stakeholders at the supranational level presupposes well-functioning communication between the EU-level association and the member organizations "all the way down to the grassroots."[58] Nevertheless, an easy flow of information and communication is difficult to achieve precisely because of the multi-level structure of European organizations. This may be because several of these groups are still in the process of "consolidating their organizational structures." The same study also suggests that market-related actors have "a long history of dealing with the EU and their predominantly hierarchical structure makes communication across levels easier" compared to the complexity of NGO confederations.[59] This highlights the structural impediment inherent in having an EU-level federation represent associations in twenty-eight member states. Therefore, my concerns persist irrespective of recent trends that show a growth of EU citizen interests organizations relative to the entire constituency of EU groups.[60]

These observations map well onto the case study in this book and the constellation of domestic actors in the telecommunications sector. Consistently with the general literature discussed above, we find that large firms have the organizational and resource capacity to participate directly in policymaking at the EU level. For instance, the BT group has a European Affairs office that is responsible for BT's relationships with the EU institutions. Nonetheless, even strong domestic actors, such as OTE, the former incumbent operator in Greece, acknowledged in interviews the difficulty of engaging on all issues at the EU level. Instead, they participate directly in a limited number of EU public consultations that affect them to a great extent. Furthermore, they normally attempt to have their voice heard by providing input on and trying to influence the common positions of the larger consortia that are active in Brussels and to which they belong.[61] In OTE's case, these are the Deutsche Telekom group (of which OTE is a subsidiary) that operates in fifty countries around the world, as well as the European Telecommunications Network Operators (ETNO), the peak organization for operators in Europe.[62] There are parallels on the NGO side as well. Visible consumer groups in France, Greece, and the United Kingdom referred in interviews to the need to be selective in terms of the public consultations in which they participate at both the national and the EU levels, primarily due to resource constraints. Therefore, they often try to feed into the position papers of BEUC, the European Consumers' Organization.[63]

In other words, national actors from both sides of the table recognize that participating through EU (con)federations may be the most effective way to get their message across at the EU level. However, this raises the inner-organizational challenge discussed earlier. That is, national firms and associations have a greater likelihood of success if the EU-level association accepts their point of view. Their message, however, may be diluted in the process of reaching a common position within an EU group that brings together many members from different countries with interests that may not coalesce.[64] If even the voices of traditional (and often relatively strong) domestic actors run the risk of being lost in the noise within pan-European groups, one can imagine the additional challenges facing smaller national civil society groups and individuals when they seek a seat at the table.

In conclusion, at this stage of development of EU interest groups, the aggregation of regulatory decision-making in the hands of a "hard" EU telecoms regulator would aggravate the challenge of equal representation and ultimately result in losses in democratic accountability. Therefore, the wisest policy choice at this point would be to keep the decentralized institutional structure in place. This is not to say that no changes are needed in a future reform of the EU regulatory framework or the way in which the system currently operates. In fact, Section B outlines a proposal that harnesses the accountability benefits of the EU regulatory architecture in a more conscious way.

B. If it ain't broke, don't fix it (but tweak it): Reinforcing the accountability-enhancing effect of EU law

The previous three chapters focused on the impact of institutional and procedural EU provisions on national administrative governance against the backdrop of the public law history and culture as well as the traditional state-society relations in France, Greece, and the United Kingdom. These case studies documented the accountability-enhancing effect of EU mandates being "downloaded" and implemented at the national level. In closing the inquiry, it is submitted here that the impact of EU law on domestic administrative governance should not be viewed only as a one-way street. This would ignore the dynamic interactions between the member states and the European Union.[65] Instead, my proposed account "closes the circuit" as depicted in Figure 6.1.

The bulk of the previous analysis explained the upper right part of Figure 6.1 (domestic transposition of EU mandates), described as "downloading." The missing piece was the "uploading" that may occur within the decentralized EU regulatory regime. The first elements of this "uploading hypothesis" were spelled out in chapter 2. More specifically, my claim was that EU law (especially the second-generation directives) provides for what was termed the "EU floor"—namely, baseline accountability mechanisms operating at the member-state level. This means that every member state is free to experiment with accountability tools that would further participation, provided that it meets the minimum EU requirements. This diversity may, in turn, result in the emergence of innovative governance models in certain member states. These could then feed back into (or, according to Figure 6.1, be uploaded onto) the EU level in a bottom-up

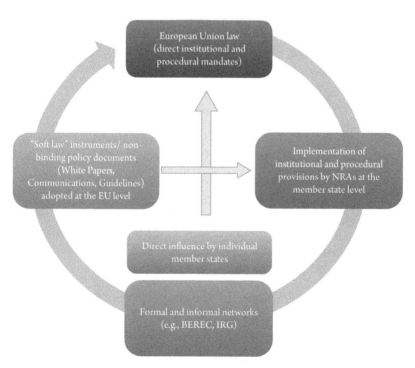

Figure 6.1 "Closing the circuit": Feedback loops in the decentralized EU regime

fashion, potentially via NRA networks; subsequently, they could spread to or be downloaded in the rest of the EU members.

Therefore, the pluralism generated by the decentralized EU regime, and the opportunities for experimentation and innovation deriving therefrom, may develop a jurisgenerative function; this advocates in favor of the existing regulatory architecture. Indeed, the feedback loops I describe did operate when it came to the evolution of EU provisions on NRA independence. It was explained in chapter 2 that the third-generation regulatory package (specifically, Directive 2009/140/EC) enhanced the political independence strand of the EU institutional requirements.[66] These reforms built on the experience from NRA operations and the challenges to independence posed by specific examples in certain member states (e.g., without cause removals of NRA officials). Hence, from this perspective, Figure 6.1 may actually represent a descriptive account. By contrast, we did not witness a similar evolution in the case of participatory requirements. The 2009 reforms did not alter the national public consultation mandates of the 2002 regulatory framework. This should not preclude the possibility that the system portrayed in Figure 6.1 is applicable to regulatory processes as well. It suggests only that what follows is a normative account at this stage. My proposal to tweak, not fix, the existing system taps into the member states as repositories of useful knowledge on administrative governance. Furthermore, it activates the feedback loops of the decentralized EU structure—only this time in the service of developing and diffusing novel accountability processes. I will explore this idea by addressing three questions: First, what does innovation mean in the context of administrative accountability in the case studies? Second, how should innovative practices spread? Third, what role should the EU play in encouraging good administrative governance?

As to the first question, we saw that Article 6 of the Framework Directive imposed a specific set of obligations on NRAs, i.e., obligations to: give interested parties the opportunity to comment on draft measures within a reasonable period; publish their national consultation procedures; ensure the establishment of a single information point through which all current consultations can be accessed; make publicly available the results of the consultation procedure subject to business confidentiality. The previous three chapters demonstrated how the regulators in France, Greece, and the United Kingdom have built on these requirements. For instance, all three agencies often publish syntheses that group together and summarize the responses to public consultations. Nonetheless, the NRAs have not followed this practice with the same degree of consistency— Ofcom, for example, would score better on this metric. Notwithstanding these gaps, the publication of such overviews at the end of the consultation procedure provides useful insights on the authorities' decision-making processes and enhances reason giving.

Another practice consistent with the ideal of reasoned administration is the use of multiple (commonly two) rounds of consultation. The regulators in both France and the UK have on several occasions, usually involving significant issues, resorted to iterated consultations. The first phase of the consultation generally invites public input on broader questions or initial thoughts of the agencies, while the final stage pertains more narrowly to the draft measure itself. A related deliberation-enhancing method that we encountered in the British case study was the "comment-on-comments" exercise. This was a practice that Oftel had often followed until 2001, whereby it would set aside a formal 14-day period for respondents to comment on the views expressed by others during the first consultation round. In other words, the agency would not publish separate consultative documents, which is the case in the French and UK multi-phased consultation examples described earlier. Besides these methods, NRAs have experimented with other tools to provide information and solicit feedback from the public. For instance, chapter 3 described online chat sessions that the ARCEP has held.

The member states have also been sites of institutional experimentation and innovation. In particular, the UK showcases two such examples. First, the position of the consultation champion. As discussed in further detail in chapter 5, an Ofcom official is in charge of ensuring that the regulator follow its own guidelines and reach out to the largest number of people and organizations interested in its decisions. Ofcom's consultation champion is also the main person that stakeholders can contact with views on the way the agency runs public consultations. The second institutional novelty is the creation of the Competition Appeal Tribunal, namely, the "specialist regulatory court" with cross-disciplinary expertise in law, economics, business and accountancy that decides many appeals against Ofcom's decisions. The previous chapter elaborated on the role of this body and its implications for regulatory governance.

Even if one is not inclined to describe all the above as path-breaking institutional and procedural innovations, the country cases show that NRAs did build on the momentum generated by the EU's minimum requirements, thus enhancing open access, transparency, reason giving, and judicial review. Having demonstrated that member states can display a degree of institutional and procedural creativity, we can now turn to the second question, the modalities of diffusion of new regulatory processes.

There are different potential channels through which new accountability mechanisms can travel across borders or be uploaded onto the EU level. These avenues are depicted in Figure 6.1 above. For instance, novel procedures implemented by a member state could be picked up by networks of NRAs, notably the IRG or BEREC, which could then advise the Commission to incorporate them either in a "soft law" document (e.g., a White Paper) or directly in a "hard law" instrument (most likely, a directive). Alternatively, various intermediate stages may be bypassed if, for example, certain member states exert direct influence on EU institutions,[67] or the Commission develops new initiatives based on member-state experience albeit without the mediation of NRA networks.

The question then is: what is the appropriate form of policy diffusion for each new type of regulatory processes? We assume that direct copying from one state to another does not pose particular difficulties as individual countries can decide which models to adopt provided that this would not contravene EU law provisions. The more challenging question concerns the appropriate level at which new requirements can be included in EU documents so that they can then be downloaded back to the member states. The answer to this question will vary depending on the specific institutional or procedural innovation at stake. Some general guiding principles, however, could be the following: as a default rule, the EU should respect the institutional and procedural autonomy of the member states and impose hard law requirements only when member-state experience indicates that the process to be formalized at the EU level has been effective and already widely implemented, thus its formalization would cause minimal disruption. Imposing rigid binding rules without much experience from widespread prior application across many states might run the risk of no or *pro forma* implementation. Moreover, the premature imposition of very detailed strict mandates of general applicability would neutralize the useful operation of states as sites of experimentation with regulatory processes. This, in turn, suggests that the threshold for including new processes in soft law documents should be lower, as this alternative promotes experimentation at the EU level while still allowing for national variation and the consideration of local particularities. This approach is another manifestation of a broader point—namely, the importance of considering the conditions of implementation of EU law through regulatory networks. These conditions determine, as has become apparent through the case studies, how common EU mandates will be translated into the diverse member states. Importantly in this context, however, they also offer useful insights into how EU policy reform can be empirically grounded in a way that harnesses these conditions of implementation.

Applying these principles to specific cases would suggest the following results: The time is ripe for the inclusion of an explicit mandate in a fourth-generation directive requiring NRAs to issue a synthesis at the end of every public consultation. This would facilitate the consistent cross-national implementation of a practice that is already, as the three country cases have shown, widespread and beneficial. This requirement would promote the justification of administrative policymaking but would not be exactly the same as the express introduction of a general reason-giving requirement; as we saw, none of the three countries impose the latter for administrative rulemaking. Whether the recommended EU mandate for the publication of a consultation overview might develop in practice into a full-blown reason-giving requirement would hinge on how national institutions, especially courts, would respond to it. However, this is not something that the EU would dictate; rather, it would be the result of the operation of each domestic public law system in conformity with member-state institutional autonomy.

The second example of a provision that would be recommended for a future EU legislative reform would read: "Member states shall ensure that national regulatory authorities designate a member responsible for monitoring the correct implementation of the consultation and transparency mechanisms, and for receiving comments from interested parties on the national regulatory authorities' decision-making processes." Although the position of a "consultation champion" has not been widely adopted by the member states, at least not officially, the UK case study suggests that the proposed provision would contribute both to a more effective and consistent enforcement of existing participatory requirements as well as to the development of better practices. Furthermore, the establishment of such a position would be minimally disruptive, for the NRA staff member in charge of this function could also have further duties, as is the case in the UK.

My proposal with respect to multi-phased public consultations would be different. This should be kept at a soft law level. For instance, a Commission White Paper could "encourage" NRAs to consult throughout the policy chain and as early as possible. The incorporation of this language in a non-binding policy document would promote a practice for which several (but not all) domestic stakeholders have expressed some support. At the same time, it would not deprive NRAs of the flexibility to decide whether the importance of the issue at stake, national stakeholder preferences, and local market conditions warrant multiple rounds of public consultation.

By contrast, at this point it would be advisable for the EU not to interfere in the appeals process in the direction of mandating a specialist regulatory court akin to the Competition Appeal Tribunal in the UK. The adoption of any language to this effect, even in a soft law document, would have implications for both the judicial and the administrative structures of the European countries; it would therefore be significantly intrusive from the standpoint of member-state procedural and institutional autonomy. The provision for a specialist appellate body possessing appropriate technical expertise and sitting outside the ordinary court structure (even if ultimately reviewed by generalist courts) might translate into higher-quality review of regulatory decisions. However, the conclusion of chapter 5 also pointed to the flipside of this: intensive expert review on both procedural and substantive grounds may introduce further delay in the administrative process, and thus result in what I termed as "ossification squared." As chapter 2 noted, the Commission is already (and has been for several years) concerned with delays associated with the appeal process in several countries. The trade-offs between effective appellate review, on the one hand, and efficient and timely administrative action, on the other, are complicated. Consequently, the EU should abstain from stepping in and dictating, or encouraging, specific institutional choices before more satisfactory answers to these complicated questions have been worked out domestically.

The last of our three questions raises the issue of the role that EU bodies could and should play in encouraging the development and diffusion of good administrative governance domestically. Both this chapter and chapter 2 alluded to the function that BEREC can perform in this regard. This EU network constitutes an excellent forum in which NRA officials could exchange views not only on substantive regulatory interventions but also on good governance practices, and therefore learn from each other and influence the further development of the EU regulatory framework. As chapter 2 maintained, reputational competition among NRAs can have a procedural component as well, and NRA networks are fertile sites for this to play out. This further recalls the discussion regarding the conditions that may promote institutional and procedural experimentation and innovation in the context of the EU decentralized regime. Chapter 2 described the idea of "policy evangelism," whereby national officials may experiment with novel accountability practices because they wish to see them spread or because innovation may enhance their social status among their peers.

Interestingly, the early UK model of the Director General of Telecommunications (DGT) may fit that description. Chapter 5 explained that the United Kingdom was at the forefront of the development of regulatory structures to implement the post-liberalization regime. This, in turn, resulted in other national governments and agencies as well as the Commission seeking to draw on the knowledge and experience that the British regulator had gained as an international pioneer in the field.[68] Don Cruickshank in particular, the third DGT and a salient public figure, was personally credited with the development of accountability mechanisms, and especially the use of public consultations. In other words, it was easier for individual DGTs (supported by Oftel) to develop personal policy agendas, which notably included regulatory processes as well, and reap the reputational benefits of innovation both domestically and across borders. Nevertheless, the "policy evangelism story" needs to take account of current cross-national institutional realities, namely, the fact that NRAs now generally follow the regulatory commission model. This model presents distinct advantages (outlined in the discussion of "the cult of the individual regulator" in chapter 5); however, it also creates additional obstacles for the reputational competition account since the establishment of regulatory boards means that any reputational benefits are now dispersed.

The diminished incentives for innovation that this situation may create should, in turn, underscore the role that the Commission could play in stepping up and fostering procedural competition and innovation. Even though my interviews with NRA officials suggested that regulatory processes are normally not high on the agenda of meetings with other NRAs and the Commission, the latter could create incentives for experimentation with accountability tools by rewarding innovation. These rewards should not be monetary[69] but should be structured in a way that sustains an informal reputational competition among NRAs. For instance, the Commission could raise regulatory governance issues in meetings with NRAs (including in the context of BEREC) or present a "reasoned request" to BEREC to prepare a report on these topics. Furthermore, the Commission can publicly highlight innovative experiments carried out by specific NRAs and feature those in conferences.

This discussion and the earlier proposals for amendments to the EU regulatory framework and soft law documents raise a broader and critical point. The EU, primarily the Commission, should be more consciously and actively involved in the process of encouraging administrative democracy at the member-state level. The support for good administrative governance should not only be a side effect to the promotion of the internal market, which, chapter 2 suggested, may have been the key motivational force behind the 2002 regulatory package. Instead, administrative accountability should be a primary goal, one that is acknowledged and thought through during every opportunity for reform at the EU level. My reform proposals point in this direction, but the current system affords such opportunities as well. For example, when Commission officials visit the member states and convene NRA officials and stakeholders, as interviews indicate is the case, they should consider adding regulatory governance to the agenda of these conversations. They should also solicit input from domestic actors on the current operation of participatory processes and whether stakeholders believe that their voices are heard in the regulatory process. Article 25 of the Framework Directive, which is still in effect, provides that the "Commission shall periodically review the functioning of this Directive and report to the European Parliament and to the Council." These progress reports should include a clear section on administrative governance and track the development of national accountability processes.

In conclusion, Part II put forth a set of proposals that can attain the best of both worlds. On the one hand, they keep the decentralized EU institutional architecture in place and activate the feedback loops illustrated in Figure 6.1. On the other hand, they allow for greater procedural harmonization by incrementally incorporating further EU-level requirements that do not, however, infringe impermissibly on member-state institutional autonomy because they stem from long experience at the national level. In other words, in the proposed scheme, now that the channels for public participation have been opened and formalized, the EU does not further *mandate* administrative democracy but does not stay inactive either. Instead, it taps into the member states' institutional and procedural creativity (which in many cases the EU itself had stimulated originally by means of baseline procedural requirements) and enlists them as partners in the joint enterprise of sustaining and increasing the democratic surplus in regulatory governance. In the best of EU traditions, both national and EU institutions collaborate not only toward the goal of market integration but that of democratic administrative integration as well.

Notes

1. *Cf.* VIVIEN SCHMIDT, DEMOCRACY IN EUROPE. THE EU AND NATIONAL POLITIES 110 (2006) (concluding that "[a]daptation to EU policymaking processes has been particularly difficult for simple polities with statist policymaking processes, and arguably harder for France than Britain").

2. *Supra*, chapters 3 and 4.

3. MARK THATCHER, THE POLITICS OF TELECOMMUNICATIONS: NATIONAL INSTITUTIONS, CONVERGENCE, AND CHANGE IN BRITAIN AND FRANCE 319 (1999).

4. R. DANIEL KELEMEN, EUROLEGALISM: THE TRANSFORMATION OF LAW AND REGULATION IN THE EUROPEAN UNION 243 (2011) (inviting future studies that will explain the conditions under which and the extent to which the adversarial mode of governance takes root).

5. In other cases, interviews buttressed and contextualized information that was available from content analysis of regulatory agency documentation or the jurisprudence of courts and appellate bodies. Furthermore, interviews have enriched other aspects of the book, including, among others, discussions of the role of consultative committees and bilateral meetings between stakeholders and regulators as potentially antagonistic or complementary to public consultations, the explanation of the breakdown of actors participating in consultation exercises, and deficiencies in these participatory processes.

6. Examining telecommunications in Britain and France, Mark Thatcher described a "pattern of enduring arrangements subject to rare but rapid and substantial alteration [that] matches a model of 'punctuated equilibrium' rather than institutional reform taking place in a gradual, piecemeal manner" (THATCHER, *supra* note 3, at 314). He also added an important qualification to the position that national institutions are resistant to change and convergence by arguing that "resistance can be overcome if countries become closely interlinked through ideas, supranational institutions, and market integration" as suggested by the "case of British and French telecommunications during the 1990s" (*id.* at 319). Having explored three cases over the course of several decades with an emphasis on administrative accountability, my conclusion is that EU law set the defining points on this "punctuated equilibrium."

7. *See, e.g.*, András Sajó, *The Impacts of EU Accession on Post-communist Constitutionalism*, 45 ACTA JURIDICA HUNGARICA 193 (2004); Zdeněk Kühn and Michal Bobek, *What about that 'Incoming Tide'? The Application of EU Law in Czech Republic*, *in* THE APPLICATION OF EU LAW IN THE NEW MEMBER STATES—BRAVE NEW WORLD 325 (Adam Lazowski ed., 2010).

8. *See, e.g.*, Michal Bobek, *Thou Shalt Have Two Masters: The Application of European Law by Administrative Authorities in the New Member States*, 1 REVIEW OF EUROPEAN ADMINISTRATIVE LAW 51 (2008).

9. *See* Cristina Elena Parau, *Impaling Dracula: How EU Accession Empowered Civil Society in Romania*, 32 WEST EUROPEAN POLITICS 119 (2009).

10. Francesca Bignami, *Three generations of participation rights before the European Commission*, 68 LAW AND CONTEMP. PROBS. 61, 79 (2004).

11. *See* Kenneth Dyson, *West Germany: The Search for a Rationalist Consensus*, *in* POLICY STYLES IN WESTERN EUROPE 17, 18, 24 (Jeremy Richardson ed., 1982).

12. SUSAN ROSE-ACKERMAN, CONTROLLING ENVIRONMENTAL POLICY. THE LIMITS OF PUBLIC LAW IN GERMANY AND THE UNITED STATES 87 (1995).

13. SUSAN ROSE-ACKERMAN, STEFANIE EGIDY & JAMES FOWKES, DUE PROCESS OF LAWMAKING 161–215 (2015).

14. Federal Network Agency for Electricity, Gas, Telecommunications, Post and Railway, Annual Report 2007, p. 20.

15. Telekommunikationsgesetz vom 22. Juni 2004 (BGBl. I S. 1190), §12.
16. *See* DORIT RUBINSTEIN REISS, REGULATORY ACCOUNTABILITY: TELECOMMUNICATIONS AND ELECTRICITY AGENCIES IN THE UK, FRANCE AND SWEDEN 38 (2007) (Doctoral dissertation, UC Berkeley, on file with author).
17. *See* Damien Geradin & Nicolas Petit, *The Development of Agencies at EU and National Levels: Conceptual Analysis and Proposals for Reform*, 01/04 JEAN MONNET WORKING PAPER 1, 29–30 (2004). For the electricity sector, see Directive 96/92/EC (first generation) and Directive 2003/54/EC (second generation). For the natural gas sector, see Directive 98/30/EC (first generation) and Directive 2003/55/EC (second generation).
18. For the electricity sector, see Directive 2009/72/EC of 13 July 2009 concerning common rules for the internal market in electricity and repealing Directive 2003/54/EC, Articles 37(2) and 22(4). For the natural gas sector, see Directive 2009/73/EC of 13 July 2009 concerning common rules for the internal market in natural gas and repealing Directive 2003/55/EC, Articles 41(2) and 22(4).
19. See Directives 2001/12/EC, 2001/13/EC.
20. Directive 2004/49/EC of 29 April 2004 on safety on the Community's railways and amending Council Directive 95/18/EC on the licensing of railway undertakings and Directive 2001/14/EC on the allocation of railway infrastructure capacity and the levying of charges for the use of railway infrastructure and safety certification, Article 17(1) ("Decision-making principles") provides that "[t]he safety authority shall carry out its tasks in an open, non-discriminatory and transparent way. In particular it shall allow all parties to be heard and give reasons for its decisions. . . . In the process of developing the national regulatory framework, the safety authority shall consult all persons involved and interested parties, including infrastructure managers, railway undertakings, manufacturers and maintenance providers, users and staff representatives."
21. Directive 2012.34/EU of the European Parliament and of the Council of 21 November 2012 establishing a single European railway area (recast), Article 56(7) ("The regulatory body shall, regularly and, in any case, at least every two years, consult representatives of users of the rail freight and passenger transport services, to take into account their views on the rail market").
22. *Cf.* Geradin and Petit, *supra* note 17, at 29 (welcoming this evolution in the field of rail).
23. *See* KELEMEN, *supra* note 4, at 243–44.
24. Mark Thatcher, *The Commission and national governments as partners: EC regulatory expansion in telecommunications 1979–2000*, 8 JOURNAL OF EUROPEAN PUBLIC POLICY 558, 571 (2001) (with citations to the press of that time).
25. See Directive 97/51/EC of the European Parliament and of the Council of 6 October 1997 amending Council Directives 90/387/EEC and 92/44/EEC for the purpose of adaptation to a competitive environment in telecommunications, OJ L 295/23, 29 October 1997, Article 8: "The Commission shall examine and report to the European Parliament and to the Council on the functioning of this Directive, on the first occasion no later than 31 December 1999 . . . . The Commission shall also investigate in the report the added value of the setting up of a European Regulatory Authority to carry out those tasks which would prove to be better undertaken at Community level." See NERA & Denton Hall, Issues Associated with the Creation of a European Regulatory Authority for Telecommunications—Report for the European Commission (DG XIII) (April 1997) ["NERA/Denton Hall 1997 Study"]; Eurostrategies & Cullen International, Executive Summary on the Possible Added Value of European Regulatory Authority for Telecommunications—Prepared for the European Commission (October 1999) ["Eurostrategies/Cullen International 1999 Study"].
26. NERA/Denton Hall 1997 Study, *supra* note 25, at 117, 21–22.
27. Eurostrategies/Cullen International 1999 Study, *supra* note 25, at 46.
28. Communication from the Commission to the Council, the European Parliament, the Economic and Social Committee and the Committee of the Regions of 10 November 1999. Towards a new framework for Electronic Communications infrastructure and associated services—The 1999 Communications Review, COM(1999) 539 final, 10 November 1999, at x.

29. *Id.* at 56.

30. *See* Communication from the Commission, The results of the public consultation on the 1999 Communications Review and Orientations for the new Regulatory Framework, COM(2000) 239 final, 26 April 2000, at 19.

31. Proposal for a Directive of the European Parliament and of the Council on a common regulatory framework for electronic communications networks and services, COM(2000) 393 final, OJ C 365 E/198, 19 December 2000, Article 21.

32. Common Position (EC) No 38/2001 adopted by the Council on 17 September 2001, OJ C 337/34, 30 November 2001, at 53.

33. *See* Commission Decision 2002/627/EC of 29 July 2002 establishing the European Regulators Group for Electronic Communications Networks and Services, OJ L 200/38, 30 July 2002.

34. Nina Boeger & Joseph Corkin, *How Regulatory Networks Shaped Institutional Reform under the EU Telecoms Framework*, 14 CAMBRIDGE YEARBOOK OF EUROPEAN LEGAL STUDIES 49, 53 (2012).

35. Eurostrategies/Cullen International 1999 Study, *supra* note 25, at 56.

36. Viviane Reding, From Service Competition to Infrastructure Competition: The Policy Options Now on the Table, ECTA Conference 2006, Brussels, 16 November 2006 (available at http://europa.eu/rapid/press-release_SPEECH-06-697_en.htm).

37. Proposal for a Regulation of the European Parliament and of the Council establishing the European Electronic Communications Market Authority, COM(2007) 699 final, 13 November 2007.

38. Communication from the Commission to the European Parliament, the Council, the European Economic and Social Committee and the Committee of the Regions—Report on the outcome of the Review of the EU regulatory framework for electronic communications networks and services in accordance with Directive 2002/21/EC and Summary of the 2007 Reform Proposals, COM(2007) 696 final, 13 November 2007, at 3, 9.

39. See the notification regime of Article 7a of the Framework Directive (as amended by Directive 2009/140/EC).

40. *See* Regulation (EC) No 1211/2009 of the European Parliament and of the Council of 25 November 2009 establishing the Body of European Regulators for Electronic Communications (BEREC) and the Office, OJ L 337/1, 18 December 2009, at Recital 6.

41. Boeger & Corkin, *supra* note 34, at 56–57. Pursuant to Article 3(3c) of the Framework Directive (introduced by Directive 2009/140/EC), NRAs must "take utmost account of opinions and common positions adopted by BEREC when adopting their own decisions for their national markets."

42. Regulation (EC) No 1211/2009, at Recital 6.

43. Ian Walden, *European Union Communications Law, in* TELECOMMUNICATIONS LAW AND REGULATION 143, 177 (Ian Walden ed., 2012).

44. Boeger & Corkin, *supra* note 34, at 54–73 (further noting, at p. 58, that the NRAs "had long cooperated with one another in the IRG, the ERG and other transnational institutions, resulting in a reasonably cohesive transnational community of expertise that was perfectly capable of building its own coalitions to mobilise against the proposed reforms"). Ultimately the NRAs asserted themselves as "independent, political players . . . and by assuming such a role they managed to head off a further push towards greater centralisation" (*id.* at 71).

45. Communication, *supra* note 38, at 3.

46. *See* Report on the proposal for a directive of the European Parliament and of the Council amending Directive 2002/21/EC on a common regulatory framework for electronic communications networks and services, Directive 2002/19/EC on access to, and interconnection of, electronic communications networks and associated facilities, and Directive 2002/20/EC on the authorisation of electronic communications networks and services (COM(2007)0697—C6-0427/2007—2007/0247(COD)), 22 July 2008 (citing the Opinion of the Committee on Economic and Monetary Affairs).

47. *But see* José Carlos Laguna de Paz, *What to keep and what to change in European electronic communications policy?*, 49 COMMON MKT. L. REV. 1951, 1954 (2012) ("At present, *it would*

316 "DEMOCRATIC DEFICIT" TO "DEMOCRATIC SURPLUS"

be unrealistic to consider strengthening the EU powers by establishing a European sectoral authority. Moreover, it seems appropriate that NRAs are able to make tailor-made interventions, adapted to very different national circumstances. Thus, the way to encourage European integration seems to be by fine-tuning regulation and ensuring that rules are applied consistently across all Member States") (emphasis added).

48. Proposal for a Directive of the European Parliament and of the Council establishing the European Electronic Communications Code (Recast), Brussels, 14.09.16, COM(2016) 590.

49. Jones Day, *Commentary: A New Telecoms Code for Europe* (September 2016), at 4.

50. According to its website (http://berec.europa.eu/eng/news_consultations/Closed_Public_Consultations/), BEREC concluded seven public consultations in 2015, five in 2014, two in 2013, eleven in 2012, four in 2011, and seven in 2010.

51. David Coen, *Empirical and theoretical studies in EU lobbying*, 14 JOURNAL OF EUROPEAN PUBLIC POLICY 333, 335 (2007) (with further citations).

52. Rainer Eising, *The access of business interests to EU institutions: towards élite pluralism?*, 14 JOURNAL OF EUROPEAN PUBLIC POLICY 384, 395 (2007).

53. *Id.* at 399 (emphasis added).

54. Andreas Dür & Gemma Mateo, *Who lobbies the European Union? National interest groups in a multilevel polity*, 19 JOURNAL OF EUROPEAN PUBLIC POLICY 969, 971 (2012).

55. Sabine Saurugger, *Interest Groups and Democracy in the European Union*, 31 WEST EUROPEAN POLITICS 1274, 1282–83 (2008). *See also* Cornelia Woll, *Lobbying in the European Union: From sui generis to a comparative perspective*, 13 JOURNAL OF EUROPEAN PUBLIC POLICY 456, 459 (2006) (noting that the multi-level nature of the EU polity aggravates the collective action problems of interest groups, and summarizing literature which concludes that "effective collective action at the supranational level is difficult even for groups of large and powerful actors such as firms, which are none the less more successful in providing selective incentives than are social or public interest associations").

56. Jan Beyers & Bart Kerremans, *Critical resource dependencies and the Europeanization of domestic interest groups*, 14 JOURNAL OF EUROPEAN PUBLIC POLICY 460, 464 (2007). The authors argue that "a low level of perceived budget competition corresponds with a lower dependency on a critical resource provider as well as with a more Europeanized orientation among interest groups" (*id.* at 472). Moreover, they observe that "a dependency on government subsidies in particular constrains Europeanization" (*id.* at 477).

57. JUSTIN GREENWOOD, INTEREST REPRESENTATION IN THE EUROPEAN UNION 13–14 (3rd ed. 2011).

58. *See* Beate Kohler-Koch, *How to Put Matters Right? Assessing the Role of Civil Society in EU Accountability*, 33 WEST EUROPEAN POLITICS 1117, 1128 (2010).

59. *Id.* at 1128–29.

60. *See* GREENWOOD, *supra* note 57, at 13 (finding that in 2011 around one-third of all associations constituted at EU level were citizen interest organizations, compared to 20% in 2000. Relatedly, business interest associations constituted a little more than half of the entire constituency of EU associations, compared to two-thirds in 2000).

61. Interviews n. 45001 and 45003.

62. According to its website, ETNO has been in operation since 1992 and has 39 members and observers (https://etno.eu/).

63. Interviews with UFC-Que Choisir, KEPKA and Which.

64. *See also* GREENWOOD, *supra* note 57, at 163 (noting that common platform building within BEUC is not easy).

65. *Cf.* Judith Resnik, *Categorical Federalism: Jurisdiction, Gender, and the Globe*, 111 YALE L.J. 619, 624 (2001) (noting, in the context of US federalism, that "[t]he contemporary debate about whether to prefer, a priori, the states or the federal government for certain forms of lawmaking misses dynamic interaction across levels of governance. In practice, federalism is a web of connections formed by transborder responses (such as interstate agreements and compacts) and through shared efforts by national organizations of state officials, localities, and private interests").

66. As a brief reminder, the 2009 directive inserted paragraph 3a in Article 3 of the Framework Directive stating that NRAs must "act independently" and "not seek or take instructions from any other body in relation to the exercise of [their] tasks." Furthermore, the head or board members of NRAs may be dismissed only if they no longer fulfill the conditions required for the performance of their duties that are laid down in advance in national law.

67. *Cf.* Mark Thatcher, *Independent Regulatory Agencies and Elected Politicians in Europe, in* REGULATION THROUGH AGENCIES IN THE EU. A NEW PARADIGM OF EUROPEAN GOVERNANCE 47, 61 (Damien Geradin & Rodolphe Munoz & Nicolas Petit eds., 2005), (noting that "[t]he EC level of decision making also allows a complex game to be played. On some issues, [independent regulatory agencies] have allied themselves with their domestic governments, notably in seeking to 'export' national models of regulation to the EU level.") This line of analysis could well apply to "exporting" national models of regulatory processes as well.

68. *See* CLAIRE HALL, COLIN SCOTT & CHRISTOPHER HOOD, TELECOMMUNICATIONS REGULATION: CULTURE, CHAOS AND INTERDEPENDENCE INSIDE THE REGULATORY PROCESS 66, 95–96 (2000).

69. See the original, but not aptly applicable in this specific EU regulatory context, proposal of Susan Rose-Ackerman, *Risk Taking and Reelection: Does Federalism Promote Innovation?*, 9 J. LEGAL STUD. 593, 615–16 (1980) (discussing systems of grants and prizes to innovative low-level governments), and, more recently, Michael Abramowicz, *Speeding Up the Crawl to the Top*, 20 YALE J. ON REG. 139, 191–92 (2003).

Appendix

INTERVIEWS

Interviewee	Position at Time of Interview/ Other Relevant Current & Past Positions	Place and Date of Interview
Stéphane Desselas	Founder and Director, Athenora Consulting	Brussels, Belgium April 11, 2011
Laetitia Adhemar	Special assistant to the President (*Chargée de mission auprès du Président*), ALTAVIA/Secrétaire exécutif at CEO Office, Alliance Renault Nissan	Paris, France April 4, 2011
Stéphane Hoynck	Legal Counsel (*Directeur des Affaires Juridiques*), ARCEP	Paris, France April 15, 2011
Martine Georges-Naïm	Attorney at law/Member of the *Commission consultative des réseaux et services de communications électroniques*	Paris, France May 19, 2011
Jacques Beltran	Senior Vice President— International Network Asia Pacific, ALSTOM/Vice President for public affairs and business intelligence, ALSTOM	Paris, France May 24, 2011
Laurent Laganier	Director of regulation and relations with local authorities, Iliad	Paris, France May 31, 2011

Interviewee	Position at Time of Interview/ Other Relevant Current & Past Positions	Place and Date of Interview
Jacques Pomonti	President, AFUTT (French Association of Telecommunications Users)	Paris, France June 17, 2011
Cédric Musso	Director of institutional relations, UFC-Que Choisir	Paris, France June 23, 2011
Edouard Barreiro	Deputy Director, Department of Studies	Paris, France June 23, 2011
Michel Derdevet	Director of communication, RTE (French power-grid operator)	Paris, France March 31, 2011
Philippe Maze-Sencier	Managing Director, APCO	Paris, France March 17, 2011
Anne Petit	Project manager, ADEIC	Paris, France July 1, 2011
Claude Douare	General secretary, ADEIC	Paris, France July 1, 2011
Ariane Pommery	Legal counsel, ADEIC	Paris, France July 1, 2011
André Mérigoux	Public Affairs Director, Global Government & Public Affairs, Alcatel-Lucent	Paris, France July 11, 2011
Marc Lebourges	Directeur du Département Europe & Economie au sein de la Direction de la Réglementation, Orange-France Telecom)	Paris, France July 11, 2011
Constantine S. Delicostopoulos	Vice-President, EETT	Athens, Greece January 12, 2012
Vassilis Kondylis	Legal Advisor, EETT	Athens, Greece January 12, 2012
Panos Karaminas	Director of the Telecommunications Division, EETT	Athens, Greece January 13, 2012
Chrisoula Michailidou	Legal officer, EETT	Athens, Greece January 13, 2012

Interviewee	Position at Time of Interview/ Other Relevant Current & Past Positions	Place and Date of Interview
Nikos Kitonakis	Member of the International & Public Relations Department, EETT	Athens, Greece January 13, 2012
Viktoras Tsiafoutis	Legal Advisor, EKPOIZO	Athens, Greece January 13, 2012
Christina Kelaidi	Head of Strategic Analysis and Regulatory Relations Department, OTE	Athens, Greece January 13, 2012
Ioannis Bougos	Attorney, Head of the Sub-directorate of Legal Regulatory Framework, OTE	Athens, Greece January 13, 2012
Anna Matsouka	Physicist, Head of Department of International Regulatory Affairs, OTE	Athens, Greece January 13, 2012
Vassiliki Papadaki	Head of Regulatory Affairs & Products and Services Department, Cosmote	Athens, Greece January 13, 2012
Nikolaos Tseberlidis	President, Consumer Protection Centre (KEPKA)	Thessaloniki, Greece July 4, 2012
Vicki Nash	Director of Scotland office (Third consultation champion), Ofcom	London, UK July 19, 2011
Graham Howell	Director England and Secretary to the Corporation, Fourth consultation champion, Ofcom	London, UK July 19, 2011
Bob Warner	Chair, Communications Consumer Panel	London, UK July 19, 2011
Fiona Lennox	Executive Director, Communications Consumer Panel	London, UK July 19, 2011
Rob Reid	Senior Policy Adviser, Which?	London, UK July 19, 2011
Antony Clark	Regulatory Strategy & Planning Manager, BT Group	London, UK July 19, 2011

BIBLIOGRAPHY

Abramowicz, Michael, "Speeding Up the Crawl to the Top," 20 *Yale Journal on Regulation* 139 (2003).

Ackerman Bruce A., "The Storrs Lectures: Discovering the Constitution," 93 *Yale Law Journal* 1013 (1984).

Ackerman, Bruce A., "Beyond Carolene Products," 98 *Harvard Law Review* 713 (1985).

Ackerman, Bruce, *We the People: Transformations* (Harvard University Press, 1998).

Ackerman, Bruce, "The New Separation of Powers," 113 *Harvard Law Review* 633 (2000).

Adinolfi, Adelina, "The 'Procedural Autonomy' of Member States and the Constraints Stemming from the ECJ's Case Law: Is Judicial Activism Still Necessary?," in Hans-W. Micklitz and Bruno De Witte (eds.), *The European Court of Justice and the Autonomy of the Member States* 281 (Intersentia, 2012).

Allan, T. R. S., *Law, Liberty, and Justice: The Legal Foundations of British Constitutionalism* (Oxford University Press, 1993).

Allison, J. W. F., *A Continental Distinction in the Common Law: A Historical and Comparative Perspective on English Public Law* (Oxford University Press, 2000).

Arancibia, Jaime, *Judicial Review of Commercial Regulation* (Oxford University Press, 2011).

Arthurs, H. W., *"Without the Law": Administrative Justice and Legal Pluralism in Nineteenth-Century England* (University of Toronto Press, 1985).

Auby, Jean-Bernard, "Remarques introductives au colloque 'Vers une démocratie administrative? Des administrés aux citoyens'" (Pôle Européen d'Administration Publique, Strasbourg, 19–20 Mars 2010).

Aucoin, Peter, "Contraction, Managerialism and Decentralization in Canadian Government," 1 *Governance* 144 (1988).

Austin, Rodney, "The Freedom of Information Act 2000—A Sheep in Wolf's Clothing?," in Jeffrey Jowell and Dawn Oliver (eds.), *The Changing Constitution*, 5th edn. (Oxford University Press, 2004).

Austin, Rodney, "The Freedom of Information Act 2000—A Sheep in Wolf's Clothing?," in Jeffrey Jowell and Dawn Oliver (eds.), *The Changing Constitution*, 6th edn. (Oxford University Press, 2007).

Ayres, Ian, "Supply-Side Inefficiencies in Corporate Charter Competition: Lessons from Patents, Yachting and Bluebooks," 43 *University of Kansas Law Review* 541 (1995).

Baczko, Bronislaw, "The Social Contract of the French: Sieyès and Rousseau," 60 *Journal of Modern History* S98 (suppl. 1988).

Baggott, Rob, "Regulatory Reform in Britain: The Changing Face of Self-Regulation," 67 *Public Administration* 435 (1989).

Barron, Anne and Scott, Colin, "The Citizen's Charter Programme," 55 *Modern Law Review* 526 (1992).

Bavasso, Antonio F., "Electronic Communications: A New Paradigm for European Regulation," 41 *Common Market Law Review* 87 (2004).

Baxter, Hugh, "Autopoiesis and the 'Relative Autonomy' of Law," 19 *Cardozo Law Review* 1987 (1988).

Baxter, Hugh, "Habermas's Discourse Theory of Law and Democracy," 50 *Buffalo Law Review* 205 (2002).

Baxter, Hugh, "System and Lifeworld in Habermas's Theory of Law," 23 *Cardozo Law Review* 473 (2002).

Bellamy, Sir Christopher, "Focusing on the European Perspective of Judicial Dialogue: Issues in the Area of Competition Law," 39 *Texas International Law Journal* 461 (2004).

Berle, A. A., Jr., "The Expansion of American Administrative Law," 30 *Harvard Law Review* 430 (1917).

Beyers, Jan, and Kerremans, Bart, "Critical Resource Dependencies and the Europeanization of Domestic Interest Groups," 14 *Journal of European Public Policy* 460 (2007).

Bignami, Francesca, "The Democratic Deficit in European Community Rulemaking: A Call for Notice and Comment in Comitology," 40 *Harvard International Law Journal* 451 (1999).

Bignami, Francesca, "Three Generations of Participation Rights before the European Commission," 68 *Law and Contemporary Problems* 61 (2004).

Bignami, Francesca, "Creating European Rights: National Values and Supranational Interests," 11 *Columbia Journal of European Law* 241 (2005).

Bingham of Cornhill, Lord, "Dicey Revisited," 2002 *Public Law* 39.

Bingham, Lord, "The Rule of Law," 66 *Cambridge Law Journal* 67 (2007).

Bingham, Tom, *The Rule of Law* (Allen Lane, 2010).

Birkinshaw, Patrick, *Freedom of Information: The Law, the Practice and the Ideal*, 4th edn. Cambridge University Press, 2010).

Birkinshaw, Patrick, "Regulating Information," Jeffrey Jowell and Dawn Oliver (eds.), *The Changing Constitution*, 7th edn. (Oxford University Press, 2011).

Birkinshaw, Patrick, Harden, Ian, and Lewis, Norman, *Government by Moonlight: The Hybrid Parts of the State* (Unwin Hyman, 1990).

Black, Julia, and Muchlinski, Peter, "Introduction," in Julia Black, Peter Muchlinski, and Paul Walker (eds.), *Commercial Regulation and Judicial Review* 1 (Hart, 1998).

Blair, Tony, *A Journey: My Political Life* (Alfred A. Knopf, 2010).

Blondel, Jean, *Comparative Legislatures* (Prentice Hall, 1973).

Bobek, Michal, "Thou Shalt Have Two Masters: The Application of European Law by Administrative Authorities in the New Member States," 1 *Review of European Administrative Law* 51 (2008).

Boeger, Nina, and Corkin, Joseph, "How Regulatory Networks Shaped Institutional Reform under the EU Telecoms Framework," 14 *Cambridge Yearbook of European Legal Studies* 49 (2012).

Bon, Pierre, "L'association du public aux décisions prises par l'administration," 2016 *Revue Française de Droit Administratif* 27.

Botsi, Foivou I., "O Koinovouleutikos Elegxos ton Syntagmatopoiimenon Aneksartiton Archon (Parliamentary Control of the Constitutionalized Independent Authorities)," 2007 *Efimerida Dimosiou Dikaiou (Journal of Public Law)* 361.

Bradley Anthony, "The Sovereignty of Parliament—Form or Substance?," in Jeffrey Jowell and Dawn Oliver (eds.), *The Changing Constitution*, 7th edn. (Oxford University Press, 2011).

Braibant, Guy and Stirn, Bernard, *Le droit administratif français*, 7th edn. (Dalloz, 2005).

Brans, Marleen and Rossbach, Stefan, "The Autopoiesis of Administrative Systems: Niklas Luhmann on Public Administration and Public Policy," 75 *Public Administration* 417 (1997).

Breger, Marshall J. and Edles, Gary J., "Established by Practice: The Theory and Operation of Independent Federal Agencies," 52 *Administrative Law Review* 1111 (2000).

Bryce, James, *The American Commonwealth*, Vol. I (Macmillan,1888).

Bryce, James, *Modern Democracies*, Vol. II (Macmillan, 1921).

Burdeau, Georges, Traité de science politique—Tome IX (Les façades institutionnelles de la démocratie gouvernante), 2nd edn. (L.G.D.J., 1976).

Cananea, Giacinto della, "The European Union's Mixed Administrative Proceedings," 68 *Law and Contemporary Problems* 197 (2004).

Cane, Peter, *Controlling Administrative Power: An Historical Comparison* (Cambridge University Press, 2016).

Carbonnier Jean, "La passion des lois au siècle des Lumières," in Jean Carbonnier, *Essais sur les lois*, 2nd edn. (Defrénois, 1995).

Carsberg, Sir Bryan, "Telecommunications Competition in the United Kingdom: A Regulatory Perspective," 37 *New York Law School Law Review* 285 (1992).

Cassese, Sabino, "European Administrative Proceedings," 68 *Law and Contemporary Problems* 21 (2004).

Cave, Martin, "The Evolution of Telecommunications Regulation in the UK," 41 *European Economic Review* 691 (1997).

Chalmers, Damian and Tomkins, Adam, *European Union Public Law: Text and Materials* (Cambridge University Press, 2007).

Chapus René, *Droit administratif général* (Tome 1), 15th edn. (Montchrestien, 2001).

Chapus, René, *Droit du contentieux administratif*, 12th edn. (Montchrestien, 2006).

Chester, Norman, *The English Administrative System 1780–1870* (Oxford University Press, 1981).

Chevallier, Jacques, *Science administrative*, 4th edn. (Presses universitaires de France, 2007).

Chrysanthakis, Charalambos G., "I Leitourgia ton Aneksartiton Archon stin Chora mas: Mia Apotimisi (The Operation of Independent Authorities in our Country: An Assessment)," 2009 *Theoria kai Praksi Dioikitikou Dikaiou (Theory and Practice of Administrative Law)* 5.

Clarke, John, "Consumerism and the Remaking of State-Citizen Relations in the UK," in Greg Marston and Catherine McDonald (eds.), *Analysing Social Policy: A Governmental Approach* 89 (Edward Elgar, 2006).

Clarke, John, Newman, Janet, Smith, Nick, Vidler, Elizabeth, and Westmarland, Louise, *Creating Citizen-Consumers: Changing Publics and Changing Public Services* (SAGE, 2007).

Clarke, John, McDermont, Morag, and Newman Janet, "Delivering Choice and Administering Justice: Contested Logics of Public Services," in Michael Adler ed., *Administrative Justice in Context* 25 (Hart, 2010).

Coen, David, "Empirical and Theoretical Studies in EU Lobbying," 14 *Journal of European Public Policy* 333 (2007).

Coglianese, Cary, "Assessing Consensus: The Promise and Performance of Negotiated Rulemaking," 46 *Duke Law Journal* 1255 (1997).

Cohen, Joshua and Sabel, Charles, "Directly-Deliberative Polyarchy," 3 *European Law Journal* 313 (1997).

Cohen, Joshua and Sabel, Charles F., "Global Democracy?," 37 *NYU Journal of International Law and Politics* 763 (2005).

Cosgrove, Richard A., *The Rule of Law: Albert Venn Dicey, Victorian Jurist* (University of North Carolina Press, 1980).

Cover, Robert M., "Nomos and Narrative," 97 *Harvard Law Review* 4 (1983).

Craig, Paul P., "Formal and Substantive Conceptions of the Rule of Law: An Analytical Framework," 1997 *Public Law* 467.

Craig, Paul, "Prerogative, Precedent and Power," in Christopher Forsyth and Ivan Hare (eds.), *The Golden Metwand and the Crooked Cord. Essays on Public Law in Honour of Sir William Wade QC* 65 (Oxford University Press, 1998).

Craig, Paul, "Competing Models of Judicial Review," 1999 *Public Law* 428.

Craig, Paul, *EU Administrative Law* (Oxford University Press, 2006).

Craig, Paul, "Perspectives on Process: Common Law, Statutory and Political," 2010 *Public Law* 275.

Craig, Paul, *Administrative Law*, 7th edn., (Sweet & Maxwell, 2012).

Croley, Steven P., "Public Interested Regulation," 28 *Florida State University Law Review* 7 (2000).

Cronin Ciaran and De Greiff, Pablo, "Editors' Introduction," in Jürgen Habermas (Ciaran Cronin and Pablo De Greiff, eds.), *The Inclusion of the Other. Studies in Political Theory* (MIT Press, 1998).

Cuéllar, Mariano-Florentino, "Rethinking Regulatory Democracy," 57 *Administrative Law Review* 411 (2005).

Curtin, Deirdre, "Delegation to EU Non-majoritarian Agencies and Emerging Practices of Public Accountability," in Damien Geradin, Rodolphe Munoz, and Nicolas Petit eds., *Regulation through Agencies in the EU. A New Paradigm of European Governance* 88 (Edward Elgar, 2005).

Cushman, Robert E., *The Independent Regulatory Commissions* (Oxford University Press, 1941).

Custos, Dominique, "The 2015 French Code of Administrative Procedure: An Assessment," in Susan Rose-Ackerman, Peter Lindseth, and Blake Emerson (eds.), *Comparative Administrative Law*, 2nd edn. (forthcoming, Edward Elgar, 2017).

Czapanskiy, Karen Syma and Manjoo, Rashida, "The Right of Public Participation in the Law-making Process and the Role of Legislature in the Promotion of this Right," 19 *Duke Journal of Comparative & International Law Journal* 1 (2008).

Dagtoglou, Prodromos D., *Geniko Doikitiko Dikaio (General Administrative Law)* (Ant. N. Sakkoulas, 2004).

Dagtoglou, Prodromos D., "Constitutional and Administrative Law," in Konstantinos D. Kerameus and Phaedon J. Kozyris (eds.), *Introduction to Greek Law*, 3rd ed., (Kluwer/Ant. N. Sakkoulas, 2008).

Dahl, Robert A., *A Preface to Democratic Theory* (University of Chicago Press, 1956).

Dahl, Robert A., *Pluralist Democracy in the United States: Conflict and Consent* (Rand McNally, 1967).

Damaška, Mirjan R., *The Faces of Justice and State Authority: A Comparative Approach to the Legal Process* (Yale University Press, 1986).

Davidson, Nestor, "Cooperative Localism: Federal-Local Collaboration in an Era of State Sovereignty," 93 *Virginia Law Review* 959 (2007).

Dehousse, Renaud, "Constitutional Reform in the European Community: Are There Alternatives to the Majoritarian Avenue?," 18 *West European Politics* 118 (1998).

Dehousse, Renaud, "The Legitimacy of European Governance: The Need for a Process-Based Approach," 1 *Cahiers Européens de Sciences Po* 1 (2001).

Dehousse, Renaud, "Misfits: EU Law and the Transformation of European Governance," 2/02 *Jean Monnet Working Paper* (2002).

Dellis, George, *Koini Ofeleia kai Agora. Tomos A. To Telos tonn Diachoristikon Grammon: I "Agorakentriki" Dimosia Rythmisi ton Koinofelon Drastiriotiton (Public Utilities and the Market. Vol. I. "Market-oriented" Regulation for Public Utilities)* (Ant. N. Sakkoulas, 2008).

Dellis, George, *Koini Ofeleia kai Agora. Tomos B. To Dimosio Dikaio ton Ypo Apeleftherosi Koinofelon Ypiresion (Ilektronikes epikoinonies, Energeia, Tachidromeio, Metafores, Radiotileorasi) (Public Utilities and the Market. Vol. II. Liberalized Utilities Law (Electronic Communications, Energy, Post, Transport, Broadcasting)* (Ant. N. Sakkoulas, 2008).

Delvolvé, Pierre, "L'été des ordonnances," 21 *Revue Française de Droit Administratif* 909 (2005).

Desselas, Stéphane, *Un lobbying professionnel à visage découvert. Enquête sur l'influence des Français à Bruxelles* (Palio, 2007).

Diamandouros, P. Nikiforos, "Transition to, and consolidation of, democratic politics in Greece, 1974–1983: A tentative assessment," 7 *West European Politics* 50 (1984).

Dicey, A. V., *Lectures Introductory to the Study of the Law of the Constitution* (Macmillan, 1885).

Dicey, A. V., "Will the Form of Parliamentary Government Be Permanent?," 13 *Harvard Law Review* 67 (1899).

Dicey, A. V., *Lectures on the Relation between Law and Public Opinion in England during the Nineteenth Century*, 2nd ed. (Macmillan and Co., 1914).

Dicey, A. V., "The Development of Administrative Law in England," 31 *The Law Quarterly Review* 148 (1915).

Dicey, A. V., *Introduction to the Study of the Law of the Constitution*, 10th edn. (Macmillan, 1959).

Dolowitz, David P. and Marsh, David, "Learning from Abroad: The Role of Policy Transfer in Contemporary Policy-Making," 13 *Governance* 5 (2000).

Drewry, Gavin, "Citizen's Charters," 7 *Public Management Review* 321 (2005).

Drossos, Yianis Z., *Dokimio Ellinikis Syntagmatikis Theorias (An Essay on Greek Constitutional Theory)* (Ant. N. Sakkoulas, 1996).

Duguit, Léon, *Les transformations du droit public* (Colin, 1913).

Duguit, Léon, "The Concept of Public Service," 32 *Yale Law Journal* 425 (1923).

Duguit, Léon, *Traité de droit constitutionnel, Tome I: La règle de droit—Le problème de l'Etat*, 3rd edn. (E. Boccard, 1927).

Dunn, John, "Situating Democratic Political Accountability," in Adam Przeworski, Susan C. Stokes, and Bernard Manin (eds.), *Democracy, Accountability, and Representation* 329 (1999).

Dür, Andreas and Gemma Mateo, "Who Lobbies the European Union? National Interest Groups in a Multilevel Polity," 19 *Journal of European Public Policy* 969 (2012).

Dyson, Kenneth, "West Germany: The Search for a Rationalist Consensus," in Jeremy Richardson (ed.), *Policy Styles in Western Europe* 17 (Allen & Unwin, 1982).

Eising, Rainer, "The access of business interests to EU institutions: towards élite pluralism?," 14 *Journal of European Public Policy* 384 (2007).

Eldersveld, Samuel, Hubée-Boonzaaijer, Sonja, and Kooiman, Jan, "Elite Perceptions of the Political Process in the Netherlands, Looked at in Comparative Perspective," in Mattei Dogan (ed.), *The Mandarins of Western Europe: The Political Role of Top Civil Servants* 129 (Sage, 1975).

Elliott, Mark, "The Ultra Vires Doctrine in a Constitutional Setting: Still the Central Principle of Administrative Law," 58 *Cambridge Law Journal* 129 (1999).

Elliott, Mark, "The Principle of Parliamentary Sovereignty in Legal, Constitutional and Political Perspective," in Jeffrey Jowell, Dawn Oliver and Colm O'Cinneide eds., *The Changing Constitution*, 8th edn. (Oxford University Press, 2015).

Eriksen, Erik, A Comment on Schmalz-Bruns, in Beate Kohler-Koch & Berthold Rittberger (eds.), *Debating the Democratic Legitimacy of the European Union* 304 (Rowman & Littlefield, 2007).

Esty, Daniel "Revitalizing Environmental Federalism," 95 *Michigan Law Review* 570 (1996).

Esty, Daniel C. and Geradin, Damien, "Introduction," in Daniel Esty and Damien Geradin (eds.), *Regulatory Competition and Economic Integration: Comparative Perspectives* xix (Oxford University Press, 2001).

Farber, Daniel A. and Frickey, Philip P., "The Jurisprudence of Public Choice," 65 *Texas Law Review* 873 (1987).

Farina, Cynthia et al., "Rulemaking vs. Democracy: Judging and Nudging Public Participation that Counts," 2 *Michigan Journal of Environmental & Administrative Law* 123 (2012).

Faucher-King, Florence and Le Galès, Patrick, *The New Labour Experiment: Change and Reform Under Blair and Brown* (Gregory Elliott trans., Stanford University Press, 2010).

Faulkner, David, "Public Services, Citizenship and the State-the British Experience 1967–97," in Mark Freedland and Silvana Sciarra (eds.), *Public Services and Citizenship in European Law: Public and Labour Law Perspectives* 35 (Oxford University Press, 1998).

Featherstone, Kevin, "Introduction: 'Modernisation' and the Structural Constraints of Greek Politics," 28 *West European Politics* 223 (2005).

Featherstone, Kevin and Papadimitriou, Dimitris, *The Limits of Europeanization: Reform Capacity and Policy Conflict in Greece* (Palgrave Macmillan, 2008).

Feintuck, Mike, *The Public Interest' in Regulation* (Oxford University Press, 2004).

Fesler, James W., *The Independence of State Regulatory Agencies* (Public Administration Service No. 85, 1942).

Fiorina, Morris P. and Noll, Roger G., "Voters, Legislators and Bureaucracy: Institutional Design in the Public Sector," 68 *American Economic Review, Papers and Proceedings* 256 (1978).

Fitzsimmons, Michael P., *The Remaking of France: The National Assembly and the Constitution of 1791* (Cambridge University Press, 1994).

Follesdal, Andreas and Hix, Simon, "Why There Is a Democratic Deficit in the EU: A Response to Majone and Moravcsik," 44 *Journal of Common Market Studies* 533 (2006).

Forbath, William E., "Habermas's Constitution: A History, Guide, and Critique," 23 *Law & Social Inquiry* 969 (1998).

Foster, C. D., *Privatization, Public Ownership and the Regulation of Natural Monopoly* (Blackwell, 1992).

Frankfurter, Felix, "Foreword," 47 *Yale Law Journal* 515 (1938).

Freedland, Mark, "Law, Public Services, and Citizenship-New Domains, New Regimes?," in Mark Freedland and Silvana Sciarra (eds.), *Public Services and Citizenship in European Law. Public and Labour Law Perspectives* 1 (Oxford University Press, 1998).

Friedman, Barry, "Valuing Federalism," 82 *Minnesota Law Review* 317 (1997).

Fuchs, Gerhard, "Policy-Making in a System of Multi-level Governance—the Commission of the European Community and the Restructuring of the Telecommunications Sector," 1 *Journal of European Public Policy* 177 (1994).

Funk, William, "When Smoke Gets in Your Eyes: Regulatory Negotiation and the Public Interest-EPA's Woodstove Standards," 18 *Environmental Law* 55 (1987).

Furet, François and Halévi, Ran, *La Monarchie Républicaine: La Constitution de 1791* (Fayard, 1996).

Galle, Brian and Seidenfeld, Mark, "Administrative Law's Federalism: Preemption, Delegation, and Agencies at the Edge of Federal Power," 57 *Duke Law Journal* 1933 (2008).

Galle, Brian and Leahy, Joseph, "Laboratories of Democracy? Policy Innovation in Decentralized Governments," 58 *Emory Law Journal* 1333 (2009).

Gaudemet, Yves, *Traité de Droit Administratif (Tome I)*, 16th edn. (L.G.D.J., 2001).

Gaus, John M., "The Report of the British Committee on Ministers' Powers," 26 *The American Political Science Review* 1142 (1932).

Geradin, Damien and McCahery Joseph A., "Regulatory Co-opetition: Transcending the Regulatory Competition Debate," in Jacint Jordana and David Levi-Faur (eds.), *The Politics of Regulation: Institutions and Regulatory Reforms for the Age of Governance* 90 (Edward Elgar, 2004).

Geradin, Damien and Petit, Nicolas, "The Development of Agencies at EU and National Levels: Conceptual Analysis and Proposals for Reform," 01/04 *Jean Monnet Working Paper* (2004).

Gerken, Heather K., "Foreword: Federalism All the Way Down," 124 *Harvard Law Review* 4 (2010).

Gerontas, Apostolos, *I Symmetochi ton Politon kai ton Koinonikon Foreon sti Diadikasia Lipsis Dioikitikon Apofaseon (The Participation of Citizens and Civil Society Actors in Administrative Decisionmaking)* (Sakkoulas, 1986).

Gerstenberg, Oliver, "Law's Polyarchy: A Comment on Cohen and Sabel," 3 *European Law Journal* 343 (1997).

Gerstenberg, Oliver and Sabel, Charles F., "Directly-Deliberative Polyarchy: An Institutional Ideal for Europe?," in Christian Joerges & Renaud Dehousse (eds.), *Good Governance in Europe's Integrated Market* 289 (Oxford University Press, 2002).

Giddens, Anthony, *The Third Way: The Renewal of Social Democracy* (Polity Press, 1998).

Giddens, Anthony, *The Third Way and Its Critics* (Polity Press, 2000).

Goldsworthy, Jeffrey, *The Sovereignty of Parliament: History and Philosophy* (Oxford University Press, 1999).

Goldsworthy, Jeffrey, *Parliamentary Sovereignty: Contemporary Debates* (Cambridge University Press, 2010).

Gordon, Michael, "The Conceptual Foundations of Parliamentary Sovereignty: Reconsidering Jennings and Wade," 2009 *Public Law* 519.

Graham, Cosmo, *Regulating Public Utilities: A Constitutional Approach* (Hart, 2000).

Graham, Cosmo and Prosser, Tony, *Privatizing Public Enterprises: Constitutions, the State, and Regulation in Comparative Perspective* (Oxford University Press, 1991).

Greenwood, Justin, *Interest Representation in the European Union*, 3rd edn. (Palgrave Macmillan, 2011).

Guettier, Christophe, *Institutions Administratives*, 5th edn. (Dalloz, 2010).

Habermas, Jürgen, *The Theory of Communicative Action. Reason and the Rationalization of Society* (Thomas McCarthy trans., Beacon Press, 1984).

Habermas, Jürgen, *The Theory of Communicative Action. Lifeworld and System: A Critique of Functionalist Reason* (Thomas McCarthy trans., Beacon Press, 1987).

Habermas, Jürgen, "Further Reflections on the Public Sphere," in Craig Calhoun (ed.), *Habermas and the Public Sphere* 421 (MIT Press, 1992).

Habermas, Jürgen, *Between Facts and Norms. Contributions to a Discourse Theory of Law and Democracy* (William Rehg trans., MIT Press, 1996).

Habermas, Jürgen, "Does Europe Need a Constitution? Response to Dieter Grimm," in Jürgen Habermas (Ciaran Cronin and Pablo De Greiff eds.), *The Inclusion of the Other: Studies in Political Theory* 155 (MIT Press, 1998).

Habermas, Jürgen, "Three Normative Models of Democracy," in Jürgen Habermas (Ciaran Cronin and Pablo De Greiff eds.), *The Inclusion of the Other. Studies in Political Theory* 239 (MIT Press, 1998).

Habermas, Jürgen, "On the Internal Relation Between the Rule of Law and Democracy," in Jürgen Habermas (Ciaran Cronin and Pablo De Greiff eds.), *The Inclusion of the Other. Studies in Political Theory* 253 (MIT Press, 1998).

Habermas, Jürgen, *Europe: The Faltering Project* (Ciaran Cronin trans., Polity, 2009).

Hall, Claire, Scott, Colin, and Hood, Christopher, *Telecommunications Regulation: Culture, Chaos and Interdependence Inside the Regulatory Process* (Routledge, 2000).

Hambleton, Robin and Hoggett, Paul, "Rethinking Consumerism in Public Service," 3 *Consumer Policy Review* 103 (1993).

Haquet, Arnaud, *La loi et le règlement* (L.G.D.J., 2007).

Harlow, Carol, "Public Service, Market Ideology, and Citizenship," in Mark Freedland and Silvana Sciarra (eds.), *Public Services and Citizenship in European Law. Public and Labour Law Perspectives* 49 (Oxford University Press, 1998).

Harlow, Carol and Rawlings, Richard, *Law and Administration*, 3rd edn. (Cambridge University Press, 2009).

Harlow, Carol and Rawlings, Richard, "Administrative law in context: restoring a lost connection," 2014 *Public Law* 28.

Harter, Philip, "Negotiating Regulations: A Cure for Malaise," 71 *Georgetown Law Journal* 1 (1982).

Hauriou, Maurice, "An Interpretation of the Principles of Public Law," 31 *Harvard Law Review* 813 (1918).

Hayward, Jack, "Institutional Inertia and Political Impetus in France and Britain," 4 *European Journal of Political Research* 341 (1976).

Heald, David, "The United Kingdom: Privatisation and its Political Context," 11 *West European Politics* 31 (1988).

Herman, Valentine and Lodge, Juliet, "The European Parliament and the 'Decline of Legislatures' Thesis," 13 *Journal of the Australasian Political Studies Association* 10 (1978).

Hewart of Bury, Lord, *The New Despotism* (E. Benn, 1929).

Hofmann, Herwig C. H., "Mapping the European Administrative Space," 31 *West European Politics* 662 (2008).

Hood, Christopher, "The Politics of Quangocide," 8 *Policy and Politics* 247 (1980).

Hood, Christopher, "A Public Management for All Seasons?," 69 *Public Administration* 3 (1991).

Houillon, Grégory, *Le lobbying en droit public* (Vol. I) (Doctoral dissertation, Université Paris-Descartes (Paris 5) 2008).

Ioakimidis, P.C., "The Europeanization of Greece: An Overall Assessment," in Kevin Featherstone and George Kazamias (eds.), *Europeanization and the Southern Periphery* 73 (Frank Cass 2001).

Irvine, Lord, "Judges and Decision Makers: The Theory and Practice of *Wednesbury* review," 1996 *Public Law* 59.

Jennings, W. Ivor, "In Praise of Dicey: 1885–1935," 13 *Public Administration* 123 (1935).

Jordan, Grant and Richardson, Jeremy, "The British Policy Style or the Logic of Negotiation?," in Jeremy Richardson (ed.), *Policy Styles in Western Europe* 80 (Allen & Unwin, 1982).

Jowell, Jeffrey, "The Rule of Law and its Underlying Values," Jeffrey Jowell and Dawn Oliver (eds.), *The Changing Constitution*, 7th edn. (Oxford University Press, 2011).

Kagan, Robert A., "Should Europe Worry about Adversarial Legalism?," 17 *Oxford Journal of Legal Studies* 165 (1997).

Kagan, Robert A., *Adversarial Legalism: The American Way of Law* (Harvard University Press, 2001).

Kaminis, Giorgos, "Oi Aneksartites Arches Metaksy Aneksartisias kai Koinovouleutikou Elegxou (The Independent Authorities Between Independence and Parliamentary Control)," 50 *Nomikon Vema (Legal Tribune)* 95 (2002).

Kamtsidou, Ifigeneia, *I Epiylaksi Yper tou Nomou, os Periorismos, Eggyisi kai Diamesos ton Eleftherion (The Reservation of Law, as Restriction, Guarantee, and Mediation of Liberties)* (Sakkoulas, 2001).

Kay, John and Vickers, John, "Regulatory Reform: An Appraisal," in Giandomenico Majone (ed.), *Deregulation or Re-regulation? Regulatory Reform in Europe and the United States* 223 (Pinter, 1990).

Kechri, Antoni S., "Skepseis epi tis ennoias 'Aneksartiti Dioikitiki Archi' (Thoughts on the notion of of 'Independent Administrative Authority')," 2007 *Efimerida Dimosiou Dikaiou (Journal of Public Law)* 353.

Keeler, John T. S., "Review: Situating France on the Pluralism-Corporatism Continuum: A Critique of and Alternative to the Wilson Perspective," 17 *Comparative Politics* 229 (1985).

Keeton, G. W., *The Passing of Parliament* (Ernest Benn, 1952).

Kelemen, R. Daniel, "Suing for Europe: Adversarial Legalism and European Governance," 39 *Comparative Political Studies* 101 (2006).

Kelemen, R. Daniel, "Adversarial Legalism and Administrative Law in the European Union," in Susan Rose-Ackerman and Peter Lindseth (eds.), *Comparative Administrative Law* 606 (Edward Elgar, 2010).

Kelemen, R. Daniel, *Eurolegalism: The Transformation of Law and Regulation in the European Union* (Harvard University Press, 2011).

Kelemen, Daniel and Sibbitt, Eric C., "The Globalization of American Law," 58 *International Organization* 103 (2004).

Kemmitt, Helen, and Angel, John, "The Telecommunications Regime in the United Kingdom," in Ian Walden (ed.), *Telecommunications Law and Regulation* 93 (Oxford University Press, 2012).

Kemp Allen, Sir Carleton, *Law and Orders: An Inquiry into the Nature and Scope of Delegated Legislation and Executive Powers in England*, 3rd edn. (Stevens, 1965).

Kersell, John E., *Parliamentary Supervision of Delegated Legislation: The United Kingdom, Australia, New Zealand and Canada* (Stevens & Sons, 1960).

Kerwin, Cornelius M., *Rulemaking: How Government Agencies Write Law and Make Policy*, 3d edn. (CQ Press, 2003).

Klucka, Ján, "The General Trends of EU Administrative Law," 41 *International Law* 1047 (2007).

Kohler-Koch, Beate, "How to Put Matters Right? Assessing the Role of Civil Society in EU Accountability," 33 *West European Politics* 1117 (2010).

Kondylis, Vassilios, "The Creation of an Independent Authority as a Measure of Compliance with European Law and Balancing between Independence and Accountability: The Case of the Hellenic National Telecommunications" and Post Commission (EETT)', Workshop "Public Administration in the Balkans—from Weberian bureaucracy to New Public Management" (5–6 February 2010, Athens, Greece).

Kontogiorga-Theocharopoulou, Dimitra, *I Dioikitiki Organosi tou Kratous (Apo Apopsi Dioikitikou Dikaiou kai Dioikitikis Epistikis) [The Administrative Organization of the State (From the Perspective of Administrative Law and Administrative Science)]* (Sakkoulas, 2002).

Kontogiorga-Theocharopoulou, Dimitra, "To 'Meteoro Vima' tou Management ston Dimosio Tomea (The 'Suspended Step' of Management in the Public Sector)," 2011 *Theoria kai Praksi Dioikitikou Dikaiou (Theory and Practice of Administrative Law)* 372.

Kühn, Zdeněk, and Bobek, Michal, "What about That 'Incoming Tide'? The Application of EU Law in Czech Republic," in Adam Lazowski (ed.), *The Application of EU Law in the New Member States—Brave New World* 325 (T.M.C. Asser Press, 2010).

Labetoulle, Daniel, "Le code des relations entre le public et l'administration: Avant-propos," 2016 *Revue Française de Droit Administratif* 1.

Laguna de Paz, José Carlos, "What to Keep and What to Change in European Electronic Communications Policy?," 49 *Common Market Law Review* 1951 (2012).

Landis, James M., *The Administrative Process* (Yale University Press, 1938).

Langbein, Laura I. and Kerwin, Cornelius M., "Regulatory Negotiation: Claims, Counter Claims and Empirical Evidence," 10 *Journal of Public Administration Research and Theory* 599 (2000).

Lavdas, Kostas A., *The Europeanization of Greece: Interest Politics and the Crises of Integration* (St. Martin's Press, 1997).

Lavdas, Kostas A., "Interest Groups in Disjointed Corporatism: Social Dialogue in Greece and European 'Competitive Corporatism'," 28 *West European Politics* 297 (2005).

Lazarakos, Grigorios G., *To Dikaioma Prosvasis sti Dimosia Pliroforia. Anoikti Dioikisi kai Koinonia tis Pliroforias (The Right of Access to Public Information. Open Administration and Information Society)* (Nomiki Vivliothiki, 2006).

Lazer, David, "Regulatory Capitalism as a Networked Order: The International System as an Informational Network," 598 *Annals of the American Academy of Political and Social Science* 52 (2005).

Laws, John, "Law and Democracy," 1995 *Public Law* 72.

Lawson, Gary, "The Rise and Rise of the Administrative State," 107 *Harvard Law Review* 1231 (1994).

Le May, Godfrey Hugh Lancelot, *The Victorian Constitution: Conventions, Usages, and Contingencies* (Duckworth, 1979).

Levi-Faur, David and Gilad, Sharon, "The Rise of the British Regulatory State: Transcending the Privatization Debate," 37 *Comparative Politics* 105 (2004).

Levy, Jonah D., *Tocqueville's Revenge. State, Society, and Economy in Contemporary France* (Harvard University Press, 1999).

Lewis, Norman D, *Choice and the Legal Order: Rising above Politics* (Butterworths, 1996).

Lijphart, Arend, Bruneau, Thomas C., Diamandouros, P. Nikiforos, and Gunther, Richard, "A Mediterranean Model of Democracy? The Southern European Democracies in Comparative Perspective," 11 *West European Politics* 7 (1988).

Lindseth, Peter, "Democratic Legitimacy and the Administrative Character of Supranationalism: The Example of the European Community," 99 *Columbia Law Review* 628 (1999).

Lindseth, Peter, "'Always Embedded' Administration: The Historical Evolution of Administrative Justice as an Aspect of Modern Governance," in Christian Joerges, Bo Stråth, and Peter Wagner, (eds.), *The Economy as a Polity: The Political Constitution of Contemporary Capitalism* 117 (UCL Press, 2005).

Lodge, Juliet, "EC Policymaking: Institutional Considerations," in Juliet Lodge (ed.), *The European Community and the Challenge of the Future* 26 (St. Martin's Press, 1989).

Loughlin, Martin, *Legality and Locality: The Role of Law in Central-Local Government Relations* (Oxford University Press, 1996).

Loughlin, Martin, "Why the History of English Administrative Law is not Written," in David Dyzenhaus, Murray Hunt, and Grant Huscroft (eds.), *A Simple Common Lawyer. Essays in Honour of Michael Taggart* 151 (Hart, 2009).

Loukis, Euripidis, Macintosh, Ann, and Charalabidis, Yannis, "Editorial," 13 *Journal of Balkan and Near Eastern Studies* 1 (2011).

Lowell, A. Lawrence, *Governments and Parties in Continental Europe*, Vols. I, II (Mifflin, 1896).

Lubbers, Jeffrey S., *A Guide to Federal Agency Rulemaking*, 4th edn. (ABA, 2006).

Luhmann, Niklas, *Essays on Self-Reference* (Columbia University Press, 1990).

Luhmann, Niklas, "Operational Closure and Structural Coupling: The Differentiation of the Legal System," 13 *Cardozo Law Review* 1419 (1992).

Luhmann, Niklas, "Quod Omnes Tangit. Remarks on Jürgen Habermas's Legal Theory," in Michel Rosenfeld and Andrew Arato (eds.), *Habermas on Law and Democracy. Critical Exchanges* 157 (University of California Press, 1998).

Lyrintzis, Christos, "Political Parties in Post-junta Greece: A Case of 'Bureaucratic Clientelism'?," 7 *West European Politics* 99 (1984).

MacDonagh, Oliver, "The Nineteenth-Century Revolution in Government: A Reappraisal," 1 *The Historical Journal* 52 (1958).

Majone, Giandomenico, "Theories of Regulation," in Giandomenico Majone (ed.), *Regulating Europe* 28 (Routledge, 1996).

Majone, Giandomenico, "The Rise of Statutory Regulation in Europe," in Giandomenico Majone (ed.), *Regulating Europe* 47 (Routledge, 1996).

Majone, Giandomenico, "Regulatory Legitimacy," in Giandomenico Majone (ed.), *Regulating Europe* 294 (Routledge, 1996).

Majone, Giandomenico, "Europe's 'Democratic Deficit': The Question of Standards," 4 *European Law Journal* 5 (1998).

Majone, Giandomenico, "Two Logics of Delegation: Agency and Fiduciary Relations in EU Governance," 2 *European Union Politics* 103 (2001).

Malberg, Raymond Carré de, *La loi, expression de la volonté générale* (Sirey, 1931, reed. Economica, 1984).

Manin, Bernard, Przeworski, Adam, and Stokes Susan, "Elections and Representation," in Adam Przeworski, Susan C. Stokes, and Bernard Manin (eds.), *Democracy, Accountability, and Representation* 29 (1999).

Manitakis, Antonis, *Kratos Dikaiou kai Dikastikos Elegxos tis Syntagmatikotitas (Rule of Law and Judicial Review of Constitutionality)* (Sakkoulas, 1994).

Manitakis, Antonis, *I Idrysi Syntagmatikou Dikastiriou (The Establishment of a Constitutional Court)* (Sakkoulas, 2008).

Manley, John F., "Neo-Pluralism: A Class Analysis of Pluralism I and Pluralism II," Robert A. Dahl, Ian Shapiro and José Antonio Cheibub eds., *The Democracy Sourcebook* 381 (MIT Press, 2003).

Marquand, David, *Parliament for Europe* (Jonathan Cape, 1979).

Marquand, David, *The Unprincipled Society: New Demands and Old Politics* (Jonathan Cape, 1988).

Marquand, David, *Decline of the Public: The Hollowing-Out of Citizenship* (Polity, 2004).

Marshall, Geoffrey, "The Constitution: Its Theory and Interpretation," in Vernon Bogdanor (ed.), *The British Constitution in the Twentieth Century* 29 (Oxford, University Press, 2003).

Mashaw, Jerry L., *Due Process in the Administrative State* (Yale University Press, 1985).

Mashaw, Jerry L., "Prodelegation: Why Administrators Should Make Political Decisions," 1 *Journal of Law, Economics and Organization* 81 (1985).

Mashaw, Jerry L., "Reasoned Administration: The European Union, the United States, and the Project of Democratic Governance," 76 *George Washington Law Review* 99 (2007).

Mavrogordatos, Giorgos Th., *Between Pityokamptis and Procrustis: Professional Associations in Today's Greece (Metaksy Pityokampti kai Procrousti: Oi Epaggelmatikes Organoseis sti Simerini Ellada)*, 2nd edn. (Odysseas, 1998).

McCormick, John P., *Weber, Habermas, and Transformations of the European State: Constitutional, Social, and Supranational Democracy* (Cambridge University Press, 2007).

McHarg, Aileen, "Regulation as a Private Law Function?," 1995 *Public Law* 539.

Mendelson, Nina A., "Rulemaking, Democracy, and Torrents of E-Mail," 79 *George Washington Law Review* 1343 (2011).

Mendelson, Nina A., "Should Mass Comments Count?," 2 *Michigan Journal of Environmental & Administrative Law* 173 (2012).

Mendes, Joana, *Participation in EU Rule-Making: A Rights-Based Approach* (Oxford University Press, 2011).

Mény, Yves, "De la démocratie en Europe: Old Concepts and New Challenges," 41 *Journal of Common Market Studies* 1 (2002).

Mény, Yves and Surel, Yves, "The Constitutive Ambiguity of Populism," in Yves Mény and Yves Surel (eds.), *Democracies and the Populist Challenge* 1 (Palgrave Macmillan, 2002).

Milbrath, Lester W., "Citizen Surveys as Citizen Participation Mechanisms," 17 *Journal of Applied Behavioral Science* 478 (1981).

Miller, Nicholas R., "Pluralism and Social Choice," in Robert A. Dahl, Ian Shapiro and José Antonio Cheibub eds., *The Democracy Sourcebook* 133 (MIT Press, 2003).

Miller, David and Dinan, William, "The Rise of the PR Industry in Britain, 1979–98," 15 *European Journal of Communication* 5 (2000).

Mitchell, J. D. B., "The Causes and Effects of the Absence of a System of Public Law in the United Kingdom," 1965 *Public Law* 95.

Moran, Michael, *The British Regulatory State: High Modernism and Hyper-Innovation* (Oxford University Press, 2007).

Moravcsik, Andrew, *The Choice for Europe: Social Purpose and State Power from Messina to Maastricht* (Cornell University Press, 1998).

Moravcsik, Andrew, "Despotism in Brussels? Misreading the European Union," 80 (3) *Foreign Affairs* (May/June 2001).

Moravcsik, Andrew, "In Defence of the 'Democratic Deficit': Reassessing Legitimacy in the European Union," 40 *Journal of Common Market Studies* 603 (2002).

Moravcsik, Andrew, "The Myth of Europe's 'Democratic Deficit'," *Intereconomics: Journal of European Economic Policy* 331 (November–December 2008).

Morgan, Bronwen, "Technocratic v. Convivial Accountability," in Michael W. Dowdle (ed.), *Public Accountability: Designs, Dilemmas and Experiences* 243 (Cambridge University Press, 2006).

Morgan, Kevin, and Webber, Douglas, "Divergent Paths: Political Strategies for Telecom munications in Britain, France and West Germany," 9 *West European Politics* 56 (1986).

Mutz, Diana C., *Hearing the Other Side: Deliberative versus Participatory Democracy* (Cambridge University Press, 2006).

Needham, Catherine, *Citizen-Consumers: New Labour's Marketplace Democracy* (Catalyst Forum, 2003).

Needham, Catherine, The Reform of Public Services under New Labour: Narratives of Consumerism 1–2 (Palgrave Macmillan, 2007).

Neill, Patrick, "The Duty to Give Reasons: The Openness of Decision-Making," in Christopher Forsyth and Ivan Hare (eds.), *The Golden Metwand and the Crooked Cord: Essays on Public Law in Honour of Sir William Wade QC* 161 (Oxford University Press, 1998).

Nicolaïdes, Phedon, "Regulation of Liberalised Markets: A New Role for the State? (or How to Induce Competition Among Regulators)," in Damien Geradin, Rodolphe Munoz, and Nicolas Petit eds., *Regulation through Agencies in the EU: A New Paradigm of European Governance* 23 (Edward Elgar, 2005).

Oates, Wallace E. and Schwab, Robert M., "Economic Competition among Jurisdictions: Efficiency Enhancing or Distortion Inducing?," 35 *Journal of Public Economics* 333 (1988).

Oberdorff, Henri, *Les institutions administratives*, 6th edn. (Dalloz, 2010).

Odent, Raymond, *Contentieux administratif* (Tome 2) (1978, reed. Dalloz, 2007).

Oliver, Dawn, *Common Values and the Public-Private Divide* (Butterworths, 1999).

Oliver, Dawn, "Regulation, Democracy, and Democratic Oversight in the UK," in Dawn Oliver, Tony Prosser, and Richard Rawlings (eds.), *The Regulatory State: Constitutional Implications* 243 (Oxford University Press, 2010).

Pagoulatos, George, *Greece's New Political Economy: State, Finance and Growth from Postwar to EMU* (Palgrave, 2003).

Pagoulatos, George, "The Politics of Privatisation: Redrawing the Public–Private Boundary," 28 *West European Politics* 358 (2005).

Pararas, Alexis P., "Oi Aneksartites Dioikitikes Arches Simera (The Independent Administrative Authorities Today)," 2006 *Efimerida Dimosiou Dikaiou (Journal of Public Law)* 123.

Parau, Cristina Elena, "Impaling Dracula: How EU Accession Empowered Civil Society in Romania," 32 *West European Politics* 119 (2009).

Parris, Henry, "The Nineteenth-Century Revolution in Government: A Reappraisal Reappraised," 3 *The Historical Journal* 17 (1960).

Parris, Henry, *Constitutional Bureaucracy: The Development of British Central Administration since the Eighteenth Century* (Allen & Unwin, 1969).

Pierce, Richard J., Jr., "Seven Ways to Deossify Agency Rulemaking," 47 *Administrative Law Review* 59 (1995).

Pikrammenos, Panayiotis, "To Elliniko Symvouleio tis Epikrateias kai oi Gnomodotikes Armodiotites tou (The Greek Council of State and its Advisory Competences)," 2011 *Theoria kai Praksi Dioikitikou Dikaiou (Theory and Practice of Administrative Law)* 361.

Pollack, Mark A., "Learning from the Americanists (Again): Theory and Method in the Study of Delegation," in Mark Thatcher and Alec Stone Sweet (eds.), *The Politics of Delegation* 200 (Cass, 2003).

Pomonti, Jacques, *L'aventure du téléphone: une exception française* (Hermès-Lavoisier, 2008).

Posner, Richard A., *The Federal Courts: Crisis and Reform* (Harvard University Press, 1985).

Prévédourou, Eugénie, *L'Évolution de l'autonomie procédurale des États membres de l'Union Européenne* (Esperia Publications, 1999).

Prevedourou, Eugenia V., "O Akyrotikos Elegxos ton Dioikitikon Prakseon ypo to Prisma tis Europaikis Symvaseos ton Dikaiomaton tou Anthropou (Annulment Review of Administrative Acts through the Lens of the European Convention on Human Rights)," 2010 *Theoria kai Praksi Dioikitikou Dikaiou (Theory and Practice of Administrative Law)* 858.

Prosser, Tony, *Law and the Regulators* (Oxford University Press, 1997).

Prosser, Tony, "Public Service Law: Privatization's Unexpected Offspring," 63 *Law and Contemporary Problems* 63 (2000).

Prosser, Tony, *The Regulatory Enterprise: Government, Regulation, and Legitimacy* (Oxford University Press, 2010).

Psygkas, Akis, "Anichnevontas kai Epananoimatodotontas ti 'Theoria ton Politikon Zitimaton' stin Elliniki Ennomi Taksi" ("Tracing and Redefining the 'Political Question Doctrine' in Greece"), 47 *Dikaiomata tou Anthropou (Review of Human Rights)* 743 (2010).

Psygkas, Athanasios Efstratios, "Revitalizing the 'Liberty of the Ancients' Through Citizen Participation in the Legislative Process. Thoughts on Doctors for Life International v the

Speaker of the National Assembly & Others," 5 *Annuaire International des Droits de l'Homme/ International Yearbook on Human Rights* 719 (2010).

Psygkas, Athanasios, "The 'Double Helix' of Process and Substance Review before the UK Competition Appeal Tribunal: A Model Case or a Cautionary Tale for Specialist Courts?," in Susan Rose-Ackerman, Peter Lindseth and Blake Emerson (eds.), *Comparative Administrative Law*, 2nd edn. (Edward Elgar, 2017).

Pünder, Hermann, "Democratic Legitimation of Delegated Legislation—A Comparative View on the American, British and German law," 58 *International & Comparative Law Quarterly* 353 (2009).

Putnam, Robert D., *Making Democracy Work: Civic Traditions in Modern Italy* (Princeton University Press, 1993).

Rabkin, Jeremy, "Revolutionary Visions in Legal Imagery: Constitutional Contrasts between France and America," in Ralph C. Hancock and L. Gary Lambert (eds.), *The Legacy of the French Revolution* 219 (Rowman & Littlefield, 1996).

Rait, Robert S., *Memorials of Albert Venn Dicey: Being Chiefly Letters and Diaries* (Macmillan, 1925).

Rawlings, Richard, "Changed Conditions, Old Truths: Judicial Review in a Regulatory Laboratory," in Dawn Oliver, Tony Prosser, and Richard Rawlings (eds.), *The Regulatory State: Constitutional Implications* 283 (Oxford University Press, 2010).

Raynaud, Philippe, "The 'Rights of Man and Citizen' in the French Constitutional Tradition," in Ralph C. Hancock and L. Gary Lambert (eds.), *The Legacy of the French Revolution* 199 (Rowman & Littlefield, 1996).

Reich, Robert B., "Public Administration and Public Deliberation: An Interpretive Essay," 94 *Yale Law Journal* 1617 (1985).

Resnik, Judith, "Categorical Federalism: Jurisdiction, Gender, and the Globe," 111 *Yale Law Journal* 619 (2001).

Revesz, Richard L., "Rehabilitating Interstate Competition: Rethinking the 'Race-to-the-Bottom' Rationale for Federal Environmental Regulation," 67 *N.Y.U. Law Review* 1210 (1992).

Revesz, Richard, "Federalism and Regulation: Some Generalizations," in Daniel Esty and Damien Geradin (eds.), *Regulatory Competition and Economic Integration: Comparative Perspectives* 3 (Oxford University Press, 2001).

Robson, William A., "The Report of the Committee on Ministers' Powers," 3 *The Political Quarterly* 346 (1932).

Roger-Lacan, Cyril, "Remarques," 2010/23 *Revue Lamy de la Concurrence* 162 (2010).

Rohr, John A., "Dicey's Ghost and Administrative Law," 34 *Administration & Society* 8 (2002).

Rosanvallon, Pierre, *Le modèle politique français: La société civile contre le jacobinisme de 1789 à nos jours* (Seuil, 2004).

Rosanvallon, Pierre, *Democracy Past and Future* (Samuel Moyn ed., Columbia University Press, 2006).

Rosanvallon, Pierre, *The Demands of Liberty: Civil Society in France since the Revolution* (Arthur Goldhammer trans., Harvard University Press, 2007).

Rosanvallon, Pierre, *La légitimité démocratique: Impartialité, réflexivité, proximité* (Seuil, 2008).

Rose-Ackerman, Susan, "Risk Taking and Reelection: Does Federalism Promote Innovation?," 9 *Journal of Legal Studies* 593 (1980).

Rose-Ackerman, Susan, *Rethinking the Progressive Agenda: The Reform of the American Regulatory State* (Free Press, 1992).

Rose-Ackerman, Susan, "Consensus versus Incentives: A Skeptical Look at Regulatory Negotiation," 43 *Duke Law Journal* 1206 (1994).

Rose-Ackerman, Susan, "American Administrative Law under Siege: Is Germany a Model?," 107 *Harvard Law Review* 1279 (1994).

Rose-Ackerman, Susan, *Controlling Environmental Policy: The Limits of Public Law in Germany and the United States* (Yale University Press, 1995).

Rose-Ackerman, Susan, *Corruption and Government: Causes, Consequences, and Reform* (Cambridge University Press, 1999).

Rose-Ackerman, Susan, *From Elections to Democracy: Building Accountable Government in Hungary and Poland* (Cambridge University Press, 2005).

Rose-Ackerman, Susan, "Introduction," in Susan Rose-Ackerman (ed.), *Economics of Administrative Law* (Edward Elgar, 2007).

Rose-Ackerman, Susan, "Regulation and Public Law in Comparative Perspective," 60 *University of Toronto Law Journal* 519 (2010).

Rose-Ackerman, Susan and Perroud, Thomas, "Policymaking and Public Law in France: Public Participation, Agency Independence, and Impact Assessment," 19 *Columbia Journal of European Law* 225 (2013).

Rose-Ackerman, Susan, Egidy, Stefanie, and Fowkes, James, *Due Process of Lawmaking* (Cambridge University Press, 2015).

Rossi, Jim, "Participation Run Amok: The Costs of Mass Participation for Deliberative Agency Decisionmaking," 92 *Northwestern University Law Review* 173 (1997).

Rousseau, Jean-Jacques, *The Social Contract and Other Later Political Writings* (Victor Gourevitch ed. & trans., Cambridge University Press, 1997).

Rubin, Edward L., "Getting Past Democracy," 149 *University of Pennsylvania Law Review* 711 (2001).

Rubinstein Reiss, Dorit, *Regulatory Accountability: Telecommunications and Electricity Agencies in the UK, France and Sweden* (Doctoral dissertation, UC Berkeley, 2007).

Rubinstein Reiss, Dorit, "Participation in Governance from a Comparative Perspective: Citizen Involvement in Telecommunications and Electricity in the United Kingdom, France and Sweden," 2009 *Journal of Dispute Resolution* 381.

Rubinstein Reiss, Dorit, "Administrative Agencies as Creators of Administrative Law Norms: Evidence from the UK, France and Sweden," Susan Rose-Ackerman and Peter Lindseth (eds.), *Comparative Administrative Law* 373 (Edward Elgar, 2010).

Ruffert, Matthias, "The Transformation of Administrative Law as a Transnational Methodological Project," in Matthias Ruffert (ed.), *The Transformation of Administrative Law in Europe* 3 (Sellier, 2007).

Sajó, András, "The Impacts of EU Accession on Post-communist Constitutionalism," 45 *Acta Juridica Hungarica* 193 (2004).

Saurer, Johannes, "Supranational Governance and Networked Accountability Structures: Member State Oversight of EU Agencies," in Susan Rose-Ackerman and Peter Lindseth (eds.), *Comparative Administrative Law* 618 (Edward Elgar, 2010).

Saurugger, Sabine, "Interest Groups and Democracy in the European Union," 31 *West European Politics* 1274 (2008).

Scharpf, Fritz W, "Democratic Policy in Europe," 2 *European Law Journal* 136 (1996).

Schmidt, Susanne K., "Commission Activism: Subsuming Telecommunications and Electricity Under European Competition Law," 5 *Journal of European Public Policy* 169 (1998).

Schmidt, Vivien A., *From State to Market? The Transformation of French Business and Government* (Cambridge University Press, 1996).

Schmidt, Vivien, *Democracy in Europe: The EU and National Polities* (Oxford University Press, 2006).

Schmitter, Philippe C., "Still the Century of Corporatism?," 36 *Review of Politics (Special Issue: The New Corporatism: Social and Political Structures in the Iberian World)* 85 (1974).

Scott, Colin, "The Juridification of Regulatory Relations in the UK Utilities Sector," in Julia Black, Peter Muchlinski, and Paul Walker (eds.), *Commercial Regulation and Judicial Review* 19 (Hart, 1998).

Scott, Colin, "Accountability in the Regulatory State," 27 *Journal of Law and Society* 38 (2000).

Seidenfeld, Mark, "A Civic Republican Justification for the Bureaucratic State," 105 *Harvard Law Review* 1511 (1992).

Seiller, Bertrand, "Pour un contrôle de la légalité extrinsèque des déclarations d'utilité publique," 59 *Actualité Juridique, Droit Administratif* 1472 (2003).

Shapiro, David, *Federalism: A Dialogue* (Northwestern University Press, 1995).

Shapiro, Martin, *Who Guards the Guardians? Judicial Control of Administration* (University of Georgia Press, 1988).

Shapiro, Martin, "The Problems of Independent Agencies in the United States and the European Union," 4 *Journal of European Public Policy* 276 (1997).

Shonfield, Andrew, *Modern Capitalism: The Changing Balance of Public and Private Power* (Oxford University Press, 1965).

Sieberson, Stephen, "The Proposed European Union Constitution—Will It Eliminate the EU's Democratic Deficit?," 10 *Columbia Journal of European Law* 173 (2004).

Sieberson, Stephen, "The Treaty of Lisbon and Its Impact on the European Union's Democratic Deficit," 14 *Columbia Journal of European Law* 445 (2008).

Siedentop, Larry, *Democracy in Europe* (Columbia University Press, 2001).

Siegel, Jonathan R., "Law and Longitude," 84 *Tulane Law Review* 1 (2009).

Skouris, Vasileios, *Chorotaksiko kai Poleodomiko Dikaio (Planning Law)* (Sakkoulas, 1997).

Sotiropoulos, Dimitri A., "A Colossus with Feet of Clay: The State in Post-Authoritarian Greece," in Harry J. Psomiades and Stavros Thomadakis (eds.), *Greece, The New Europe, and the Changing International Order* 43 (Pella, 1993).

Sotiropoulos, Dimitri A, "Southern European Public Bureaucracies in Comparative Perspective," 27 *West European Politics* 405 (2004).

Spanou, Calliope, "On the Regulatory Capacity of the Hellenic State: A Tentative Approach Based on a Case Study," 62 *International Review of Administrative Sciences* 219 (1996).

Spanou, Calliope, "European Integration in Administrative Terms: A Framework for Analysis and the Greek Case," 5 *Journal of European Public Policy* 467 (1998).

Spanou, Calliope, and Sotiropoulos, Dimitri A., "The Odyssey of Administrative Reforms in Greece, 1981–2009," 89 *Public Administration* 723 (2011).

Spiliotopoulos, Epaminondas, "Judicial Review of Legislative Acts in Greece," 56 *Temple Law Quarterly* 463 (1983).

Spiliotopoulos, Epaminondas, *Greek Administrative Law* (Ant. N. Sakkoulas, 2004).

Spiller, Pablo T. and Vogelsang, Ingo, "The United Kingdom: A Pacesetter in Regulatory Incentives," in Brian Levy and Pablo T. Spiller (eds.), *Regulations, Institutions, and Commitment: Comparative Studies of Telecommunications* 79 (Cambridge University Press, 1996).

Stassinopoulos, Michel, *Le droit de la défense devant les autorités administratives* (L.G.D.J., 1976).

Stebbings, Chantal, *Legal Foundations of Tribunals in Nineteenth-Century England* (Cambridge University Press, 2006).

Stern, Jon, "What the Littlechild Report Actually Said," in Ian Bartle (ed.), *The UK Model of Utility Regulation: A 20th Anniversary Collection to Mark the "Littlechild Report". Retrospect and Prospect* 7 (University of Bath, 2003).

Stewart, Richard B., "The Reformation of American Administrative Law," 88 *Harvard Law Review* 1669 (1975).

Stewart, Richard B., "Pyramids of Sacrifice? Problems of Federalism in Mandating State Implementation of National Environmental Policy," 86 *Yale Law Journal* 1196 (1977).

Stigler, George J., "The Theory of Economic Regulation," 2 *Bell Journal of Economics and Management Science* 3 (1971).

Stokes, Susan C., "What Do Policy Switches Tell Us about Democracy?," in Adam Przeworski, Susan C. Stokes, and Bernard Manin (eds.), *Democracy, Accountability, and Representation* 98 (1999).

Sunstein, Cass R., "Factions, Self-Interest, and the APA: Four Lessons since 1946," 72 *Virginia Law Review* 271 (1986).

Sunstein, Cass R., "Constitutionalism after the New Deal," 101 *Harvard Law Review* 421 (1987).

Sunstein, Cass R., "Deliberative Trouble? Why Groups Go to Extremes," 110 *Yale Law Journal* 71 (2000).

Szydło, Marek, "National Parliaments as Regulators of Network Industries: In Search of the Dividing Line Between Regulatory Powers of National Parliaments and National Regulatory Authorities," 10 *International Journal of Constitutional Law* 1134 (2012).

Teubner, Gunther, *Law as an Autopoietic System* (Zenon Bankowski ed., Anne Bankowska & Ruth Adler trans., Blackwell, 1993).

Thatcher, Mark, "Institutions, Regulation and Change: New Regulatory Agencies in the British Privatised Utilities," 21 *West European Politics* 120 (1998).

Thatcher, Mark, *The Politics of Telecommunications: National Institutions, Convergence, and Change in Britain and France* (Oxford University Press, 1999).

Thatcher, Mark, "The Commission and National Governments as partners: EC Regulatory Expansion in Telecommunications 1979–2000," 8 *Journal of European Public Policy* 558 (2001).

Thatcher, Mark, "Independent Regulatory Agencies and Elected Politicians in Europe," in Damien Geradin, Rodolphe Munoz, and Nicolas Petit eds., *Regulation through Agencies in the EU. A New Paradigm of European Governance* 47 (Edward Elgar, 2005).

Thatcher, Mark, "Regulatory Agencies, the State and Markets: A Franco-British Comparison," 14 *Journal of European Public Policy* 1028 (2007).

Thatcher, Mark and Stone Sweet, Alec, "Theory and Practice of Delegation to Non-majoritarian Institutions," in Mark Thatcher and Alec Stone Sweet (eds.), *The Politics of Delegation* 1 (Cass, 2003).

Thompson, C. Bradley, "The American Founding and the French Revolution," in Ralph C. Hancock and L. Gary Lambert (eds.), *The Legacy of the French Revolution* 109 (Rowman & Littlefield, 1996).

Tiebout, Charles, "A Pure Theory of Local Expenditures," 64 *Journal of Political Economy* 416 (1956).

Tomkins, Adam, *The Constitution after Scott: Government Unwrapped* (Oxford University Press, 1998).

Tomkins, Adam, "In Defence of the Political Constitution," 22 *Oxford Journal of Legal Studies* 157 (2002).

Tomkins, Adam, *Our Republican Constitution* (Hart, 2005).

Trantas, Georgios, Zagoriti, Paraskevi, Bergman, Torbjörn, Müller, Wolfgang C., and Strøm, Kaare, "Greece: 'Rationalizing' Constitutional Powers in a Post-dictatorial Country," in Kaare Strøm, Wolfgang C. Müller, and Torbjörn Bergman (eds.), *Delegation and Accountability in Parliamentary Democracies* 376 (Oxford University Press, 2003).

Tzimapiti, Anna, "Oi Kanonistikes kai Apofasistikes Armodiotites ton Aneksartiton Dioikitikon Archon: Symperasmata apo tin Elliniki Pragmatikotita (Rulemaking and Decisionmaking Competences of Independent Administrative Authorities: Conclusions from the Greek Reality)," 2009 *Theoria kai Praksi Dioikitikou Dikaiou (Theory and Practice of Administrative Law)* 1166.

Veljanovksi, Cento, "The Need for a Regulatory Charter," 1 *Journal of Financial Regulation and Compliance* 355 (1993).

Venizelos, Evaggelos, "Poiotita Nomothesias, Koinoniki Synainesi kai Antagonistikotita tis Ellinikis Nomothesias (Legislative Quality, Social Consensus and Competitiveness of the Greek Legislation)," 2006 *Efimerida Dimosiou Dikaiou (Journal of Public Law)* 374.

Vialettes, Maud and Barrois de Sarigny, Cécile, "Questions autour d'une codification," 2015 *Actualité Juridique, Droit Administratif* 2421.

Vigoda, Eran, "From Responsiveness to Collaboration: Governance, Citizens, and the Next Generation of Public Administration," 62 *Public Administration Review* 527 (2002).

Wade, H.W. R., *Administrative Law*, 1st edn. (Oxford University Press, 1961).

Wade, Sir William and Forsyth, Christopher, *Administrative Law*, 10th edn. (Oxford University Press, 2009).

Wald, Patricia M., "Judicial Review in Midpassage: The Uneasy Partnership Between Courts and Agencies Plays On," 32 *Tulsa Law Journal* 221 (1996).

Walden, Ian, "European Union Communications Law," in Ian Walden (ed.), *Telecommunications Law and Regulation* 143 (Oxford University Press, 2012).

Walker, Geoffrey de Q., "Dicey's Dubious Dogma of Parliamentary Sovereignty: A Recent Fray with Freedom of Religion," 59 *Australian Law Journal* 276 (1985).

Walker, Geoffrey de Q., *The Rule of Law: Foundation of Constitutional Democracy* (Melbourne University Press, 1988).

Weatherill, Stephen, "National Parliaments as Regulators of Network Industries: A Reply to Marek Szydło," 10 *International Journal of Constitutional Law* 1167 (2012).

Webb, Sidney and Beatrice, *English Local Government: Statutory Authorities for Special Purposes* (Longman, Greens, 1922).

Weber, Yves, *L'administration consultative* (L.G.D.J., 1968).

Weiler, J. H. H., "The Transformation of Europe," 100 *Yale Law Journal* 2403 (1991).

Weill, Rivka, "Dicey was not Diceyan," 62 *Cambridge Law Journal* 474 (2003).

Wheare, Kenneth C., *Legislatures*, 2nd edn. (Oxford University Press, 1968).

Willis, John, *The Parliamentary Powers of English Government departments* (1933, repr. Lawbook Exchange, 2003).

Wilson, Frank L., "French Interest Group Politics: Pluralist or Neocorporatist?," 77 *American Political Science Review* 895 (1983).

Woll, Cornelia, "Lobbying in the European Union: From sui generis to a Comparative Perspective," 13 *Journal of European Public Policy* 456 (2006).

Woolf, Harry, Jowell, Jeffrey, and Le Sueur, Andrew, *De Smith's Judicial Review*, 6th edn. (Sweet & Maxwell, 2007).

Ziamou, Theodora, "Public Participation in Administrative Rulemaking: The Legal Tradition and Perspective in the American and European (English, German, Greek) Legal Systems," 60 *Zeitschrift für ausländisches öffentliches Recht und Völkerrecht* 41 (2000).

Ziamou, Theodora Th., *Rulemaking, Participation and the Limits of Public Law in the USA and Europe* (Ashgate, 2001).

Zoller, Elisabeth, *Introduction au droit public* (Dalloz, 2006).

INDEX

Note: Page references followed by a "*t*" indicate table; "*f*" indicate figure